Manchester
England

The Story of
the Pop Cult City

Dave Haslam

FOURTH ESTATE • *London*

For Jack and Raili

This paperback edition first published in 2000
First published in Great Britain in 1999 by
Fourth Estate
A Division of HarperCollins*Publishers*
77–85 Fulham Palace Road
London W6 8JB
www.4thestate.co.uk

The Author and Publisher are grateful to the respective proprietors for permission to quote lyrics from the following works: to Howard Devoto for the Buzzcocks 'Boredom' and Magazine 'The Light Pours Out of Me'; to IMP Ltd for the Smiths 'Hand in Glove' (Morrissey/Marr) © 1984 Warner Chappell Music Ltd, London W6 8BS; to IMP Ltd for A Certain Ratio 'All Night Party' (Moscrop/Kerr/Topping/Johnson/Terrell) © 1979 EMI Virgin Music Ltd, London WC2H 0EA; and to Zomba Music Publishers for the Stone Roses 'She Bangs the Drums' (Brown/Squire).

10 9 8 7 6 5

A catalogue record for this book is available from the British Library.

ISBN 1-84115-146-7

Typeset by Rowland Phototypesetting Limited,
Bury St Edmunds, Suffolk.
Printed in Great Britain by Clays Ltd, St Ives plc

Contents

Manchester:

Past Imperfect, Present Tense, Future Uncertain

> The inhabitants are of a good sort, being pretty much of the old English temper, hearty and sincere in their affections and expressions, given to hospitality, very kind and civil to their friends, but very stiff and resolute against their enemies, well disposed to religion and very zealous in whatever they engage.
>
> **William Stukeley on Manchester, 1724**

> The city does not tell its past, but contains it like the lines of a hand, written in the corners of the streets, the gratings of the windows, the banisters of the steps, the antennae of the lightning rods, the poles of the flags, every segment marked in turn with scratches, indentations, scrolls.
>
> **Italo Calvino, *Invisible Cities***

We were in Ancoats, a district just north of Manchester city centre, looking for evidence of ruin and industrial decay. The names of some of the narrow streets in the neighbourhood – Cotton Street, Loom Street, Silk Street, Bengal Street – are a reminder of past glories when the cotton trade in Manchester created an Empire-building wealth for Britain. Born during the industrial revolution, Manchester's power grew so huge that a hundred and fifty years ago the city was one of the richest places in the world. Now it's come to this: empty Ancoats buildings, smashed windows, bleak silence. There are several giant, half-derelict seven- and eight-storey cotton mills, some occupied at ground or first-floor level by small-scale textile firms and embroidery companies, but most are deadly quiet. The mills stand solitary or cling together via overhead chutes and walkways, immense above the surrounding wreckage, broken walls and makeshift car boot sale sites.

I was with a crew from a German satellite TV station filming an insider's view of Manchester, a kind of shopping and clubbing guide. Ten hours of wandering would be edited into a three minute segment, fronted by me. It took an age getting it all right, doing the right cut-aways, inside and outside the Velvet bar on Canal Street, Café Pop on Oldham Street and Wear It Out in the Royal Exchange Shopping Centre. Also they needed a context for the story, they told me, something very Manchester, very Northern. So we'd driven up to Ancoats, in search of the perfect wasteland.

Wandering these streets, the German TV crew kept the camera rolling, the lens hungrily devouring bleak, corroded old Ancoats. We parked up close by the site of McConnel & Kennedy's huge mill complex on Redhill Street. Once the envy of the world, now bushes (not just weeds) were growing out of the mortar halfway up the seven-storey walls, and whole window frames were smashed open, gaping. Someone had stuck up a hand-written sign in blue biro: 'Guard Dog On Premises'. The mill was silent, the dog – if it existed – was sleeping. 'Yes', the German director said. 'In Germany we know about the music and Manchester United, but when we think of how Manchester looks we think of this.'

The cotton trade, the merchants, the riches are gone. The cotton exchange shut up shop more than half a century ago. 'Cottonopolis', as the city was dubbed, has been rubbed off the map. The former mainstay of Manchester is a memory, and nothing could more graphically illustrate the city's movement away from its role as a leading manufacturing and commercial city than what we filmed that day on the streets of Ancoats. Twentieth-century changes have created a sense that the city and its people have been deserted and abandoned, like the uneconomic ruins of another era; like an Ancoats mill, the shell of the city is intact, but its heart emptied, its reason for living unclear.

Later that evening I took the German film crew down to the Haçienda, possibly the most famous symbol of modern Manchester, and one of the most talked-about nightclubs in the world. I'd built a career, a life, DJ-ing there, and no modern guide to the city could be complete without a pilgrimage to its doorstep. The film director wanted more humour, though, and kept complaining that I was looking too stern (wouldn't you be looking stern if you had to deliver two under-rehearsed, cynical sentences about the Haçienda in full view of ten doormen with walkie-talkies and a queue of a few hundred people waiting to hear Allister Whitehead and Matt 'Jam' Lamont?).

When the Haçienda was finally put up for sale, some months later, in June 1997, the news was covered in the music magazines and the daily broadsheets, just as earlier incidents in the club's history had been: the rave explosion, the enforced closure in 1991, the careers of New Order, Happy Mondays and M-People.

We've got used to regular eruptions of interest in what goes on in Manchester. Sometimes it's connected with *Coronation Street*, the longest-running soap on British TV, set locally and delivered three times a week to audiences of upwards of fifteen million, or it's connected with the city's plans to host major sports events like the Commonwealth Games. Occasionally it's huge news – the bombing of the city centre by the IRA in June 1996, for instance – or shopping news – the opening of the Trafford Centre in September 1998. On another occasion, when the Bridgewater Hall, the new concert venue built for the Hallé Orchestra, was opened in Manchester, the news media hovered, set up cameras across the road and interviewed the architects. Special attention was paid to the shock absorbers built into the structure to protect against the rumble of traffic, trams and trains. Granada TV marked the occasion with a half-hour special programme, and the Hallé Orchestra's organist was profiled in *The Times*. The BBC's *Nine O'Clock News* described the opening of the Hall as 'a great day for Manchester'.

Restaurant openings are another favourite media target, but most often when Manchester hits the headlines it's to do with football, pop music or some sensationalist brew of drugs, gangs and urban chaos; violence on the street, a gangland shooting, a crisis at Manchester City Football Club, the sale of Manchester United, and more success, or more controversy, for the city's pop groups.

The image of Manchester, fabricated as much from preconceptions as from reality, is invariably gloomy; where once the Manchester myth was based on cobblestoned streets, belching chimneys and George Formby, it's now gangsters in clubs, contaminated E and empty factories. And incessant rain remains such an intrinsic part of everybody's definition of Manchester that any media portrayal of the city becomes virtually unidentifiable without it. Yet the image of the city gleaned from films like *A Kind of Loving* and *A Taste of Honey*, working-class films set in Northern England in the early 1960s, is still particularly potent, intensified by those regular doses of *Coronation Street*, created in the same era. Such films required authenticity; the depiction of the North of England had to persuade. In *A Kind of Loving* there's hardly one outdoor shot or landscape that doesn't include a smoking mill or factory chimney; every street is cobbled. The director, John Schlesinger, toured the North of England for months looking for the right locations. In his search for a church for the wedding of Vic's elder sister to a schoolteacher, he settled on St Mary's in Beswick, east Manchester. In November 1961 he filmed there, and in nearby Devon Street, co-opting locals as extras. Quite where the realistic, the authentic and the downright hackneyed begin and end, I don't know; it wasn't raining in Manchester that day, but the script had called for a wet wedding, so the Fire Brigade were employed to douse the streets and roof-tops with water.

Between visits from film crews, and eruptions of interest from the media, the city, of course, endures, meandering through damp weeks until the next sudden downpour of headlines. But the story of what happens beyond and behind the headlines – the longer story – is seldom heard; this book aims to fill the gaps, and document some of the thousands of rumours and reports, tall tales and buried details which make up a bigger picture of Manchester.

It's obvious; both to understand the present and to prepare for the future, we have to go back over the past. So I'm backtracking some of the time, digging about in what remains. It's like an excavation, peeling back layers of the city's culture, searching for clues, following connections, looking behind facades, trying to discover how Manchester has changed. First famed and feared a hundred and fifty years ago as it became the first industrial city in the world, Manchester has been reinventing itself for a new century, on an experimental journey from despair to where. It's time to take a walk, leave the Capitol; time to get concrete, check out the bricks and mortar, see what's happening, and get close to the streets.

The hidden stories of the city, and its people, reach back, hidden in a street, a sound, a building. The stories lead us on a journey, an inquisitive wander, out of Ancoats, up and down Oldham Street, across Piccadilly, down Canal Street, along Peter Street and Deansgate, through the town at night, under bridges, on street corners, in basement bars and round the back of shady nightclubs. The stories become pieces in a jigsaw; you begin to think all the pieces might fit together. At the back of the Kendal's store on

Deansgate there's a narrow street called Southgate. In 1843 Frederich Engels, co-author of the communist manifesto, worked there in an office. In 1963 Dave Lee Travis worked at the Kendal's store as a window dresser, until he got a job as a disc jockey at the Manchester Cavern. In their heyday the Stone Roses had a manager called Gareth Evans. His real name was Eric, and he started out thirty years ago as a hairdresser (he now owns a golf range). Friends from that time refer to him as 'Eric the Mod'. In 1992 Manchester United launched a new cuddly mascot; a red devil named Fred the Red. You wonder if Eric the Mod and Fred the Red are somehow related. Or if, indeed, Frederich Engels, communist, is the real Fred the Red. It's possible. Anything's possible.

And if I insist on being complicated, that's just Manchester. Nothing behind a headline is simple. Like England itself, Manchester is haunted by history, loved and hated by its citizens, unsure whether we've never had it so good or whether things have never been worse. I'm not quite sure we've arrived where we want to be; past imperfect, present tense, future uncertain. So what follows is both a celebration and an obituary, a whim and a business plan, a love letter and hate mail, a reveille and a requiem.

As in other cities, Manchester communities can feel transient; it's like we're all somehow strangers, rubbing together, making it up as we go along. Unlike London, which was a thriving metropolis three hundred years ago, Manchester is a hybrid town, born all in a rush one hundred and fifty years ago, when those arriving looking for work in the fast-growing factories, workshops, warehouses and foundries included large numbers of Catholic Irish, as well as Scots, and German and East European Jews. These migrations have been replicated since, with incomers from the Caribbean in the 1950s and from the Asian sub-continent in the 1970s. Then there are the students, appearing every September, many not staying more than three years, but others relocating here permanently.

There's an identity crisis at the heart of the story of the modern city. Manchester, like England, is now re-creating itself, looking for a new role, a life without manufacturing industry. Like a middle-aged man made redundant after a lifetime in a factory, Manchester is either facing years drawing charity, welfare and government handouts, or it's going to retrain, reorganise, and find something to keep it occupied.

The new roles, we're advised, are to be found in entertainment, tourism, finance and the service industries. Through the 1980s and

1990s plans to bring bright new buildings into the abandoned acres of Ancoats were being announced, withdrawn, repackaged. Strategies to turn the old mills into loft apartments and wasteground into piazzas were set in place at the end of 1998, but it's a job for the new century, the long, challenging resurrection of Ancoats.

Two hundred years ago, before work in the mills and factories brought thousands of people into Ancoats and other parts of the town, Ancoats was in the countryside, all corn fields and country lanes, gardened cottages and the occasional inn. Before the mills and factories Manchester itself was a small market town. The culture of England was different; stable, and rural. In Manchester, England, over the last two centuries, that culture has changed; it's now unstable, and urban. Our lives aren't measured by the ancient rhythms of harvesting, planting and wintering out, but the booms and slumps of the economy, or the football season, or when the students are around. It seems unnatural, this urban living. For the migrants to the city in the early nineteenth century it probably felt even more so. They were uprooted, then thrown together.

In the nineteenth century Ancoats was one of the busiest commercial and manufacturing districts in Manchester, buoyed by a population which increased from around ten thousand to fifty thousand in the first fifty years of the century. Alongside the Irish and the Scots, another visible community in Ancoats at the time was the Italians. Houses were routinely crammed next to factories; there was no demarcation between industrial and residential areas. The air was polluted by smoking chimneys, open drains, chemical works, soap and bone works, and a horse-slaughtering compound. Worst of all, the city's authorities had sited the Health Works, for the collection of household sewage and other waste from the city's homes and businesses, in Ancoats; the horse-drawn refuse vans passed through the area 625 times a day, carrying 8,000 pails of refuse daily. Not one house in Ancoats in the nineteenth century had a built-in bath. Death rates in the district were higher than anywhere else in Manchester. The people of Ancoats were creating the wealth of Manchester but were left to live like pigs.

This new urban, industrial Manchester became a model for a new England, a class-based England; 'Two Nations' was the Victorian phrase describing the division of bosses and workers in the middle of the nineteenth century. Manchester was where this new version of social division was first made manifest, as merchants and mill-owners became millionaires on the backs of the working poor. But working to reverse this, Manchester was also home to the Chartists, the first organised working-class protest movement in Europe. Into the twentieth century Manchester provided a base for the suffragettes seeking voting rights for women. By the time Walter Greenwood drew on the Salford strikes and demonstrations of 1931 in his novel *Love on the Dole*, the history of industrial unrest in Manchester and Salford stretched back over a hundred years. In the second half of the twentieth century, as the textile industry disappeared along with most of the manufacturing base of the North of England, the gulf between the masters and the men remained, replicated in the gulf between those financing the tourist trails, thriving from marketing schemes and service industry bonanzas, and those locked out of the story. The rich and the poor; those in work, those without work; the suits and the unsuitable.

But from the first, noisy, unruly early years of the industrial city, something had to be made out of this alienation. To the mill-hands and the factory apprentices, work and wages were important, and there was no going back to the land. Throughout the nineteenth century the new Mancunians found life-affirming pleasure, even in Ancoats. A short-lived publication, *The Manchester Figaro*, in 1880 reported on a visit to the Star Music Hall, Pollard Street, Ancoats: 'Where the ill paid curate and the city missionary fight their fiercest warfare with crime, in those hideous recesses behind the gaily painted scenes, where wealthy Manchester hides the pallid and despairing forms it dare not bring to light, the one solitary bright spot in the midst of an horizon of dreadful gloom is situated the Star Music Hall.'

From the 1830s and 1840s, as the burgeoning industries provided work for an ever-growing population, so a new urban, industrial culture developed, based on music and nightlife, street life, singing and drinking. Public houses acting as music venues were very much a part of Manchester life in this early era, with singing saloons – drinking with music on the side – developing into fully blown music halls – a charge being made for the entertainment – by the 1850s.

One of the earliest entertainment venues in Manchester was the music hall in Victoria Street, popularly known as 'Ben Lang's' – Ben Lang was the original owner – close to Victoria Bridge, almost opposite the Cathedral. In the 1840s it established itself as a popular haunt of the working classes in the area, and huge audiences of over two thousand people would often attend, entertained by singing, comic songs, and various turns and games, including sack races across the stage. Prizes of butter coolers and cups (said to be silver-plated) were handed out to the best and worst comic singers from the audience; the entertainment value amplified by every singer being compelled to sing while carrying a live goose under one arm.

Manchester, you might think, is noisy by day; wild, and a bit sleazy, at night. Certainly a century ago it was. According to Arthur Shadwell, writing in 1906, 'What most human beings like is companionship, life, things going on, the presence and stir of other human beings. You get these things in Manchester to a pre-eminent degree. In the main arteries where the tide of life runs at the full, it runs with a roar and a stir and a bustle which are not exceeded by any other town, not even by New York or London itself.'

By the time Shadwell was writing, drunkenness had become an inescapable fact of Manchester life. As England caught up with Manchester and industrialisation took hold from Liverpool to Newcastle, Glasgow to Birmingham, so did the drink. By the beginning of the twentieth century Shadwell was lamenting that the scenes of alcoholic insensibility he witnessed in Manchester were nothing new or rare: 'I am afraid this sort of thing is typical of England, and, undeniably, Manchester is very English.'

Manchester was defined by work and hooked on pleasure. Improvised street entertainment and the cheap delights of the music hall entertained the masses in the nineteenth century. In the twentieth century pride of place must go to the amusement park at Belle Vue; as many memories are buried in Belle Vue as Southern Cemetery. Belle Vue is at one end of the 53 bus route, a route skirting the south side of the city, from Old Trafford close by the Manchester United football stadium via Chorlton, Moss Side, Rusholme and Longsight. A zoo opened there in the 1830s, and the site grew to encompass gardens, concert halls, rides and rollercoasters. Between about 1920 and 1960 Belle Vue was in its heyday. Thousands traipsed there at weekends, and bank holidays especially.

After the Free Trade Hall was destroyed by German bombs during air raids in December 1940, the Hallé Orchestra needed rehearsal space and when he came upon an old church building on Hewitt Street, the Orchestra's conductor, John Barbirolli, decided to use the top-floor assembly room. Intrigued by the industrial heritage surrounding them, the players in the Orchestra dubbed the room 'The Factory'; it was cold, though, with only one coal fire heating the entire eighty foot room. Meanwhile, the Hallé Orchestra gave concerts at Belle Vue, at the King's Hall. Situated right in the middle of the zoo and amusement park site, performances by the Hallé were sometimes interrupted by the shouts and screams of the passengers on the Scenic Railway and the big dipper – or the 'Bobs' as it was known because it cost just one shilling a ride – or even drowned out, it was said, by the roars of the lions from the lion house.

The 'Bobs' took 10 trains at 60 miles per hour to a height of 80 feet and drops of 45 degrees. The older Scenic Railway – another rough ride equally as popular and scary – was the highlight of Belle Vue's first guide book in 1928 ('The Scenic Railway dominates Belle Vue. It takes you emotionally, as well as physically from the depths to the heights'), and in the search for the hysterical thrills of the big dipper, generations augmented trips to Belle Vue with visits to Blackpool; in the 1927 film *Hindle Wakes* the young lovers escape to Blackpool and the camera travels with them on the Blackpool rollercoaster, and the film *Love on the Dole* (completed in 1941) changes the site of Harry and Sally's holiday from a ramble in the countryside (as happens in the 1933 book) to a trip to Blackpool and a ride on the rollercoaster. Now the zoo at Belle Vue has gone; the last lion has roared, and the rest of the amusement park – once the biggest in Britain – closed piecemeal through the late 1970s. These days Mancunians take a trip to Nemesis, the dizzying big dipper ride at Alton Towers ('The World's Most Intense Ride Experience', a sign promises) and Blackpool's The Big One, perhaps unaware that the history of uppers and downers goes back a long way.

Fifty years ago lives stretched little further than the corner shop at the end of the street, or the terminus of the 53 bus route. Manchester, like other world cities, has since spread; there's been further movement out, the suburbs eating up the surrounding countryside. Manchester is now firmly joined to Stockport in the south and Salford in the north, and – as an aerial view would show – there's been widespread road-building and multiple extensions to the airport. Alcohol was once described as the quickest way out of Manchester, but these days around twelve million people leave Manchester International Airport every year for the sun (mainly the Mediterranean). The shift in power out of the centre of cities, the growth of suburbs, airports, outer shopping centres – the '100 mile city' (of which Los Angeles is the prime example) described by Deyan Sudjic – has changed the look of Manchester, but the urge to escape never dims.

Consuming not manufacturing is the city's *raison d'être*. Across the Rochdale Canal from the old McConnel & Kennedy mill, land has been cleared for a series of flat, squat, grey and red superstores, among them Children's World, CarpetRight and Toys R Us ('The world's biggest toy superstore'). Ancoats is obviously no longer a manufacturing quarter; anyone in this part of Ancoats is more likely to be a consumer than a producer.

Leisure is our lifeblood. Fifty years ago, Manchester Corporation commissioned a film called *A City Speaks*, documenting the city at work and play. The portrayal of the city's leisure activities – football, music and dancing – is tacked on at the end, after the stolid reality of the cotton industry, housing problems, education and health funding, and the structure of local government. Fifty years later, you can't draw even a fine line between leisure and business in the city. Football, for instance, has become both big business and one of Manchester's most famous tourist attractions. But Manchester United isn't the only example of the way the city's leisure activities feed into the city's commercial life and leave both economic and physical marks. Belle Vue was a wasteland until 1989, when the Massachusetts-based Showcase Cinemas Limited invested in the building of the Cineplex cinema, a multi-screen complex with a huge floodlit car park, mainstream blockbuster movies, fizzy drinks, popcorn crumbs under the seats. It was the arrival of the cinema which prompted companies like Burger King and Deep Pan Pizza Co. to move there and give Belle Vue some life again.

Nightclubs pull fifteen thousand people into the city centre every Saturday night, they provide somewhere in the region of five hundred jobs, their high profile nationally and internationally boosts the city, their success encourages spin-off industries like bars and record shops, and their effect on the built environment is obvious; Sankey's Soap took over Beehive Mill on Jersey Street in Ancoats, the Boardwalk occupied the same old church building on Hewitt Street once used by the Hallé, the Haçienda transformed an old yacht warehouse, Discotheque Royale is housed in the old Theatre Royal on Peter Street. The Theatre Royal was erected in 1845 after a fire destroyed its previous home on Fountain Street. Its subsequent history has followed almost precisely the changing face of popular entertainment in Manchester, being converted from a theatre to a cinema in 1923, from a cinema to a bingo hall in 1972, and from a bingo hall to its current use as a nightclub.

Manchester is full of old buildings waiting for new uses. As the booms and slumps of the cotton trade turned into one long, slow-burning slump, available space in mills and warehouses increased dramatically. By 1983 there was an estimated twenty million square feet of empty industrial floor space, much of it old cotton mills, all of it potentially available for repair and refurbishment. In the last decade and a half the trend has been to build in, and around, the old industrial buildings.

The alternative is to knock down the broken buildings of old industrial and Victorian Manchester and replace them with shale car parks or shopping centres. In Manchester's city centre thirty years ago the planners tore down a maze of back streets and alleyways between Market Street and Shudehill in order to site the Arndale Shopping Centre. It was that era – between 1963 and 1977 – when most of the worst architectural excesses in Manchester occurred. In 1968 the public inquiry into the shopping centre began, and in 1971 planning permission was granted. By the time shoppers started using the Arndale, criticisms were deafening. In June 1976, replying to complaints that the grey, grim Arndale looked like a gigantic public toilet – the 'hyper loo' it was dubbed – Council Leader Norman Morris admitted, 'It stands out like a sore thumb ... We hope it can be improved even at this late stage', adding that the exterior decor was chosen because 'it is resistant to soot and dirt'. Another Manchester first: the first public building in the world deliberately designed to blend in with the surrounding pollution.

On other occasions spanning the history of the city, Manchester's planners, developers and architects have recycled buildings. Five hundred years ago they looted stones from the Roman settlement at Castlefield to make bridges and churches. More than a hundred years ago, in 1886, as a result of an initiative taken by a young court reporter, Lex Devine – who in the 1870s and 1880s had witnessed the problems caused on the Manchester streets by the so-called 'scuttlers' (youths wearing metal-tipped clogs, brass-studded belts and bell-bottoms who intimidated the local populace by hanging around street corners) – the first Boys' Club was opened in a disused Hulme factory on Mulberry Street. This effort to get the hoodlums off the streets was a huge success; on the opening night two thousand queued to get in, but only five hundred could be catered for.

City life is built on change. In Manchester physical evidence of our links, debts and intimate relationship with the past is all around, especially in the buildings. Cities more than two centuries old are like a collage in their design; bits glued on, added, covered over. Improvisation and piecemeal progress means Manchester has been left with an ever-present past. It hasn't been a case of rip it up and start again; there's some continuity. The Royal Exchange Theatre is suspended in the vaulted splendour of the old cotton exchange. On the corner of Oldham Street and Church Street there's a building with a long retail history; first developed as the proud home of Affleck & Brown, a huge retail company during the 1860s and 1870s, it's now Affleck's Palace, a warren of second-hand clothes stalls, hat shops, shoe shops, bric-a-brac emporia, record shops and barbers.

The Corn Exchange building was founded in 1837 by Manchester's powerful corn merchants. It was enlarged in the years up to 1903 to make room for the growing Grocery Market – the largest of its kind in England – which took place in the grand central hall. At the time of the IRA bombing in June 1996, the central hall was home to a clutter of second-hand stalls. These businesses were destroyed by bomb damage, and the building was turned into the hands of property developers. The Corn Exchange had featured Manchester's most popular clairvoyant: Avril. Forced out by the bombing, she was one of thirty-five traders who moved from the Corn Exchange to new units created in the Coliseum on Church Street (originally a 1920s textile warehouse). With her psychic powers, the clairvoyant had an advantage over other traders; 'I have been out of business since the June explosion', she said, 'but I can foresee this venture will prove to be a colossal success.'

G-Mex, built in the shell of the former Central Station, was one of the first prestigious developments in Manchester city centre in the modern era. In 1969, as a result of the Beeching changes, Central Station closed, its platforms became used for car parking and its structure deteriorated considerably. It was eventually acquired and developed by Greater Manchester County Council, and converted to an exhibition centre. Subsequently, its uses have broadened to include fun-fairs, motor shows and ice shows. The first major pop concert there was the 1986 Festival of the Tenth Summer. No one at that 1986 concert, however distracted by the records Mike Pickering and I were playing, or the sight of Morrissey's white jeans, or Paul Morley's speech, or New Order's fabulous concluding set, would have come away believing that G-Mex was purpose-built; as the sun set through the massive windows, the improvisation that has characterised urban architecture for a hundred and fifty years was obvious.

In Manchester history and modernity struggle for dominance, buildings are recycled, old ideas renewed, and nostalgia remains potent. It's like a series of time loops. In 1992, in an initiative aimed at modernising transportation in Manchester, a new version of old trams surfed the new Metrolink after nearly half a century off the rails. Walk into his shop and hear my barber discussing football with his customers, and it takes a good ten minutes to realise that they're still fighting old battles, still unsure about the effectiveness of two wingers, still criticising team selection from 1963, and still marvelling at the exploits of Bert Trautmann. 'Bring back Joe Corrigan', they say. It's all about Manchester City; yearly the crises come and go, the well paid fuck up, talent goes unnoticed. In life, as in football.

In Café Pop the walls are covered with memorabilia from the 1960s and 70s; trash *Top of the Pops* record sleeves vie with George Best portraits for space. On Deansgate, the former Gaumont cinema becomes a vast pub, the Moon Under The Water. The Refuge Assurance Building is turned into a hotel. Barclays Bank becomes KFC. If they're not recycling the past, they're borrowing from it. Oasis are rock music's equivalent of Café Pop; they celebrate and recondition recent history, drawing on the Beatles, glam rock and the Stone Roses for inspiration.

The slow death of manufacturing industry released dozens of warehouses in the city centre, many ripe for refurbishment; the Britannia Hotel, for example. The Britannia occupies what was once one of Manchester's finest warehouses, built for drapers S. & J. Watts, opened in 1858 and designed in an extravagant imitation of the grand *palazzi* of Renaissance Italy. Host in its time to everybody from Frankie Goes To Hollywood to Madonna, the Britannia Hotel, by the middle of 1995, was trading on these associations; 'Hang out with the rock stars' trumpeted its publicity material, although it's unlikely that in reality guests would want to share the lifts with American heavy metal groups or run the risk of being flattened by TV sets falling from the upper floors.

And it's not just hotels like the Britannia or nightclubs like Sankey's Soap and the Boardwalk which are housed in old nineteenth-century buildings; residential city centre flats built in the 1980s and 1990s occupy old warehouses, like Chepstow House (on Chepstow Street). In 1996 Mash & Air was opened by London-based entrepreneur and restaurateur Oliver Peyton. And so it goes on, more old buildings discovering new uses: McDonalds on the ground floor of the Oxford Picture House cinema; take-aways, café bars and garages under railway arches; the Air & Space Museum in the old Campfield markets on Liverpool Road; second-hand bookshops, Thai, Mexican and Chinese restaurants in former warehouse basements; and the Goyt Mill in Marple providing a home for a snooker club and a restaurant.

Like the McConnel & Kennedy mills, not all buildings, of course, find a future; on Cheetham Hill Road, for instance, the Assembly Rooms were demolished in 1966, and the Town Hall is wrecked. Some stay empty, some get occupied illegally. In October 1995 police found a cannabis farm in an old mill on Back Piccadilly, including a thousand plants growing under special lamps, fed by an intricate irrigation system, spread over four hundred square yards of factory space, exhibiting a wonderful entrepreneurial spirit.

When it comes to housing, though, traces of the past are less easy to find. In a reflection of the hard-headed priorities of nineteenth-century Manchester, the business premises were well built and often the height of elegance, and the prestigious public buildings – which gave a gravitas and legitimacy to the city – were also lavish. Housing, however, has been poorly constructed in the city. Since the huge rush to Manchester for work, when the city boomed in the early nineteenth century, the incoming workers haven't been so much housed as stored, funnelled into rows of terraced streets or stacked in high-rise blocks like cut-price commodities on supermarket shelves.

The Hulme estate, just south of the city centre, was the biggest example of this housing nightmare. By the late 1950s Manchester's housing problem was immense; surveys suggested that within inner Manchester and Salford a quarter of a million houses were slums – leaky, damp and many with no indoor toilets or running hot water – with no future other than demolition. These were the final years of the Victorian terraced streets – built in the main in the decades that followed the introduction in 1867 of local housing regulations (a concept pioneered in Manchester) – and the changeover was painful and prolonged. Morrissey lived in Hulme, at 17 Harper Street, until the summer of 1965, just a mile or so from the city centre. Hulme had already been targeted for demolition; by 1965 some streets had already gone.

The period of transition in the mid 1960s, as old terraced Hulme was turned into high-rise Hulme, was caught by the camera of Shirley

Baker and reproduced in her collection entitled *Street Photographs*. In the introduction she notes that there was no dialogue between the council and the householders. She claims that those at the Town Hall were considered to be 'spies and the arch enemy of the people who resented having to leave their homes and move away from families and friends'.

Shirley Baker's photographs document Hulme and Salford during a time of limbo, with houses falling apart, some occupied by squatters and some demolished or burnt out. Families and businesses were moving out of the blighted area, the churches and pubs often left stranded in a desert of dust heaps as the houses collapsed around them.

The same blind, destructive impulses which led to the Arndale lay behind the formation of these new estates. Continuity was sacrificed; communities were deprived of their roots. Similar battles occurred in the 1960s and continue to occur in other cities, as laboriously self-created communities, especially in poorer neighbourhoods, come under pressure to fall in with the grand schemes of those seeking to modernise cities. What Ralph Ellison told a Federal Committee in 1966 when he argued that what Harlem residents wanted was not relocation but urban renewal, could just as easily have been applied to the Hulme, Salford and Moss Side of the time: 'They would just like to have a more human life there. A slum like Harlem isn't just a place of decay. It is also a form of historical and social memory.'

The redevelopment in the 1960s of Hulme and Moss Side set new records as the biggest piece of radical urban renewal that had been attempted in Europe; during the transitionary years documented by Shirley Baker, thirty thousand people were extracted and rehoused. The Morrissey family had moved on to Queens Square in Moss Side, but this area too was redevelopment territory, and they were rehoused by the City Council at 384 King's Road, where Morrissey lived until fame and London called. And this change affected all inner city Manchester. Over in Ardwick, Johnny Marr (then Maher) grew up at 12 Highfield Street. In 1973 all the local council tenants there and in the surrounding terraced streets were moved to an estate in Baguley, part of the Wythenshawe area.

But the Hulme redevelopment was a massive failure. Initially there was glee as the contractors – John Laing Concrete Ltd – built new houses at a frantic rate, making concrete panels at their Heywood factory, transporting them the seven miles to the site, and then, in the words of one report of the time, slotting them 'together like a child's construction kit'. But this factory-built system, based on a Danish method, though quick – Laing finished two or three years sooner than anyone using traditional building methods would have done – was unsound. The architect's concepts were wrong, the raw materials were wrong.

The new Hulme was a prison, or – in the words of one young mother in the mid 1970s – 'It's more a sort of Remand centre. We'll get out eventually. It's just that the remand is longer than most sentences.' The populace, like the housing blocks, was cracking up. Antisocial behaviour inevitably intensified in such a claustrophobic environment. Destructive boredom set in. The high-rise flats, crescents and deck-access flats, built using methods that had attracted such awe ten years before, were falling apart. The damp percolated through cracked concrete; the skirting boards and dividing walls were host to hordes of cockroaches; the underfloor heating system proved disastrously expensive and inefficient to run. And with the piss-filled lifts permanently broken, leaving access only along unsafe walkways and up stairwells swarming with cries and whispers, Hulme became a mugger's paradise.

The degeneration of the area was exacerbated by poverty and rising unemployment during the mid 1970s. In 1977, of the 916 dwellings in the Crescents more than half were occupied by supplementary benefit claimants. In 1977 Paul Hannon of the charity organisation War on Want was moved to comment: 'It is not necessary to go as far as South Africa to observe the reality of second class citizenship. Deprived families, herded together, are to be seen in every major British inner city. Manchester's Hulme bears all the sociological characteristics of a Bantustan reservation.'

By the mid 1970s nobody could hide the mental distress suffered by Hulme tenants; in 1977 the six doctors in the Hulme House Group Health Practice prescribed a (literally mind-numbing) quarter of a million tranquillisers and anti-depressants per month. By the end of the 1970s the Council had put any decision on dynamiting the tower blocks to one side, despite a report by the Hulme People's Rights Centre in October 1977 which concluded that 'Demolition is the only answer to Hulme'; instead it was decided that families would no longer be allocated dwellings in the Crescents or higher blocks.

The world had turned its back on Hulme, but in June 1978 the beginning of a new era for the area was marked by the opening of

Factory's Friday nights at the Russell Club, a joint venture by Tony Wilson and Alan Erasmus which, in turn, led to the formation of Factory Records later in the same year. Factory Records went on to become the most influential record label the city has ever seen, dominating the 1980s, selling New Order to the world and financing the Haçienda. The Factory name bore no relation to Barbirolli's draughty Hewitt Street rehearsal room, of course, and was thought at the time to be an attempt to grab the lustre still shining from Warhol's New York Factory. However, according to Alan Erasmus, it had a more direct Manchester connection, reflecting the death of the city's industry and the movement of its defining spirit from manufacturing to music:

> I was driving down a road and there was a big sign saying 'Factory For Sale' standing out in neon, and I thought, 'Factory, that's the name' because a factory was a place where people work and create things, and I thought to myself, these are workers who are also musicians and they'll be creative. 'Factory' was nothing to do with Andy Warhol because I didn't know at the time that Warhol had this building in New York called the Factory.

In part because of the pioneering location of the Russell Club, and certainly helped by the easy evasion of confused Council rent collectors, its proximity to the college campuses and its design for communal living, Hulme became a magnet for squatters, students and artists. They mixed, often well, occasionally traumatically, with those working-class tenants from the first era. Record labels and fanzines thrived in Hulme in the mid 1980s, and bands as diverse as the Inca Babies, James, Big Flame and the Ruthless Rap Assassins did their thang. 'Hulme found its own identity. We were just left to get on with it', says Jim Glennie of James, who rehearsed in his flat during the making of their first two singles for Factory Records.

Despite the improvisation evident in the way this particular generation of Hulmites worked – a perfect example of the way Manchester's youth has always been willing to thrive in whatever conditions they find the city in, to turn alienation into creativity – living in Hulme in the mid 1980s felt to me like living on borrowed time. The Council found the cost of maintaining and repairing the blocks impossible to meet, and merely embarked on a series of superficial retouches –

window frames painted pastel pink and green, for instance. In 1992 the blocks began to be demolished and yet another era for Hulme began.

Change kills off treasured routines, old ways of living, destroys old communities. Ironically, just as older residents hung on to their idealisation of the terraced streets, so the younger Hulme residents – who had made do, enjoyed and exploited the high-rise blocks – fought against a wholesale return to low-level housing when consultations about the new experiment began; indeed, part of Hulme's 1990 plans included deck-access flats.

The sense of loss felt by many Mancunians as the waves of change crash over the city is undeniable. Bernard Sumner of Joy Division, and later, New Order – and, later still, Electronic – grew up in Lower Broughton in Salford, just a few hundred yards from a huge chemical factory and right next to the polluted and stinking River Irwell. He remembers playing out in the street, safely, late at night, old ladies chatting on doorsteps and a great sense of community. But the terraces were demolished and his family were moved over the river into a towerblock. This dislocation – together with some early experiences of death in his family – he now agrees played a part in delivering the darkness to Joy Division's music. He is eloquent and expressive on the subject of the neighbourhood traumas: 'By the age of twenty-two, I'd had quite a lot of loss in my life. The place where I used to live, where I had my happiest memories, all that had gone. All that was left was a chemical factory. I realised then that I could never go back to that happiness. So there's this void. For me Joy Division was about the death of my community and my childhood.'

Bernard Sumner's life has been grounded, inflamed, fabricated by pop music. Indeed, the recent life of Manchester itself has been inescapably caught up in pop music. Without it, in fact, the modern city of Manchester would be dead. From the names of fifteen years ago – New Order, Simply Red, the Smiths – to the star acts of today – M-People, Oasis – from the teeny bop idols Take That to the club-centred pioneers 808 State, from the Buzzcocks to Happy Mondays, the Fall to Electronic, local bands have been a priceless part of the life of the city. Factory gave a focus to Hulme. Sankey's Soap began the regeneration of Ancoats. You can't write about pop music without writing about Manchester and you can't write about Manchester without writing about pop music.

It used to be claimed that if Dublin were destroyed, all you would need in order to rebuild it could be found in the works of James Joyce. The same is true of Manchester and its pop music. Visionaries like Mark E. Smith of the Fall have practically defined modern Manchester, both for itself and for strangers to the city. We had two Dutch boys staying once who had chosen to spend their holiday wandering round the canals and docks, the streets and the shops. They were amazed; 'It was just like Fall country!' they exclaimed during tea.

Travel the world and Manchester is known for two things: pop music and football. Mention to a stranger abroad that you're from Manchester and even a half-fan of football will lighten up and drool at the glorious reputation of Manchester United, intoning magic words: Best, Charlton, Cantona, Giggs. In the words of one BBC commentator, 'Manchester United have the greatest name in the world, recognised wherever a kid in a slum kicks a football.'

A few years ago a book was published in which fans of the Smiths wrote about their favourite Smiths songs. There were contributions from Japan, Canada, Wyoming, Utrecht, Lancashire, Kent, France, Spain, Scotland. Many of them reveal a love for Manchester or, rather, for a version of the city mythologised by Morrissey. Mostly they're people who feel that the records have connected with them; of the song 'Jeane' one correspondent writes 'I am Jeane'. Mostly the young writers match Morrissey; they're sentimental, morbid, enthusiastic (only about Morrissey) and very well read.

Pop music and football obsess the people who live here, that's obvious. Pop music is a greater divider of the generations than football, but the recent successes of Happy Mondays, the Stone Roses and Oasis, and the rise of club culture, led by the Haçienda, have intrigued even the generations long past going out or buying records. Down Market Street there used to be an old man on a flower stall and throughout the Madchester years (1989 and 1990), he kept trying to inveigle me into conversations about the Haçienda. He'd seen my picture in the paper and he knew I DJ-ed there. Come the darker days and the bankruptcy of Factory Records, the banter didn't stop; 'How's your mate Tony Wilson?', he'd shout.

As well as obsessing and entertaining, pop music and football employ people, inspire them. It's not just musicians (or DJs), there are the hundreds of associated jobs in the city which depend on pop music: clubs, record shops, leaflet designers, record sleeve designers, studio engineers, fashion retailers. When they dug up, re-laid Market

Street and erected the obelisk outside McDonalds in the summer of 1994 the flower stall got moved on, and my heckler ended up getting a job at the Man City training ground.

Irvine Welsh has said that when he was growing up all he wanted to do was be a footballer or a musician; two classic escape routes for working-class kids. He turned out not to be too good at either, so he drifted into writing. Noel Gallagher of Oasis, brought up in Burnage, recalls similar feelings: 'Me, if I didn't have football and the guitar, God knows what I would have become. I got the talent to write songs and live from it. So I do my best to amuse people. Because I know that's all I can do for them. Three and a half minutes of happiness in a gloomy and banal life, I'm afraid that's my only contribution.'

The dreams and imagination of Manchester people have always needed sustenance. The ambitious or the dissatisfied growing up in the narrow confines of an industrial city, with prospects as bleak as their environment, have always been haunted by dreams of escape. Throughout, and well beyond, his adolescence Morrissey was immersed in pop music, writing and dreaming. For previous generations the cinema served as a conduit for flights of the imagination, and for older generations still, the world of the music hall and, specifically, the promise of a life on the stage, was a lifelong dream. That great star of the Edwardian stage, Phyllis Dare, reports in her autobiography that she once received a letter from an aspiring young girl in Manchester. Writing some time around 1906, her correspondent hits an authentic Morrissey-esque note: 'At present I am engaged in a dressmaker's shop, and earn ten shillings a week, working eleven hours a day. Oh, Miss Dare, do help me get an engagement, for I am so miserable that life does not seem worth living.'

From the pub to the cinema, from the rollercoaster to the discotheque, from Victorian Manchester to Manchester in the 1960s, the urge to fly free of work, poverty, Manchester or domestic disaster has underpinned popular culture in the city. The city centre, especially, has always been the site of uncontrollable mania. In parts of Manchester in the 1840s the average life expectancy was seventeen years; there didn't seem much reason to hold back, so why not go for it? The widespread drug use in Manchester, England, Scotland and elsewhere is down to the poor quality of straight life. When explaining the background to *Trainspotting*, Irvine Welsh said: 'The main issue for me is that so many people are using drugs negatively, to get as far away from the horror and dullness of straight, mainstream life as possible, rather than positively, as life enhancers.'

The explosion of creativity in pop culture in Manchester is partly because of this impulse to escape and also partly the result of so few other choices, generally, for the young in this part of England. As Noel Gallagher recalls, 'When my generation left school, they had only three choices offered them: football, music or the dole. That's why there are so many big rock groups from the North.' Partly we're also benefiting from the long tradition that in Manchester you make your own entertainment. This is perhaps down to the circumstances in which the city was born; no facilities were laid on and London was a four-and-a-half-day carriage-ride away, so self-sufficiency was a necessity. The do-it-yourself spirit in the city, redefined for the modern age in the punk years, is now the most important driving force Manchester possesses.

What gives further flavour to pop music in Manchester is perhaps because it's a hybrid town, specialising in hybrid music (M-People's mash of house and supper-club soul, Black Grape's mix of black street-wise crackery and white indie shuffle, Audioweb's dub and rock collision, the jungle-meets-Joni Mitchell sound of Lamb). Perhaps it's the size; Manchester is too small to be unwieldy and impersonal, but too big to be weedy and insignificant. Perhaps it's to do with the city's entrepreneurial spirit; it's not a question of making things, it's also one of marketing them, selling them. There's an attitude too: defiant, determined, cocky, canny.

The city's historical links with other countries and cultures, via migration and trade, have left Manchester with open-minded attitudes. It's one of the least insular music cities in the world; it can love its local bands without being deaf to the charms of others. Pop music at its most vital talks person to person, ghetto to ghetto, flying free of geography, making links and connecting experiences, and just as people in Utrecht, Wyoming or wherever can connect with music made in Manchester, so people here thrive on what they hear from elsewhere; from Chicago blues and Detroit soul in the 1960s, to New York disco in the 1980s, and Nirvana and REM in the 1990s (walk through the park behind Stepping Hill Hospital in Stockport and you can't miss graffiti memorialising REM painted in yard-high white paint on the wall of the brick-built bowls pavilion; MICHAEL STIPE IS GOD it reads). Just as Manchester music fans get into these sounds from out of town, Manchester musicians – and you can trace this back decades – have a well-developed consciousness of what's going on elsewhere, and an inclination to bring these outside influences to bear on their music. Just as the city used to import raw material – cotton – and turn it into something else, so modern Manchester finds itself importing, refashioning and exporting pop music.

Wherever the music business moguls may be (in all probability behind desks in London, answerable to more senior executives in Japan or New York), Manchester has been at the heart of English pop music creativity for at least three decades. Where once the Manchester mill-owners and merchants, mill-hands and factory operatives created the wealth that financed the Empire, now the city dominates English pop culture, trading in music, the sounds from the city's streets resonating around the globe.

Away from the centres of political power – and you can't get much further away than a bedroom in Burnage or a dancefloor in Ancoats – Manchester's mavericks and misfits have created a magnificent unofficial, underground culture. Even in a society where school-leavers with a handful of qualifications, or – even more tragically – a host of great ideas (poems, maybe, or songs, or designs, or drawing skills), still end up listless, penniless; even in that uncaring, crabbed and confined society, and even amidst several ongoing, relentless recessions, young Manchester has expressed itself: in 1958 Shelagh Delaney, a teenage playwriting prodigy from Salford, stormed theatreland with *A Taste of Honey*; in 1965 three Manchester bands had top five hits in America; between 1977 and 1985 three Manchester songwriters – Ian Curtis, Mark E. Smith and Steven Patrick Morrissey – revolutionised the vocabulary and scope of pop music; in 1990 the Haçienda was the most famous nightclub in the world; in 1996 Oasis were so successful there was no indoor arena in England big enough for them; in December 1998 Longsight-born Chris Ofili became the first black artist to collect the £20,000 Turner Prize.

Shelagh Delaney was eighteen when *A Taste of Honey* was first produced, in May 1958. The story of an illegitimate teenage mother (Jo), a 'semi-whore' (Helen, her mother), a homosexual art student (Geof) and a black National Serviceman is still a moving, exuberant play. The local media greeted the news that it was to be staged in London gushingly, but as the play's content became clear local reaction changed. The *Salford City Reporter* letters page was filled with denunciations of the play; it was a side of Salford no one wanted the rest of the world to see. The play and its author were both attacked in a bitter front-page comment column on 20 June 1958.

Delaney was telling the truth, her work unfaked and not sanitised. And that remains a conundrum; the music scene in Manchester is high profile, successful, resourceful, but fronted by the likes of Morrissey, Mark E. Smith, Shaun Ryder and the Gallaghers – all a law unto themselves – it's a scene that can't be controlled. Pop musicians aren't the most natural ambassadors of a city. In 1996 the Black Grape singer, Shaun Ryder, wasn't doing the City Council's marketing department's bidding when he told *Q* magazine, 'Manchester is a Disneyland for drugs.' I remember Martin Moscrop from A Certain Ratio telling me the band were often asked about Manchester on their travels abroad. And what did he tell them? 'I tell them it's a shit-hole.'

Drowning in urban anonymity, alienated from the centres of political and cultural power, the urge to prove that you can do it, that you are somebody, is a major driving force for survival in a city like Manchester. In the late 1960s the social critic Andrew Kopkind observed the basic political statement in the riot-torn cities of North America: 'Take me seriously. LISTEN!' In Manchester a history of self-assertion goes back over a century and a half, from the earliest days of trade unionism in England, to the Chartist crusades and the city's leading role in the suffragette movement. It might be fanciful, or it might not be, to see a connection between the political struggles and the powerful position of Manchester's pop music, between the Chartists and the chart hits; the shared craving for self-assertion and self-expression.

Out of Hulme came 'Voodoo Ray', out of Burnage came 'Wonderwall'. Creativity takes root in the unlikeliest, scuzziest places, often in the minds of off-the-rails types, the ones who've been shunned, mocked, given up for dead. Novelist Jeff Noon – author of *Vurt* and *Pollen* – has recalled the circumstances he found himself growing up in in north Manchester: 'On the streets of Droylsden I was a total loner. Ashton and Droylsden are very difficult places to be creative in; they just think you are a madman or a homosexual.'

But despite all the talk of pop culture glory, in Manchester there are still more drug deals than record deals. The old mass-employing industries are only half replaced by part-time, insecure jobs. A get-up-and-do attitude is not always encouraged. Poverty and unemployment, too much heartache at the DSS, too much queuing at the post office, rents too high, hopes too low, trapped in small lives, daily routines strangling like a ligature; for the many, opportunities are few.

So it's no wonder that the urge to be somebody, make your mark, make a few bob, can end up breeding a life of criminality. For every youngster with aspirations to be the next Oasis, there's another watching the life of the local head, the local gangster, and seeing him seemingly safe, with money, respect, a Frontera, a souped up Golf GTI, a black, smoked-glass BMW.

The city's pop music is soaked in the chaos, boredom and violence of modern Manchester. The Bridgewater Hall, the new home of the Hallé, on the other hand, appears untouched by the city around it, detached and uninterested. Such prestigious developments in Manchester deny the bad news; they're so high profile they cut out a view of the streets. Sanitised, bright, well lit and clean, insulated from reality as much as it is from the rumble of traffic, the Bridgewater Hall is the complete opposite of the city it sits in; a city of unhealthy, tangled discord. It's a passive experience, as well; it doesn't draw us in, define and enlarge our dreams. It's a shrine to worship at. It shines out a message that culture is something polished and expert, something good for us, merely a soothing massage.

You can have all the privileges in the world, and nothing to say. Maybe there's some part of the human imagination that responds better to adversity, insecurity and boredom than to comfort and perfection.

Maybe if Manchester was less of a shit-hole then creativity in the city would die, the culture of the city would shrivel, and gone would be the poems of Lemn Sissay, the novels of Jeff Noon, warehouse parties, Oasis albums, Fall singles, the shared world of domino players in Moss Side, the clubs, the pubs, the monkey run, reminiscences of old Harpurhey, DJ-ing, a day at the cricket, shopping on Market Street, meeting outside the library, singing a comic song with a live goose under one arm.

Out of the trauma of the city comes energy. The positives and negatives of life in Manchester power the imagination and creativity of the city. Out of the disharmony of Manchester, England comes rock & roll. The disharmony you can't miss; it's in the collisions of race and class, the geography of the city, the architecture, the traffic, the pollution. It's another world to the Four Seasons, the England of the National Trust, the tranquil gardens of stately homes, or the untouched moors and mountains; for that, try Vivaldi, Elgar. There's a clashing disharmony in the very life, sight and sound of cities, certainly, and probably now more than ever, in what one journalist has called 'the rushing, shoving, screaming, shouting, swearing sonata that Manchester city centre has become'.

Charlie Gillett called his definitive book on rock music *The Sound of the City*, but it's a title that could subsequently have been claimed for punk, or house, or rap, or jungle (the opening track of Goldie's definitive 1995 jungle LP *Timeless* begins with a fierce rhapsody to inner city life sung by Manchester singer Diane Charlemagne). Witness, too, the MC5 in Detroit, gabba techno in Berlin, heavy metal in Birmingham, hip hop in New York. Imagine a soundtrack for modern Manchester, international, local; something as thrilling as Nemesis; as beaten up as Ancoats; something dreaming of escape; something by M-People or the Stone Roses; maybe 'Live Forever' by Oasis or 'The Reno' by A Guy Called Gerald. Maybe 'Atmosphere' by Joy Division.

PART **ONE**

Immigrants, Merchants, Anarchists:

the Birth of the City

Manchester a hundred and fifty years ago had a reputation for wild nightlife, for a special kind of raw, noisy and gregarious weekend culture. The street had a special kind of vibe, an edge. There was drunkenness, violence and vice. And there were pubs, beer-shops and music halls catering to the urban masses, especially around Ancoats, Shudehill Market, Red Bank and down near the Irwell. There was even a ballad from the early nineteenth century, 'Victoria Bridge on a Saturday Night', which celebrated the pleasures of a night on the town in Manchester; Victoria Bridge was some kind of latter-day Whitworth Street or Canal Street, thronged at the weekend with drunks, gangs, even thieves and tarts. It wasn't a refined night out.

One of the big attractions in the area around Victoria Bridge was Ben Lang's music hall. In the early days of industrial Manchester there was a huge demand for the kind of entertainment the music hall provided; songs, comedy routines, freak shows and magicians all under one roof in one evening's hectic schedule. The working people led bitterly downtrodden lives, and all opportunities to enjoy a night of public, cheap, spectacular entertainment were taken up. Urban culture had developed suddenly in the city, with no traditions on which to draw. The citizens would work hard (perhaps), and play hard (certainly); the workers lived for the weekend.

Ben Lang's was probably the most popular music hall in nine-teenth-century Manchester, and certainly one of the cheapest. Originally it was licensed as an inn and known as the Trafford Arms, but the inn was transformed by 1840 as impromptu informal tavern

3

singalongs developed into regular concert performances and comic shows. At Ben Lang's hall were the first stirrings of a music hall circuit which would remain intact for decades, and an urban popular culture in Manchester which can be traced from the very earliest days of the city right through the city's history, via nineteenth-century street life, jazz, the cinema and the 1960s, to standing in the rain at the front of the queue outside the Haçienda, and getting chased through Rusholme after an Oasis gig at Maine Road.

One day Victoria Bridge may benefit from its position on the edge of the redevelopment plans for the city centre formulated in the wake of the IRA bomb attack in 1996, but it's currently one of the ugliest ways of approaching Manchester; a forgotten, stubby little bridge, the brown stone washed with dirt, with a gruesome bus station and a shuttered toilet hutch on the Salford side, and dual carriageways, car parks and vacant grey office blocks on the Manchester side. On Saturday nights there are a few people looking for somewhere to park close to the Manchester Evening News Arena, but during weekdays there's no bustle, just a few lost shoppers. In the mid nineteenth century there was housing right up close, bunched in old cobbled streets around the Cathedral and up towards Shudehill – this was where medieval Manchester was centred – and over the river the workers were housed in cramped streets and courts clustered around Greengate.

Ben Lang's was well placed to meet the local demand, and attracted numbers in excess of any nightclub in the city today; despite a front entrance no bigger than a shop doorway, over two thousand people attended some Fridays and Saturdays. Admission to the gallery seats was 2d, and to the pit 3d. Alcohol was available from the beer-house attached to the hall, despite the view voiced by a local magistrate that tea, coffee and ginger beer should be sufficient refreshment for the patrons. The authorities never really knew what went on in these halls, although there were always rumours that they were frequented by prostitutes and known criminals. It took a disaster on a huge scale for Mancunian popular culture even to register in the lives of the well-to-do.

On the last day of July 1868, Ben Lang's was packed with Friday night revellers enjoying a programme of comic songs and talent contests. Just before 10pm a jet of flame from a broken gas pendant near the left of the stage sparked a rumour of fire, and as the audience fled, their panic exacerbated by a fear of leaking gas, twenty-three people were killed; most of the deaths occurred when a banister on

4

the packed staircase out of the building collapsed. Eye-witness reports spoke grimly of crushed bodies being hauled out at the bottom of the stairs, including those of teenage children. After the accident there was chaos outside as crowds descended on the scene, blocking hansom cabs sent to ferry the injured to the Infirmary. Some men who had hurried to assist ended up dragging the injured on their backs, running through the streets.

It was a disaster that must have shaken the working-class people of Manchester, but there's little trace of it now. There's no memorial, and few mentions in the history books, but in truth there was little made of it at the time too; a mirror image of the underground cultures of today.

Despite the great loss of life in the centre of the city, coverage of the disaster gets but a quarter of the space allotted to reports from the Cotton Supply Association annual meeting in the *Manchester Guardian*. In the reports the victims are described as 'street Arabs', although details of the injured reveal that most of them had a job of one sort or another: factory operatives, a founder, a weaver, a moulder, and a fifteen-year-old spindle and fly maker. Ben Lang's catered for the poorest of the working class, that mass of factory fodder who lived lives in so different a world to the newspaper's readers. There's clear prejudice against them. Workers or 'street Arabs', to them it's all the same: unwholesome. The poor are an embarrassment, ten a penny, dispensable.

Victoria Bridge is one of the bridges that span the River Irwell between Manchester and Salford. Undoubtedly the Salford heartlands are poorer, rougher and less well off than most (but not all) of Manchester, but England is a thousand-piece jigsaw of cheap shots and timeworn prejudice, and thus Salford looks on Manchester as Northerners look on Southerners, as Liverpool looks on the rest of Lancashire, as north Manchester looks on south Manchester; softer, pushier, posher. Manchester, meanwhile, treats Salford like an ambitious mother treats her unruly son: suspiciously. In truth, the two cities are closely related, share the same gene pool, grew up together. Their lives have merged.

Manchester and Salford were built on the sweat of migrant labour. One migrant, Ewan MacColl, the actor, singer and writer of 'Dirty Old Town' among other songs, changed his name in the 1940s. He was born as Jimmy Miller, in Salford in 1915, two and a half years after his parents moved down from Scotland looking for work. His father had gone on to Australia searching for prosperity but the plan to move the family there was abandoned when he was deported after being involved in a foundry strike. The Millers were just one of thousands of families who moved to Manchester and Salford looking for work, the pattern set a century or so before when thousands of new workers arrived to fill those streets around the Cathedral and up and down Greengate.

The cotton trade was the great employer in the area. Lancashire's natural hilly, rain-sodden landscape provided water and coal – key essentials in the manufacture of textiles – and the foundations of weaving, spinning, wool, linen, silk and hat-making industries had been laid centuries earlier, in towns and villages throughout Lancashire and Cheshire, in Bolton, Rochdale, Bury, Ashton-under-Lyne, Oldham, Macclesfield, Stockport and Salford.

Manchester's great leap forward in the early nineteenth century was the result of the industrialisation of the cotton trade. Profit-making in the industry had always ridden on the ability of new inventions to transform manufacturing processes, but the introduction of steam power in the 1780s, using the technology created by Boulton and Watt at their Soho works in Birmingham, brought huge change to the cotton industry. Science plus commerce equals Manchester.

The replacement of small-scale, old-style cotton manufacture with great mills, and the opportunities for new engineering factories using steam power for the production of iron and other metals, required large capital investment. Those who set up the new mills and factories, the powerful capitalists of the nineteenth century, needed, recruited and hired workers to run the machines. A new relationship became the dominant relationship in English society; that between owners and operatives; bosses and workers; capital and labour.

Coal-driven steam power ushered in a new age; this was the age of the industrial city, an age when advances in technology and manufacturing were transforming lives. Cotton led the way, developing and benefiting from industrialisation like no other trade in England at the time. Small towns became huge cities in the space of a generation. Rural workers throughout Europe migrated in their millions like refugees from a worn-out world, seeking work in the new industries based in the burgeoning cities. The pace of change was nowhere in the world greater than it was in Manchester, England, and the gulf between bosses and workers nowhere wider. It was not so much the movement of free labour, as forced labour.

In addition to the social division in this industrial society, there was a wildness at the heart of city life. The Manchester streets were virtually a brutal, bloody battlefield in the early part of the nineteenth century. On roads now jammed with traffic, troops fought pitched battles with local citizens. The sites of our shops, arcades, clubs and housing developments witnessed skirmishes, shootings and class war. And the painful birth of the city via the chaotic experiences of uprooted families and exploited workers has left a legacy of trauma, recurring in new guises over different generations, to the redevelopment of Hulme and Moss Side in the 1960s, manufacturing's final death spasms in the 1970s, and the ongoing massive changes in employment patterns.

The look of the place has never stayed the same for long. The markets and merchants of Manchester benefited hugely as the steam age brought not just new methods of manufacture, but transport too; canals and railways opened up vast new trade routes. During the 1820s and 1830s something like eight hundred warehouses were built in the town in order to display and store raw cotton, spun yarn and finished cloth. To a landscape with chimneys, a skyline already being refashioned by mills, factories, canals and, increasingly, railways, came the bulky, four- and five-storey warehouses.

Manchester became part of a global network. In the era of rock & roll this would be just as crucial as in the days of cotton and coal. As lines of transport and communication improved across the thirty miles of Lancashire to the port of Liverpool, so international markets expanded and Manchester's economy boomed. Within the first few decades of the nineteenth century, the city's merchants had worldwide contacts, with no dependency on the largesse of London. They had created their own wealth, become economically self-sufficient, as had other parts of England; the steel-makers of Sheffield, the engineers of Birmingham. Critically, the authority of London was undermined by the wealth, power and self-begotten independence of the big provincial cities.

By the end of the 1830s, after the industrialisation of cotton manufacture, Lancashire was responsible for 90 per cent of the cotton manufactured nationwide. England needed Manchester. Manchester was at the vanguard of wealth creation in the country; cotton had become hugely important to the national economy, accounting for nearly 50 per cent of all export earnings. Liverpool had become the most important cotton port of its age, and Manchester the greatest cotton market.

Before industrialisation, though, cotton had been one of the more minor products that passed through Liverpool. More lucrative had been goods like tobacco and sugar. Most lucrative of all had been the slave trade. During the late eighteenth century around thirty thousand slaves a year were transported through Liverpool, rising to fifty thousand by the beginning of the nineteenth. The trade made huge profits for Liverpool.

Cotton and slavery were inextricably linked. From Africa slaves were purchased from the local tribal chiefs in exchange for metal goods, guns, gold, cowrie shells and brightly printed cotton goods provided from the Indian sub-continent, but increasingly from Lancashire. The slave-exploiting plantations of the West Indies provided most of the raw cotton for the Lancashire-based cotton industry. The huge leap in demand for raw cotton as the industry became industrialised was a major factor in the founding and maintaining of new plantations in Virginia and the other southern states of America from 1790 onwards. The industrialisation of Lancashire developed and maintained slavery in America.

The slave trade was outlawed in 1806, but that didn't stop the Lancashire mills using cotton from the existing slave plantations. Meanwhile, analogies between the rapidly worsening lot of the workers in England and the slaves on the plantations were pointed out by William Cobbett, Richard Oastler and others. Mills run by the notorious factory owner William Douglas on the site of Pendleton Old Hall on Whit Lane in Salford had such a bad reputation for exploiting the workers, especially the young (pre-teenage) apprentices, that the mills became known locally as the 'White Slave Mills'. Children who tried to escape their work there were dragged back, put in irons and manacled to their beds at night.

Manchester's population boom, as industry expanded and the poor came looking for work, brought massive housing problems. Families were crushed into shoddily constructed back-to-backs, often built next to the unchecked sprawl of industrial factories, chemical and dye-works, and railway goods yards. Some of the worst living conditions were in the squalid cellars of old middle-class housing which had fallen into ruin and been converted for the use of several families. Those close to the canals and rivers suffered seeping water. Over twenty thousand people lived in cellars in the 1830s.

Manchester suffered the kinds of disease associated with such poor conditions: cholera, smallpox and typhus. A great cholera epidemic swept Europe in 1832, from the Mediterranean to the Black Sea, and Manchester and Glasgow were both hard hit. The epidemic's first reported casualty in Manchester was James Palfreyman, living in Somerset Street; altogether 790 people died from cholera in Manchester and Salford between 1831 and 1833. The disease was almost exclusively confined to the poorer districts; the shanty towns of Angel Meadow, Little Ireland and Red Bank. In this era the middle class abandoned their homes in the disease-ridden and sewage-strewn streets of the town centre and moved to quiet places like Didsbury (then a hamlet among open fields), but too many new Mancunian families lived a life cursed with poor health, easy death and high fatalities among the young; over half of all children in Ancoats died before their fifth birthday.

'This English Nation, will it get to know the meaning of its strange new to-day?', asked Thomas Carlyle in 1843 in *Past & Present*, a widely influential essay much concerned with what was going on in Manchester. As the Victorians sought to get a grasp on the almighty changes which their society was undergoing, Carlyle's anxious essay told them this much: the key to understanding the condition of England was buried somewhere among the mills, masses and myths of Manchester.

Novelists such as Elizabeth Gaskell, Benjamin Disraeli and Charles Dickens, as well as the social critics of the age such as John Ruskin and Alexis de Tocqueville, all filed writings from the pioneering city, and with their descriptions of Lancashire's industrial growth – the onward march of machinery and the giant factories, the money-making merchants and manufacturers, and sulphurous, dangerous slums – set the scene for Manchester's life story and, by implication, England's too. What the writers, journalists and commentators found in Manchester one hundred and fifty years ago fixed the image of the city as a grimy, industrial hell-hole.

You couldn't deny that life and the environment in Manchester and Salford have frequently been grim – Edmund Frow has described the Salford of the 1930s as 'arguably the most grim place in the North of England' – and that grimness has been valuably, vividly reflected by many voices; from the cheerless realism of *Love on the Dole* to the pinched, slouched workers in the Lowry wasteland, to the warped tales of mental and environmental disorder so beautifully pinned down by Mark E. Smith. But alternative visions have surfaced, different perceptions of Manchester. For instance, the pop music from the city during the late 1980s re-created Manchester by challenging this one-dimensional view so forcefully that it required the renaming of the city: 'Madchester'. The sights and sounds of Madchester – from the thrilling, rolling drum beats of the Stone Roses' celebratory 'I Am The Resurrection', to Central Station's big colour sleeve and poster designs – were qualitatively different to old Manchester.

But whatever changes, complications and alternatives have developed in the last century and a half, Manchester has been fixed in the international mind, entrapped in its history, condemned to live forever in a landscape of rusting iron bridges, rivers the colour of lead, rain pouring down on derelict canal wharfs, and red-brown back-to-backs. The potency of Manchester's grim, rather than glam, public image remains, with out-of-towners especially happy to roll with the ready-made preconceptions. When the bids to host the 2000 Olympics were being made, the fight to prove that Manchester wasn't rainy, grimy and half-derelict was too much for the spin doctors. The winning city, Sydney, commissioned a damaging, unsubtle video which contrasted Manchester's empty warehouses and derelict, rain-swept wastelands with film of sunny Sydney harbour and glinting downtown Sydney skyscrapers.

The nineteenth-century view of Manchester focused on more than just the grim environment; Manchester was seen as a harbinger of future chaos in England. The authorities, the landed gentry, the London Parliament, spent decades trying to control Manchester and its restless population. The raw poverty, rough conditions and seething violence in everyday life fed into a general feeling that cities were a threat, that urban life was essentially unnatural, uncivilised even. Hostility against city life has a long tradition among the English ruling class, and moral panics among prosperous rural dwellers regarding 'travellers' during the 1980s were, in part, a fear of contamination, a fear that the travellers – many of whom were refugees from the inner city – brought with them lawlessness and uncontrollable city ways. In 1843 Carlyle brought home the brutality of city life with a report of Stockport parents found guilty of poisoning three children in order to collect the £3 insurance due on the death of each child. The psyche of the city was feared.

There were clearly two ways of looking at mid nineteenth-century Manchester; the rise of Manchester as a powerful town with massive buildings, newly built monuments to its own magnificence and a pioneering position in the industrial world was undeniable, yet the ugliness and distress among the working classes were conspicuous to all.

The working classes were sceptical that they would benefit from the increased profits triggered by technological progress. Manchester was likely to disprove all trickle-down theories and underline instead that the new industrial society would enrich the minority but not the masses. In Lancashire, especially in the outlying cotton towns, what became known as 'Luddite' activity – machine-breaking – became a regular occurrence as workers, fearing redundancy as trades became more industrialised, efficient and competitive, declared war on factory and mill equipment.

Between the classes there were oceans of mistrust. Mrs Gaskell's poor weaver, John Barton, describes himself as a 'slave' and is tortured by the thought that the bosses care little for him or his class: 'We pile up their fortunes with the sweat of our brows, and yet we live as separate as if we were in two worlds.' In the early years of industrial Manchester, the physical division of the operatives living cramped in the town and the middle class living outside, reflected the shape of industry; masters and men, the Cotton Supply Association and the Victoria Music Hall regulars.

Thomas De Quincey, the author, essayist and opium addict, grew up in a family which moved out of central Manchester to green fields two miles south, at what became Greenheys. He fell under the spell of opium in 1804, later describing it as 'a panacea for all human woes'. He would get dosed up on Tuesdays and Saturdays and go out listening to music, carrying with him at all times 'portable ecstasies', tinctures of laudanum (a solution of crude opium in alcohol). His anonymous memoirs, *Confessions of an English Opium Eater*, were published in two parts in 1821. Within just a few months he was held responsible for widespread copycat drug-taking and a spate of up to sixty deaths caused by opium overdose. Fifty years later he was hailed as 'Manchester's deepest thinker'.

The young Thomas was tutored by the curate of St Anne's church, who lived in Salford. Every day Thomas and his brother William walked to his home in Salford, a journey which took them past a cotton mill on the outskirts of Manchester. One morning the factory lads espied the well-to-do De Quincey brothers shod in over-refined knee-high boots with tasselled tops, and began following them, taunting them with a derisive chant of 'Boots! Boots!'. The conflict continued every time the brothers passed the mill to and from their tutor's house, a miniature class war conducted with sticks, stones and name-calling, a trivial reflection of the bigger battles of the age.

For decades Manchester was occupied by troops sent by London to subdue the local citizens. The city's reputation for wild nightlife was part of a wider perception that the city was uncontrollable. Manchester's markets were flashpoints, the locals resentful of price rises and adulterated goods. On 15 November 1757 a serious food riot occurred at Shudehill. Armed men from Oldham and Ashton came into Manchester and seized provisions from the market, motivated by hunger and outrage at the exploitation of the people by the traders. They were beaten off by soldiers; four of the rioters were killed. One of the flour mills attacked was said to have mixed 'Accorns, Beans, Bones, Whiting, Chopt Straw, and even dried Horse Dung' with its flour.

Women played a major part in the food riots. As one commentator in 1800 noted: 'All public disturbances generally commence with the clamour of women and the folly of boys.' The most notorious riot took place in 1812. On 20 April, carts were overturned, mills burned to the ground and shops looted. Among the arrested rioters, Hannah Smith confessed to three days of marauding, during which she had stopped potato and butter carts in the street and distributed the produce to the crowds. Her offences were deemed 'highway robbery' and she was hung in June at Lancaster, along with seven other people, including Abraham Charlson, a sixteen-year-old boy charged with setting fire to a weaving mill in Westhoughton.

The food riot had been a traditional means of protest, but in urban industrial society, with the supply of Manchester's food coming from as far afield as the south east of England, neither mobs nor magistrates could do much to pressurise the producers into keeping prices low. It became clear that an alternative means of maintaining living standards was not by influencing prices but by protecting wages. Thus the workplace became the focus for agitation and a new strain of trade unionism emerged out of the old guilds and craft organisations, less cowed by the power of the bosses, and highly politicised.

The authorities feared that Manchester would lead the country to a political and social revolution. Draconian measures to punish disturbances among the city's working poor were unleashed; even potato-stealing was a capital crime. But it wasn't just those taking part in riots or looting who felt the force of law, but also workers attempting to combine and organise to protect wages and conditions;

they faced violence and hostile labour laws, and the leaders risked imprisonment.

In the early decades of the nineteenth century, radicalism and political campaigns were maturing fast, amid increasing chaos and violence in Manchester. Calls to replace the whole established ruling class – the combined Church and State, the King, the unrepresentative Parliament – were growing louder. The ground was shifting under the feet of the old Establishment. Tory Loyalists called a meeting at the Exchange Hall in April 1812 which, instead, turned into an anti-Government riot. The Exchange, that great symbol of Manchester merchants, the cathedral of capitalism, where the cotton merchants gathered to haggle and deal, was the centrepiece of Manchester's commercial life. If there was ever going to be a revolution in Manchester, it was clear that the first call would be to storm the Exchange.

After the Exchange Hall riots, tension on the streets remained high, with tales of hostile gangs seeking out the well-to-do and finely dressed, and class conflict escalated. It was just a few days later that the mob headed by Hannah Smith wrought havoc in food riots. Violence was in the air; on 10 May a well-known sergeant in the militia, John Moore, and a female relative were set upon and murdered on Ancoats Bridge, their bodies tipped into the water. The murderers were never identified.

Economic unrest became further politicised in the years following the end of the Napoleonic War. The Constitution looked incapable of providing institutions that could deal with the problems of the new age. Genuine, long-lasting improvement in the lives and working conditions of the poor would only come through structural changes in the political system; to the radicals, constitutional reform was a prerequisite of social reform.

Throughout 1819 mass meetings in support of political reform were held in a number of towns in Lancashire and West Yorkshire. There was nothing more awesome in this era than the mobilisation of the masses; just a few decades earlier mobs on the streets had engineered the French Revolution. Focused, directed, collective anger was a powerful force. The ability of Henry Hunt and other orators to draw huge crowds was a tangible, terrifying threat to the authorities. On 8 January eight thousand people gathered at St Peter's Field to hear Henry Hunt affirm, 'all men are born free, equal and independent of each other' and that 'the only source of all legitimate power is in the people'.

Fearing revolution, over the next months the Government and Manchester's magistrates were in close contact, devising strategies for undermining the momentum behind these large rallies. In addition to legal constraints and the use of spies and informers, reformers' letters were intercepted. When all else failed the authorities didn't hold back from using military muscle against the people; the military were called to disperse a mass meeting in Stockport in February 1819, and when the magistrates banned a meeting due to be held in Manchester on 9 August, a spontaneous protest at New Cross degenerated into a riot lasting three nights during which two thousand people fought with a body of police and military led by the infamous Deputy Constable of Manchester, Joseph Nadin.

But the biggest gathering and the fiercest battle came a week after the confrontation at New Cross; 'Peterloo', as the episode became known. The details of the events which took place in Manchester on 16 August 1819 – the murder of protesters by mounted soldiers – were hugely controversial, with clear attempts made to play down the guilt of the soldiers. It was a showdown played out around what is now Peter Street. Peter Street would later become the site of the Free Trade Hall and Midland Hotel, and Manchester's theatreland, but in 1819 it was no more than a footpath over open fields.

Around a hundred thousand protesters had gathered from around Manchester and outlying towns, carrying flags and banners inscribed with slogans. The authorities, meanwhile, had brought together an immense body of special constables and military and artillery forces (volunteer yeomanry as well as regular troops). Under orders from the magistrates, Deputy Constable Nadin, aided by the Manchester Yeomanry, attempted to arrest Henry Hunt. Eye-witness Samuel Bamford described the Yeomanry making their way through the crowds with their swords, cutting at people: 'Their sabres were plied to hew a way through naked held-up hands, and defenceless heads; and then chopped limbs, and wound-gaping skulls were seen; and groans and cries were mingled with the din of that horrid confusion.' The violence escalated when the 15th Hussars, assembled on the corner of Windmill Street and Mount Street, joined the fray; by the end of the day at least eleven people had been killed and six hundred injured.

The violence used against the demonstrators shocked and politicised the nation. The poet Shelley was stung into writing 'The Mask of Anarchy', an indignant call to the masses to overthrow the ruling classes, reminding them, 'Ye are many – they are few'. Peterloo was the biggest single moment in Britain's struggle towards democracy, and it inspired what Shelley's biographer describes as 'the greatest poem of political protest ever written in English'.

This battle in Manchester was nothing less than a battle for the control of Britain, a fight, literally, to the death. The millions who helped to create the wealth of the country wanted their voices heard, but the authorities had dashed their hopes unmercifully. With overwhelming military force the authorities had won an infamous battle, but it was not the end of the story. The brutality on the part of the authorities was a sign of weakness not strength; after Peterloo democracy was more, not less, likely.

A symbol of the ruling elite's capacity for exploitation and violence, Peterloo has been hidden from sight. The wording on the plaque on the front facade of the Free Trade Hall marking the site of Peterloo reflects something of Manchester's unease with the uprising. The plaque refrains from using the word 'massacre', and even from mentioning the loss of life. It states simply: 'The site of St Peters Field where Henry Hunt, radical orator, addressed an assembly of about 60,000 people. Their subsequent dispersal by the military is remembered as "Peterloo".'

In 1878, when the Manchester Town Hall Committee met to decide which incidents in Manchester's history were to be depicted by Ford Madox Brown for the Town Hall murals, Peterloo was rejected; it 'did not seem to meet with favour', the minutes reported. In 1938 the organisers of a civic pageant were reluctant to include Peterloo, and suffered the criticism of the *Manchester Guardian*. The makers of *A City Speaks*, commissioned by the Corporation in the 1940s, also made no reference to Peterloo. The battles of the Napoleonic War – Waterloo and Trafalgar – are landmarks in our history books, etched on the mind of the nation, but the battles at home go unremembered. By 1999, when the Free Trade Hall looked to be at the mercy of property developers – with various plans for hotels, conference centres and luxury apartments – the obliteration of history had become an everyday event.

Peterloo was not a one-off. In the late 1820s, industrial unrest, food riots, intermittent Luddite activity and increased political radicalism had boosted Manchester's reputation for uncontrollable sedition. Strikes, riots and unrest continued; more repressive measures and the arrest and trial of the radical leaders followed. When mills in

Ancoats suffered arson attacks in April 1826, the trouble was sufficient for the Cabinet to meet in emergency session in London and again order the dispatch of troops to quell the disturbances.

Manchester had what amounted to the status of a far-flung colonial outpost of London; the city's struggles for representation in the London-based Parliament were defined as sedition; reporters sent stories back from the dark underworld, and demonised the townspeople as criminals and agitators; whenever unrest appeared the troops were deployed. The two hundred miles between the rulers and the ruled never seemed so far.

But during the late 1820s the struggle for change widened in Manchester, with the emergence of a new middle class very different from the old-style aristocratic ruling class. These manufacturers and newly rich merchants were a bright breed of Manchester entrepreneurs, often from Nonconformist religious backgrounds rather than sharing the Anglican traditions of the Tory old guard. But like the operatives, weavers, factory workers, the new middle class had no representation in Parliament, and no control over local government in Manchester. When they became involved in the push for constitutional reform, under the leadership of Richard Cobden, they brought to the movement something other than the mysterious menace of mass assembly; they wielded genuine economic power. Cobden and the self-made men of the North believed in free trade, unbridled competition and the superiority of market forces, and were incensed by measures like the highly restrictive Corn Law – which the Tory landed interest had used its monopoly in Parliament to secure, ensuring the landowners' profits – and the levying of high import duties on cotton.

Nationally, partial parliamentary reform in the 1832 Reform Bill widened the voting franchise and gave Manchester two MPs, but delivered no real influence to the Manchester middle classes. Their calls for free trade were ignored, and the Corn Laws remained. Locally, however, the long overdue granting of Manchester's borough status in 1838 – giving the city the right to elect councillors instead of being controlled by unaccountable Tory-minded local landowners and magistrates – gave Cobden a strengthened foundation for a push into national politics. Cobden and the local Liberals then focused attempts to end trade restrictions in March 1839 by establishing the Anti Corn Law League with other manufacturers and businessmen, with a head office in Newall's Buildings on Market Street.

The Reform Act was an even sharper disappointment to the working class. Manchester's two MPs opposed workplace regulation, factory legislation and every extension of the right to vote, and even colluded in the introduction of a stringent new Poor Law. As the economy from 1837 went into a sharp decline, the operatives were driven to increase their political agitation, and their aims were summed up in the People's Charter, published in May 1838.

The Chartist movement was the first sustained working-class movement in Europe in the industrial era. Chartism drew considerable strength from battles past, including, of course, the massacre at Peterloo. It sought to concentrate unrest among the labouring poor on six key Charter demands: universal suffrage, annual Parliaments, vote by ballot, equal electoral districts, no property qualification and the payment of MPs. One commentator has described the Chartist movement as 'divided, ill-organised, and abysmally led', but one of its earliest meetings mobilised thousands; on 15 September 1838 an estimated fifty thousand people attended a Chartist rally on Kersal Moor, near Manchester, the biggest gathering in the area since Peterloo.

At first, the Chartist movement was a threat to the status quo. Although in retrospect it's clear that the Chartist demands were the blueprint for modern democracies, at the time they were fiercely resisted by the authorities. The House of Commons rejected a national petition, Chartist leaders were arrested and charged with conspiracy and, after rumours of a huge armed Chartist insurrection, General Sir Charles Napier was asked to strengthen the Manchester garrison with more troops.

The one thing that both the Chartists and the Anti Corn Law League had in abundance was a belief in self-organisation. Away from real political power in London, they understood that to make progress they needed to build alternative networks. To the workers in the new industrial cities of England, self-organisation – whether in the trade unions that were formed by workers earlier in the century, or the Cooperative movement which was soon to follow – was increasingly important. Urban networks flourished. The powerful propaganda propelled by the League from the city over the next months identified Manchester at the vanguard of change and further loosened the city's dependence on London. According to one non-Mancunian historian, 'Manchester spoke, of course, in the name of the provinces, and the provinces spoke in the name of England.'

That's not to say that Manchester presented a united front. In other cities reformers formed alliances, but in Manchester the working-class agitators and the middle-class radicals were frequently at loggerheads; a riot occurred between the Anti Corn Law League and the Chartists in Stevenson Square in June 1841. The split went back to Peterloo and the ambiguous role played by the manufacturers, but was also a reflection of deep ideological differences. The Chartists were the oldest of old Labour, fervent advocates of the interests of working men and women; the Anti Corn Law League, on the other hand, were unembarrassed bosses, capitalists and free marketeers.

Richard Cobden is now commemorated with a statue in St Ann's Square, close to businesses like Dixons and W. H. Smith, and within hailing distance of the Royal Exchange. In a baggy coat and sturdy shoes, he presents the image of grounded, successful Manchester man, his left hand snugly, smugly nestling under his waistcoat, his right hand flourished in an oratorical style, apparently pointing in the direction of what is now the Disney shop. The Disney empire is a natural extension of Cobden's free market beliefs. Only recently an expert was analysing the company's success at cut-throat international competition: 'I don't think that Disney work with people, they either take them over or put them out of business.'

When the IRA bomb exploded in the centre of the city in June 1996, the Exchange was badly damaged. By the middle of 1997 its internal walls were being supported by miles of scaffolding. The bomb had temporarily destroyed all attempts to produce the kind of safe, sanitised city centre – clean, tidy, free of beggars and derelict buildings – demanded by the tourist trade and the retail sector. But it was, in one way, a reminder of the reality of the early days of industrial Manchester; an age of anxiety, dirt and shored-up buildings. Hastily and badly built, many homes were unsafe; in July 1814 three people drowned when their houses at Hunt's Bank slid into the River Irwell, and in July 1834 unsafe houses on Long Millgate collapsed, killing two boys and a girl. People's places of work, those buildings which transformed the landscape, were also a threat to life, and barely a week passed without a chimney being blown down, a warehouse collapsing or fire destroying buildings. The fall of an iron beam at the factory of Mr Nathan Gough caused the death of nineteen workers in October 1824. A fire at Messrs Macintosh & Co.'s patent cloth factory in Chorlton-upon-Medlock in April 1838 killed three people. Employers took safety risks to boost profits. It took persistent pressure from workers to win regulations such as limits on working hours and minimum age requirements for dangerous jobs.

At the sharp end of life fluctuations in wages could throw whole communities into chaos. Several weeks of strikes in August 1842 in various parts of the region – from Stalybridge to Salford – became known as the 'Plug Riots', the most concerted set of disturbances that Manchester had witnessed, when strikes spread through the cotton districts. This spontaneous protest against wage cuts was fortified by food riots, and revived calls for a general strike. Throughout August there were battles between workers and the military, including clashes between marchers and soldiers near where the BBC now stands, widespread looting and arson, and the destruction of a police station; a Chartist rally attended by fifteen thousand people in Granby Row Fields was dispersed by troops, two six-pounder cannons and five hundred special constables sworn in the previous day. The strike lasted five weeks, with fifty thousand strikers closing two hundred places of work.

The year 1842 was the hardest of all hard times in Manchester's economic history, with massive distress among the operatives, falls in wages, loss of jobs. The economy of the city was riding a rollercoaster of boom and slump, creating instability for masters and men alike. In the summer of 1842 the *Manchester Times* was reporting, 'The picture which the manufacturing districts now present is absolutely frightful. Hungry and half-clothed men and women are stalking through the streets begging for bread.' Manchester, a city at the vanguard of the industrial revolution, had dissolved into near-anarchy, beset with mobs battling with soldiers on the streets. Into this chaos came Frederich Engels.

Engels detailed and analysed social and economic conditions in Manchester in his book *The Condition of the Working Class in England*, first published in May 1845, a vivid, indignant, eye-witness polemic which provided the raw material underpinning Karl Marx's *Das Kapital*, and the joint works of Marx and Engels, including *The Manifesto of the Communist Party*. The hold that capitalist market values had on Manchester, and the poverty and exploitation of the workforce, was particularly strong in the city. But Engels was also influenced by Manchester's unique history of political dissent and social disturbance. His belief in the power of the proletariat to re-create society, abolish private property and take their share of the social advantages of industrialisation was undoubtedly, specifically, stimulated by civil unrest in Manchester in the decades up to the 1840s. He came to a city steeped in a tradition of riot and resistance, Luddite uprisings, Chartist demonstrations, spontaneous disturbances. And Peterloo – just a generation earlier – was still vivid in the collective memory.

Engels came to Manchester on the wish of his father, who wanted his son to prepare for a career in the family's textile factory back home in Barmen, Germany, by witnessing first hand the workings of his second factory, the cotton company Ermen & Engels, which had been established in 1837 by Engels Senior and the brothers Ermen on the outskirts of Manchester near Weaste Station on the Manchester to Liverpool Railway. Engels spent most of his time at the company's warehouse and offices at 7 Southgate, just a short walk from the Royal Exchange. The offices the young Engels worked in overlooked the yard of the Bush Inn, but Engels preferred drinking at the nearby Golden Lion. In October 1852, writing to Marx, he asked him to send his reply via the Golden Lion's landlord, James Belfield.

His work for Ermen & Engels positioned him firmly in the bourgeois world of business and commerce, but he led something of a double life. While in Manchester he established strong links with local Chartists and other subversives. Also, Engels engaged in a clandestine relationship with a local Irish factory girl, Mary Burns. He kept an official, respectable home and he also kept a separate home with Mary. When she died in January 1863, he lived with his sister, Lizzie. His advice to Marx to write via the Golden Lion is evidence of just how much weaving and dodging there was, as Engels drifted between the go-getting world of the prosperous business classes and the world of the poor. He must have been the only member of the Exchange who went home for tea in a two-up-two-down in Hulme.

But his links across the social classes gave Engels a perfect perspective when it came to dissecting life in the industrial city. On the one hand, without his life as a businessman, Engels would have had far less insight into the bourgeois mind and the practical workings of capitalist life – the mundane economics of costs, profits, trade, turnover – and, on the other, without Mary Burns, it's unlikely that he would have been so well informed about the lives of Manchester's factory workers, or that he could have gained safe passage in the more squalid areas of the town, many of which were virtual no-go areas for strangers, especially German-speaking businessmen. As it was, during his wanderings Engels found traumatic evidence of the appalling conditions that the mass of Manchester's inhabitants endured in a low-lying area just to the west of Oxford Road known as Little Ireland, surrounded on all sides by factories, mills and the smells of the River Medlock, with its shit heaps a-plenty; a mass of damp, trampled back-to-backs and collapsing new buildings.

For Engels, opposing Luddite views, it wasn't machines that dehumanised society, but the exploitation of the working class by the factory owners. For him, the distress of Manchester's working poor was a direct result of middle-class prosperity, a product of impersonal market forces let loose in a money-motivated society, the bourgeoisie regarding the workers as commodities not people, as 'hands' not human beings; 'The relation of the manufacturer to his operatives has nothing human in it; it is purely economic.'

Engels laid out evidence that the hugely magnified social divisions in society and the particular strains of the new, urban industrial age had forced the working poor 'to think for themselves' and to organise. In Manchester, he concluded, the exploitation and poverty, and the particular new set of social relations engendered by industrialisation, had spawned class consciousness among working people. They were now a new force, the industrial proletariat; 'a compact group with its own ways of life and thought and outlook on society'. Workers, he wrote, would one day grab 'their share of the advantages of the new era'. Engels predicted the revolution of the proletariat with unswerving certainty. The proletariat was driving itself irresistibly forward towards its ultimate emancipation. Emancipation by force, that is; as far as he was concerned, in Manchester, in 1844, revolution was just a stone's throw away.

But he underestimated the power of the authorities. They had hit back hard during the Plug Riots, with two thousand troops brought by train into Manchester to strengthen the garrison. In the period immediately following the riots, up to fifteen hundred local and national Chartist leaders were arrested and imprisoned. On 21 March Fergus O'Connor and fifty-eight other Chartists were tried at Lancaster.

In a sense, the Plug Riots marked the beginning of the decline in industrial and social unrest in Manchester, not – as Engels had predicted – the beginning of greater ferment. Constant defeat and harassment led, inevitably, to the demoralisation of Manchester's Chartist movement. The Chartists' third national petition of 1848 was the national leadership's final attempt to mobilise the masses, but on this occasion the march was held in London. Further meetings in Manchester dissolved in the face of huge military operations against them. Again, leaders were arrested. Without Manchester stoking the furnaces, the Chartists nationally lost their momentum.

As well as moving against Chartist leaders, street-level disorder was much more effectively policed from 1842, when Manchester's New Police began operating in a far more aggressive way than the old system of watchmen had allowed. In areas with a reputation for crime a policy amounting to a version of zero tolerance was implemented; every street gathering was dispersed, loiterers moved on and beer-shops regularly closed. The new regime in Manchester proved effective, although high-profile policing triggered rioting on various occasions, including May 1843, when off-duty soldiers and citizens clashed with police in Ancoats and broke into Kirby Street Police Station, attacking the police inside.

In addition, in the latter part of the 1840s the economy went through one of its boom periods, and the conditions of extreme distress ebbed away. In times of improved economic performance, the bosses were more generous in their concessions to the workers. A shift in the methods of Manchester-based employers began even before national legislation; they instigated what overseas competitors called 'the English week', and thus a free weekend from at least midday Saturday became the norm in Manchester and other parts of Lancashire in the 1840s, spreading to London in the following decade, and although the smaller firms tended to maintain sweatshop conditions, bigger industrialists began to accept legal supervision of working conditions.

Against the background of a buoyant local economy and a more efficient, Liberal-controlled local government, the authorities instigated building and sanitation programmes to relieve the conditions in the worst quarters of the city. Prosperity bought for Manchester the luxury of respectability. In the pincer movement of concessions – on the one hand – and suppression – on the other – the middle classes successfully tamed the working class. The mill workers of Lancashire remained passive even in the face of the cotton famine of the 1860s. Two more Reform Acts further increased the electorate (although about two million men and all women were still denied the vote). By the time the first authorised English edition of the *Condition of the Working Class* was published in 1892, Engels acknowledged that as wealth had increased 'a new spirit came over the masters, especially the large ones, which taught them to avoid unnecessary squabbles'. There was no denying that Manchester's international reputation for revolutionary disorder melted away as the nineteenth century progressed.

It was not the Manchester Chartists but the movement of middle-class businessmen in the Anti Corn Law League who maintained their national profile in the years after the Plug Riots. The League had held a banquet at the Free Trade Hall on Peter Street in January 1840, attended by nearly four thousand people; the first public meeting held there. They had erected a temporary wooden building constructed for the purpose by a hundred men in eleven days. A more permanent structure was built in 1856. By this time the Free Traders had won their victory; in 1846 Sir Robert Peel, a Lancashire man, had repealed the Corn Laws. The strength of the middle class reflected the strength of their economic position. Their riches had been fed into the campaign with a vigour and efficiency which would shame a modern political pressure group; a drive for funds in the crucial months at the start of 1846 had raised over a quarter of a million pounds (enough, at 1846 prices, for example, to build ten Town Halls).

The Royal Exchange had survived riots and continued to attract up to six thousand dealers in its great hall. Furthermore, the industries growing through the middle decades of the nineteenth century broadened the base from purely cotton and textile manufacture. The proximity of the coalfields meant that trades such as metal and engineering were increasingly fruitful, as well as the production of food and drink, glass, munitions and armaments, railway engines, chains and chemicals. In a further social shift, within a few decades the employment base had so changed that more women were employed in domestic service than in Manchester mills. The mill-towns of Lancashire retained their one-industry culture, but in Manchester shop-owners – not factory barons or mill-owners – came to dominate local politics. In 1899 Beatrice Webb noted that Manchester's City Council consisted largely of 'hard-headed shopkeepers'.

One reason for the shopkeepers' domination of the Council was that the big players in business, commerce and manufacture had continued to move out of the city, further into the suburbs and outside the Council's reach. The parallel orbits of the operatives and the monied classes continued, with middle-class networks developing an invigorated culture of art galleries, concert halls and social clubs. And shopping, too, of course. Shopping as a leisure activity had evolved from visits to the market on a Saturday night into the beginnings of our era's obsession; brightly lit department stores first hypnotised Manchester more than a century ago.

In 1890 a writer in a local magazine describing the joys of 'shopping' at Kendal Milne's – the activity of 'shopping' was so novel that the magazine felt compelled to enclose the word in inverted commas – and Lewis's (the 'great show place' of Manchester) is transfixed by the special displays; the new, sparkling, fashionable goods; the crowds of visitors. The range of goods, the architecture, space, height (nine floors), the lights ('The premises are illuminated by more than a thousand powerful electric lamps', then an extreme novelty in itself) were awe-inspiring. The means by which the writer conveys his excitement are striking: 'For people to come to Manchester without seeing Lewis's would be as great an anomaly in the eyes of many as to come away from Rome without seeing St. Peter's.' As a shrine to shopping, no expense was spared. The result: 'shopping' had become a religion.

In March 1890 a shop selling Bovril, and only Bovril, was opened on the corner of Princess Street and Mosley Street, opposite the Art Gallery. It was one of five Bovril branches, the others being in London, Liverpool, Edinburgh and Paris. The drink was acclaimed thus in the local press: 'A splendid essence which has invigorated millions and revolutionised the drinking tastes of thousands.'

In contrast to Engels's grand hopes, it seemed by the 1890s that little more had been revolutionised in Manchester than the drinking tastes of the local population, an impression strengthened by the emergence of Vimto, a pick-me-up tonic invented in 1908 by Noel Nichols of Granby Row. Sold as a concentrated syrup to which hot or cold (and, later, carbonated) water was added, Vimto – said to impart 'vim' or vitality – became the local drink of choice at herbalists and temperance bars.

Yet political protest lived on. Over several Sundays in October and November 1893, the self-styled 'Ardwick Anarchists' held meetings at Ardwick Green which were vigorously targeted by police clampdowns. Although there are indications that the crowd included a sizeable number of sightseers who considered the meetings and inevitable police activity good Sunday afternoon entertainment, the meetings began attracting several thousand people. Nevertheless, after a couple of cold, rainy winter Sundays (and a more cunning police tactic of ignoring the meetings), the numbers dwindled, but not before letter-writers to the local newspapers had denounced the 'reckless, lawless, insurrectionary firebrands'.

Protests also continued around one of the big unresolved questions in Manchester, England: the failure of parliamentary reform to grant the vote to the female population. During the nineteenth century the struggles for democracy in Manchester had been bloody and prolonged, and the battles against privilege and patronage fought by reformers and radicals had brought a degree of success, but hadn't established universal suffrage. At Peterloo banners had called for 'Universal Suffrage' and votes for all was a Charter demand, and although it was quietly dismissed by later Chartists as a hindrance to their cause and too preposterous to be worth fighting for, the idea hadn't died. Given the rich traditions of protest and idealism in Manchester, it's not surprising that the city, and Lancashire generally, provided a base for campaigns for voting rights for women well before the issue of suffragettes pitched into the spotlight in the early twentieth century.

In Manchester the National Society for Women's Suffrage was formed in 1867 by stalwarts from the recently disbanded Anti Corn Law League and other progressives, including Dr Richard Pankhurst. The movement gained momentum when Dr Richard married Emmeline and Mrs Pankhurst joined the fray, but the struggle for universal suffrage was still marginalised, despite the best efforts of Lydia Becker, the local organiser, born in Cooper Street, Manchester, the most highly regarded figure in the movement until her death in 1890.

A second local strand of independently minded working-class women and radical suffragettes came from the cotton towns of Lancashire. In Blackburn, Burnley and Preston, three-quarters of unmarried women, and a third of married women, worked but, despite their importance to the cotton industry, they had neither equal pay nor the right to a vote. In relation to female workers in the rest of England, however, the female cotton workers of Lancashire were relatively well paid, well versed in survival strategies, and had traditions of organising and female protest on which to draw.

Suffrage campaigns regained momentum locally thanks to key individuals spreading the word and working towards uniting the strands of protest. The joint efforts of Esther Roper, who lived in Victoria Park, and an Irish poet, Eva Gore-Booth, had a huge impact on the lives of the Pankhurst family; Emmeline, Sylvia and especially

Christabel. The Pankhursts lived in Victoria Park during part of the 1890s, until they moved to a house in Nelson Street, just off Oxford Road. It was Christabel who introduced headline-grabbing tactics to the suffragette campaign, starting at the Free Trade Hall in 1905, when she and Annie Kenney disrupted a meeting addressed by Winston Churchill. Those with roots in the cotton towns campaigned over broader issues; even after 1918 when women over thirty were granted the vote and pressure from the Pankhursts eased off, radical Lancashire women continued to press for equal pay, for instance, and divorce law reform.

Novelists and commentators still found material in Manchester to illuminate life in England. In the early 1930s Walter Greenwood set his novel *Love on the Dole* at a time of chronic unemployment (a third of all the adult population of Salford was unemployed), highlighting the 1931 Salford demonstrations against cuts in public expenditure, reduced unemployment benefit and the introduction of the dreaded Means Test. A film version was delayed because of the sympathetic way he portrayed the National Unemployed Workers' Union and socialist agitators involved in the protests.

The pivotal moment of the Salford demonstrations of 1931 was a march to a protest meeting outside the Salford City Council offices at the Town Hall in Bexley Square. The event attracted nearly ten thousand marchers, but once in Bexley Square the deputation was spurned and mounted police charged the crowd, which included Walter Greenwood himself, Edmund Frow (who was arrested) and a young Jimmy Miller (Ewan MacColl). A demonstration in Manchester a week later attracted thousands of marchers, but the police blocked roads leading to Albert Square, and turned fire hoses from Whitworth Street Fire Station on demonstrators at the junction of London Road and Whitworth Street.

By the early 1930s, political activity had become part of life for MacColl, who was then unemployed. He and his Young Communist League friend, Bob Goodman, an amateur boxer who had lost his job at a rubber stamp-moulding workshop, walked the Derbyshire hills on Sundays and spent the week selling papers outside Metropolitan Vickers in Old Trafford, distributing leaflets at factory-gate meetings, treating themselves to the occasional 3*d* lunch at Yates's Wine Lodge on Oldham Street, and trekking round Salford, over the Irwell and through Ancoats. MacColl realised he was walking the same streets that Engels had walked during the making of *The Condition* *of the Working Class in England.* He wasn't convinced that much had changed in the intervening ninety years, and the book was a guide through his life; 'Engels' book became our Baedeker to the city'.

MacColl understood that having a vote wasn't the same as having a voice. Having a voice, making yourself heard, required a different approach; his first theatre group he called the Red Megaphones. In the Theatre of Action manifesto of 1934, MacColl noted how the working class was 'debarred from expression in the present day theatre'. He later explained that his determination to take an explicitly political line in his theatre and songwriting came from his kinship with 'the people who wanted to tear it all down and make something better'. The roots of his beliefs came from what he saw in his young days in Salford, the unemployment, the social inequalities, the repression: 'All the time I was living on a thread of anger, which was eating me away.'

In the early 1930s as well as sharpening his political beliefs, Mac-Coll was discovering jazz and blues. He began composing songs, satirical, political pieces. He formed the Theatre of Action with Joan Littlewood. Among their early performances was a stage version of Shelley's poem, 'The Mask of Anarchy', inspired by Peterloo and praised by Engels. Later, in the 1950s, just before a Theatre Workshop tour of South Wales, he wrote *Landscape With Chimneys*, which included 'Dirty Old Town'. Noel Gallagher of Oasis has declared it to be his all-time favourite song.

Manchester has many traditions of self-representation and self-expression, giving a voice to those shut out or marginalised, or the misfits, or the masses made miserable by work or lack of it, or those for whom 'shopping' is not everything, and those never touched by wealth; traditions of making a better life, imagining a new world, pursuing an individual vision. In Manchester millions have struggled to make the last farthing count, and imagined and then created a better world for themselves.

In the case of one great discontented visionary, the search for a better life meant a move away from Manchester, England. Ann Lee was a young, illiterate textile worker who joined a sect of dissenting Christians who had broken away from the mainstream Churches in 1747 and began to worship in private homes. The forms of worship included trances, convulsions, shouting and shaking; they became known as the 'Shakers'. Her ardour brought accusations of witchcraft and heresy and led to her imprisonment on several occasions. In

1774, instructed by a vision, she led a group of followers to Liverpool, from where they sailed to America, the New World. There they formed communities based on agriculture, crafts and cottage industries, underpinned by new-style – spiritual rather than biological – 'family' relations, a communal sharing of possessions, pacifism and celibacy.

Others have stayed in the city and still managed to get a glimpse of freedom via political or religious endeavour, or simple good times. Thus Ewan MacColl acknowledged various traditions and inherited two forms of self-expression from previous generations: 'Singing and politics were the two great passions of my father's life', he recalls. One appeal of political militancy was the thrill of collective action; the crowds of marchers at Peterloo unfurled dozens of banners and were accompanied by bands of musicians. In *Hard Times* a circus company brings colour to the uniformly drab world of Coketown.

Fired by the utopian and socialist ideals of Robert Owen – an enlightened industrialist who had lived in Manchester in the last decade of the eighteenth century – Owenites met regularly at the Hall of Science on the corner of Byrom Street and Tonman Street. Engels reports hearing John Watts delivering a lecture there one Sunday, noting the mix of radical thought and 'superabundant humour'; the meetings were the 'occasion for much laughter'. Twenty-six years after he first came to Manchester, even Engels reveals himself far from dour in a list of confessions given to Eleanor Marx. His favourite virtue? 'Jollity.' His motto? 'Take it easy.'

The hedonistic impulse in Manchester has always been strong, especially in hard times. It's a city still full of ideas, and dreamers hanging on to optimism even in the face of overwhelming evidence to the contrary (recurrent uncertainty and poverty, random violence and suffocating preconceptions from out of town). The unsettled, rarely united communities in Manchester have never been denied their pleasure, or their search for something better.

A century and a half after the birth of industrial society, and decades of struggle by the self-made, the survivors and the visionaries, Manchester is still one of the least content, least passive places in England. There's a line in 'Hand in Glove', the first Smiths single: 'The good life is out there somewhere, so stay on my arm you little charmer.' The search goes on, for something more than Chopt Straw and dried Horse Dung in our flour; if not a better world, at least a great night out.

CHAPTER 2

Madame Chester and One-Armed Dick

'Street Life is the Only Life I Know'

Life is a wait. For a job, or a better job. For a change in the weather, for a sugar daddy, or a National Lottery win. Time flies when you're having fun, but when you're not, then it drags. You skin up, shut up, lie down, can't be bothered; feel alienated, poverty-stricken, sad. Maybe you have the luck and the wherewithal to shape your own destiny, with a job you love and enough money to please yourself. But more likely, you don't. More likely you're trapped in a job you don't much like and which pays a wage you can't live off; insurance, telesales, shelf-stacker.

In a city of a million people you can be lonely. You can be bored. For plenty of people, city dwellers past and present, a lone parent on an estate, a fifteen-year-old struggling with school work, an unemployed would-be musician – 'time flies, time crawls; like an insect up and down the walls' (in the words of Howard Devoto in Magazine's 'The Light Pours Out Of Me'. In his previous group he had penned another ode to Manchester life; 'Boredom').

Crap job, or no job, a night out gives you something more, and – if you're lucky – reveals a sense of what a city can offer, and liberates you from the whims of your employer, the landlord or your own routine. You take to the streets, you head for the pub or the cinema or the betting shop, or you take the bus into town, make a night of it, take in some clubs, stagger home.

This is urban popular culture in the raw, going out, having a good time, painting the town red. What follows is the story of beer-shops and music halls; of nineteenth-century gangs bringing strife to the city centre; of Manchester's unrelenting hedonism; of brothels and brothel-keepers, drunkards and thieves. Throughout the city's history, as a market town, a manufacturing phenomenon, or the dance music capital of England, the mass of Mancs have been mad for it.

Often the entertainment is homemade and improvised, and sometimes it's been commercial. Ours is not the first generation to work hard to find ways of entertaining itself. The urge to go out, get drunk, fall over, meet a girl, meet a boy, listen to music, have a laugh; that urge has been in Manchester for generations. As far back as 1561 the Court Leet attempted to regulate the ale-houses in Manchester, and in 1573 were insisting that anyone found drunk should be locked in a dungeon overnight and ordered to pay 6d to the poor. If the drunkard couldn't pay the fine, the publican had to pay it for him. By the end of the sixteenth century the county authorities based in Lancaster had begun an inquiry to determine why Manchester was becoming such a drinker's paradise. The history of getting out of our heads goes back five hundred years.

Poverty encourages the hedonistic urge – drink your troubles away, why not? – but poverty is also an obstacle to a social life, especially in a society like the one we have in the 1990s in which commercial forms of leisure predominate – the bar, the cinema, the concert. Robert Roberts, writing about life in Salford before the First World War, gives us a vivid description of an Edwardian couch potato: 'Summer leisure for men without the few coppers to go into a tavern meant long, empty hours lounging between kitchen chair and threshold. How familiar one grew in childhood with those silent figures leaning against door jambs, staring into vacancy waiting for bedtime.'

Having come to Manchester to work, only to become one of the many unemployed in the 1920s, Ewan MacColl's father, as his son recognised, was ground down by unemployment, reading the paper in the library in Peel Park, hoping his luck would turn. Ewan was young at the time, and life was still an adventure. He began exploring the world outside his home, the streets, primarily, as well as railway embankments, canals and rivers. Life, for him, started on the streets.

The world outside his home was unsafe; that might even have been part of the buzz. He frequented Strawberry Hills, bleak dumps behind Strangeways prison, troughs filled with water, in which, one tragic summer, according to MacColl, four children were drowned. As an older kid it was on the streets where he first felt liberated, first indulged his imagination: 'The street was our stage, our race-track, our gymnasium. It was our jungle, our prairie, our untamed ocean. It was anything we wanted it to be.'

When we're young our carousing and courting days are in full swing; not for us nights leaning against door jambs. In our unwaged and irresponsible years the search for some informal and inexpensive means of meeting invariably leads to an evening on a street corner. Throughout Manchester it's usual, around dusk, to find groups of kids in their middle teens on street corners, hanging out, chatting, indulging in petty acts of vandalism. For them – as for generations before them – going out is merely a matter of escaping the house, parents, little brothers and sisters.

In the Robert Roberts era street-corner life was hugely important, especially for young people for whom the pub held little attraction (being the haunt of their fathers) and commercial entertainment (such as the dance hall) needed spare cash. Frequently street corners were claimed by regular gangs. Roberts credits these street-corner gangs with many positive virtues: 'an open-air society, a communal gathering which had great importance socially, culturally, and economically ... During each nightly meeting the young worker, once fully-integrated, listened, questioned, argued and received unawares an informal education.'

Thus the gangs gained a degree of formality. Territory was marked, a male space, a union of peers, and it was not all so innocent; corner gangs frequently incurred the wrath of the district with noise, the harassment of local girls and gambling. For those reasons, corner lads were forever getting moved on by the police (who had powers to charge offenders with loitering or obstructing the footpath). The *Salford City Reporter* in August 1920 reported:

> Seeing a crowd of youths in Robert Hall Street, Salford, late on Friday night, Police Constable Howard investigated and found they were singing, playing a banjo, dancing, and creating a terrible noise. As he approached they ran away, but they later returned and commenced the racket again. He rushed and succeeded in arresting Harry Singleton, aged 21, of New Bury Street, Salford, who was now fined 20s, or thirteen days for being drunk and disorderly.

The less grave charge of loitering was frequently brought against young men who, with no money and living in cramped, damp living conditions, had barely any other options than to take up with a street-corner gang. When you hear some cases, you realise that they're loitering out of necessity more than anything else. In May 1930 the *Salford City Reporter* told of a nineteen-year-old youth who had been charged with loitering. He came from a family in which the father, mother and six children slept in just one room in a house in West Wellington Street. When Lex Devine opened his Boys' Club it's no wonder there was such a high demand.

But the street is a public space. Throughout the history of Manchester control of the street has been a battle fought between the people and the authorities. Coming down hard on loiterers was part of a battle to remove conspicuous evidence of disorder on the streets. In the 1840s, discussing child labour, Cooke Taylor describes those who oppose child labour as 'sentimentalists'. If the children weren't at work, he writes, 'their only resource would be the street with all its perils and all its temptations', revealing the classic bourgeois anxiety about street life. But for the people who lived there, street wisdom was obligatory; survival depended upon it. Moreover, many city dwellers weren't fazed by the unchecked energies of the street; they came to accept that life was rough around the edges, savoured the unpredictable bustle.

A trip to town and a walk round the markets was a favourite way to spend Saturday nights throughout the nineteenth century and the first decades of the twentieth, a kind of promenading. All human life was there, a frenzy of noise, the promenaders simultaneously consumers and participants in the Saturday night spectacle. In the 1830s Deansgate from Bridge Street to St Mary's Gate was very narrow and on a Saturday evening was thronged with people from the outskirts of town coming to look at the shops. There were families, drunks and courting couples. Out on the streets beggars were conspicuous. Some were (or claimed to be) ex-servicemen, some begged with their children, some were blind or maimed, some sold bootlaces or matches. A blind woman sold matches at the corner of St Mary's Gate. Organ grinders took pitches every few yards. There was a noisy rawness about the city streets.

The centre was the city's troubled soul. Through the early part of Manchester's life, the middle classes abandoned the city centre, escaping perils and temptations, crime and cholera, and moving into the cleaner spaces of the suburbs. The city centre itself, the site of the city's warehouses, civic buildings and markets, was also dangerous. As today, the fear of crime was more widespread than crime itself; received and written opinion thrived on stories of an urban underworld overflowing with vagrancy, violence, vice. As the middle class moved out, in the words of the French writer, Leon Faucher, they abandoned the town to the 'operatives, publicans, mendicants, thieves and prostitutes'.

At the end of the nineteenth century the favoured focus for a Saturday night in town was around the top end of Market Street along Oldham Street, and in Shudehill. The main Manchester market at Shudehill traded all through Saturday, and provided plenty of entertainment and free amusement for families, couples, women and children. Shudehill – and also the Flat Iron and Cross Lane markets in Salford – came alive on a Saturday evening, with crowds of shoppers and sightseers, and stallholders entertaining and cajoling with their spiel. Most shops were open, and the main streets were lit up and packed, the town brightly gas-lit and bustling, and there was the added incentive that nearing closing time at midnight food became cheaper. And, again, the big crowd – in a single day in 1870 it was estimated that as many as twenty thousand people went to Shudehill – attracted beggars, musicians and entertainers seeking an audience. Just to the south of Shudehill, the area around Tib Street and Stevenson Square was a favourite pitch of various political orators.

Rewind and tune in to the soundtrack of nineteenth-century Manchester; a heady mix of the shouts and sounds of human crush, and the commotion of commercial industry. Arthur Shadwell, in 1906, as mentioned, found the stir of life and bustle in Manchester greater even than in New York or London. In Manchester, according to him, 'the tide of life runs at the full'. Hectic trade preoccupies Manchester and its citizens, writes Shadwell:

> The signs of trade are over it all – movement and wealth and power. The streets are thronged with loaded drays rumbling along and impeding the quicker traffic. Many of the side streets consist entirely of tall warehouses, with bales swinging overhead in mid air, ascending or descending all day long between the upper floors and the drays which stand lining the roadway below. This is the business of Manchester; the factory element is in the background.

The particular atmosphere of Manchester's street life was due to more than just industrious business. If, as Shadwell says, what most human beings crave are 'things going on', that buzz can't be gained solely by watching loaded drays all day. The hectic bustle of incessant commerce is mingled with a rawer street life; what Shadwell calls 'pauperism, vice and misery'. He ventures an opinion as to why vice abounds: 'Buyers and sellers come from everywhere, strangers with money and leisure when business is over but no friends or anywhere to go. The hotels are full of them, and they want amusement.' Thus, he says, 'Vice abounds'.

From its first beginnings, Manchester has had as much of a reputation for depravity as industry. The Lancaster worthies couldn't halt the city's drinking habit; by 1843 it was calculated that Manchester had 502 public houses and 781 beer-houses, or 'jerry shops' as they were known, and plenty of 'hush-shops' – secret, unlicensed drinking places, often served by secret distilleries, rarely visited by the police. Drunkenness in the street was commonplace, although one reason for the large amount of alcohol being consumed by the urban poor was that fresh drinking water was impossible to find in most areas of Manchester. The brewing process, on the other hand, removed water impurities; the city's drunks could console themselves with the knowledge that they weren't going to succumb to cholera from drinking a jug of ale.

Saturday night in town at the end of the twentieth century is still a sight to behold, but extravagance, intoxication and all-night partying is nothing new. Engels reported thus in the 1840s: 'On Saturday evenings, especially, when wages are paid and work stops somewhat earlier than usual, when the whole working class pours from its own poor quarters into the main thoroughfares, intemperance may be seen in all its brutality. I have rarely come out of Manchester on such an evening without meeting numbers of people staggering and seeing others lying in the gutter.'

For these forty-eight hour party-people, there's more: 'On Sunday evening the same scene is usually repeated, only less noisily. And when their money is spent, the drunkards go to the nearest pawnshop, of which there are plenty in every city – over sixty in Manchester, and ten or twelve in a single street of Salford, Chapel Street – and pawn whatever they possess.' Thus Engels sees the extent of intemperance among the workers of England. According to Lord Ashley, during a sitting of the Lower House at Parliament in February 1843, the working class spent something in the region of twenty-five million pounds a year on intoxicating liquor.

In the 1850s, the Committee of the Manchester & Salford Temperance Society investigated the drinking habits of the Manchester people on a Sunday. They divided the city into sections and wards, and over a period of some months they visited a grand total of 1,437 beer-houses, public houses and gin vaults, observing and making notes. They concluded that far too much drinking went on; the policing of the drinking places and the enforcement of legal opening hours was virtually nil; and that a culture of vice and violence had developed, especially in the poorer areas of the city. Children were sucked into this world, often sent out to get ale and whisky to take back to the family home. At the Tullochgorum in Little Ireland, inspectors counted eight two-gallon bottles being taken out by children in the space of two hours one Sunday afternoon. Sorely vexed by what they found in the Angel Street area ('a district crowded with men, women, and children, in rags and filth, some drinking in the streets, others gambling'), the inspectors and superintendents from the Temperance Society took a very poor view of the local inhabitants, reporting a high proportion to be 'thieves, beggars, and prostitutes'. As you might expect, the locals didn't take too kindly to the inspectors either, as the report confesses: 'Most of the men taking this ward had to be changed every half hour, or hour; some were driven off by mobs, others stoned.'

The temperance movement fought a long fight against the evils of drink throughout the nineteenth century. As the first medical practitioner ever to join the Temperance Society, a local man, Dr Grindrod, gained a degree of notoriety. He lived at 5 Great Ancoats Street, just two doors down from the Crown & Kettle, while a beer-shop was at No. 7 and the Nelson Tavern at No.9; whether his beliefs arose because of his close proximity to temptation isn't clear. He took part in various temperance drives throughout the 1830s, once featuring in a great open-air debate in Stevenson Square with Mr Youil, a brewer. Three thousand people were estimated to have attended, but Engels was scathing about temperance drives in the city. Thousands of workers take the pledge, he said, but most of them are back on the drink again within a month; 'If one counts up the immense numbers who have taken the pledge in the last three or four years in Manchester, the total is greater than the whole population of the town.'

Engels describes a Sunday evening trip to his Owenite haunt, the Hall of Science, where there were 'tea-parties where young and old, high and low, men and women, sat together and partook of the customary supper, bread-and-butter and tea', but his evenings weren't always so wholesome. Engels himself was a bit of a drinker, and generally revelled in some of life's livelier leisure pursuits. In 1859 he was embroiled in a drunken argument in a pub near the Royal Exchange, and struck out after receiving an insult: 'I hit out with an umbrella I was carrying and the ferrule got him in the eye', he reported in a letter to Karl Marx.

Engels socialised with a drinking crowd, many of them exiled Germans, including Wilhelm Wolff, or Lupus as he was nicknamed, a sometime secretary of the *Neue Rheinische Zeitung* newspaper launched by Engels and Marx in Cologne. He had fled to England via arrest and imprisonment in Belgium and exile in Switzerland; Engels's letters to Marx tell of a series of scrapes involving Lupus and his landladies, and drunken escapades at the Chatsworth Inn, a favourite haunt of 'German clerks and English philistines', according to Engels. His network of friends extended also to Ernst Dronke (an apt name, as we shall see).

Dronke was working as a clerk in Bradford and he often made the trip over the Pennines to join his German buddies. In June 1854, Dronke – 'drunk as usual', according to Engels – was run over and injured by a cab. A few weeks later, at one o'clock one morning, during another drinking session, recounted Engels, Dronke made a 'grab at a female in the street; she, a married, middle-class woman, boxed his ears, whereupon he KNOCKED HER DOWN'. The police apparently refused to get involved, although the woman's husband instigated a private prosecution; Engels paid Dronke's fine.

Aside from drunkenness, beer-houses and public houses had other perils. Angus Bethune Reach toured Manchester and the textile districts in 1849 and reported that the Dog & Duck on Charter Street was the haunt of swell mobsmen 'and the superior class of thieves' ('swell mobsmen' being the vagabonds who dressed in finery, passed themselves off as gentlemen and indulged in what would now be called white-collar crime; infiltrating the banking system, defrauding members of the Cotton Exchange and money-forging, for instance. According to Reach, criminals of this kind in Manchester frequently had connections in Paris, London, New York even), but there were plenty of less prestigious vagabonds and thieves in Manchester in the middle of the nineteenth century. The criminal classes swarmed over the city.

A career in crime was easy to fall into. Street urchins aged six or seven were known for their petty pilfering and pickpocketing, and with a frightening number of lost or abandoned children in Manchester at any one time in the 1830s (estimates frequently putting the number at more than a thousand), this kind of activity was widespread. Some would be trained up by older criminals in order for them to join horse-stealing gangs, or gangs of what were called 'sneaksmen', who would steal from shop windows and unattended wagons and carts. Fences – receivers of stolen goods – thrived in the city, including one known as 'One-Armed Dick', who operated from a shop off Oldham Road in the 1840s, and Joe Hyde, the landlord of the London Tavern.

Manchester was full of strangers and travellers. The cotton industry was renowned for its use of casual labour, hiring and firing, taking on labour during busy periods, laying off labour later, so the city had a shifting populace. Manchester has never been lucky enough to be the kind of settled community that guarantees a crime-free environment. The Chaplain at Preston Gaol used his report of 1849 to warn that, owing to its size, anonymity and reputation, Manchester was in danger of becoming out of control, a city 'to which both idle profligates and practised villains resort as a likely field for the indulgence of sensuality or the prosecution of schemes of plunder'.

The cotton industry also relied on the mill girls, who famously worked hard and played hard. Villainous rumours spread about their moral health. According to one source in the middle of the nineteenth century,

> There are various opinions afloat as to the extent of female immorality in the mills. It is the sincere conviction of a millowner in a town about thirty miles to the north of Manchester – a gentleman who has devoted a great deal of attention to the study of the social state of the cotton operatives – that there is hardly such a thing as a chaste factory girl, at least in the large towns. But this is an assertion the correctness of which is generally, and I believe with truth, denied.

Although the same writer goes on to make it clear that 'there appears, however, no doubt whatever that prostitution is rare among the mill girls', the same can't be said of Manchester as a whole. In 1795 the inhabitants of Back Turner Street and Brick Street (adjacent to Shudehill) wrote to the magistrates describing the activities of 'a large Quantite of Bad Girls' in two nearby houses, and asking for action to be taken. Cooke Taylor, in 1842, was claiming that Manchester had 309 brothels. By the following year the police believed there were 330 brothels and 701 common prostitutes in Manchester (or one per hundred inhabitants, or approximately one per fifteen Manchester lads).

In the nineteenth century many of the commonest crimes committed were those associated with prostitutes working in league with gangs of thieves. In 1837 Ellen Reece, a twenty-four-year-old shoplifter and prostitute-thief held in Salford Gaol, admitted, 'None of the girls think so much of prostitution but as it furnishes opportunities of robbing men ... most girls will rob by violence and especially drunken men.' Jane Doyle, Ellen Reece's companion, admitted they would pick a punter's pockets while his trousers were round his ankles and make their getaway while he was prevented from giving chase.

By the middle of the nineteenth century many parts of the city centre had already established themselves as recognised areas of prostitution, the haunt of street walkers, Bad Girls and makeshift brothels. One was the neighbourhood of Canal Street, Minshull Street and Richmond Street; it was in the midst of this area that Manchester's homosexual community was to materialise. A second was the other side of Piccadilly Gardens, along Back Piccadilly. These areas were out of bounds to polite society. Jerome Caminada believed that any middle-class person immoral enough to succumb to temptation could be sucked into greater danger via these haunts of iniquity: 'These plague spots were terrible agencies for recruiting year by year to the ranks of dangerous society from our middle-class population, and many a clerk and other respectable young man has begun a criminal career by becoming a secret pilferer from the till to obtain the means of gratifying his appetite in such haunts of sin.'

Jerome Caminada, of Italian/Irish parentage, was born in Deansgate and lived in Mount Street in Moss Side. His memoirs of his days in the police force, *Twenty Five Years of Detective Life*, deal mainly with the 1870s. At this time he describes Wood Street or, as it was called by the fraternity, 'Timber Grove', Spinning Field, Hardman Street, Dolefield, and the adjacent courts and alleys on the one side, and Fleet Street, Lombard Street, Lad Lane and Bootle Street on the other side of Deansgate as the worst scenes of vice. It was reckoned that within this small area either side of Deansgate there were twenty-two brothels; 'The neighbourhood of Deansgate also was the rendez-vous of thieves and was a very hot-bed of social iniquity and vice. The women of the locality were of the most degraded class, and their chief victims were drunken men, collier lads, and country "flats", whom they picked up and rifled with impunity.'

There's plenty of material uncovering one corner of Manchester's vice history in the small book *Memoirs of Madame Chester* by Polly Evans, published in 1865. Born in North Wales, she spent time while she was just fifteen with soldiers in Chester, Liverpool and Dublin, and when the 12th Lancers were transferred from Dublin to Man-chester Polly moved with them. 'I had not been in Manchester more than a month before I was sought after by all the rich men of this wealthy city; for money at that time was no object.' Her gentlemen (she never refers to them in any way that might infer that they're clients or customers; they're always 'visitors' or 'gentlemen') included one, early in her Manchester career, who, though more than thirty years older than the sixteen-year-old Polly, fell hopelessly in love with her and began promising her the earth in return for a life with her. He tried to turn her head with a bouquet of moss roses and fern leaves wrapped up in a £500 bank note. But even as early as the party she threw to celebrate her good fortune, she began to regret taking his money, reminded of what she was going to be missing by the company at the party ('All his friends were young and hand-some'), and threw the money back at him. 'I never saw him after that evening', she writes, 'But I heard from a friend of his that he had sailed from Liverpool to America.'

Yet Polly made money, plenty of it, and soon decided to take a 'house' of her own; by which she means 'brothel' (but, again, such words are avoided in her decorous narrative). Having found herself serving the higher echelons of society – those who would prefer to sit around for hours drinking wines and ports, rather than those out for a cheap quickie round the back of Deansgate – she proceeded to deck out the brothel with fine bronzes, ornate bedsteads, furniture, clocks and crystal chandeliers. The soldiers stationed locally remained regular visitors to the house; at least someone was gaining from the city's status as a garrison town during the turbulent years of social unrest. The 11th Hussars were particularly favoured by Polly, includ-ing a young cornet player who managed to woo her for himself. She ran away with him down South, but complaining her mind was too unsettled for married life, she returned to Manchester to set up a new house, this time in Major Street (which runs parallel to Canal Street, two blocks up Sackville Street, in the heart of the action). Her most profitable period came after the end of the Crimean War, when the returning 7th Fusiliers and 1st Royals were making merry in Manchester.

Apart from soldiers, her trade fed off the appetites of the young, and sometimes not so young, well-to-do. One of her regular visitors was a young gentleman from Ashton whom Polly calls Harry N—, who is described as 'the son of a very rich cotton lord'. Most of her business came either from idle, monied sons who had more money than sense, or the retired rich. She caused mayhem by attending every day of the Art Treasures Exhibition of 1857, meeting there many charming young men and handsome officers, though drawing more than one scowling glare from the wealthy ladies there. It's clear that she was known, recognised in the public domain as a keeper of a brothel; and she was alleged to be the long-term mistress of Manchester's mayor.

Harry N— was about twenty-eight years of age, Polly tells us, and 'Being fond of display, and having large sums of money constantly at his command, could indulge his eccentric fancies to an unlimited degree'. The details of his eccentric fancies in the bedroom are left to our imagination, but one of his other habits is documented: throwing full decanters of port from upstairs windows. This extravagance often drew a crowd outside, but it didn't trouble Polly; she billed him for the drink, whether swigged, savoured or slung to the street below. Some of these young gentlemen took to staying at her house for days and nights on end; 'I have known my house to be full of gentlemen for weeks at a time playing all manner of pranks and spending endless money.'

Polly's memoirs seem to have been stimulated by the notoriety she attracted during a court case involving a Birmingham merchant who brought a court action against her to recover the half of a £50 Bank of England note which, he alleged, had been illegally detained by her at her house at 3 Boundary Street, Greenheys (Lupus, incidentally, lived at No. 59). The details of the court proceedings were made into a bootleg pamphlet which sold in its thousands, even – reports a shocked Polly – reaching the hands of troops stationed in India. Her memoirs go over the same ground, with the uproarious nature of the evidence providing much mirth in the court, especially when it becomes clear that the merchant's memory of the evening's events proves much marred by the copious amounts of alcohol he had drunk.

In many areas of the city, especially the poorer areas, prostitutes plied their trade in the community. Charter Street in Ancoats attracted all manner of thieves, and prostitutes, for example, as did that part of Ardwick where the Apollo Theatre and the Pitz five-a-side football ground are now sited. The minutes of the Watch Committee in the 1850s record many reports by the Chief Constable of complaints received against prostitutes by shopkeepers and local residents. In 1857, when the Committee wished to follow up the complaints, the Chief Constable defended the lacklustre efforts of the police by confirming that vice, along with violent crime, was endemic in parts of the city. Habitual law-breakers seemed unrestrained by police action: 'The annoyance it is to be feared, is one which the police have it not in their power entirely to remove. They may exercise the greatest vigilance, they may report all cases that come under their notice, summons the offenders before the Nuisance Committee, but the class of person of whom your memorialists complain are unhappily but little affected by fine and punishment.'

Cultural and social changes of the early twentieth century wiped out some of the insularity and also the wealth of nineteenth-century Manchester. On the one hand, there were improvements in the transport network, with the arrival of trams and the increased ownership of cars, as well as the growing leisure developments like the cinema and jazz dancing; on the other, the textiles industry stuttered, and mass unemployment brought misery in the 1930s. Prostitution, however, didn't disappear. As the city expanded out from the centre, into mid Victorian terraces and Edwardian suburbs, so prostitution entered even so-called 'respectable' neighbourhoods. One scandal in the 1930s centred around the activities in a house on Leopold Avenue in leafy West Didsbury. In February 1933 two men and two women were charged with various offences, including keeping a disorderly house and living on immoral earnings. They denied all charges, but the police had kept a watch on the house. PC Owen said he had seen men visiting the house at late hours. On one occasion, upon looking through the front window, he saw one of the accused, Mrs Marjorie Yellow, misconducting herself with a man. Defending, Mr Judson explained that the nineteen-year-old Mrs Yellow had lived 'an adventurous life'. She had even been told she should write a book, and a newspaper had offered her £50 for her life story. Mr Judson said that no man had entered the house for improper purposes. He claimed that the men the officer had seen had gone to the house to help Mrs Yellow write her book.

Another fundamental part of the soundtrack of Manchester, in addition to the bustle of commerce, conviviality, vice and violence, was, of course, the sound of music. In 1849 Angus Bethune Reach toured the textile districts:

> In returning, last Sunday night, by the Oldham Road, from one of my tours, I was somewhat surprised to hear loud sounds of music and jollity which floated out of public house windows. The street was swarming with drunken men and women and with young mill girls shouting, hallooing and romping with each other. Now I am not one of those who look upon the slightest degree of social indulgence as a downright evil, but I confess, that last Sunday in the Oldham Road astonished and grieved me. In no city have I ever witnessed a scene of more open, brutal and general intemperance. The public houses and gin shops were roaring full. Rows and fights and scuffles were every moment taking place within doors and in the streets. The whole street rung with shouting, screaming and swearing, mingled with the jarring music of half a dozen bands.

You couldn't get a quiet drink in Manchester in the middle of the nineteenth century. Licensed beer-houses like the Old Ship, the Pat McCarthy, the Green Man, the Dog & Rat and the Red, White & Blue were in full swing. Out on the town, there'd be informal sing-songs, nights spent listening to mechanical organs, perhaps with accompanying drums and tambourines. Public houses acting as music venues were very much a part of early Manchester life. This close link between drink and music, as well as the bawdy nature of the popular songs (especially those heard late in the day as the drink took hold) caused consternation among many observers. The early days of the music hall were closely linked with the general demand that public houses provide a music space or a singing saloon.

The textile industry was the first to introduce shorter working days (the so-called 'Manchester week') and it also provided regular, family employment, giving the bulk of the local Manchester populace time to fill and small amounts of money to spend, especially at the weekend.

This guaranteed the swift rise of a local entertainment industry, a headstart in hedonism in the world's first industrial city. Local entertainment primarily served the bulk of the city, the urban working class, but the city had a broader population profile too, and the range of music on offer in this period reflected this. The growth of the Hallé Orchestra, part of the network of clubs and art venues established by the emergent middle classes, fulfilled that group's ambition that Manchester should enjoy high art on a par with that of any other city. Even down among the concert halls, theatres and music halls there were niche markets. The music halls provided a variety of entertainment on each night's bill. Some charged upwards of 6d and included songs from operas as well as comic capers, ballet, gymnastic displays, and dramatic sketches and tableaux. Most included a degree of knockabout farce and slapstick, and all featured songs; many patriotic and sentimental, some rousing and some satirical. Many of the most popular songs dealt with public gossip and local events.

In the first half of the nineteenth century music hall ballads and broadsides reflected the changing lives of the listeners. In the 1850s John Beswick, Parish Jack, was a singer, flute-player and fiddler popular at 'stirs' and merry-makings. In one of his compositions he declared his sorrow at what he claimed was the degeneration of Gorton as it became a poorer, rougher place than a few decades earlier. Another popular song around that time was 'Manchester's Improving Daily', a cynical commentary contrasting the reality of life in the city with the public hype, and wondering where the revolutionary, fighting spirit of the Manchester people had gone. The bloody battles against the bourgeoisie were over; 'All that bleed now, good people, hark it / Are the cows and pigs in Shudehill Market.' Those at the lower end of the scale concentrated on comic songs, patter, turns and onstage high jinks of various sorts. These less sophisticated halls were particularly a feature of Manchester life. As one local paper remarked at the time, 'In no place in England, probably, are concert halls better supported, as far as the lower classes are concerned, than in Manchester.'

Although prostitutes were known to frequent the lower kinds of music hall, the high numbers of women and children in the average audience generally kept proceedings decent. On occasions magistrates and police would close down intemperate premises, but in general the authorities would take a more relaxed attitude – or perhaps realistic is the word. Most of the middle class knew nothing of the lives and leisure pursuits of the urban poor, so seldom showed any interest in what was happening at the music halls. Those commentators who were aware of the music halls understood the place they had in working-class communities: 'After the labours of the weeks, it is but natural to suppose that that relaxation so much desired by those in confined occupations should be sought after by those engaged in the operations of a cotton mill', said one local paper, pointing out that 'No entertainment in the city appeared to be such a place of general resort among young mill hands as the Victoria Music Hall'.

At the inquest following the accidental deaths at the Victoria Music Hall in 1868, the wife of the beer-house proprietor gave a spirited defence against charges that the Hall was unruly and the crowd often drunk, telling the Coroner that 'No complaint has ever been made of the house as a beerhouse, nor in the matter of overcrowding. Our performances, I am able to state, afford a great deal of pleasure to a great many poor people. We endeavour to prevent, as far as possible, drunkenness and disorderly conduct.' Superintendent Gee, of A Division, in reply to the Coroner, said this was so.

Drunkenness may not have been an issue in the investigation of the incident, but overcrowding certainly was. The Licensing Act then in force made no reference to the quality or quantity of the exits, but it's clear that although overcrowding was accepted practice, and presented no problem on an orderly, normal night, the only staircase provided couldn't cope with the pressure of the stampede; it was only five foot wide. A contributory factor was that the steps were faced with iron – to reduce the wear and tear caused by the effect of clogs – but this rendered the steps slippery. At the inquest it was revealed that there was a second means of escape from the galleries, a staircase that went via the pit. However, in a move which was devious but not strictly illegal, the management had locked the door to this staircase to stop customers who had paid 2*d* for a gallery place from sneaking down into the 3*d* pit. In August 1868 the *Manchester Courier* drew an inevitable conclusion: 'The great desirability of compelling the proprietors of music halls and places of amusement to provide proper means by which speedy egress might be made in cases of panic.'

Later in the century there were many attempts to bring more respectable music to the people by reformers who viewed music as a force for social and moral good, but entrepreneurs and impresarios ruled the roost, so social engineering was unlikely unless someone could make a few bob out of it. In 1883 the aims of the People's

Entertainment Society were 'to cultivate a taste for good, high class amusement among the poorer classes in the hope of withdrawing them from lower places of resort, to introduce an element of brightness into their lives, and to establish a better feeling between the different classes by bringing them into clear contact with each other'.

Many music hall proprietors boasted of middle-class customers, often to assuage doubts of the decency of their establishments, and late in the nineteenth century variety bills with a greater appeal for the middle class developed – with elements borrowed from the straight theatre – but most establishments drew their custom from the locality, and this hindered any real barrier-breaking. The working class and the middle class lived unrelated lives, separated by geography as much as economics. To the likes of Robert Roberts, the working class living in the classic slum were never a uniform mass anyway; the barriers among the working class, between the tradesman and the factory worker, or the craftsman and the unemployed, were as great as between the proletariat and the bourgeoisie, as evidenced by his description of a full house at the local theatre: 'Shopkeepers and publicans in the orchestra, stalls and dress circle, artisans and regular workers in the pit stalls, and the low class and no class on the "top shelf" or balcony.'

You'd be hard pushed to deny that the quality of the entertainment on offer at the music hall was poor. It was better than nothing, though, and undoubtedly a laugh. It contributed to a well-developed entertainment infrastructure in the city; for a while, Manchester's theatreland was far developed enough to support a periodical covering its news, the *Manchester Figaro*. The formula was successful, and the poverty-stricken regulars were happy to pay for what was offered. Felix McGlennon was one of a number of successful local songwriters in the last decades of the nineteenth century. He was a Manchester-based Scotsman, responsible for a string of popular ditties, including the tune to 'My Old Man Said Follow The Van'. Many music hall songs were repetitive and derivative; in fact, the bulk of them, according to Robert Roberts, were 'of a wretched quality, with airs painfully banal and lyrics of an inanity that even the sub-literate rejected'. The 'turns' were little better. Roberts tells a tale of a Houdini-like entertainer who invited members of the audience to tie him with ropes, guaranteeing to be free 'in a trice'. Two dockers then trussed him up so effectively that after a few minutes stage-hands had to carry him off like a parcel, the imitation Houdini bent double and almost asphyxiated.

As well as often providing rooms for music and song, beer-houses laid on all kinds of other entertainment, including prize-fighting, well organised and formal, with a roped off area and inter-district competitions. This was one activity, however, that Caminada and the other local police did their best to put an end to; after the police clampdown, most fighting went on at fairs, but other activities, including betting, gambling and dog-fights, continued. Events like dog-fights drew the middle class 'swells' to these beer-houses, although Caminada says that they often regretted mingling with the vagabonds and pick-pockets: 'Swells who did not mind paying for the spectacle used to put in an appearance – sometimes to their own discomfiture through the loss of a watch or some other article of value.'

The trip to town on a Saturday night was made by young men and women, in groups, gangs and alone. There were opportunities for meeting, and courting, and adventure. Charles Russell, writing in 1905, picked up on the element of social display in this Saturday night out: 'Working lads generally change into their Sunday clothes, or, in their own expressive language, "toff themselves up", for Saturday night, and even if they have been to a concert, a theatre, or a music hall, will take a tour round the market before finally going home.' Russell, it seems, wasn't naive; the implication is that the lads went down to the market if they had failed to find a girl earlier in the evening. Shudehill, no doubt, had the kind of reputation as a cattle market that various clubs and bars now have in the city centre.

In the late nineteenth century the lads who hung around the streets in groups, intimidating some of the city's sober citizens and being harried by the police, became known as 'scuttlers'. In their heyday, the Northern scuttler and his 'moll' achieved a level of infamy on a par with any gang in modern times. The scuttler had his own look: hair well plastered down, a peaked cap worn at an angle, a loose white scarf, a union shirt, a heavy leather belt with a large steel buckle, thick, iron-shod clogs and, most strikingly of all, coarse cotton trousers cut – like a sailor's – with 'bell-bottoms'. Their method of operation, much like steaming, was working *en masse*, knocking down passers by in order to rob them. It earned them a fearsome reputation.

Rival gangs frequently clashed on slum streets. 'Vicious and purposeless violence', Robert Roberts called it; 'Deprived of all decent ways of spending their little leisure, they sought escape from the

tedium in bloody battles with belt and clog – street against street.'
Charles Russell, in his 1905 study of Manchester lads, attributes the
activities of the scuttlers to a mixture of merry high spirits and a
desire for the gangs 'to assert the supremacy of their own particular
district against that of some neighbouring one'. As well as turf wars,
the spark for gang disturbances, according to Russell, often arose
from attentions paid to the sweetheart of a member of one gang by
a member of another, leading to a pitched battle: 'Gangs, twenty
or thirty strong, armed sometimes with heavily buckled belts and
mineral-water bottles, would from time to time engage in set combat,
in which serious injuries were often inflicted.'

There was some blurring between gangs which indulged in overtly
criminal activity, and those simply consisting of lads who'd grown
up together and hung out together. Whichever, the gangs were a
product of the overcrowded working-class communities, the densely
packed neighbourhoods and the significance of the street as a meeting
place, a demotic university of life. Henry Grimshaw, the son of a
tailor in Chorlton-on-Medlock, recalls his young life:

> You were born in a gang if you lived in that area. There were
> so many children in the streets, they looked like one of Lowry's
> paintings, you see. So wherever you were born, in that area
> you automatically had ten, twenty, children to play with all the
> time, and that was the gang. You didn't realise you were in a
> gang; you were just playing with children, see. There was the
> Cogan Gang, the Kendall Street Gang. I was in the Willesden
> Street gang. We did use to fight each other.

In 1892 local papers were filled with outrage at 'another of those
disgraceful scuttling cases which have long been notorious in Manchester and Salford'; on this occasion a murder had been committed.
Three sixteen-year-olds were charged with the murder of Peter Kennedy in Ancoats. The assailants, said to be from the Lime Street
Gang, had targeted their victim (from the Bradford Street Gang)
some days before they attacked him. After following him through the
streets on 23 April, they cornered him in Alum Street, attacked him
with broken bottles and stabbed him with a pocket knife in the left-
hand side of his back. Kennedy died a fortnight later in the Infirmary.
William Willan was discovered to be the ringleader of the gang; he
had struck the fatal blow with a knife purchased for 2d a fortnight

before the attack. The jury acquitted his two accomplices, but found Willan guilty of murder. The judge ignored the jury's plea for mercy and sentenced Willan to death. The prisoner was terror-stricken, and was said to have cried out, 'Oh master, have mercy on me, I'm only sixteen!'

Similar incidents occurred for another decade or more (including a serious gang-related affray on Jersey Street in Ancoats in January 1903), but Robert Roberts believed that this kind of mass brutality calmed down in the first years of the twentieth century. Nevertheless, after the scuttler came other working-class tribes, each generation, or each location, inventing a new look, a new style and a new label. In the first decade of the twentieth century the 'ikey lad' was the successor of the 'scuttler', sharing a similar reputation for hanging around and fighting, but evolving a different look and more solitary methods of mugging. In other cities at the time other groups of aggressive working-class lads were labelled, like the London 'hooligans' or the 'peaky blinders' of Birmingham.

At the sharp and violent end, the scuttlers and their descendants have viewed the street as 'turf', but for many in Manchester the street has been their playground, the street corner their community centre, a site for socialising not fighting, and as the urban young became used to getting toffed up and promenading the streets, the parade became more ritualised; thus was born the so-called 'monkey parade' or 'monkey run'. A cross between loafing and cruising, the monkey parade is mentioned by Charles Russell in 1905: 'On Sunday evenings there are three main points of attraction for working lads; Oldham Street, Market Street, and Stockport Road. From Hulme, from Ardwick, and from Ancoats they come in, in the main well dressed, and frequently sporting a flower in the button-holes of their jackets.'

Russell's reports were specifically focused on lads, but the monkey parade was for the benefit of both sexes. The parades had varying, and local codes of behaviour – in the early part of the twentieth century most parts of Manchester had their own parade routes, or monkey runs (Regent Road, Cross Lane, Eccles New Road in Salford, and a triangle formed by Rochdale Road, Conran Street and Moston Lane in Harpurhey) – often with lads parading down one side of the street, while girls went down the other. Ewan MacColl remembers watching his cousin, John, leave the house for the monkey parade; 'a preliminary mating ritual', he calls it. Russell again: the boys 'exchange rough salutations with the girls, who seem in no way less vigorous than the boys themselves, and whose chief desire, one would think, was to pluck from the lads' button-holes, the flowers which many of them wear'.

The monkey parades described by Russell developed in the mid nineteenth century (there's written evidence in reports during 1869 in *The Shadow*), and continued unabated through the 1930s, and despite some evidence that the activity began falling off in the wake of the Second World War, one local man, Stan Whittaker, still harbours happy memories of the Harpurhey monkey run in the 1940s. His wanderings weren't limited to Sundays; most nights he and his friends would do the monkey run, right through until eleven o'clock, by which time the chip shops had closed and the teenagers subjected to strict curfews had wandered home.

He used to meet his friends at Gotelli's, the local drinks shop. Such places evolved from herbalists, where they'd make sarsaparillas, and dandelion and burdock and sell them in a big glass. Gotelli's sold ice cream as well. They were an Italian family, remembers Stan Whittaker:

> The daughter who was of our age bracket was called Rose, and they were a nice couple, although they had a bit of persecution at the beginning of the War because they were Italians. Not real persecution, they just got a few stupid people having a go, but they were as British as us. Anyway, we were called Gotelli's lot. There was about thirteen of us altogether, one or two characters amongst them. We used to meet more or less from about half past six onwards in there and we'd have a Vimto, or whatever you fancied, a packet of crisps, an Eccles cake.

Gotelli's was on Conran Street, a long street which changed at its top end to Upper Conran Street. A mile or so up there was a left into Moston Lane, then back down the busy Rochdale Road, which joins back on to Conran Street. Gotelli's lot would walk the triangle maybe five or six times in a night, although they might cut through the back streets which intersected the main roads to head off other groups:

> We might meet somebody and ask, 'Have you seen such-and-such a body?' and if it was some girls that we fancied and

we'd got to know, they might say, 'Oh, we've seen them near Balf's [a chemist]' or somewhere, whatever shop, and depending which way they were going we would turn off the main road and go down the next side-street and head them off so we were waiting for them. Of course, you got to know everybody, although you stuck to your own group. It was a way of meeting people. It was something we enjoyed doing.

The monkey parade was a way of passing the time, something of a display, a catwalk and courtship ritual in one. The chat-up lines were no less unsophisticated than those from the 1990s; 'The conversational gambits were generally uninspired, consisting of the kind of clicking sounds that are used to encourage a horse to go faster, or remarks like "Going far?" or "fancy a walk?"', remembers Ewan MacColl.

The parades attracted dedicated followers of fashion, among them many too poor to do much more than customise their work clothes. Others missed a week or two if their best suit was at the pawnshop. Stan Whittaker was an apprentice plumber, a reserved occupation on call for vital war work, so he avoided being called up into the forces. He wasn't one to worry about the way he looked: 'With clothes being rationed, if you had two shirts you were very lucky. You always had a best shirt which you'd wash and iron when you needed to put it on, so you might change into that, or a decent pullover. But clothes, we didn't have a lot of clothes because you couldn't get them even if you could afford them.'

One way to maintain the parading habit despite a lack of money was to improvise. Decades later the practice of customising clothes was to become an important part of many eras – the tie-dye t-shirt of the 1960s and the safety pins of the punk era – but this is one woman talking about the parade at Boggart Hole Clough in north Manchester:

You know the toreador hats – with the tassels? My friend and I got one of those. It was only about five shillings. Sometimes we hadn't even money to buy powder. It was a tiny box and it was only about tuppence. So we used to put flour on our face. With those hats on – flour on our face! We did that for years, every Sunday night. Two hours of walking up and down. And you hadn't two ha'pennies for a penny in your purse.

The tradition of the monkey run evolved from street-corner society. It maintained that close contact with your mates, it avoided trouble with the police for loitering by staying on the move, and it was free. It was a potent, improvised courtship ritual with only one big drawback, in fact: it was not well suited to the traditional Manchester climate. Caught in the rain, groups would take refuge in shop doorways or on street corners, or nip into Turner's temperance bar or Gotelli's ice-cream shop for a drink of hot Vimto at 2p a shot. The chance to pair off was key to it all, though. One woman remembers the monkey run in Salford: 'All up Regent Road on either side there were lads and girls . . . till they got to Cross Lane, the Eccles New Road, that's where they picked these lads up. My mother copped me once with a lad, and I got a damn good hiding.'

Stan Whittaker, though, resists attempts to put a sensationalist gloss on the goings-on on the monkey run. He maintains that times and attitudes were very different fifty years ago, and has a story to tell to prove how innocent his intentions were. On one occasion the monkey run dispersed when an air-raid warning siren sounded and one of the girls requested that he should walk her home:

> She was a bit forward for her age this girl, as you might say. And I got talking to her stood in the entry near where she lived and she says to me – this shows how naive I was at this time, and I must have been seventeen, easily – she says to me, 'If you could have anything you like, now, right at this moment, what would you have?' She was a big girl, big bust and everything, and I said, 'Oh, I think I'd like a nice car', and she said, 'No, right now, at this moment', and I said everything bar what she wanted me to say. She says to me 'Wouldn't you like to introduce me to Fagin?' Now, to this day, this isn't a phrase I'm familiar with, but what she was suggesting was sex, like. But I said, 'What do you mean?', and she just looked at me and said 'Don't be so bloody stupid' and walked off.

Some of the older generation found it hard to differentiate high spirits from low intentions. In March 1924 the *Salford City Reporter* reported testimony from the local police that the Salford parades had become rowdy, the youths walking abreast on the footway singing 'Yes, We Have No Bananas', jostling passers-by off the pavement and into the roadway. But these groups of lads usually weren't gangs in any accepted anti-social sense; Stan Whittaker is most insistent on this point. According to his testimony, the lads in those days were a harmless bunch:

> Amongst our lot, our gang, there'd perhaps be ten lads and six girls. We never swore in front of these girls and we never heard them swear and they never smoked in the street. That's a difference I've noticed a lot now. Even though we came from a so-called 'low area', Collyhurst, Harpurhey, where it's supposed to be a bit rough, we was quite well mannered, as you might say, and we respected old people. We had park-keepers in them days, and if you were in the park at night – we used to go there at night because it was still light – but if you went on the swings, which were only for children, the park-keeper, who was a pensioner, generally, would chase you. Now you can imagine that happening today; they'd chase the pensioner wouldn't they?

In most areas, for most young people, the monkey parade tradition-ally happened on a Sunday. This remained unchanged even when the twin pleasures of the dance hall and the cinema began to attract huge interest in the 1920s and 30s, principally because before the Second World War licensing laws did not allow dancing or film shows on a Sunday.

At the end of the twentieth century cable and satellite television bring the world into our living rooms, but a hundred years ago the street was the limits of your world. Your community confined you; Robert Roberts once met a woman who hadn't travelled further than a five minute walk in eighteen years of marriage. The young took to the streets, having no more alternatives than they had bananas.

The street is where people collide. All manner of them, depressing and desperate people, and jovial, chirpy successful people. We've almost insulated ourselves courtesy of the motor car, but city life can't help involving encounters with the people around us. Once we've left the sanctuary of the four walls of our house to venture out into the streets, the sparks inevitably start flying; a greeting here, a mad stare there. In most parts of the city the street has never lost its edge or its menace. And there's still a battle over possession of the streets, arguments about whether winos should be moved off benches, tension between local residents and street prostitutes, and still thousands of people spilling out of halls late at night every weekend.

Music halls died a slow death in the middle of this century. One venue, Liston's Music Hall, was operating in the mid 1950s, but the material had evolved into something more like today's cabaret circuit than the old-style variety shows. The atmosphere in working men's clubs and karaoke bars bears similarities with the early days of the music hall, and the public's appetite for musical turns, endless catchphrases and dancing girls lives on in at least half the TV programmes on the Saturday night schedules.

Monkey runs began to die out after the war, including the well-mannered monkey run in Harpurhey frequented by Gotelli's lot, as the thrills of dance halls and the cinema began to dominate. From 1947 Sunday cinema was allowed in Manchester. A strong further reason for the decline of the monkey runs was the break-up of the old communities that sustained them. Acres of Harpurhey got demolished, the residents relocated to large overspill estates like Langley and Wythenshawe.

Soon after the war Stan Whittaker married Edna, the sister of one of his friends, and together they moved to Wythenshawe. In 1996 he wrote to the *Manchester Evening News* requesting old friends from the Harpurhey monkey run to get in touch. There's talk of a get-together. Edna joined us when I went round to reminisce. I asked her if they really walked for hours. 'Yes', she replied. 'You could look in all the shop windows. We didn't have much. You couldn't do that now, though, could you? They're all shuttered up.'

CHAPTER 3

'If That's Music, I'm the Shah of Persia':

Jazz and the Cinema (the Cultural Revolution)

There was a cultural revolution in England in the first four decades of the twentieth century. Two forces transformed Mancunian lives and the culture of the city. Superficially, the rise of cinema and jazz might be regarded simply as mere changes in leisure habits, but they weren't peripheral; they gripped, became central to existence, more important than work, better than sitting at home or getting drummed out of school.

By the end of the nineteenth century Manchester already had traditions of merry-making – public house stirs, the music hall, local songs, humorous skits, organ grinders on the streets, brass bands and the monkey parade – and there was also an infrastructure catering for middle-class tastes (the Hallé Orchestra, the art galleries and private clubs). The First World War, however, had had a major impact on life in the city, and by the 1920s old traditions were further marginalised by the arrival of cinema and jazz.

Neither nights at the Hallé nor a lifetime devotion to the music hall prepared the people of Manchester for the sound of jazz. With its syncopated rhythms, accent on volume, unconventional instrumentation and reliance on improvisation – and, most of all, with its obvious debt to Afro-American black culture – jazz hit the city with a rattling jolt. In its own way, the coming of jazz was as much of a shock to Manchester as the industrial revolution. In fact, to some it seemed a fundamental part of the same journey, another leap away from rural, quiet, immutable, conservative England. According to historian Eric Hobsbawm, when jazz arrived it was recognised as a 'symbol of modernity, the machine age, a break with the past'. Dance halls multiplied as demand for the new sound of jazz grew.

The cinema also weaved a spell. The cinema couldn't provide permanent escape from the drudgery of day-to-day life, but it met the needs and dreams of the masses like nothing before it. The big cinema buildings – or 'dream palaces', as they were called – changed Manchester's environment, and the movies transformed the landscape of the imagination.

The cinema and jazz flourished in the 1920s and 30s, economically two of the least stable decades in history, the decades of the General Strike, the Wall Street Crash, *The Grapes of Wrath*, *Love on the Dole*, the Bexley Square demo, the Jarrow marches. They were decades wracked by the effects of economic booms and slumps, and by unprecedented levels of unemployment in key manufacturing industries: shipbuilding, coal and cotton.

Some parts of England thrived in the 1930s, however; the image of uniform poverty throughout the country is wide of the mark. Average living standards rose, and several large new industries – car manufacture, for instance – provided good wage levels and less weekly hours than the older industries. And in some parts of Manchester – Wythenshawe, for example (Manchester's showpiece garden suburb) – council house dwellers enjoyed new and better-equipped housing. Nevertheless, mass unemployment and dire poverty were widespread in parts of England, especially the North.

Locally, both the slump and the long-term decline in the cotton industry were devastating. Between the wars the export market for textiles collapsed. By 1937 the volume of exports was down to just one third of its 1913 level. India had begun to export cotton goods to Britain, reversing nineteenth-century trade patterns. On occasions in the 1930s a third of all cotton workers were without work, and many of those still employed were on reduced hours and reduced pay.

Significantly, though, both the cinema and the dance hall were relatively cheap nights out. The cultural revolution was undimmed, perhaps even illuminated, by the decades of depression. Even in the midst of poverty, the young stayed on their feet; on the dancefloor at least.

By the end of the 1930s the cinema and dance boom had grown into mass commercial industries, but their roots had been established in an earlier age – the late Victorian and Edwardian era, the days when the Empire ensured that there was money about, even in working-class areas. This was when the big spectator sports began to take hold; organised, professional football in England dates from this same era.

Foreshadowing the rise of the cinema and dance halls, football locally grew from tangled roots in the nineteenth century to a mass spectator sport. In 1913 Charles Russell homed in on the obsession with football among the boys of Manchester: 'From the days when they begin to go to school this is the one game which absorbs their attention ... In courts and alleys, on vacant plots of land, on brick-fields, indeed where any open space at all may be found, attempts are made to play the game, even though the football be but a bundle of tightly rolled-up, string-bound papers.'

Professional football in England was thirty years old when Russell wrote those words, and Manchester United had come a long way in a short space of time, evolving from the Newton Heath Lancashire & Yorkshire Railway FC in 1878, and surviving near bankruptcy in 1902, to become a major commercial enterprise in the first decade of the twentieth century. Success on the pitch had already become a habit – they won the Championship in 1908 and 1911, and the FA Cup in 1909 – and the crowds flocked to their new ground at Old Trafford (opened in 1910).

Manchester City Football Club also had their first great team in the mid 1900s, winning the FA Cup in 1904. Their ground at the time, on Hyde Road, had a considerable capacity of around forty thousand, but it still wasn't big enough to cope with the weekly demand. A fire at the ground finally precipitated a move to a newly built ground at Maine Road in Moss Side in 1923. Fifty-six thousand people saw the first game at Maine Road, against Sheffield United. Maine Road was a state-of-the-art stadium, with high stands and lush turf cut and carted from the best pastures in Cheshire. Before the match the band played 'Ours Is a Nice House, Ours Is'.

Football moved from street to stadium in the space of a generation as popular culture began influencing the architecture and look of Manchester as conspicuously as the warehouses, mills and chimneys had seventy years previously. Cinemas, in their turn, followed a similar pattern. Among the plushest picture houses in Manchester was the Palais de Danse on Rochdale Road in Harpurhey, opened in 1927 by the Lord Mayor with guest celebrity the silent screen star Reginald Denny. When Joe Kay remembers the investment made by the cinema companies which provided a Palais de Danse of such grandeur and opulence, he cannot but help compare it with the real world of depression-hit Harpurhey: 'In retrospect, all this luxury amongst the humble dwellings of Harpurhey, and amid the depression and unemployment, seemed to be, as the saying goes, "one thing laughing at another".'

Well before Hollywood, the 1930s and the mega-venues, cinema began transforming Manchester, England. At the end of the nineteenth century, the first movies introduced the Manchester masses to a life beyond gossip from the corner shop. Whether it was newsreel of boxing from Carson City, or short fiction features like *A Trip to the Moon* – or later, the films of James Cagney, Fritz Lang and Greta Garbo – the cinema pitched Mancunians out of their confined neighbourhood mindset, and into a wider, bigger world. According to Robert Roberts, the cinema, together with the First World War, destroyed the 'stifling parochialism' of Edwardian Salford. It was a huge leap in cultural development; 'for us in the village the world suddenly expanded'.

Film shows in Manchester were sporadic, and at makeshift venues. Limitations of the early technology meant that for the first ten years of cinema history, up to 1905 or so, most films were short snippets lasting just a few minutes. Most screenings included a compere to entertain the audience while the reels were changed, and musicians and singers were employed to provide accompaniment, being presented as part of a bill of various other kinds of entertainment, often as part of touring shows brought to Manchester by travelling showmen, local entrepreneurs and promoters established on the music hall or fairground circuits.

In May 1896 films were first shown in Manchester; at St James's Theatre on Oxford Street and at the old YMCA building at the top of Peter Street. In the same month, using material from the French film pioneers, Auguste and Louis Lumière, local showman (and sometime juggler and hand-shadow performer) 'Professor' Lucien Trewey promoted a film show at the Lesser Free Trade Hall. All these early films were little more than a demonstration of the technique, flickering examples of what the new technology could achieve; the Lumière shows included footage of card playing in a Paris café and the antics of Buffalo Bill's Circus. Sport was a favoured cinema topic, especially racing, cricket and boxing. The first large-scale showing at the Free Trade Hall took place in June 1898, when an estimated audience of fifteen thousand people viewed five showings of the Corbett–Fitzsimmons boxing world championship bout.

As the technology advanced and demand grew apace, the importance of the film camera as a documentary tool was soon acknowledged and the cinema became a prime news deliverer. Newsreel film of the big international events – the San Francisco earthquake, the death of King Edward – was made available by Gaumont and Pathé, but a blurring of fact and fiction was also accepted, or undetected, by early audiences; 'dramatic reconstructions' of the Boer War were filmed by the Blackburn-based Mitchell & Kenyon film company by employing local actors and staging mock battles on the moors around Blackburn and Darwen.

Other local film-makers regularly filmed communal events (some staged for the benefit of the cameras) in order to capture as many locals on film as possible. Church processions, especially the Whit walks, were a favourite subject for the camera crews. In this era – decades before the disposable camera, the snapshot or the camcorder – most of the working class were without the means to make a private record of their lives. They formed the hardcore of cinema goers, though, and were naturally eager to see themselves on the silver screen, thus ensuring big box office returns for the documenters.

By 1909, before the regulation of cinemas, an infrastructure for the movie industry was in place in Manchester. There were regular shows at all the main theatres, and one-offs elsewhere. Production companies and companies renting and repairing films were all over the city, with clusters of activity around Deansgate and Great Ducie Street.

The pattern of building had changed in Manchester. The working class had moved out of the city centre to make way for railways and railway stations, the canal, and commercial and office developments, and in response to new housing regulations. The Corporation had taken a lead in new housing; the first wave of terrace streets – the traditional *Coronation Street* look – went up in the 1860s and 70s, housing covered by new bye-laws situated in new areas, developing new communities. Twentieth-century Manchester evolved with a commercial centre, working-class areas in an inner city ring, with middle-class suburbs developing further out of town. It was in the inner ring, among the terraced streets, that the first permanent, purpose-built cinema venues appeared; among the earliest were the Longsight Picture Palace on Stockport Road, the Alhambra in Higher Openshaw and the King's Hall in Hulme.

The Cinematograph Act of 1909 regulated British cinema, requiring safety standards and operating licences. The Tivoli Music Hall (the old Folly on Peter Street) was one of the first theatres to be granted one of the new licences, and later became the Winter Garden Cinema. The Grand became a full-time cinema and underwent several name changes: the Palladium, the Peter Street Picture House and the Futurist. The Act also stimulated a round of purpose-built cinemas in the city centre, including the Picture House in 1911 (in a building now used by McDonalds and the Leisure Time slot machine and video game arcade; the Picture House name is still visible on the fascia above the top of the current frontages). Seating a thousand people, with an inclining floor and balcony, and incorporating ornate and spacious design features, the first owners declared it to be 'the largest and finest cinematograph theatre in the UK'.

Other purpose-built cinemas that opened in the city before the First War include the Scala in Withington, opened in 1912, which is now Cine City, and one on the site currently used by the Cornerhouse to house its main screen, the Kinemacolor Palace. It opened in 1910 – its name proclaiming its cosmopolitan modernity – and showed hand-tinted colour as well as black and white films. Another was the Deansgate Picture House and Café Rendezvous, which was decorated in an ornate style, with tapestries hanging from the higher walls and oak panelling. This later became a Cannon cinema.

Manchester and Salford were wild for the new cinema experience. Demand was huge. In 1913 Manchester had 111 licensed cinemas, serving a population of 714,000; this was a larger number of cinemas per head than any other area of Britain. By 1914 and the outbreak of the First World War, weekly cinema audiences for the country as a whole were twenty million. The early, silent days of the cinema proved a problem for some of the less literate in the audiences, who couldn't follow the words flashed up between episodes.

After the Great War the popularity of the cinema was rivalled only by the rise of the dance hall as a vital part of the entertainment of the day, especially for the young, free and single. Dance halls grew during the early years of the twentieth century, and reached their peak of popularity in the two decades between the wars. Dancing itself wasn't new, but the scale of participation was, as was the change in the music to a jazz-based sound, the close identification of the new dance scene with a new and international culture, and, as in the cinema boom, the investment made in setting up and promoting venues. The inter-war years, the so-called 'Long Weekend', were the dancing decades, the Jazz Age.

We know there were wild song-and-dance sessions in the beer-houses and public houses of Manchester in the nineteenth century, but sedate affairs catering for the middle classes have a long history too. 'Grand balls' and 'select dances' had been held in the city for years. In 1792, for instance, the Assembly Rooms opened opposite the Portico Library on Mosley Street, with office space, tea rooms and a ballroom. Strict rules were published and enforced regarding the ballroom dancing; for example, gentlemen were to change partners every two dances and no couple were to leave a dance until it was concluded. While the artisans danced on the tables in nearby taverns, the Assembly Rooms remained restrained; the middle classes who resisted regulation in the workplace preferred it on the dancefloor.

The big boom in dancing which blew away bourgeois, buttoned-up ways of behaving came after the First World War. The war had shocked society with its unprecedented violence and the huge loss of life on the front line. There was a mania around during the Long Weekend, perhaps even denial; the traumatic experiences of those soldiers who fought in the trenches remained largely unspoken, unexplored, for decades. The constituency that detonated the boom were the young, those too young to have fought, or too lucky to die. Although the birth of rock & roll in the late 1950s is often credited as the era which brought the birth of 'youth' as a separate, distinguishable social group and the point at which the generation gap was created, a generation gap was certainly apparent in the 1920s. In the 20s and 30s the cinemas and dancehalls of England were most enthusiastically embraced by the younger generation, especially by the unmarried young; those traditionally most dedicated to going out.

Leisure – a concept previously the preserve of the idle rich – began to play an important part in the lives of all classes. An article in the *Manchester Guardian* in 1926 upbraided what it called the 'Age of Luxury', in the kind of shocked and horrified tones we have since heard turned against long-haired hippies and drug-guzzling ravers:

> Short skirts, lipsticks, vulgar films . . . sex novels, jazz, the Eton crop . . . There is almost no end to the list of abominations . . . Before the war and in the uneasy years which immediately followed it, luxury was mainly a matter of means. Now any

young typist from Manchester or Kensington can keep her hair trimmed and waved and her busy feet in fine silk stockings and pale kid shoes.

Jazz was the greatest abomination of them all. Music from the plantations had been around England for a century or more in a variety of forms. One was the gross comic caricature minstrels of the music hall, and a second was the sentimental attraction for Victorian audiences of 'Negro' spirituals and religious songs.

Jazz was different; it had been filtered through urban America and the accent on rhythm demanded foot-tapping, at least. When the Original American Ragtime Octet took a residency at the London Hippodrome in 1912 they made a sensational splash.

Ragtime was the first form of jazz to reach England. It was seized upon by the press, who wrote it up as a 'craze', part of the tradition of novelty and comedy which the minstrels had embodied, and on a par with other consumer crazes of the time; ice skating, for example. But the music kept coming. The Original Dixieland Jazz Band arrived in England in 1919, pandering a little to the novelty angle expected, and billing themselves as 'Untuneful Harmonists Playing Peppery Melodies' and 'The Creators of Jazz'.

As jazz in the 1920s developed and enveloped the dancehalls of England, so shrill criticism of the new sound was also heard. The press slammed jazz. The noise annoyed ('a boiler factory at full blast', said *Musical Mail*), and it was a menace to morals declared church-men ('a national humiliation', said Bishop Weldon), although, like other crazes, the controversy seemed merely to fuel fascination with the new big thing, and the journalists played up the scandal for all it was worth. Doctors, teachers, and the great, good and worthy were all mounting soapboxes to denounce jazz.

Connections were made between jazz and the jungle. It was the product of a 'Negro' culture already degraded and damned as primitive by the ruling class. It was like the revenge of the slaves, this all-conquering sound from Africa via America. Jazz was untamed; 'It is not likely to be continued by decent people', wrote Sir Dyce Duckworth in the *Evening News* in March 1919.

Whereas the fruits and rewards of carefree luxury had been a preserve of the richer classes, popular culture was, in a sense, democratising society. The masses could actually be more *avant garde* in their tastes than the artistic elite; the defenders of a more traditional, insular culture were wedded to a canon of acceptable art and touch-stones of spiritual health. But in the cities, mass culture was dominating. England was changing forever; not just the environment, but in its mentality, its culture. Lipsticks, cinemas, typists at dancehalls, peppery melodies; there was no going back.

That *Manchester Guardian* writer focused criticism on young women. The battles for female emancipation fought by the suffragettes had borne fruit in 1918, when women over thirty won the vote. Various other Acts between 1919 and 1925 had aimed at giving women equality under the law. In 1928 the vote was extended to all working women over twenty-one. Many social critics resented young women apparently flaunting their newly won economic and political freedoms with their liberated dress and demeanour.

The new freedoms for women wouldn't have necessarily benefited women in all families. Married women, especially, had been invested with too many mundane responsibilities to enjoy the Jazz Age. In many communities in Manchester and the rest of Lancashire it was the women who were in charge of the family budget, scooping up the men's wages (minus beer money). In that sense, society was matriarchal. Whatever the latest dance craze, or new Act of Parliament, wives would carry the burdens of the family as they always had done.

For working women, the independent young and urban middle-class women, lives were changing, especially their social lives. Much was made of their changing habits: going out without the old-style whalebone corsets; dancing without gloves (they had become too expensive); wearing not just lipstick, but rouge, and mascara too; drinking cocktails; smoking cigarettes. The noisy, imported syncopated sounds, and the new informalities on the dancefloor, underlined this break with the past. The fact of change was the cause of regret for some, but rejoicing for others. Most of the rejoicing was done by the young; out of the ruins of the First World War, they were taking charge.

In the 1920s young wage-earners were targeted by the rapidly expanding film industry; a young, new artform for a new generation, and one ripe with the allure of modern technology. Throughout the decade films were shown in Manchester cinemas that were made and marketed with the young in mind; another piece of evidence suggesting that a culture belonging to the 'youth' was born well before 'Good Golly Miss Molly'. In January 1920, for instance, the Tower

Picturedome in Broughton showed both *The Echo of Youth* and *The Blindness of Youth*. At the far end of the decade, in November 1929, the Manchester Hippodrome screened *Movietone Follies of 1929*, which, according to a local film brochure of the time, was about a 'jazz-mad flapper', and its theme was 'Youth with a capital Y'.

Youth with a capital Y was also well acquainted with dancehalls in the 1920s, much to the disgust of those guarding older traditions. Behind many forms of youth culture there's a lust for life and pursuit of the sweet smell of sex. The dancehalls were great meeting places; dark and noisy, with the allure of the illicit. The appeal crossed classes; the sedate and the wanton were coming together. An article by the fashionable young Pat Sykes in the *Manchester Evening News* in 1929 noted a falling-off of interest in set-piece dances that required hours of practice, acknowledging that the new styles were more individual and expressive, the new dancehalls were less formal, looser. Jazz dancing, freed from the restrictions of booking dancers and pairing off with partners of the opposite sex, brought an entirely liberated form of going out to the young. The formalities were breaking down.

In *The Classic Slum* Robert Roberts describes the popularity of the dancehalls which opened in the working-class districts of Manchester in the 1920s. Youth with a capital Y was there in force:

> In the explosive dancing boom after the war, the young from sixteen to twenty-five flocked into the dancehalls by the hundred thousand; some went 'jigging' as often as six times a week. The great 'barn' we patronised as apprentices held at least a thousand . . . At 6*d* per head (1/– on Saturdays) youth at every level of the manual working-class, from the bound apprentice to the 'scum of the slum', fox-trotted through the new bliss in each other's arms.

The growth in demand for dancehalls during the 1920s stimulated the growth of a certain kind of dance music, creating an environment in which the new kinds of jazz flourished. By the mid 1920s 'jazz' was widely used as a generic term for popular dance music. Nearer and nearer the dancers stepped, until jazz dancing brought accusations of virtual sexual congress. Bigger and bigger the dancehalls became. Intriguingly, local pianist Frank Pritchard suggests that practical considerations – the necessity to reach all corners of the big new dance venues – influenced the evolution of jazz in Manchester. The extra raw volume required to reach right round the big halls would have further alienated older, more sedate audiences. Raucous music was now the predominant soundtrack for a night out: 'The new dances demanded a more raucous tone of music, so the saxophones and trumpets took on a leading role in the modern dance band ... the violin was relegated to a doubling instrument, used mostly by sax players in the romantic modern waltzes.'

From the arrival of the new jazz sounds and onwards, there was always a frenetic turnover of dances and styles. Dances which saw the light of day in the 1920s include the Black Bottom and the Charleston. To bring the dancers back week in and week out – as in today's clubland – new sounds and new ideas were essential. Every week the dancefloor needs to be filled; a commercial imperative which has ensured the ongoing evolution of dance music, relentlessly reinventing itself, staying fresh.

Although it was ragtime which shook English culture in the 1920s, jazz was already fragmenting into various forms, many of which were commercialised, modified to appeal to as wide a number of people as possible. New, untamed forms developed to counter commercialisation; when the intensely anti-commercial be-bop revolution occurred in the 1940s, it shocked and polarised the jazz industry as well as the fans. 'Be-bop had immediacy, and it was almost as savage as seeing Jimi Hendrix for the first time', says local jazz musician, Bruce Mitchell.

The key to the survival of jazz was the turnover of styles. Ways of reacting to music in England, like so much in English society, had been bound by tradition, but jazz thrived on change. Terence Blanchard – composer of the *Malcolm X* film score – once explained his view that the turnover of jazz styles was an evolution driven by reaction and revolution. Dizzy Gillespie came out of Roy Eldridge, Coltrane came out of Dexter Gordon, Charlie Parker came out of Don Byas, and Clifford Brown out of Fats Navarro. 'The whole notion of jazz is to break the tradition ... That's what all the great musicians have done all the time', he said; 'Breaking the tradition; that *is* the tradition.'

Those of us who have witnessed the invention, dedication and self-confidence of girl dancers in soul and house clubs won't be surprised to hear that the more complicated dances in the 1920s – like the Tango – became something of a speciality of the girls. 'On Friday nights I used to go with three or four of my mates to Merrie Mac's, over the Co-op shop on Moss Lane West', remembers Frank Pritch-ard. 'When the dreaded tango was announced, that was the signal for all us lads to dash to the doorkeeper for a "pass out". This cost tuppence, but it was worth it as it provided the means of escape to the happiness of a quick couple of pints in the pub across the road. Our return fifteen minutes later was always greeted with ironical cheers from the girls.'

Music had created not a gender gap but a generation gap, even in the early 1930s. Ewan MacColl's cousin, John, had just started becoming a regular on the Regent Road monkey parade. He also harboured a desire to be a singer. He and the young Ewan (then aged around eleven) set about learning some of the pop songs of the time. Once rehearsed and polished they presented a performance in front of John's father and some of his cronies. They were bewildered by the duo's material. His Dad's friend, Jock, couldn't get his head round it; 'If that's music, then I'm the Shah of Persia', he said.

Going dancing was not an activity much encouraged by parents. This could cause tension in households which included young wage-earners still living at home and subject to the authority of their parents, yet who yearned to break out. The dancehalls didn't supply anything stronger than coffee, but that didn't assuage parental fears, as Joe Kay recalls: 'Going to the dance-halls, fox-trotting and jazzing was regarded with a great deal of suspicion by older people. Young women especially were looked upon by some folk as being "flighty pieces" or even "scarlet women".'

Girls knew that once they were married they would come under severe social pressure to buckle down; so it's unsurprising that, despite parental anxiety about the perils and temptations of the dancehalls, the girls grabbed their few years of fun. Joe Kay's sister, Ethel, was fifteen in 1927; 'She was considered by Dad to be too young to go dancing, but she went secretly at first. After coming home from work and getting ready to go out with her friends, if Dad was in the house she would throw her dance shoes over the backyard wall. Later she would go out that way and pick the shoes up in the back entry.'

But by the mid 1920s jazz was being heard at home. Changes in communications technology, coupled with the advent of public broadcasting in 1922, meant that radio – or, rather, the wireless – played an important part in spreading the gospel of jazz and dance-band music. 'Radio transformed the life of the poor as nothing else had ever done. It brought the world into their room', writes

Hobsbawm. And it brought music; thus began the process whereby music was disseminated, popularised and sold to the masses. Music was a daily companion. In the 1920s Manchester and Salford had their own music station, 2ZY, with a studio at the Metro Vickers plant in Old Trafford. A world away from the niche marketing of the 1990s, a typical evening on 2ZY reflected the chaotic variety of early music radio, and reflected the fluidity of the culture and the society: a piano recital relayed from the Piccadilly Picture Theatre, a Bach concert from St Annes On Sea, live appearances by bands such as the Amazon Six and the Garner Schofield Orchestra, and programmes of recorded jazz like *Syncopation* presented by J. H. Ambrose.

This variety was reflected in the repertoire of dance bands playing live; in Manchester in the mid 1920s this often meant moving from Dvorak through souped-up, jazzed-up versions of old-time standards, to a novelty fox-trot like 'The Doll Dance' by Nacio Herb Brown, all within a short set. There was plenty of work for the bands in these decades of high demand: weddings, office outings, church socials, and regular Friday and Saturday public dances.

Venues for public dances in the city centre in this era included the Grosvenor Hotel and Deansgate Hotel (at the northern end of Deansgate), UCP Coniston Rooms (Market Street), Parker's Restaurant (St Mary's Gate), the State Café (corner of Piccadilly and Market Street), and the nearby basement of the Piccadilly Picture House (between the corners of Tib Street and Oldham Street). Most districts out of town were well catered for. On the south side of the city, the Rusholme and Moss Side area had the Casino Ballroom on Wilmslow Road, Cowan's Dance Hall (on the corner of Raby Street and Bickley Street), Merrie Mac's, the Rialto (Denmark Road) and the RB Ballroom (on Monton Street).

There was an obvious hierarchy among the many venues. Shorrocks's Super Ballroom, situated on Brunswick Street, charged 2/– entrance fee (half a shilling more than most) and had a reputation for being 'toffee-nosed', whereas Grimshaw's (near All Saints) was more populist. Grimshaw's, like many other dancehalls, had started out as a dance school in the days when formal training in dance steps was mandatory. The Ritz on Whitworth Street was the top spot. According to Frank Pritchard, the Ritz 'was mainly frequented by first class dancers, who were assured of finding good partners'. In the 1930s it was described as 'The Hall of a Thousand Delights'.

Some of the venues were purpose-built, but others made do, reorganised or customised existing spaces. Shorrocks's Ballroom and the resident band, the Syncopated Six, occupied two adjoining houses in a terraced row of large, three-storey houses. Merrie Mac's and the Rialto were both above Co-op shops. Among the purpose-built dancehalls were Levenshulme Palais on Stockport Road and Chorlton Palais near Chorlton Bus Terminus, both with a capacity of three hundred. Among bigger new halls was, of course, the fabulous Ritz, and the Palais de Danse in Harpurhey.

By this time the cinema had also grown into a huge endeavour that touched every Mancunian. Films had become more sophisticated as the technology – fed by commercial pressures – advanced and as international companies took a grip on an increasingly lucrative industry. In America, Hollywood had moved into full-scale, full-on production and in the 1930s distributors like the Odeon (a German-based company, its name an acronym of Oscar Deutsch Entertains Our Nation) and (the French-owned) Gaumont chains were beginning to dominate. The cinema was international, and, as such – compared with the indigenous music hall – it held a magical allure. By this time the cinema industry had been boosted by a further innovation: the 'talkies'. The first talkie in Manchester was screened at the New Oxford Picture House; *Uncle Tom's Cabin* in November 1928.

By the end of the 1930s, the number of cinemas in Manchester had grown to 129, among them a whole new generation of 'picture palaces', including the Piccadilly Picture Theatre overlooking Piccadilly Gardens, which housed a restaurant, café and dance hall, as well as a cinema. As the leisure revolution stimulated competition between and among music hall theatres, cinemas and dancehalls, design played a big part in creating the best, most opulent, surroundings. Escapism lay at the heart of the appeal. Money invested and made by cinemas was huge, and designs grew grander still, and grander. The Paramount (now the Odeon) on Oxford Street was pure state-of-the-art opulence. The dream palaces mirrored more closely the relentless glamour of 1930s Hollywood than the real world outside.

For many, the modernity of the cinema industry marked an American influence on Manchester, an influence represented not just on Hollywood-derived celluloid but in spirit, and in bricks and mortar too. As Arthur Donbavand, who worked as a cinema electrician at the Paramount, recalls: 'The super cinema, as it was classed at the time, was really something out of this world to the people of the period who'd been used to the local cinema or the old converted theatres into cinemas that was happening in the city. When the super cinema came along with all the American razzmatazz and what-have-you, you can quite understand there was a lot of real interest in it.'

Outside the city centre there were fewer picture palaces, but still plenty of local houses, flea-pits, or bughouses. Most districts had more than one cinema. As a young boy, Anthony Burgess had the choice of two cinemas on Queens Road, near his Lodge Street home in Miles Platting. His Saturday afternoons at the Electric were the beginnings of a lifetime's devotion to the cinema. Burgess, like other children with good reading ability, read the words out loud so that those around him could follow.

When Burgess moved to Moss Side his affections were split between the Palace Cinema on Princess Road, run by a Jewish entrepreneur from north Manchester called Jakie Innersfield, and the Claremont on Claremont Road. At the Palace he saw *The Great Gatsby* and *The Wizard of Oz*, but it was Fritz Lang's film *Metropolis* which most impressed him. For Burgess, seeing *Metropolis* at the age of ten at the Palace Cinema, Moss Side always remained 'one of the major artistic experiences of my life'.

Metropolis caused a big stir in Manchester. Burgess remembered publicity leaflets distributed around the city and 'COMING SOON' posters appearing on billboards. But did Fritz Lang draw inspiration for *Metropolis* from Manchester, as Burgess was to do later in writing his novel *A Clockwork Orange*? According to Deyan Sudjic in an article in the *Guardian* in September 1994, he did: 'Manchester was the first industrial metropolis and the world had seen nothing remotely like it. What made it so powerful and so alarming was that it seemed to represent the future . . . To Fritz Lang, Manchester was still resonant enough to inspire his cinematic image of the modern city in *Metropolis*.'

The film reflected perennial anxieties about urban life felt from Manchester to Berlin to New York; those changes wrought by the coming of the machine had changed civilisation forever, and civilisation's ability to cope with the continuing changes was still in doubt. And the massive class divisions analysed by Engels and others in early industrial Manchester were still the prevailing model of industrial society; a state of affairs at the heart of *Metropolis*, set in the year 2000 in a city controlled by an industrial magnate, a city divided between a decadent master-class and the common labourers living underground. What remains most striking about the film is its visual depiction of the city itself, the thronging masses in thrall to the infernal machines, the landscape dominated by skyscrapers. In fact, it's more likely to have been a trip to New York – and, specifically, a view of New York's skyline – which inspired Lang to make a film of a city set far into the future.

When the 'talkies' came, Jakie Innersfield at the Palace didn't believe the new fad would last, and hung on to a programme of silent films. So Burgess took to going to the Claremont. The stars inspired him and his friends: 'One lad adored Maurice Chevalier in *Innocents of Paris*, dressed his hair in the Chevalier style, thrust out his lower lip, and spoke English with a French accent ... We worshipped Marlene Dietrich in *The Blue Angel*. The German language, which was not taught in school, took on an exotic glamour and some of us formed little groups to learn it.'

Like millions of people growing up in the first half of this century, it's clear that Anthony Burgess's world was widened and his imagination sparked by the films shown at the local cinemas. Cinema was gratefully grabbed as a space of escape from home, work and worries. Dark, half public and half private, it was the venue for courting, and has remained so, even when audience numbers plummeted after the Second World War.

Cinema touched more than just the Maurice Chevalier fans at Burgess's school. One researcher in the 1930s claimed that girls had adopted a 'Hollywood accent', and some imitated the hairstyles, dress and mannerisms of their favourite actresses; the 'Cagney look' was popular among Manchester lads between the wars. Writing in the *Manchester Evening News* in 1937, columnist Robert Blatchford bemoaned the spread of American slang into the English language, criticised English youths for picking up the 'slatternly synonyms and tortured metaphors of alien illiterates', and pointed to the use of phrases like 'Sez you' and 'OK' as evidence that 'Bowery barbarisms' had infiltrated the native English language through their use in films.

By the 1930s movies had also begun to influence local fashion. Decades before Elvis or Teddy Boys, dressing up correctly among both boys and girls was an important part of going out. Manchester had been known as a 'flash' city from its early days (William Cobbett remarked on this reputation as far back as 1826). One man remembers just how flash his fashion-conscious street gang was in the 1930s: 'If you could afford it, you had trousers with a twenty-four inch bottom, with an inch turn-up. And if they were anything under twenty-four inches, you didn't want to know them ... Bell-bottom trousers with a twenty-four inch bottom, and a haircut to match.'

You'd think from the 1980s/1990s style bibles that before New Order young Mancunians had flat caps, George Formby and nowt else, but there were ever-changing fashions in hats, buckles and jackets. The street gangs and the monkey run regulars considered the cut of their clothes to be an important part of their culture. There was the haircut, in the case of our 1930s gang member 'cut in a special style, what they call a "jazzer's" haircut' (music was influencing fashion even then). And the look was completed with a hat and coat, influenced by cinema: 'The one that I wore was what they call an at-a-boy. That was like a Stetson and you pulled it down low, like a gangster effect. And a black belt, and a short belted overcoat.'

Gangster films of that era attracted the disapproval of local moral guardians, reasoning that if young people's hairstyles and trouser widths could be influenced by the cinema, so could their morals. One of the first talkies to be shown in Manchester caused controversy and led to alleged, and more serious, anti-social influences; *The Perfect Alibi* was shown at the Hippodrome in August 1929 (an estimated sixty-five thousand people paid to get in during the first fortnight). In January 1933 members of Bury Town Council denounced *Scarface* as 'degrading' and questioned whether the local Watch Committee were right to allow it to be shown in the town. The chairman of the Watch Committee, Councillor Hoyle, defended the film; it wasn't degrading, it was 'noisy', he said. The Watch Committee had recommended it for adult viewing only.

More innocuous fare in the 1930s was provided by a rising number of Manchester movies and homegrown Lancashire film stars. These were unashamedly light, knockabout films – some made by Mancunian Films, others by Ealing Studios using Northern-based writers and actors – which have since become known, mortifyingly, as 'Jollywood'. Often these films were as much a commercial calculation as the Hollywood epics, and made a direct appeal to older audiences; those who wanted to see some of the spirit, and some of the stars, of the dying variety circuit.

George Formby was nothing if not typecast. In his films he was a good-hearted simpleton, a little man against the world. His music hall background was strong, and his 1930s films, with their hit songs, were a huge success. His songs reflected a quaint version of Lancashire ('A

Lad Fra' Lancasheer'), and some had a smattering of saucy innuendo ('My Little Stick of Blackpool Rock'). In 1934 he was working with John E. Blakeley's Mancunian Films. Blakeley was from a family of cinema entrepreneurs and ran a rental company in Manchester at the turn of the century. Mancunian Films made a total of twenty-five films, although in its early days it worked out of small London studios. The company also had trouble holding on to its stars; many signed to Ealing, as Formby did after two films.

Gracie Fields was as strong as Formby was weak, perhaps reflecting the strong influence wielded by women in working-class communities. She had a no-nonsense persona, in contrast to George Formby, who was all nonsense. Born over a chip shop in Molesworth Street in Rochdale, Gracie Fields was a big stage star in the 1920s, and she too sang about the local community (songs like 'The Clatter of Clogs' and 'Lancashire Blues'). Formby and Fields represented cheery, decent, hard-working, patriotic Lancashire, and Fields, especially, was marketed as classless. The majority of Northern films of the time were only superficially realist. No boats were rocked; in the midst of the Depression, in 1934, the theme of the film *Sing As We Go*, starring Gracie Fields, was an unrecognisable reconciliation between bosses and workers.

Mancunian Films were generally coarser than the later films of Formby and Fields, and cheaper too. Storylines would feature stock characters: the dim toff, the gormless Lancashire lad and the toothless, gossipy old matron (played by Norman Evans – for example, in *Over the Garden Wall* – an early-doors Les Dawson). Dialogue would be catchphrase-dependent, as in music hall. Sandy Powell was renowned for his 'Can you hear me mother?' catchphrase; he was the star of *Cup-Tie Honeymoon* (which also featured Pat Phoenix, then Patricia Pilkington, later of *Coronation Street*). The leading in-house star in the 1940s was Frank Randle, born in Wigan. The films didn't travel well; Randle was a regional, rather than national success, playing more combative, disruptive characters than Formby ever did. He was particularly able playing lecherous old drunks; 'Bah, I've supped some ale tonight' he would roar as he made a play for the busty leading lady.

The films had a knack of appearing old-fashioned. Their links to *Coronation Street*, the least heavy of the TV soaps, are strong; inclined to comedy or sentimentality, clearly repetitive, happily unsophisticated, loved by the public. They were born of an insular culture, one that regretted the swift changes of the twentieth century. This catchphrase-crazy, happy-go-lucky cinema with its roots in the music hall is hilariously captured by Paul Whitehouse's Arthur Atkinson character in BBC2's *The Fast Show*; see him and watch Mancunian Films wither. It was the cinema of limited expectations. These films clearly lacked the glamour of *The Blue Angel*, the visceral anger of *Scarface*, or the ambition and explosive imagination of *Metropolis*.

There were other representations of local life on celluloid, including film versions of *Love on the Dole* and *Hobson's Choice* (the best one, starring Charles Laughton, John Mills and Brenda de Banzie, was released in 1954). These too were conspicuously down to earth compared with the glitz and glamour of escapist cinema, and combined the influence of the 1930s documentary movements with older theatre traditions; specifically, the theatre tradition that spawned *Hobson's Choice*.

In 1894 the Independent Theatre Committee was formed in Manchester with the aim of presenting works by the likes of Ibsen and Shaw; 'the new revolutionary drama', as it has been described. They used the Gentlemen's Concert Hall on Peter Street for four years, ending with a performance of Shaw's *Candida* in 1898. The baton for *avant garde* drama was taken up by the Playgoers Theatre Company formed by Iden Payne; they performed Shaw, Rostand and Maeterlinck at the Midland Hotel.

It was in the midst of this scene that probably the most important figure in Manchester's theatre history appeared: Annie Horniman, who came to Manchester from Dublin where she had helped set up the Abbey Theatre. In 1907 she bought the Gaiety Theatre on Peter Street. She gathered around her actors from the local independent groups, and created the first recognisable repertory company in the country. With an artistic vision matched by great marketing skills, she ran the Gaiety until 1921, keeping prices low, presenting children's shows and building a clear identity as a base for the new drama. She also championed local dramatists in a way no impresario had previously dared. Three local authors came to prominence: Stanley Houghton (*Hindle Wakes*, which caused a stir in 1912), Allan Monkhouse (*Mary Broome* and *The Conquering Hero*) and Harold Brighouse (*Hobson's Choice*).

The writers of the so-called 'Lancashire school' had become, under Miss Horniman's guidance, the most dynamic force in English theatre. The school, and the Company, were known for realistic, working-class, family dramas with characters very much of the street rather than the drawing room, with accents and priorities very different to mainstream theatre traditions. They were clear forerunners of the Northern films in the 1960s, the kitchen-sink era epitomised by the gritty, witty *A Taste of Honey*.

It's clear, too, that a strong female sensibility is at work in this writing tradition; from Mrs Gaskell via Annie Horniman to Shelagh Delaney, there's a rejection of grand gestures or fantasy writing, and instead a light touch and a focus on social crises impacting on families, the close-knit community in a struggle against a hard-faced world. But the cinema boom ate into the audience for drama, and Miss Horniman moved from the Gaiety in 1921.

While the rise of the cinema decimated the demand for music hall and live theatre, it boosted the spread of the jazz word; jazz and popular songs were an integral part of the films of the 1920s and 1930s and fuelled each other's growth, just as the cinema was to do again with the rise of rock & roll in the late 1950s (the success of 'Rock Around The Clock', for instance, was assured by its high profile in more than one film).

In our modern era, where music seeps from speakers in supermarkets, lifts, hotel lobbies and shopping precincts, it's hard to imagine an environment like that of pre-war Manchester when music wasn't ubiquitous. The increases in radio ownership in the 1920s and the advances made by the talkies fed demand for the new syncopated dancefloor sounds, and thus played an integral part in the jazz boom. It was through the household gramophone that Ewan MacColl first heard jazz. His mother got a job at the traditionally minded Cunningham Dance Academy in the autumn of 1930, and any discs unsuitable for the fox-trot or the two-step weren't used at the Academy, so Mrs Miller would scoop them up and take them home. Young Ewan got to hear Bessie Smith, Louis Armstrong and Jelly Roll Morton.

Jazz became the sound of now, the new sound fit for the new technology. Whereas once the young Mancunian would have to go looking for music, music had now arrived on the doorstep. Joe Kay recalls hearing a record shop-owner playing a record of Al Jolson singing 'Sonny Boy' at a volume loud enough to attract passers-by. This must have been around 1929. Joe Kay was enraptured, and he wasn't alone; 'People coming home from work, or getting off tramcars, stopped to listen and gathered round the open door or loitered nearby.'

The cultural life of Manchester changed dramatically in the first four decades of the twentieth century, especially for the great mass of Mancunians who now had access to forms and varieties of entertainment that previous generations had never had. Occasionally access to this new world of ideas was denied through poverty, but the old parochialism, inward-looking and narrow-minded, was most definitely dying.

In the late 1920s and 30s young Mancunians were breaking out of their neighbourhood in search of a good night out. Girls from Salford would venture into Manchester, or down to Sale (especially Sale Lido). Others would dance regularly locally, and then take a trip to the Ritz for a special night out. The more adventurous dance fans were even travelling out of town, on what was dubbed the 'dance train'. This took Manchester's most dedicated revellers to ballrooms in Blackpool and back, for half a crown return. The dancers would set off around six, and get back at two or three in the morning; ancestors of the famous roving ravers of the late 1980s who would travel from the Haçienda in Manchester to Shelly's in Stoke, to Quadrant Park near Liverpool in search of the perfect piano anthem, and partying at motorway service stations *en route*.

Throughout the nineteenth century districts had kept themselves to themselves, with life revolving around the insular, mini-circle of street, local work, local shop, local boozer, local church. But this insularity began breaking down as the twentieth century unfolded. As well as changing habits brought about by the dance boom, transport improvements were important too. All-electric tramcars ran on over a hundred miles of line throughout Manchester by 1903, providing widespread and cheap travel. Shopping habits created by the rise of the city centre department stores meant that people were travelling further than the edge of their neighbourhood. Psychologically, creatively, physically, Manchester was changing.

The breakdown of neighbourhood territories had one unfortunate by-product. In some areas Manchester and Salford gangs frequented neighbourhood dancehalls and defended 'their' territory with violence. These gangs were sometimes based on youth clubs (like the Adelphi Lads' Club) or districts (Hanky Park, Salford, Swinton; all had clearly defined gangs). The secure, close-knit communities, and the street-corner gatherings of the young, had created such a strict sense of local identity that strangers were not always tolerated. Subsequent gang violence in Manchester clubs has continued to be drawn from gangs based on localities: Cheetham Hill, Salford, Moss Side.

Dancing and courting went on in the dancehalls, but there was violence around too. Memories of this period differ in their recollection of violence. Joe Kay, for instance, remembers the 1930s as an unblemished decade: 'I frequented the dances and had a great time – there's nowhere like it today for the young ones. There was definitely no fighting or rowdyism.'

Others have a different view; that the violence which bubbled under the surface of daily life, especially in working-class areas of Manchester and Salford, frequently infiltrated the dancehalls. Various Salfordians recall fights at the Empress, and Dyson's (or 'The Jig', as it was known) in Liverpool Street. Underlining the threat of violence feared by many licensees, bouncers were used by many dancehalls in the 1930s; at Dyson's, 'Nipper' Cusick, a renowned local boxer, worked the door. In the rougher parts of town, the threat of violence was never far away, and if local turf wars spilled into the dancehalls, usually somewhere in the story you could bet there was also a dispute over girls. MacColl, on The Jig again: 'If you went there you took your partner with you. If you walked across the floor to ask a girl to dance and she was, say, a member of the Percy Street mob, a dozen blokes would converge on you. And you were lucky if you got out without being beaten up.'

In Ancoats there is evidence of many violent acts carried out by the so-called 'Napoo Gang' in the years during and immediately following the First World War. They had a nihilistic sense of drama; they took their name from army slang meaning 'good for nothing' (which could also be used as a verb – to Napoo – meaning 'to kill') and believed to have derived from the French 'il n'y *en a plus*' (literally, 'There is no more'). They were known for their distinctive clothing influenced by the American gangster-look in the films of the day. Gang members wore a navy blue suit, a trilby and a pink neckerchief; the kind of look Cagney made popular, and followed too by the gangsters in Graham Greene's *Brighton Rock*. According to Henry Grimshaw, whose own Willesden Street Gang were small beer in comparison, the Napoo were much feared, their reputation carrying all before them: 'They did all sorts of things, smashing windows, fighting everybody they could fight, and they had razors stuck out of their waistcoat pockets, cut-throat razors, that sort of business. But you never got the truth of it. It was always second hand; it was what people said.'

Public events – Henry Grimshaw remembers in particular a firework show at Belle Vue – were disrupted by Napoo Gang fights, or just a rumour that the Gang were on their way which sent people scurrying for the trams home. The Napoo Gang – in behaviour forty years later to be associated with Teddy Boys – also ripped up cinema seats at the Cosy Corner picture house in Ancoats, but they were most renowned for frequently and violently breaking up dances at Belle Vue.

The threat of violence doesn't seem to have deterred the young from going out dancing. A more potent obstacle to the good life was poverty. The divisions in England in the 1930s had a conspicuous geographical emphasis. The North West and the North East – home to the declining shipbuilding, coal and cotton industries – consistently suffered from much higher rates of unemployment than the national average. The Midlands survived on the back of car manufacture. The South East, as ever, benefited from favoured investment; almost half of all new factories opened in Britain between 1932 and 1937 were sited in Greater London.

Within the regions there were more localised fluctuations. Manchester itself had a reasonably diverse economy, but the retail sector took a knock in a far from cash-rich economy. Workers reliant on Salford docks suffered with the fall in trade, as did coalfields around Wigan. Worst hit were other surrounding towns in Lancashire, those reliant on one key industry: textiles. In Blackburn, a virtually one-trade town, where 60 per cent of jobs were in textiles, almost exactly half the entire workforce were unemployed in 1931.

Families in Manchester were hard hit by the Depression in the 1930s, and although it's obvious that unemployment and poverty curtailed the activities of the young, there is also plenty of anecdotal and statistical evidence that going out was often the last thing a young person would sacrifice.

In the 1930s youngsters with a job who were still living at home invariably managed to lead a busy social life, keeping a good proportion of their wages back as 'spends', with the rest surrendered up to mothers as 'keep'. This was as true of young women as men. Individual families differed, of course. In some wages would never reach the young. In others husbands drank or gambled the family into poverty. In some the womenfolk might be expected to stay at home. Nevertheless, in spite of everything, girls and women did have plenty of opportunities for leisure and entertainment; in fact, they became the main consumers of the cinema.

By the end of the 1930s, there was still a thriving network of boys' clubs and an irremovable street-corner society (and, of course, monkey parades), but there were other options as well. A major change had occurred in the breakdown of regional insularity. The consumption of commercialised leisure activities – dancing and movie-going – was part of this new freedom, a taste of the good life that previous generations of the less well-off had never had. It was a kind of freedom. Young unemployed Harry in Walter Greenwood's *Love on the Dole* is thrown into deep despair when he is too poor to buy two seats at the cinema. He feels imprisoned, back to the bleak insularity of the street.

As culture relocated from the streets to the stadia, from the street corner to the picture palace, young people without a job, or those tied to decreasing family budgets, were at a disadvantage in the spread of commercial popular culture. Often sympathetic cinema managers would allow hard-up kids reduced price, or even free, entry to local picture houses. Nevertheless, one of the central images of city life since industrialisation remains the marginalised individual, the families or communities untouched by commercial culture. It's probably truer now than ever, at the end of the twentieth century, that a satisfying life has to be bought, and for those without the means to do so, city life remains purely one of potential, of promise unfulfilled.

For millions, going out had become a way of life; a way to life. In the 1930s few wanted to give up visits to the cinema, which could cost as little as one penny on Saturdays; this so-called 'penny crush' was still in operation in mid 1950s Salford when Shelagh Delaney had just started going out. In the 1930s a visit to the cinema or the dancehall was worth saving up for, worth missing a meal for, a dedication shared by today's giro jugglers well schooled in making sure that they don't miss out on Saturday nights out. Youth culture has always been like that; don't forget James Brown and Fred Wesley in 1972, 'Givin' Up Food For Funk'.

In the 1930s a major economic depression wasn't going to dampen the ardour of the young, and the entrepreneurs knew that. There's always been big money invested in the venues and sites of popular culture, as shown by the building of dream palaces and dancehalls in the first decades of this century, as well as the recent development of the Printworks on Corporation Street, or the rise in nightclub and café bar-building during the late 1990s. The same is true of products;

in the making of films like *Metropolis*, the recording and marketing of hit albums, or the signing of key football stars.

Life's possibilities seemed enhanced by movies, music and going out, and Manchester now had more to offer. Manchester's first self-confident steps into the international arena were in the nineteenth century, with the city a major player in the network of free international trade, with merchants and manufacturers making considerable links to markets overseas. The city had been born as part of a network of trading partners. Now the free trade of goods was being bolstered by the free trade of ideas. The village mentality which had persisted into the first years of the twentieth century was broken down by the arrival of films from Germany and Hollywood, rhythms from Africa, music out of Harlem and America's Deep South.

Jazz, dance, movies; they connected with the needs and desires of Mancunians in a way which high culture never had. Hobsbawm: 'The twentieth century, it was increasingly clear, was the century of the common people, and dominated by the arts produced by and for them.' The new popular culture disrupted the nineteenth-century notions of social order. The rapid infiltration of cinema and radio into the lives of the lower classes threatened the old traditions. The notion of culture had changed; the rarefied, refined culture denied to anyone lacking a classical education had no meaning. The new technologies of the cinema and the wireless were providing means of escape, debate, and the transmission of ideas and values which belonged to a bigger and more complex world.

Hobsbawm identified the early twentieth-century obsessions with jazz and the cinema as evidence of a break with the past, as big a rupture as the industrial revolution. Throughout the nineteenth century, the idea that the new England created by industrialisation was blotting out the old had been a recurring theme. In the twentieth century the idea that a cultural revolution was the next stage in this development was just as strong. In 1933 J. B. Priestley reported on his journey through England. He first laid out the qualities of rural old England ('the cathedrals and minsters and manor houses . . .'), and secondly described the industrial England of coal, steel, cotton, railways; the England of the Northern towns, 'thousands of rows of little houses all alike, sham Gothic churches, square-faced chapels'. This England was under threat; 'it is not being added to and has no new life poured into it'. The third England, he concluded, has roots in America: 'This is the England of arterial and by-pass roads, of filling stations and factories that look like exhibition buildings, of giant cinemas and dancehalls and cafés, cocktail bars, motor-coaches, wireless, factory girls looking like actresses.'

There are no Year Zeros in the development of England, it's evolution, and a rubbing together of influences, trends, decades. It's like the adjustments of tectonic plates, the story of these eras and revolutions, linked, slow and gradual, the eruptions and earthquakes masking the deeper movements, the bucklings and shifts.

The battles at the arrival of jazz had foreshadowed arguments which would rage decades later; for many social commentators across the political spectrum, the influence of the American entertainment industry was having a negative effect on English life. The old champion of the left, Robert Blatchford continued to criticise 'alien' artforms. D. H. Lawrence hit out at the 'plaster-and-gilt' horror of the cinema as another nail in the coffin of Shakespeare's England, another ugly victory of trade over passion. In the 1950s liberal left critics like Richard Hoggart claimed that the spiritually dead 'shiny barbarism' of American culture was creating a 'candy-floss world'; Hoggart's *The Uses of Literacy* often reads like a plea for the world to stop turning, to go into a reverse spin, in fact, to bring us back to a cosy world of neighbourly back-to-backs.

Certainly, England in the middle part of this century was undergoing an invasion of American influences. Now, thanks to its huge communications and entertainment companies, America has become pre-eminent among exporters of attitudes. Early on, the process tends to be one of the receiving culture indiscriminately sponging up the American influences. Societies, like individuals, can react to the shock of the new in a range of ways.

The notion that a society might change under pressure from the new influences gives some a cause for fear. Although indiscriminately sponging up at first, a society's response to outside ideas imported through whatever medium (books, records, satellite TV or films) isn't necessarily one of passive acquiescence; the reaction to the new ideas, and their meshing with native traditions, means that the exchange isn't purely one sided or one way.

The cultural revolutions of the twentieth century were changing English identity. It was a battle for the hearts and minds of the nation. The Arts Council was launched in 1946 in direct opposition not just to American culture, but to the very idea of *popular* culture. The aim of the Arts Council, its Royal Charter stressed, lay in 'developing a greater knowledge, understanding and practice of the *fine arts exclusively.*'

The cultural symbols cherished by the ruling class – like Glyndebourne, for instance, or the Henley Regatta, Windsor Castle or the novels of Trollope – take an exalted place in the English national identity, whereas anything issuing from a supposedly less refined culture – from the streets, from popular culture – is downgraded, undervalued or rejected.

Less predictably, but even more conspicuously, we've heard conservative voices issuing from the traditional left; from Blatchford and beyond. Although looking back at the way new ideas were pouring in from all sides some of the anxiety is explainable, should we always be afraid of change? Who wants to stay the same? From Bury Town Council to Richard Hoggart, those who perceive only negative effects in the rise of commercial popular culture; would they have denied the working class access to *Metropolis*, Duke Ellington and James Cagney just because they disapproved of *The Perfect Alibi*, shuddered at the impure souped-up versions of Dvorak, or regretted the disappearance of the fox-trot?

You can't put import controls on ideas and attitudes. In the period between the two world wars, many people connected with aspects of the new global – American-generated – culture because it made sense, or tapped desires. In *Dockers and Detectives* Ken Worpole charts the appeal of hardboiled American crime fiction writing to British men in the 1930s, and quotes an ex-docker: 'What intrigued me about the American writers was that they were talking the way we talked.' For the docker, living and working in an industrial, urban, working-class environment, the 'alien' culture of America connected with him far more directly than his 'home' culture. He was making his own culture, one that rang true to him, something that could speak to him.

By the 1930s, therefore, the incoming movies were the nearest thing to a shared culture. In 1934 903 million visits to the cinema were recorded by picture houses up and down Britain. Researchers in 1934 noted that, 'At the time of writing, girls in all classes of society wear "Garbo" coats, and wave their hair á la Norma Shearer or Lilian Harvey.' And American influence did not wane during the 1940s, especially as the physical presence of GIs was inescapable; some say that it was their presence, in fact, which finally killed off Manchester's monkey parades. But cinema-going declined with the coming of television, and Hollywood's grip on the public imagination was loosened by the 1950s.

Television would be the next means to a shared culture, and would deliver one of Manchester's most persuasive representations: *Coronation Street*. There were clearly comic, music hall roots to *Coronation Street*, with stock figures like grumpy matrons, blowsy barmaids and womanisers. But at the time of its first series, the *Street* took strength from its other roots in the gritty, Northern realist drama tradition; *Love on the Dole* and *A Taste of Honey*. The thrill and the key to the success of *Coronation Street* in the 1960s was that its portrayal of life came closer to the day-to-day experience of the ordinary viewer than anything broadcast before. Voices from outside the charmed London circle were being broadcast to a mass audience.

The balance between wit and grit was formed in the early years of *Coronation Street* by writers like Jack Rosenthal. He grew up just off Cheetham Hill Road, in prime *Coronation Street* country. His political awareness was awakened during the Second World War after his family had moved from Manchester to the Lancashire mill-town of Colne. Here he came into contact with local socialists like Len Dole who had a dream of a different kind of England; most folk had a picture of the Queen on the mantelpiece, but Len had a picture of Lenin. Rosenthal took a job at Granada TV for £7 a week at the very birth of the station. For the second series of *Coronation Street* he was given the opportunity to script an episode. It was the beginning of a magnificent career. The Bar Mitzvah Boy has a poster of Mike Summerbee on his wall.

Granada TV has remained a powerful presence in Manchester, and the BBC too; locally, the BBC used to work from a converted Wesleyan church in Dickenson Road in Rusholme, a building bought in 1954 from John Blakeley, who had opened film studios there in 1947 (thus freeing his Mancunian Films from dependence on London studios). The studios in the old church were to become the first venue for *Top of the Pops*.

By this time, the cultural revolutions of the twentieth century had come a long way. The cinema had contributed to the death of the music hall, the monkey run and other last vestiges of Victorian entertainment, and it had opened new worlds and new ideas; but now cinema itself was being threatened by television. As the demand for theatre dropped, the Gaiety had become a cinema, but with the arrival of television in the 1950s, the building was demolished (the site is now occupied by offices, a travel agent's and a typewriter shop).

Urban culture from the start had been impromptu, improvised and without models. The arrival of trains, planes and automobiles; the co-existence in the city of immigrant groups from Ireland, Eastern Europe, Germany and – into the 1950s – from Asia and the Caribbean; together with the new international dimension of mass commercial leisure; all this was giving the city a changed identity. The world wars had an impact which accelerated cultural change, and brought America and American troops, ideas, attitudes and commerce into Europe. There was no going back. The village had become a city.

Ragtime had taken the dancehalls by storm, jazz had metamorphosed, evolved, and in the decades that followed, it was to be newer forms of popular music – from be-bop in the 1950s to house music in the 1980s – which were to be America's most important cultural export to Manchester. It was the reaction of Mancunians to American popular music which was to shape going out in the last four decades of the twentieth century. Manchester's response to American popular music would reveal just how it was possible for a society to move beyond passive consumption of foreign culture; how, by absorbing imported ideas, customising them and adding a twist of authentic Mancunian genius, it could make of them something unique.

CHAPTER 4

Jimmy Savile and the Italian Consul:

Manchester Goes Mod

The billeting of American troops in Britain during and after the Second World War had many spin-offs, but one was to affect pop life in Manchester more than any other: the American Forces Network, a radio channel. Bruce Mitchell – later to become a key player in the Manchester music scene – had just started going out to clubs in 1956, and playing in jazz groups. He remembers homegrown radio being out of touch. For him, as for those who had flocked to Hollywood films during the previous decades, imported culture made an incontestable, personal impact: 'The BBC played Rosemary Clooney; it didn't play what we wanted to hear. The thing that we listened to all through the fifties was the American Forces Network. The AFN had jazz programmes, be-bop, and rhythm & blues.'

Bruce Mitchell had an ally in John Mayall. Mayall grew up in Burnage, Manchester, later the home turf of Liam and Noel Gallagher of Oasis. Mayall was a massive music fan and a cinema buff too; he'd cycle round three or four cinemas on a Saturday to pack in as many movies as possible. His music tastes were more rhythm & blues-oriented than Mitchell's, but that didn't stop them sharing good times. Bruce Mitchell describes the samizdat nature of their music listening: 'John was a very unusual sort of guy, and had marvellous energy for all his various obsessions. He ran reel-to-reel tape recorders to a tuner, and taped all the important AFN shows, and he'd annotate his tapes. He was an important focus for us. His house was the only place we could hear our kind of playlist.'

Mayall would study the tapes, learning every last chord of every last John Lee Hooker song. He assisted Bruce Mitchell in the running of clubs (designing posters advertising the shows), but moved to London early in 1963, found a mentor in Alexis Korner, and formed Britain's premier rhythm & blues outfit, the Bluesbreakers. He took with him a fellow Mancunian, the drummer Hughie Flint.

Through the American Forces Network, Mayall, Mitchell and other Manchester musicians, like Tosh Ryan, rode the waves of jazz as they reached England; 'Tosh was very strong on the be-bop musicians, black musicians', says Mitchell, 'and I was very strong on the white West Coast musicians because they were fashionable and had a very clear-cut image; people like Gerry Mulligan and Chet Baker.'

Not everybody in Manchester in 1956 wanted to hear modern jazz quintets playing cool jazz. On the margins, the raw sound of rock & roll had made an impact through teen movies like *Rock Around the Clock* but was rarely heard on radio and lacked the support of British record companies. The biggest market, though, was still for the commercial jazz groups which had dominated the dancehall, cabaret and Mecca ballroom circuit since the Second World War; in the mid and late 1950s at the Ritz on Whitworth Street the Phil Moss Band was in its heyday, winning awards, broadcasting on top radio shows (*Meet the Band, Swingalong, Ray Moore's Saturday Night Out*), and appearing in the film *A Taste of Honey*.

Bruce Mitchell preferred his music at the cutting edge, but, as a working, wage-earning jazz musician, he also confesses to too many nights playing music he wasn't interested in. For him and his cohorts, the best places to indulge their love of contemporary jazz were the black clubs in Moss Side. Among the Moss Side venues at the end of the 1950s where the house bands played harder jazz were the Reno (on Princess Road), the Nile Club, the Western Club, the Lagos Lagoon Club (on Carter Street) and various shebeens on Monton Street.

The turnover of jazz styles from the mid 1950s onwards was fast; Mitchell ended up playing in a variety of jazz groups, from trad bands to big bands, from modern jazz quartets to skiffle acts. Skiffle was England's first attempt to produce a homegrown style; it relied on the plundering of American folk and blues songs, but was reproduced in a homemade, DIY fashion (in skiffle trios, featuring just a guitar, vocals and a washboard). The purists came to loathe it, but according to Alan Lawson – author of the beat music history book, *It Happened in Manchester* – skiffle marked an important part of a process, instigated by Elvis Presley, which led to thousands of kids starting to make their own music by the early 1960s: 'Elvis Presley was everything that kids wanted and totally unlike anything else that was going, but obviously kids in Burnage or Levenshulme or Salford had no way of duplicating that sort of stuff. But Lonnie Donegan was accessible and he was playing the kind of music you could play in your front room. He was doing something they could imitate.'

As the jazz generation was succeeded by the rock & roll generation, music lovers of all kinds in Manchester still struggled to quench their growing thirst for American music. On radio, the BBC, even by 1958, had only just got round to providing a two hour programme catering for the young, with Brian Matthew's *Saturday Club*. Means to get the music were found, however. The lead singer of the beat group The Powerhouse 6, Kevin Curtis, had a relative in the navy who regularly brought records back over the Atlantic. The band were one of the first beat groups to break big in Manchester, their careful scrutiny of Elvis Presley and Ray Charles standing them in good stead; in fact, the first major live appearance of The Powerhouse 6 kicked off with a cover version of 'Hound Dog'.

Manchester's first import record shop – One Stop – didn't open until 1957. The two main means of obtaining authentic American records were either through contacts at Burtonwood Airbase near Warrington, which was manned by American soldiers until the mid 1960s, or – as Kevin Curtis did – via sailors. Both the Beatles in Liverpool and Eric Burdon of the Animals in Newcastle are known to have relied for their early music education on imports brought by visitors to the ports in their respective cities, but Manchester, too, had its docks, courtesy of the Ship Canal, which was regularly visited by ships from Montreal, New York and other ports on America's East Coast. According to Alan Lawson some sailors were on a nice little earner bringing boxes of records back: 'I met one old chap who claimed he bought his first car on the proceeds from records he bought dirt cheap in America and sold for a fortune back home.'

With a high demand for live music, jazz evolving into a variety of forms, and the beginnings of rock & roll, musicians were kept busy. 'There was a lot of action in Manchester, and so many clubs to play in', Bruce Mitchell recalls of the later part of the 1950s; 'The club scene was incredibly dramatic in those days, and was full of live acts. Sometimes we made good money, but we'd play for nothing sometimes. We were young and we could do every night of the week.

It was very busy, so busy, in fact, that musicians who wanted to make money could play two or three clubs a night.'

A new kind of venue for going out began to appear in the second half of the 1950s: the coffee bar. In Lawson's phrase, the coffee bar was 'probably the first sign of social emancipation'. As a gathering place for the youth, it had no rivals. For the young, the combined pleasures of the juke box, a chrome coffee machine and a meeting place were considerable. The coffee bars provided a focus for teenage culture. You don't need somewhere glossy, well lit, and well marketed; all you need is a space and the right soundtrack (as the success of the rave generation in turning the Haçienda from a bleak old yacht warehouse into the best club in the world was to prove thirty years later). Coffee bars marked both the territory and the victory of pop culture. It was the arrival of the juke box – with the sounds of Bill Haley and Little Richard blasting out – which gave a musical edge to the invasion of the coffee bars by the beat generation, driving out the squares, the straights and anyone over the age of nineteen.

Central Manchester had a number of conventional coffee bars – the Zanzibar, and the Cona on Tib Street, for instance – but among the first which directly appealed to the young was the 700 Club on Stockport Road, Levenshulme, which was opened in 1958 by Pauline Clegg. For a while, Glynn Ellis (later calling himself Wayne Fontana, of Wayne Fontana & the Mindbenders fame) was employed as a washer-up there. Pauline Clegg went on to run the Oasis, one of the key clubs in Manchester in the 1960s.

Coffee bar culture was another example of the English teenager customising influences from abroad; this time Italy. As if to underline the debt, when the Three Coins coffee bar and dance club opened on Fountain Street in November 1960, the Italian Consul, no less, was the guest of honour. Coffee bar culture thrived in Manchester, including the Now or Never, the New Paddock, the New Astoria Coffee Jive bar (which opened in Hyde in 1962) and La Cave (on Church Street). Some were coffee bars by day, clubs in the evening; the 2Js – at 44–47 Lloyd Street (it got its name from the initials of its owners, Jack Jackson and John Collier) – was a coffee bar which closed at 6.30, reopening an hour later as a jazz club. Manchester's most famous club in the 1960s, the Twisted Wheel, started out as a self-proclaimed 'beatnik-type' café called the Left Wing, which, in its advertising material, offered entrance for 'Feminine-type cats' at a reduced rate.

With the juke box providing the soundtrack during the day, putting bands on in the evening was a logical progression. Thus an infrastructure for the beat scene very quickly developed, as C. P. Lee, musician and historian, points out: 'The beat scene was dead easy; all you needed was a cellar, a Cona coffee machine, a few tables, and a couple of speakers and you could open a coffee bar. Then sometimes to put bands on you could build a little stage out of crates with plywood.'

Other spaces occupied by the kids were even less grand. Radio DJ Mike Sweeney spent his early adolescence in youth clubs, and at Fanny Rudd's on Ordsall, which was over a shop; 'You'd go there and you'd pay sixpence and there would be a record player there, and you could get a cup of orange squash, and they'd have a tin box with Smiths crisps in it, and you could buy a packet of those if you were flush.'

As the 50s became the 60s, the big change in going out in Manchester, according to Bruce Mitchell, was marked by the arrival of Jimmy Savile: 'The real noticeable change started to happen when Jimmy Savile took over a Mecca club on Oxford Street, the Plaza. He liked DJ-ing, he liked playing the current records. The Plaza was doing no business at all, and Mecca appointed him the manager. Savile went in there with control over the playlist, and reflected what the new generation wanted. He had the place rammed in no time.'

Jimmy Savile looks back on his time in Manchester with undisguised fondness. He arrived there in 1959 after building a reputation at the Palais in Ilford. A pioneering DJ who claims to have presided over the world's first ever disco – in the function room of an insurance company just outside Leeds in 1942 – at a time when dancing to live bands was the norm and the idea of dancing to records, he recalls, was 'literally laughed at', Savile used his creative and commercial powers to the full at the Plaza. The lunchtime dance sessions he instituted there were soon full, full of a crowd desperate to listen to what Savile called 'the new music'.

The Plaza's lunchtimes have assumed a mythical status as some of Manchester's most momentous, buzzing events. At threepence a head, from midday until 2pm, they were unmissable. The club's official capacity was four hundred and fifty but during those two hours Savile claims more than two thousand people often attended. Ray Teret (later to become a DJ himself) recalls in *It Happened in Manchester*: 'I was so bored at school I used to sneak out before the final morning lesson. I'd get the bus into Manchester and spend a couple of hours at the Plaza. Then I'd get the bus back and creep into the next lesson. I got away with this for over a year.'

Savile confesses that not a few teenage lives were changed at the Plaza: 'Monday, Tuesday, Wednesday, Thursday, Friday there were never less than six hundred any lunchtime and I got bollocked by schools and colleges and things and I had a stock reply: "You've had it too easy for too long; if you make your school more attractive than my dancehall you can keep them".' The formula was copied by other clubs, notably the Bodega, which did lunchtime sessions which served food as well; the Jive Luncheon Club it was called. But Savile didn't give his customers lunch; 'Did I bollocks; do me a favour!'

The Plaza was crowded all week, but especially on a Saturday afternoon (for the Jive Marathon, which lasted from midday to 5pm) and the big Saturday nights. Mitchell sees the key to Savile's success in the music policy; in a major change to going out in Manchester, there were no live acts. Savile and his sounds were what drew the people in; 'It was all based on records, like it would be now; no different', says Mitchell.

Savile lived in Great Clowes Street during his stay in Manchester, surrounded by acolytes and disciples; he was the first example of four decades of inspirational DJs in Manchester. There was something of a personality cult surrounding him; his followers dressed like him, behaved like him, took his music taste as gospel, and worked for him for free. Prior to his arrival the Plaza had got a reputation for trouble, but – coming from a mining town – he brought his miner friends in to run the door, ensuring that the customers now felt safe. Responding to allegations of impropriety at the Plaza, Savile is adamant that his club was clean:

> No, no, no. Listen, first of all I can tell you that in three-and-a-half years there was never one fight in the Plaza, Manchester. Not one, never. Impropriety; forget it baby! If you smelt of booze, you couldn't get in. If you had long sideburns, we kept a razor at the cash desk and if you let my lads take your sideburns off with our razor, you could come in. If you didn't; piss off. If you came incorrectly dressed, if your shoes weren't clean, trousers weren't pressed, if your shirt wasn't clean, then you were sent home; but I removed the sting by telling them they could get back in for free.

Bruce Mitchell also remembers various rumours surrounding Savile during his spell at the Plaza: 'The management couldn't work out why this twenty pound a week club manager was driving about in a white Rolls-Royce. It's pretty certain that he was playing the piano with the till to an outrageous degree. It was said that this is what led to his transfer by Mecca; they suspected him, but they didn't want to lose him.'

But give him the opportunity and Savile can explain about the Rolls-Royce. He knew a flash car would give him good publicity and help boost his reputation. 'Teenagers like to see their leaders do well', he believed, so he scraped together the deposit for an old Bentley saloon, ran it to a garage, brought in a modern Rolls-Royce radiator, and thus 'After lots of hammering, welding and spraying of paint there emerged into a startled Manchester what appeared to be a new black and cream Rolls-Royce. Belonging to me, no less!'

Savile believes that there was a simple formula for success: 'Give people a good time but stand no nonsense from anyone.' But it's clear that he rejoiced in gaining a larger-than-life persona. 'I didn't wear any particular outfit', he remembers, 'I wore sometimes very smart casual gear, sometimes outrageous gear. I used to put big fur slippers on or something like that, but that made you into a character. Because they couldn't pigeon-hole you other than calling you a "character" your image was in the minds of the people who saw you. "A" would think you were silly, "B" would think you were terrific; take your pick, you know.'

As well as getting his flash car and developing a taste for cigars, by February 1963 Savile had also developed catchphrases which were to dominate his vocabulary for years to come, 'Hi there! Guys and gals' and 'How's about that then?' included, although these came from his show on Radio Luxembourg. Despite his burgeoning TV and radio career in the mid 1960s, he also played a big part in the hugely successful Top Ten club at the Elizabethan Hall at Belle Vue (which opened in May 1963, and where he remained even after his tenure at the Plaza ended). He had considerable nous, and was driven by a love of music and a fondness for the good life. But hard work played its part. His reward was a fun-filled three-and-a-half years in Manchester spent in late-night unlicensed drinking dens – like the Motor Club at the back of Bootle Street – and DJ-ing to the quintessential teenage generation.

After the Plaza, Mecca sent Savile to manage its dancehall in Leeds, an enormous place that was also struggling to survive. Naturally, Savile soon had the place full, and the Plaza, meanwhile, deteriorated. The club later changed its name to the Tropicana, which, despite hosting one of Simply Red's early gigs and a classic hip-hop jam in 1986, never did any serious business in the 1980s, was unused in the 1990s and, when the whole block of buildings was demolished, was turned to dust in 1993.

American music continued to be influential and Jimmy Savile remembers the allure the American rock & roll greats continued to have for the Manchester youth: 'One night we were working at the Plaza and in literally the next building – which was the Odeon – Bill Haley was doing a personal appearance there. The great shock for Manchester was that a girl student was alleged to have got hold of a medicine bottle of Bill Haley's bath water and she drank it in public.'

In this era pop group managers like Harvey Lisberg (who managed Manchester's Herman's Hermits) were making regular visits to America, looking at the charts there and picking certain songs that English groups could cover. With access to authentic American records so limited, bands were making a good living filling sets with cover versions throughout the late 50s and early 60s, although the impact was somewhat diluted by bands throughout England choosing the same basic songs. How many 'Hound Dog's can you bear? It was one of Savile's traits as a DJ to dig out the original version; in this way he appealed to the in-crowd as well as the more mainstream market.

Music was moving, and DJs were picking up the cutting-edge and hard-to-get records, turning young groups on to new sounds. A new generation of music-makers was born; guitar-players, in particular, were picking up on the various strands of American rhythm & blues. Local guitarists have spoken unashamedly of how they'd listen to and imitate the sounds on discs by Elvis, Buddy Holly, Fats Domino, Little Richard; as the Beatles did, and the Rolling Stones too. Vic Farrell, for example, whose group – Jerry Lee & the Staggerlees – were to hold down a Friday residency at the Bodega during the summer of 1960, recalled in a conversation with Alan Lawson, 'The first solo I managed to learn was from "It's So Easy" by Buddy Holly.'

The British beat boom had begun. This turnover of styles naturally caused casualties among the musicians. Mitchell again:

> Every time this kind of change occurs, the old school resent what the new generation are doing; they think it's lower standards and you get a polarisation between that group of musicians and the next one coming up. When a new generation of bands come along, the older musicians always stand about saying 'They don't know how to play, they're out of tune'. It also went on in the punk days, and now you get composing musicians complaining about DJs making records.

The change isn't always a clean break, and at the beginning of 1960 beat groups were appearing on the bill at the Phil Moss Talent Competitions regularly held at the Ritz. The line-up at Platt Fields on Bank Holiday 6 August 1962 was part trad jazz, part pop (including one of Manchester's most rated beat groups, Paul Beattie & the Beats). Mitchell: 'Trad stayed strong for a while. The trad bands in club situations would be top of the bill. When I was playing in trad bands the support would often be a Merseybeat-type group, and then within about nine months the position reversed, and the beat groups were the bill-toppers.'

Promoters and club owners who'd run jazz bars suddenly scrambled to keep up as the beat boom exploded. The 2Js had always had a young audience (it called itself a Teenage and Teetotal Club), but the young were losing interest in even the most fashionable forms of jazz, and the club was forced to start featuring beat groups. In October 1960 the club hosted Manchester's first all-nighter. Eventually jazz was left off the bill altogether, and Jackson and Collier closed the club in July 1961.

Soon, though – on Saturday 4 November 1961, in fact – the Oasis Coffee Bar opened on the site of the 2Js, styling itself 'Manchester's Most Fab Club for Young People'. The Oasis opened at 10am for coffee and snacks, closed at 2pm, and then reopened from 6pm until 2am with live music and DJs, maintaining a no-alcohol policy throughout the day and night. A big local group of the time, Pete MacLaine & the Dakotas, secured a Tuesday residency, Gene Vincent played the Oasis on 15 December 1961, and the Beatles made their first Manchester appearance there, on 2 February 1962. According to the club owner, Rick Dixon, the Beatles gig was a total disaster: 'In the club there were thirty-seven people, and none of them were very impressed.'

The Beatles launched their careers with a wholesome image, and the lovable mop-tops weren't the only ones. Other groups had images based on Ivy League suits and Cuban heels, and a major fashion statement would be a band all wearing blue jeans; like the Swinging Blue Jeans, in fact. Anyone who sees Herman's Hermits appearances on TV repeated in the 1990s can't be anything but struck how spineless they look; a million miles from blowin' a fuse. 'The beat groups were all very, very smart', says Mitchell. 'The image generally appealed to Grandmas and Granddads; Merseybeat was benign in a way r'n'b wasn't, and rock & roll hadn't been. I saw Bill Haley in 1956, and there was a lot of trouble then, with Teddy Boys and their rocker image; they danced in cinemas to *Rock Around the Clock*, and then they started dancing along the tops of cars as well.'

During the beat boom years Manchester both benefited and suffered from its proximity to Liverpool. The existence of a rival scene forty miles down the River Mersey gave a competitive edge to Manchester musicians' ambitions, and the rise of the Beatles provided a role model for hundreds of groups, whether from Liverpool or not. However, many of the Manchester groups were eclipsed by the spotlight on the Beatles, and the goings-on at the Cavern. The major advantage gained by Manchester was one that the city has since managed relentlessly to exploit; from the Beatles onwards, it's been the cities outside London which have nurtured the major forces in British pop. According to Charlie Gillett, 'Until the Beatles made their first record in the fall of 1962, it had been very difficult for any group based outside London to gain access to the record companies. It had almost always been necessary for ambitious musicians, singers, and groups to move to London and hope to attract the attention of somebody who mattered.'

The beat boom marked a shift in pop culture in England. Musicians became less slavishly imitative of American music. In rock & roll's early days England's answers to Elvis Presley and Jerry Lee Lewis – Cliff Richard, say, or Tommy Steele – were an embarrassment, the sex and threat of rock & roll turned into a rootless frolic. A new process became apparent, whereby pop music was filtered through a local English consciousness. Often this still meant a dilution of rock & roll's vitality – Manchester's Freddie & the Dreamers drew on the music hall in their shows with a truly daft stage act, coming across like *Blue Peter* presenters taught to pogo by Pinocchio – but gradually English rock & roll began to have some kind of integrity of its own.

Englishness asserted itself in pop music in various ways; eventually, and more meaningfully, the Beatles began singing about their Liverpool lives. And, in Liverpool, London and Manchester, local accents were heard on pop records. This was new; this hadn't been done before. Even skiffle, big in Britain between 1956 and 1959, had been sung with an American accent, with the Glasgow-born Lonnie Donegan singing (in a whining, fake American voice) about picking cotton, sheriffs, railroads and his Dixie darling.

Skiffle stars who had hits in America (like Lonnie Donegan and Nancy Whiskey) were, in fact, the middle link in a crucial exchange. Colin MacInnes noted that some of the hit skiffle songs had crossed the Atlantic three times; 'From here to America in colonial days, from there back again to the London skiffle cellars, and now, with Mr. Donegan and Miss Nancy Whiskey, over once more to the U.S.'

Such transatlantic exchanges were to become ever more complicated. By 1965 Manchester groups were having hits in America, often playing songs written for them by American songwriters. By the 1980s Manchester was part of a vast web of creativity. New Order admit blatant imitation of New York disco hits in creating their early 80s electro sound. In the mid 1980s Detroit techno innovator Derrick May's early work (including the landmark track 'Rhythm of Life') was influenced by New Order, as well as by the German group Kraftwerk. Tracks like 'Rhythm of Life' then went on to influence another generation of Manchester musicians, including A Guy Called Gerald and an early version of M-People, T-Coy.

But back in the 50s, the influence was purely one way, and most British acts marketed as homegrown rivals to the great Elvis Presley had sung with an American accent. Crooners always had. Demotic stars like George Formby had regional accents, but as a gimmick, playing up the accents for their full novelty value. When Lonnie Donegan decided to drop the fake nasal twang, he fell straight into pantomime English for 'My Old Man's A Dustman'. Colin MacInnes, writing at the time, pointed this out:

> The battle for a place among the top twenty has been won by British singers at the cost of splitting their personalities and becoming bi-lingual; speaking American at the recording session, and English in the pub round the corner afterwards ... Now that the singers are finding an English place for themselves on the golden disc, will the English lyric writers and composers try to do so too? In other words, will they begin to write songs

in an English idiom, about English life, that the performers can
sing as Englishmen not only in body, but in voice themselves?
Can teenagers, in short, take songs about themselves?

As a discography featuring, say, 'Waterloo Sunset', 'A Day In The
Life', 'Ghost Town', *Timeless* and 'Sorted For Es and Whizz' suggests, the question posed by MacInnes in 1957 is now answered.
The early 1960s saw the dumping of cover versions and the partial
demolition of what was known as Tin Pan Alley; the culture whereby
pop songs were written not by the groups themselves, but by professional songwriters who, by and large, stuck to rigid formulas and
limited subjects. Whereas songs written by the likes of Mickie Most
and Mitch Murray were sung by Freddie & the Dreamers and the
Hollies, the Beatles and the Kinks, for instance, reacted against the
constraints of Tin Pan Alley, and wrote their own songs based on
their own lives and in their own idioms, and thus made pop music
youth's most vital form of self-expression.

Unfortunately, once English bands stopped being imitative of
American acts, they began, instead, to become more imitative of each
other. Thus, especially among the Liverpool bands of the period, too
many debts to the Beatles hampered Merseybeat bands and cut short
careers. Post-Merseybeat, as in the months that followed the Madchester music explosion in the late 1980s, being caught with what had
suddenly switched from being the right accent to the wrong one was
fatal. In the words of Nik Cohn, 'Merseybeat was huge for a time but
Liverpool was a limited city; it only had so many guitarists and, once
they'd all been snared and signed, the business had to look elsewhere
for its meat. In any case, the whole thing had only been a one-time craze
and, inevitably, it finally blew up. When that happened, thousands of
guitarists all over England dropped their scouse accents.'

The Beatles' breakthrough into the commercial charts turned beat
music into the new pop, and broadened the base of youngsters who
got turned on to music and the new culture of coffee bars, DJs and
DIY bands. Says Bruce Mitchell: 'The Beatles made all the difference.' More than thirty years later, the debt was still being paid;
in February 1994 Manchester's five-piece teeny-pop act Take That
performed a schmaltzy Beatles medley at the Brit Awards dressed
in full mop-top gear and performing on a black-and-white set in a
Ready Steady Go pastiche, and ten months later Oasis were on TV
playing a wonderful, dissonant cover version of 'I Am The Walrus',

and filling their first two albums with Beatles-inspired melodies.

Mike Sweeney is living proof of the impact the Beatles made in Manchester, and – in his case – Salford. He remembers an evening at the Dock Mission on Trafford Road in Salford in February 1963 like it was yesterday:

> It was the coldest winter since 1947, and I went there in a black t-shirt, my first leather jacket, a pair of drainpipes and winkle-pickers, totally unsuitable, really, and I was freezing. It was a sparsely attended night because of the cold. I asked the DJ to play something by the Shadows, and I remember turning round to walk back across the dancefloor and I was stopped in my tracks. He played this record, 'Please Please Me' by the Beatles, and it was as if the heavens opened-up and this hand plucked me up and said, 'This is the Beatles, and this is the future'. It changed me completely, and I wanted to be in a group from then on.

The attractions of the Beatles were wide; their impact wasn't just on music, but fashion as well. That August Sweeney went with his family on a summer holiday to Rhyl: 'I washed my hair on the Friday night to go to the Friday night dance. I'd had it in this greasy, combed-back style all week and all week I hadn't copped off with a girl. Instead of combing my hair back, I cut the fringe across with a pair of scissors, and gave my hair an embryonic Beatles cut. That night I walked into the dancehall and pulled the minute I walked in. Absolutely the first minute.'

By the end of 1963 Sweeney's young life had settled into a tidy pattern, working at Metro Vickers by day, and clubbing by night, first at the Jungfrau (which later became Pips) and then at His Excellency's in Salford, and then, through 1964, he was a regular at the Twisted Wheel. He saw the Animals at the Oasis (an unannounced Tuesday gig), Ike & Tina Turner at the Oasis, John Mayall's triumphant return to Manchester with Eric Clapton on guitar in the Bluesbreakers, the Pretty Things at the Manchester Cavern, the Kinks at the Twisted Wheel.

The speed of the Beatles' rise can be gauged by the fact that just a year after their disastrous Manchester debut, they played again at the Oasis, this time on 22 February 1963; and this time the club was packed. Sweeney, an unhesitating queue-jumper, was, for once, left out in the cold: 'I couldn't get in. It was hard. By the time I got there the queue was round the block, but the club was already full, so even though I got to the front of the queue I was turned away.'

The Oasis played host to one of Manchester's rising DJ stars, Dave Lee Travis. Travis, whose first job was as a window-dresser at Kendal Milne's, was an Oasis regular who soon started pestering Pauline Clegg for a chance to DJ. His pushiness paid off with regular slots before and after groups, and during lunchtimes. He, like Savile, took to being flash. Travis had a big jeep painted with red and white polka dots and his name emblazoned across the windscreen. By the time the Manchester Cavern opened in May 1964, Travis had worked at the Oasis, the Plaza and the Bodega. He became the Manchester Cavern's resident DJ.

Throughout the first half of the 1960s, most of Manchester's best beat-room DJs were playing an eclectic mix of tracks, reflecting the music of local bands, the domination of the Beatles (and then the Rolling Stones), the soul classics (like Otis Redding and Dionne Warwick), rougher and ever-present rhythm & blues (from John Lee Hooker to the Pretty Things), and the beginnings of Motown. A typical playlist from September 1965 could include tracks by the Small Faces ('Whatcha Gonna Do About It'), Wilson Pickett ('In The Midnight Hour'), the Hollies ('Look Through Any Window'), Manfred Mann ('If You Gotta Go Go Now'), pop like Sandie Shaw ('Message Understood') and perhaps even something by the Beach Boys ('California Girls'). As a mark of the continued and now re-emerging interest in genuine rhythm & blues, at the end of September 1965, DJ Ric Vonn's Record of the Week at the Manchester Cavern was Jimmy Smith's 'The Organ Grinder's Swing'.

The DJs in the early 1960s were using very primitive equipment; Dave Lee Travis at the Oasis was using a Dansette autochange. They talked between records, making a virtue out of a necessity as the technology to segue records neatly into one another hadn't yet been developed. Thus the patter and the personalities of the DJs became important. Jimmy Savile's one-off Disc Club at the Higher Broughton Assembly Rooms promised 'Top Pops and fun games on the stage with Jimmy'.

The excitement in the city at the time was boosted by the ongoing success of local bands in the national charts. 'Look Through Any Window' was the ninth hit single in a row by the Hollies, including a Number One with 'I'm Alive' in May 1965, although Manchester's first Number One was by Herman's Hermits, when they topped the Hit Parade in August 1964 with 'I'm Into Something Good'. The third of the big three in Manchester at the time, Freddie & the Dreamers, had had four releases in the Top Ten by November 1964.

The Beatles had opened the way for other English bands in America after their tour there early in 1964. What, up until then, had been a one-way process – with English music fans looking to America for constant inspiration – suddenly was reversed. Alan Lawson describes the turnaround as 'astronomic'. Freddie & the Dreamers, Herman's Hermits and Wayne Fontana & the Mindbenders all had huge hits in America in the mid 1960s, although only Herman's Hermits maintained anything more than temporary success there. The group's singer, Peter Noone, became a huge star in America, as did a second grinning Mancunian who went Stateside: Davy Jones, the singer in the Monkees (following TV appearances as Ena Sharples's nephew in *Coronation Street*).

In Manchester in the mid 1960s, with clubs galore, venues aplenty, bands and DJs by the score, all the ingredients for a good night out were in place. It wasn't a narrow scene, easily pigeon-holed. For some young Mancs the excitement was to be found in the more specialist soul clubs spinning the purer import sounds rather than the city's pop sensations like Wayne Fontana or the Hollies. For others, weekends were spent at folk clubs or Chicago blues jams. Some musicians wanted to be the Beatles, some Bob Dylan. C. P. Lee invokes Billy Liar: 'I think in the 60s it was Billy Liar; you wanted to get out and it was a fantasy world that you inhabited. Whether it was British modness or a pale imitation of Californian psychedelia, music was always an escape; going to a club to see a group of Manchester musicians playing Chicago blues, for that forty-five minutes or an hour you could be part of another experience.'

But the mods were definitely the dominant tribe in Manchester, extending the city's deep soul roots. Long hair was one of the defining features of Manchester mods; in 1966 Manchester mod style, according to C. P. Lee, 'would have been suits with long hair, very much like the Small Faces; parted in the middle, with long sideburns'. The first uniquely English-born youth movement, the mods were evidence of how the international world of pop culture was confronting and killing off old definitions of Englishness. Their roots lay in a broad-minded and bold melding of other cultures; their dress sense they took from American West Coast jazz icons, their music from Detroit soul and the rhythm & blues of the Deep South, and their Vespas and Lambrettas from Italy.

There is little evidence of serious mods-and-rockers trouble in Manchester, aside from Mike Sweeney hearing rumours of the odd skirmish in Albert Square, and C. P. Lee making the acquaintance of greasers in Stockport. The greasers also made their presence felt at a gig by the Shangri-La's at the Manor Lounge in Stockport, storming the mod-filled dancefloor for 'their' anthem, 'Leader of the Pack'. Alan Lawson has examined some of the press reports of such trouble and concludes that often they're no more than the local press trying not to be left out of what was then (in 1964) the most newsworthy teenage trend: 'If you had two people bumping into each other in Deansgate, one with short hair and one with a leather jacket, you'd get the *Manchester Evening News* screaming "MODS AND ROCKERS RIOT ON DEANSGATE"!' This lack of trouble seems to have been the result of a less demarcated view of pop music in Manchester and a healthy and continuing scepticism about any trends hitting the headlines in tabloids. Mods and rockers battling it out? 'It seems to be a very strangely fabricated London, southern media event which had nothing to do with what was happening up here', says C. P. Lee.

Modism has always been strong in the North West, and it provided the foundations for the Northern Soul scene (strong from the early 1970s onwards). Ian Brown of the Stone Roses, in his youth, was a member of a scooter club. I remember a mod renaissance in Manchester in 1984 at Cloud 9, a basement club on Cross Street; on a Saturday afternoon there'd be scooters parked up on Newmarket Lane – just up the road from Spin Inn's first shop – and down Back Pool Fold near the original Geese, and the strains of Dobie Gray's 'Out On The Floor' and Ramsey Lewis's 'Wade In The Water' could be heard above the Cross Street traffic. World of Twist, before they even got together to make music, were a mod-influenced bunch of lads who worked in Affleck's Palace and launched a very short-lived but spot-on club night in 1986 called 'World of Music'. Perhaps if the press had picked up on these connections, the city could have found itself being dubbed Modchester.

Dedicated followers of the Manchester club scene in the mid 1960s all recall hectic Fridays and Saturdays. In Sweeney's words, 'You'd go to town on Friday afternoon, and not get home until Sunday tea-time.' The clubs were cheap, and it was likely that a night out could include a visit to more than one club. You might start at Beat City (as the Three Coins was now called) on Fountain Street, from 8 until 11-ish, then go on to the Manchester Cavern on Cromford Court, and maybe still have the time and the shillings for a trip to the Twisted Wheel all-nighter. Even those without a wage could participate. C. P. Lee used to go to the Jigsaw, Heaven & Hell, the Jungfrau and the Twisted Wheel: 'You just went along and bought membership for about 3/6 and things would start to arrive in the post. If you worked it out properly you could go to four or five clubs in a night without paying because you got special passes for certain hours and if you figured them all out, you could do a circuit and go round and round.'

On Saturdays, Sweeney had a favourite routine:

> On Saturday morning, if you'd been out all night Friday, you might nip home for twenty minutes for a change of clothing, or you might stay in town, in coffee bars and cafés. We used to go to the café at Victoria Station, and then we'd go to Lewis's where they had record-listening booths and we'd be in there listening to records and pretending we were going to buy them. You'd hang around Lewis's café, and hang about Piccadilly Gardens, and maybe try to get a bit of kip. We must have pissed off the average middle-aged person at that time; they must have thought the world was coming to an end.

Come Saturday night, and the clubs would fill again. Sweeney wasn't flush, but he had a job and he knew what his priorities were. At Metro Vickers he was picking up the pounds and shillings equivalent of £2.80 a week, of which £1 or more was spends. Some weekday nights at the Twisted Wheel and Oasis were free, and on weekend nights entry would be between 2/6 (12.5p), and 5/× (25p) when there was a top drawer act on (Georgie Fame & the Blue Flames, say, or the Pretty Things). Sweeney:

> Kids like me had money. There was very little unemployment in Manchester in those days. The only unemployed were either the unfit or the professional dodgers, because there were plenty of jobs. We were walking in and out of jobs. I didn't get on particularly well in industry because I always wanted to be a

singer and so I wasn't into my job. I used to let them down and I never got on with the chargehands and the foremen. And when it all finally blew up I'd always say, 'Give me my cards, I'm off'. Next day at the Labour Exchange there'd be loads of vacancies, and it would just be, 'Which one do you fancy doing?'

In February 1958, in the journal *Twentieth Century*, Colin Mac-Innes put forward the notion that 'The great social revolution of the past fifteen years may not be the one which redivided wealth among adults in the Welfare State, but the one that's given teenagers economic power.' And it's undeniable that the economic boom in the early 1960s gave teenagers jobs and plentiful cash, and thus created the ideal conditions for a high-profile, fast-moving pop culture to develop, and not just in music. MacInnes points to the way various industries rely on the teenager's consumer power; the pop disc industry, for instance, as well as the clothing, scooter, and radio and TV industries, as well as the coffee bars and clubs that cater for them. He does a piece of rough mathematics, calculating that there are two million kids aged fifteen to twenty-three, each (in 1958, that is) with weekly spending money of £3, giving 'an annual teenage kitty' of £312,000,000. MacInnes exaggerates his case here – it's unlikely that more than a handful of young Mancunians had anything like £3 spends each week – but it's certainly true that teenagers enjoyed strengthening spending power in the early 1960s; thus in 1964 73 million 7" pop singles were sold in Britain (at 6s 8d each), more than in any year before or since.

Through the busy weekends the kids out on the floor would need to keep awake. The clubs, having evolved, in the main, from coffee bar culture, were not licensed to sell alcohol. Sweeney remembers:

> There were a lot of dexadrine and other amphetamines around in Manchester in the mid-60s. They arrived some time around the summer of 1963 and stayed fashionable for about three years. We all tried taking amphetamines at one period or another – you could very easily buy purple hearts and black bombers in Manchester – but I found very quickly that they made little difference to me as I was so up all the time anyway, and the coming down part was awful.

In that era the drugs were available on prescription, as slimming pills, but dealers could get hold of supplies of larger, illegally obtained batches of pills. There are few reports of the dealers being involved with violence and intimidation, as later, in the years after acid house; certainly the kids could remain unaware of any violence attached to the drug scene. What brought an end to the speed scene was when alcohol arrived in the clubs in 1966 – as a direct result of police intervention – at a time when the music was changing too. 'Suddenly it all became licensed', says Sweeney, 'And that changed the whole scene completely. Clubs were totally different once alcohol was allowed in. Everyone had a drink, and the pills disappeared not quite overnight, but very quickly.'

The mid 1960s were marked by massive police activity in Manchester's clubland. C. P. Lee has uncovered a lurid report entitled 'Coffee Beat Clubs' which was prepared by Chief Superintendent Dingwall and included in Chief Constable J. A. McKay's annual report in 1964. The Chief Constable had obviously decided that the teenage culture which had grown out of the coffee bars and cellar clubs was a menace. He went to war.

Chief Superintendent Dingwall identifies the patrons of the clubs as 'individuals of exaggerated dress and deportment, commonly known as mods, rockers or beatniks'. He claims to have received intelligence reports – presumably from the Mod Squad, as the plain clothes police cadets sent in 'undercover' were known to regular clubgoers – that drug-taking was rife. Dingwall paints a picture of a fully criminal twilight world inhabited by teenage runaways, exploitative entrepreneurs, pimps and drug dealers. He also recounts details of various raids on Manchester clubs in the period after February 1965. The Cavern was raided and a doorman and a cloakroom attendant were both found in possession of cannabis and amphetamines. When Heaven & Hell on Sackville Street was raided, one fifteen-year-old girl was charged with possession of an amphetamine capsule and 'four young persons' arrested for possession of dangerous weapons. Dingwall's report was undertaken in order to provide evidence for Chief Constable McKay's successful attempts to seek 'powers of registration and control'. These powers are enshrined in the Manchester Corporation Act of 1965. 'An astonishing piece of legislation', in the words of C. P. Lee; 'An Act of Parliament to close down the clubs in Manchester, just in Manchester.'

The Act, which came into force on 1 January 1966, resulted in the collapse of the network of coffee bars, clubs and venues; a success, as far as Chief Constable McKay was concerned, a disaster for the city's bands and music fans. Some closed down even during 1965 when the owners realised that they would never be able to meet the fire, safety and sanitation standards, nor control the clientele in the draconian manner the Act required (club owners, for instance, were liable to have their licence revoked if any illegal drugs were consumed on the premises, whether they were aware of such activity or not). Some of the clubs became late-night adult supper clubs with liquor licences. 'By 1968 only two city centre venues catered exclusively for young people', says C. P. Lee, 'the Magic Village and the Twisted Wheel. In a way, one is tempted to suggest that these two clubs were allowed to exist as symbolic outlets for teenage passions.'

By the end of 1965 the beat boom had waned; the successful bands had either moved to America or become all-round family entertainers, more at home on the pantomime circuit than in a cellar club. The Oasis began to move towards a cabaret-style entertainment policy and turned into Sloopy's, and the Monday night beat session at the Bodega was replaced by a variety bill. Meanwhile, John Mayall's instincts had been correct; rhythm & blues was beginning to dominate teenage tastes, with the Stones replacing the Beatles at the fashionable end of the pop market. Rhythm & blues had stayed underground in the years since 1956, but by the mid 1960s groups like Manfred Mann, the Spencer Davis Group and the Animals were all hit-makers. They carried the torch for teenage rebellion, maintaining a more delinquent edge than the Merseybeat groups, and their long-haired harshness fed into the sound that Jimi Hendrix was to bring from America in 1967. The shift towards rhythm & blues is witnessed in Manchester by the prominence of the Twisted Wheel in the years that followed, with regular appearances there by the likes of the Blues-breakers and the Pretty Things.

Eclecticism in clubland was lost as soul music and rock diverged. This, together with the entrance of alcohol into clubs, drove out a lot of the good vibes of the early 1960s. C. P. Lee regretted the schisms:

> There was a most definite split between rock and soul and that's when violence started creeping in. Also skinheads appeared at that time who seemed to possess a genetic impera-tive to stomp anybody who had long hair. You'd be chased up

and down Market Street by skinheads on a Saturday afternoon. I got gang-stomped in an alleyway for having long hair. This was the end of the 60s. People would have a go at you. Gangs of Irishmen would attack you in the street; a most bizarre thing being ordered out of pubs and bars just for having long hair. It sounds daft now, but it was something that upset people very greatly and I never figured out quite why.

The live scene took a battering from both venue closures caused by police activity and changing tastes as the demand for soul-based disc-only nights grew. 'By 1968 we're going towards the disco era; venues stopped putting bands on, and just played music', remembers C. P. Lee. The phrase 'disco' had arrived; in 1968 in Gore Street, off Piccadilly, there was a hardcore mod club calling itself the Blue Note Disco Bar – 'Classic soul for people who know what they want', its advertising promised – although the owner occasionally gave up Tuesday nights to make space for psychedelic happenings. Fragmentation of the scene triggered debates on the relative merits of DJs and live bands which continued through the following decades, but for Alan Lawson the rise of the DJ in the mid 1960s was a bad omen: 'The increase in the number of disc jockeys was a warning of what was to come several years later when the man playing the records, rather than the group playing the music, became the star.'

Undeniably, the beat group era was the first time the kids in Manchester stopped being consumers, and became producers and active participants in the scene. It was the first major explosion of that perfect Manchester moment when people said 'We can do this for ourselves', a rallying cry later to be declaimed during both the punk era and the Madchester boom of the late 1980s. 'Every street in Manchester had a beat group', remembers Bruce Mitchell; 'People would get home from work, pick up a second-hand guitar and save their wages as engineers, say, so they could buy the rest of the beat group gear.' And with its development of a healthy live network, and the ground-breaking chart success of its leading lights, the era laid the foundations for Manchester music and gave the city the beginnings of a self-sufficient scene. The beat era passed a considerable legacy to the generations that followed. This first flowering of pop music in Manchester gave a lie to those commentators and critics who had believed that there is only a sponge-like response by a native culture to the influence of international pop culture. Manchester began to contribute. Life became more than a wait, more than subservience to Establishment values; through pop music young England had a voice.

But not everyone was receptive to the new scene. Ewan MacColl had played a major part in kickstarting the skiffle scene with a radio series called *Ballads and Blues* which traced the links between jazz and blues and working-class folk songs from Britain and America. It was from a marginalised scene based round the radio programme and one or two associated singing clubs that skiffle emerged, and MacColl formed one of the first skiffle groups. Post-Lonnie Donegan, however, MacColl strongly disliked the direction taken by skiffle and emerging rock & roll in the late 1950s, concerned that the younger generation had become quasi-Americans, sensing the death of radical English cultural traditions, and in reaction to this he became much more of a purist. He embarked on a campaign opposing American influences; it was contrary to the spirit of the times – everyone from Elvis Presley to Big Bill Broonzy was inspiring English youth – and instead of being the champion of radical cultural traditions, as the 1960s developed MacColl ended up looking austere, backward-looking and insular.

But many other people, especially those who had played a part in the music boom in Manchester, remained enthusiastic and thrived. As the 1960s turned into the 1970s, Jimmy Savile consolidated his position as a top entertainer on BBC TV and radio, and Bruce Mitchell and C. P. Lee played in Greasy Bear, Manchester's first psychedelic band – formed in 1966 at Manchester High School for Art – and later in Alberto Y Los Trios Paranoias. In the post-punk era Bruce Mitchell went on to play drums in the Durutti Column alongside Vini Reilly (managed by Anthony H. Wilson; theirs was the first release on his resurrected Factory label in November 1994). The Twisted Wheel – which had moved from Brazennose Street to Whitworth Street earlier in the 60s – became Placemate 7, but other prime sites of teenage dreams were comprehensively buried when the Manchester Cavern, the Jigsaw and the Magic Village – as well as Brown Street with its many record shops and swinging boutiques – got demolished in the construction of the Arndale Centre. Roger Eagle, the creative force and DJ at the Magic Village, had already left, for Liverpool; he booked groups at Eric's in Liverpool during the punk era, but returned to Manchester to partner Gareth Evans at the International on Anson Road in the mid 1980s. Tosh Ryan, with Martin Hannett, went on to run Rabid Records, Manchester's premier punk label, set up the Basement Video project and now has a major role at IDEA (a digital arts lab in All Saints).

One of the city's most gifted songwriters in the 1960s was Graham Gouldman. He wrote 'For Your Love' for the Yardbirds, a swirling hybrid of pop, blues and wild inspiration which so upset the blues-worshipping purist Eric Clapton that it provoked his departure from the band; he joined John Mayall's Bluesbreakers. In 1969 John Mayall moved to Los Angeles. Gouldman went on to form 10cc with Eric Stewart from Wayne Fontana & the Mindbenders. Freddie & the Dreamers, the Hollies and similar contemporary Manchester groups were unable or unwilling to record their own songs and relied on professional songwriters and Tin Pan Alley; a state of affairs which led the frustrated Graham Nash to leave the Hollies and take himself off to America in 1968. This successful move brought him much fame as part of Crosby, Stills, Nash & Young.

Danny Betesh – whose Kennedy Street Enterprises started out as a management company for Freddie & the Dreamers – went on to become a major league rock promoter. Mike Sweeney played in a series of unsung bands in the 60s (Circuit 5, the Irwells), formed Stackwaddy, who were signed to John Peel's Dandelion label for a while ('We used to drink a lot, fall over and swear at students', remembers Sweeney), then Smiffy – Manchester's premier glam rock group – the Salford Jets and the Fabulous Thunderbirds. He went on to carry the flame for 60s music on shows throughout the commercial local radio network. Hughie Flint, ex-trainee missionary, formed McGuinness Flint after he left the Bluesbreakers, and then The Blues Band with Paul Jones from Manfred Mann. He is now a porter at an Oxford college. Peter Noone went on daytime TV in April 1997 to announce comeback plans. He'd been in America too long, he said; 'The best place to be a star is in England. People give up their parking spaces for you.'

You'd think MacColl would have lightened up in his later years, but he always maintained his belief that rock & roll was (in his words) 'politically suspect' right up to his death. He also had reservations about the American folk scene of the early 1960s, and even the radical protest songs recorded by the young Bob Dylan; he had met Dylan at a festival in Minneapolis where Dylan called him 'sir'. By the time Dylan played at the Newport Folk Festival and launched into an electric set, the folk boom was dead and he had long left MacColl behind. On his next tour of England, Dylan played at the Free Trade Hall and his electric set rocked the old building to its foundations; 'As Dylan launched into "Tell Me Mama" it was like a B-52 taking off. I'd never heard anything so loud in my life', recalls C. P. Lee.

This new Dylan fired indignation in some of the audience. He was considered a 'traitor' by the traditionalist fans of protest folk. The catcall 'Judas' just as Dylan was about to launch into 'Like A Rolling Stone' was recorded for posterity, and the Free Trade Hall gig appeared on the bootleg erroneously entitled *Live at the Albert Hall* (one of the most consistently selling bootlegs of all time). The heckler, Keith Butler – then a second-year student at Keele University, now a citizen of Toronto, Canada – came forward in February 1999 as a result of seeing publicity surrounding the long-overdue official release of the recording. He appeared on a radio documentary about the night. C. P. Lee remembers people responding by booing the booers.

Pop history, pop evolution, is a series of battles. MacColl's dictats reflected a disabling inflexibility, but the kinds of argument about defining a sound as authentic, or radical, or commercial played out in May 1966 at Dylan's gig returned in later years as, for instance, arguments about street credibility and selling out in the punk era; 'unplugged' music and computer music in the 1980s; and underground and mainstream house in the 1990s. Popular culture moves swiftly. Revolutionaries become reactionaries in a year or two, an innovation becomes a cliché in a month. Generation gaps appear daily.

When Alan Lawson casts his mind back to his beat group era, he turns misty-eyed: 'There was a gentler time in the history of the clubs of Manchester and Salford and Stockport when life was simpler and cleaner, when alcohol and drugs were not a problem, when people could actually see real groups playing real, live music, and when the public was spoiled for choice among the plethora of clubs available to them . . . That brief golden age lasted from 1958 to approximately 1965.'

Undoubtedly arguments could be advanced in favour of almost any era being considered a golden age. Sometimes it's only hindsight that makes one seem so good; more than likely it's the era when we were young, free and out on the town. In 1965, for some, the good times were still to come, with psychedelia and long nights spent at the Magic Village or the Northern Soul scene, or the rave era. Golden ages are like rows with your parents: all generations have them. Ironically enough, Frank Pritchard, in his book *Dance Band Days*, recalls precisely the era rock & roll destroyed – the Manchester of the 1930s and 1940s – in an elegy not dissimilar to Lawson's recollection of the 1960s; 'It has been my good fortune to live through those exciting times of real ballroom dancing', he writes. For him the early 1960s, far from being a golden age, was the beginning of the end. While two million teenagers spent three hundred million pounds, he yearned for a return to those days of 'rhythmic, tuneful music, when dancing folk could hold a conversation in the ballroom without shouting or being deafened'.

But the early 1960s in Manchester does seem to have retained the potent power of a mythic golden age. Every teen culture seems free and spontaneous and uncommercialised in its early years – even punk, even rave culture – but the word 'innocent' could only be used for the first flowerings of teen culture in the early 60s. 'Innocent times had been consumed and devoured by big business', for example, is how Alan Lawson describes the end of 1965.

Innocence is not particularly a virtue in pop culture, especially when it's manifested in music as naive, innocuous and jaunty as Freddie & the Dreamers'. Writing around the time of their hits – in 1966, in fact – George Melly described pop music as 'the only key to the instant golden life', but even if his definition was true then, we've since come a long way. A shift in pop music signposted by that legendary Dylan performance in Manchester – described by Richard Williams as 'the most electrifying single moment in post-war culture' – developed through the second half of the 60s. New songwriters emerged unconstricted by Tin Pan Alley, the drugs got harder and Jimi Hendrix mashed up a whole new set of possibilities. There was acid and there was Altamont. The golden life was an illusion, as the next generation of Manchester bands would articulate in a quite stunning way.

Perhaps the power of the myth is also entangled with the fact that the mid 1960s was the last era of job security and regular wages for the people of Manchester. The young had jobs, had money, had it easy. Furthermore, for working-class Mancunians the big ruptures caused by slum clearance were only just kicking in. Through the backward gaze of a million Mancunians it's all one; beat groups, the Plaza, *Ready Steady Go*, Otis Redding, 'Dancing In The Street', terraces not tower blocks, black and white television, Matt Busby, the Twisted Wheel.

But the end of 1965 marked another turning point in the city's history. In October of that year, two bodies were found on Saddleworth Moor – those of ten-year-old Lesley Downie and eleven-year-old John Kilbride – and in May 1966 Ian Brady and Myra Hindley were sentenced to life imprisonment for their murder and the hacking to death of seventeen-year-old Edward Evans. It later became clear that the couple had kidnapped, tortured and killed a total of five young Manchester children. Innocence indeed had withered. The Moors Murders cast a great shadow over the heart of the city, and Manchester would never be the same again.

CHAPTER 5

Punk, Post-Punk and the Punk Postman:

Manchester Music, 1976–86

John the Postman has tried to keep all the tickets to all the gigs he's ever attended. He still sees gigs, but most are small-scale affairs, in the back room of the Marble Arch on Rochdale Road or a Tuesday night at the Roadhouse on Newton Street; the kind of gigs no tickets are ever printed for. Sometimes he jots the bands' names down on the back of an envelope. These mementoes he keeps in a shoe box at home, under his bed. At weekends he's a dealer (in records – not drugs – that is). He takes crates of records round the record fairs of Northern England, selling Swell Maps singles to other forty-year-olds, most of whom have a wife, some kids and everything the MC5 ever recorded. John is an amiable drinker, with a preference for real ale brewed by small brewers. He chides me for drinking Budweiser. He has a plan to blow up the Budweiser factories; he knows where they are.

In among his personal archive is the ticket he bought when he went to see the Sex Pistols at the Lesser Free Trade Hall on 4 June 1976. When I first saw it, no more edifying than a raffle ticket or a ticket for the bus home, I picked it up with just the tips of my fingers, like some expert on the *Antiques Roadshow*.

Recalling Manchester in the years just prior to punk, John the Postman remembers an uninspiring and lifeless time despite the existence in the city of various individuals, sects, Bowie-clones, sixth-form rebels, American garage enthusiasts, arty types, soul boys and jaded 60s scenesters hanging on to blurred recollections of the Magic Village. His bad memories are backed up by Paul Morley, who became the chronicler of post-punk Manchester in his writings in *New Musical Express*; 'Manchester was a very boring place to be. It had no identity, no common spirit or motive. It was probably a reflection of the country at large.'

Early in 1976, or even late in 1976, the notion of Manchester as a taste-making rock & roll town was unthinkable. There were no local labels, nor small venues or rising stars. Punk changed this. Crucial to the story of this change are two Sex Pistols gigs at the Lesser Free Trade Hall (a small hall, on a floor above the Free Trade Hall proper) in the summer of 1976, the first summer of punk. The audiences who saw them play included many people who were to go on and play a major part in Manchester music in the next decade, including Pete Shelley, Howard Devoto, Richard Boon, Mark E. Smith, Bernard Sumner, Peter Hook, Linder Mulvey, Tony Wilson, and a young man from Stretford who'd just done his O Levels: Steven Patrick Morrissey. Morrissey remembers seeing the Pistols: 'The audience was very slim. It was a front parlour affair.'

For Mark E. Smith of the Fall, events at the Lesser Free Trade Hall are still fresh in his mind. He'd spent the mid 1970s working in the offices of a shipping company based at Salford Docks, bored, listless, into the Velvet Underground and Captain Beefheart, and into keeping himself entertained by any means necessary; the day Manchester United played Southampton in the 1976 Cup Final he took a load of dexadrine and went to see a Jimi Hendrix film at the Aaben Cinema in Hulme. But the day he saw the Buzzcocks with the Sex Pistols was better still; 'I saw the Buzzcocks and I thought I'd better form a group, I can do better than that! I actually remember coming out of the gig at the Lesser Free Trade Hall and thinking that.'

Unhyped and under-capitalised, the first Pistols gig in Manchester, on 4 June, was a DIY gig promoted by two young students, Pete Shelley and Howard Devoto. In June 1976 Devoto was an *NME*-reading music fan into the Velvet Underground and the Stooges who came across the Sex Pistols in a review in *NME*. Curious, Devoto and Shelley went down to see them play in High Wycombe and Welwyn Garden City. According to Devoto, 'My life changed the moment I saw the Sex Pistols. I immediately got caught up trying to make things happen. Suddenly there was a direction, something I passionately wanted to be involved in. We thought they were fantastic; it was, we will go and do something like this in Manchester.'

His enthusiasm for the Sex Pistols was translated into an active involvement. Devoto spoke to Malcolm McLaren and invited the Pistols to play at the Student Union at Bolton Institute, but the Union wouldn't agree to the gig, so he decided to put them on at the Lesser Free Trade Hall. The inspiration was on a totally different level to that of the average Pink Floyd fan. Punk was empowering. You didn't need musicianship, or a big stage show. I can remember a guy at school coming the next morning after seeing Pink Floyd at Bingley Hall in Stafford. 'Great lights', he said. We laughed. It was like going to the football and coming home and saying, 'Great pitch'.

For the second gig, on 20 July, Shelley and Devoto formed Manchester's prime punk band, the Buzzcocks, and played third on the bill, their set ending with Shelley smashing a guitar. Also on the bill that night were Slaughter & the Dogs, who performed in full glitter regalia, showing their glam-rock roots via a cover version of Roxy Music's 'Both Ends Burning'. Word had spread since the first Pistols show, and a pocket-sized community was emerging. According to Richard Boon, friend of Devoto and Shelley, and Buzzcocks manager-to-be, 'The Seventies incarnation of the mythical Manchester scene developed from there.'

Tony Wilson had been drawn there by Howard Devoto, who'd sent a tape to him at Granada TV. Wilson has always listened to people. At Granada he earned his reputation as a youth culture guru by knowing who to listen to. He's never underestimated the way that a culture that appears marginal one year can be mainstream the next. Previously Leonard Cohen was his hero, but Wilson understood that the Sex Pistols were important; 'I went to see them, and didn't know what the fuck was going on, until they played "Stepping Stone". Then it was clear that they were deeply and fabulously exciting.' He arranged for the Pistols to play on his Granada programme in the autumn. They premiered 'Anarchy In The UK'.

By the end of 1976 punk was overground, shot there by the media. On 12 November the BBC's teatime news magazine, *Nationwide*, covered the latest youth cult. Punk was 'as big as the Mods and Rockers of the 60s'; 'Punks wear vampire make-up, swastika armbands and leather trousers', viewers were told. A live interview with the Sex Pistols on Thames TV's show *Today* on 1 December dissolved into swearing (two 'shits', one 'bastard', one 'fucking', one 'fucker'). The bad language at teatime created a storm of tabloid protest.

Media reaction in Manchester was much like the rest of Britain, with the *Manchester Evening News* stoking the fires of outrage. Even though the *Today* show hadn't been seen in the Granada region, they pounced on a tenuous local link; the interviewer, Bill Grundy, had a home in Marple Bridge, Stockport, and he had been suspended for his part in the controversy. The hysteria in the media in the first week of December 1976 was sustained, somewhat obliquely, by sensations in other parts of the pop music world; on 3 December Teddy Boys rioted at a Bill Haley gig at New Victoria Hall in London, and within a week a Bay City Rollers press conference degenerated into a free-for-all. Rampaging teenagers, the uncontrollable young and their noisy pop music were sending waves of fear through the straight world. The *Manchester Evening News* ran three front-page stories about the Sex Pistols in ten days.

The Sex Pistols had a tour planned during the first weeks of December, but Manchester venues the Palace Theatre and Free Trade Hall joined others around the UK in boycotting the Pistols. Eventually they did play locally, at the Electric Circus in Collyhurst, a heavy metal venue in the middle of a Council estate. Justifying his ban, Free Trade Hall manager Ron O'Neil said at the time that during the second show at the Lesser Free Trade Hall the Sex Pistols 'had started arguments with the audience and their language was a bit strong to say the least'. He also claimed that 'one member of the audience had to be taken to hospital after an incident'. No one I've spoken to who attended the Sex Pistols show in question remembers any violence there at all.

Not only did the Palace Theatre and the Free Trade Hall ban the Sex Pistols but so did two Manchester hotels: the Midland in the city centre and the Belgrade Hotel in Stockport. At the Midland the band had booked two nights but were turned away by hotel staff on their arrival. Attempts to book in at the Belgrade failed. So the Anarchy Tour arrived at the Arosa Hotel, Wilmslow Road, Withington. The manager of the Arosa, Mr Anwar, was calm: 'I have booked them in for one night. They seem to be decent people and I will expect decent behaviour from them', he told the *Manchester Evening News*. At the venue, the police were on full alert; according to reports, 'Detectives in denims and pop gear mingled with the crowd and senior uniformed officers kept vigil from the back of the hall.'

The next day it became clear that it had all gone horribly wrong for Mr Anwar at the Arosa. The *Evening News* headline said it all:

'Pistols Are Turned Out of Hotel'. Mr Anwar had been forced to call the police; the band had paid £120 (in advance) for the rooms, but were ejected at 3.30am, an hour after they'd arrived back from the gig. A disillusioned Mr Anwar explained: 'They made a lot of noise and upset the other guests. I couldn't allow them to stay any longer. I told them when they arrived that the hotel does not allow girls in their rooms but they broke the rules.' Inadvertently, of course, he'd hit on all the things that appealed about the Sex Pistols; they made a lot of noise, and they broke the rules, and no one was going to stop the randy fuckers from having girls in the bedrooms. 'They were filthy and their language was filthy', he added.

It was clear that punk was disturbing, subverting and liberating, in dress, attitudes, music. Tosh Ryan remembers:

> It was when I first heard and saw the Buzzcocks that I knew something great was happening. They weren't working in the normal structures. And their appearance was quite disturbing; an untidy, art-school dirt kind of look and lots of safety pins. When I first met Pete Shelley he was covered from head to foot in safety pins and his hair was bleached in a really tatty way. Until then I'd thought fashion was about how well clothes were cut, and suddenly fashion was about wearing rags, safety pins and bin-liners.

What to some seemed like liberation, to others presaged the end of civilisation. One correspondent, known only as 'Mrs L. of Heaton Moor', felt panicked into writing to the *Manchester Evening News* problem page: 'Like the rest of the country, I'm sickened by this new vogue called punk rock . . . I'm really very worried about the influences that are shaping our children's future.'

The last twenty years will have been hell for Mrs L. The influence of punk rock has been huge, in Manchester, England and internationally. Enthusiasm triggered involvement; punk rock was empowering, its fans inspired to form bands, to create their own culture. The momentum behind music in Manchester today remains this punk ethic: do it yourself.

A lot of street-level activity connected with the punk explosion was a case of making a virtue out of a necessity. There was nowhere to play, so you booked your own venues. There were no labels, so you started your own. A network was building nationally, locked into by a newly energised music community in Manchester. Among the early converts, Morrissey was making plans; roused by the Sex Pistols, he put an advert in *Sounds* in December 1976: 'Dolls/Patti fans wanted for Manchester-based punk band.'

Richard Boon's New Hormones label put out the Buzzcocks' 'Spiral Scratch' EP in January 1977 on cadged money, with Martin Hannett (then known as Martin Zero) producing; the recording and mixing of the four songs took just over five hours. Boon got together a DIY cover featuring a picture of the four band members in front of the statue of Robert Peel in Piccadilly Gardens. Shelley helped him put the vinyl in the sleeves. On 3 February John Peel played the record on Radio One. Within six months it had sold sixteen thousand copies.

Devoto has since complained of his 'mickey-mouse, fake Cockney' vocals on 'Boredom', the headlining track on the EP, but the record manages to be angry, melancholy and bewildered all at once – 'I'm living in this movie / But it doesn't move me', sings Devoto – but the choruses of 'B'dom, b'dom' dose the song with humour too. *New Musical Express* described the record as 'heavily New York influenced in style', but the New York influence, or whatever, is irrelevant; it's out of Manchester and it's probably one of the most English pop records ever made. Devoto left the Buzzcocks just a week after the release of 'Spiral Scratch'. He later formed Magazine.

'Spiral Scratch' gave Manchester a high profile in the punk scene, but the independent spirit behind it intensified the record's significance. With the Sex Pistols and the Clash signed to major labels, their rhetoric about anarchy and revolution was always going to sound a little hollow, but the Buzzcocks showed just how far you could get working outside the normal structures. The Buzzcocks articulated boredom, and practised autonomy.

By going it alone, the Buzzcocks launched the independent label scene, a parallel world that was to develop through into the 1980s. It was this which was punk's biggest legacy to British music. It opened the door for Factory, Mute, Creation, Postcard, 4AD, Rough Trade. It provided the model for similar structures developing and surviving in America, and for music genres other than rock; house music's energy in the 90s has come from a plethora of small labels and one-off releases.

The independent label dream has always been hard to sustain, however; that romantic notion of going it alone, pure and untainted by hype and multinational marketeers. The Buzzcocks soon moved on to United Artists, providing an early model many later bands would follow, using independent releases as a stepping stone to a major. But the way history has developed – the Smiths falling out with Rough Trade in 1987, Factory Records collapsing in November 1992, the major/indie divide blurring in the 1990s with Oasis, for example (bought by Creation with Sony money) – disguises just how revolutionary those independent punk releases were.

Despite the dilution of London's power in pop music in the early 1960s, when the North especially – from the Beatles in Liverpool to the Animals in Newcastle – produced a series of highly successful bands, groups and their managers unavoidably looked on London as the city to go to make it in the business. It was either that or move to America, as Herman's Hermits had done. But in the punk era cities like Manchester – especially Manchester – and Liverpool, developed fierce local identities, and a business infrastructure to back them up. Independence, and a new perception that moving to London and going with a major was 'selling out', gave Manchester bands new motivation. If the Sex Pistols taught that forming a band was easy, the early success of the Buzzcocks taught the value of the independent ethic. Answering Paul Morley's lament, Manchester had finally become a rock & roll town.

In the view of Jon Savage, 'In early 1977, Manchester started to develop as England's second Punk city after London and, as the capital quickly became Punk-saturated, its most creative site.' The development of an infrastructure to support the creativity unleashed by punk was crucial. It made all the difference locally; Newcastle was held back by a lack of venues for punk, whereas Liverpool was to have Eric's – arguably as important in that city's musical history as the Cavern – and Manchester was blessed with a number of live venues, notably the Electric Circus, although another venue played a key part in providing a stage for younger, breaking bands. This was the Squat, a rundown building on land owned by the University where the Academy now stands. Home to the Royal Northern College of Music until they left it to go to bigger premises further up Oxford Road, the building was going to be demolished to make a car park, but students occupied it. The University reprieved it and it was made into a people's venue in the early 1970s, with the Albertos playing the first ever music gig there. It became important when the local band scene blossomed in the aftermath of punk, hosting Manchester's first ever Rock Against Racism gig. The Squat was still in irregular use in 1980 when New Order played a semi-secret gig. I remember Bernard Sumner falling over.

Some of Manchester's infrastructure had foundations from earlier eras. Rabid Records grew out of joint activity between Martin Hannett and Tosh Ryan, instrumental in Music Force, an agency set up in 1973. In 1977 Rabid put out records by Slaughter & the Dogs and John Cooper Clarke, among others. Tosh remembers:

> We were in it purely for the fun, the stupidity, having a laugh and a wack at major labels and not really concerned whether we were successful or not. We were successful by default; I wanted to put the Jilted John single out because it was so stupid. Demystifying the music industry; that was what it was all about. People making their own records and their own clothes. And putting on gigs for themselves.

The attitude at Rabid captivated all kinds of budding entrepreneurs and punk activists; 'There were people saying "Yeah, I can do it", and then going out and doing it, mainly as a result of Martin Hannett and Tosh Ryan starting Rabid', remembers C. P. Lee. 'I'd just go and sit at the Rabid office on Cotton Lane clocking what was going on; there'd be Ed Banger there, and John Cooper Clarke. Tony Wilson and Alan Erasmus spent a few days in the office watching how it was all done. People would come up from London to see us, or them. Nick Kent arrived, to a flurry of great laughter off everybody, looking like a wasted buffoon, with scarves tied round his arm.'

Joy Division especially benefited from the backing they got from arch-propagandist Paul Morley in his writings in *NME*. But able reflectors of the local energy ranged from Tony Wilson at Granada TV, to the grassroots fanzines, among them *Shy Talk*, *Ghast Up*, Pete Shelley's *Plaything* (3p a copy, folded after two issues) and, later, *City Fun*. One of the more unsung publications was *Modern Drugs*. *Modern Drugs* was a collaboration between Martin Fry, who went on to form the group ABC, and future house music guru, Mike Pickering.

Mike Pickering was living in Bramhall when punk broke. He rebelled, went to live in Rusholme, and started hanging out with punks, musicians and slightly oddball characters who claimed to be on art courses at the Polytechnic. His first loves were Northern Soul and Manchester City. The best days of Northern Soul had ended by the mid 1970s, and certainly by the end of 1976 Pickering was up for something more. He regularly saw the Buzzcocks, and he went to the Electric Circus to see the Pistols. 'The Pistols weren't my favourite band really; the Buzzcocks and Magazine I really liked. I thought the Buzzcocks were like Northern Soul; short, sharp pop songs.'

Manchester was an ideal breeding ground for punk. There was boredom, plenty of it, and poverty; we're talking about 1976, a year when the number of people living on or around the official poverty level had trebled over two years to more than 15 million, the biggest jump since the 1930s. The DIY spirit of punk was easily grasped in a city well used to making do, struggling to improvise a culture out of whatever's to hand. The language of punk was at home in Manchester, among the high rises and the supermarkets. And the sound of punk reflected qualities of the city; Manchester had, and still has, energy, and a hint of violence. Manchester was, and still is, the site of an intriguing working-class and art student mix; a very punk collision.

Punk flourished in the most unlikely places. Like the Ranch, for instance, where the Buzzcocks played in August 1976, and which went on to become a favoured punk hangout. Sited in Dale Street, and owned by Foo Foo Lamaar, Manchester's most prominent drag artist – who also owned the next door building, the Palace, where he preferred to appear himself – the Ranch is remembered variously by reminiscing punk heads decades later. Pete Shelley usually talks of it with fondness, but it was in a dodgy part of town. In September 1976 eighteen-year-old Michael Molloy died as a result of a fight outside the Ranch. Violence has always been part of Manchester's nightlife; it's never been safe. John the Postman didn't like the Ranch: 'It was a bit rough there. I was threatened at the Buzzcocks gig. "You looking at my bird?"; the classic line. There were certainly some heavy characters there.'

For a brief period another punk venue flourished in the first half of 1977, the Oaks on Barlow Moor Road in Chorlton. Rob Gretton, who had known Ray Rossi, the Slaughter & the Dogs manager, from watching Man City and hanging out in Wythenshawe, and had been employed by the band as a roadie, took over looking after the group with Vinny Faal when Rossi went to prison for motoring offences. The back room at the Oaks had been used previously as a disco, but Gretton and Faal put on a Slaughter gig there, made some money and started booking more bands. The Drones, the Vibrators, Ed Banger & the Nosebleeds, Wayne County, Little Bob Story all played the Oaks during the first half of 1977. On 29 March 1977 Johnny Thunders and the Heartbreakers played to a crowd of 218 people, presumably including that great New York Dolls fan, Morrissey, who was then living less than a mile from the venue. Gretton, a soul boy who felt that punk had just the sort of excitement that was temporarily drifting away from black music, was the in-house DJ at the Oaks. Later he DJ-ed regularly at Rafters. In 1977 he became manager of the Panik. He co-produced their single 'It Won't Sell'. It didn't.

The Band on the Wall hosted John the Postman's live debut when he clambered out of the crowd of fans and on to the stage at a Buzzcocks gig there on 2 May 1977 and launched into a version of 'Louie Louie'. John recalls the sequence of events that led to his stage debut:

> Well, I was down the front, of course, and I think the Buzzcocks left the stage and the microphone was there and a little voice must have been calling 'This is your moment John'. I've no idea to this day why I sang 'Louie Louie', the ultimate garage anthem from the 60s. And why I did it a cappella and changed all the lyrics apart from the actual chorus I have no idea. I suppose it was my bid for immortality. One of those great bolts of inspiration. And I was drunk, of course. I never performed sober.

The Electric Circus was even less obviously a space for something to happen, surrounded by a housing estate, deep in Collyhurst, with a track record of hosting heavy metal gigs. Mick Middles, in his 1996 book on Factory Records, paints a vivid picture of nights spent trekking along inhospitable inner city streets, dodging aggressive local youths lurching at punks from the darkness of the surrounding streets, finally arriving at the crumbling venue, assailed by grimness at every turn. The insalubrious surroundings used to freak out some of the visiting dignitaries. Andrew Lauder (who, some dozen years later, signed the Stone Roses to his Silvertone label) was there in May 1977 looking to sign the Buzzcocks to United Artists. 'I remember I had made my mind up to sign them even before I had seen them. What I remember most is that after the gig I phoned a cab to take me back to my hotel, because I didn't like the thought of walking round Collyhurst at midnight.'

John the Postman practically lived at the Circus:

> It was very scuzzy, but that suited the times; there was a great atmosphere there and it wasn't a violent place. There was no trouble there, no need for bouncers. I only saw about two lots of trouble, one involving me, in fact. The Slaughter & the Dogs manager punched me because I flicked a Park Drive dimp at the band and it hit the drummer, although there were a lot worse things being thrown by other people. One of my mates broke a Newcastle Brown bottle over his head and he crumpled to the floor apparently, although I didn't see that because I was holding my black eye, staggering round and moaning. The only other thing I remember seeing was some people throwing beer over Pauline Murray from Penetration at a gig being filmed by Wilson. Generally there was very little violence at punk gigs. I remember fighting at a Distractions gig in Dumfries, but that was probably normal practice up there.

The local kids on the estate used to goad the punks on their way to and from the Electric Circus. Punks generally were a target on the streets, though the Postman steered clear: 'Not being into the fashion thing, I got away with it. But people I did know who dressed as bona fide punks did have a lot of trouble. Denise who lived in Rochdale used to get beaten up on the all-night bus on a Friday and Saturday going back from the Ranch.'

He remembers a definite antipathy towards dressing-up to go to punk gigs:

> When the Bromley contingent came up Chelsea were playing with the Buzzcocks in November 1976. I think Vicious was there, and Steve Severin, and they were like posing. There were a lot of mirrors at the Circus, along the sidewalls, and they were stood there combing their hair while the band were on which I thought was pathetic. Most of my friends had long hair and kept their long hair because they refused to get it cut, although I actually did.

When you see footage of punk gigs from those days, the audience aren't in a uniform punk style; there's always a wide cross-section of people, flares and long hairs. John the Postman acknowledges that the Manchester punk scene accommodated all sorts: 'Definitely. The nice thing about those days was that you didn't get many students at the gigs, either. Which was good; it did seem to be a grassroots, working-class thing.'

From subsequent accounts of punk, you could be forgiven for thinking that the 'punk look' was universal and compulsory. The punk clichés – swastika armbands, spiky hair, safety pins, bondage trousers – were less evident in Manchester than London. Certainly out went kipper ties, billowing flares and Oxford bags, but in Manchester punk attitudes and ideas took precedence over concern with wearing the right clothes. In Manchester, says C. P. Lee, nobody particularly cared: 'There was a slight concession to buying stuff from Oxfam. Kids up here didn't have the money to go and buy bondage trousers; some did, but on the whole you'd go and buy a second-hand suit, maybe rip it a bit or put safety pins in it or whatever, but there certainly wasn't that kind of fashion intensity.'

The fact that punk in Manchester wasn't so uniform was its great strength. What aided Manchester's creativity in the years after punk was that formulas in music and fashion were broken by the best bands, or even ignored. Some of the bands around in 1976 and 1977 played out punk clichés, often well and convincingly, occasionally not so – the Worst, say, or Ed Banger & the Nosebleeds (mad, comic, incredibly artless) and Slaughter & the Dogs – but it wasn't these Damned soundalikes that thrived in Manchester but aberrant, singular bands like the Fall and Joy Division.

The founding members of Joy Division – Ian Curtis, Bernard Sumner and Peter Hook – began rehearsing above the Black Swan public house, near Weaste Bus Depot, even before they'd found a drummer for the band. Punk gave them iconoclastic attitudes, self-belief and the inspiration to form a band. For Bernard, who'd grown up as a skinhead ('Where I lived you had to be one or you got beaten up basically', he says), and started his musical education listening to Motown, and then the Stones and Jimi Hendrix, the Sex Pistols were the catalyst for forming a group. Ian Curtis, meanwhile, was already steeped in the pre-punk tradition of rock's angry, disordered young men. Sumner remembers: 'Ian turned me on to a lot of things, he turned me on to Iggy Pop. I loved it straight away. I guess inspirationally it was the Sex Pistols, but musically it was Iggy; Iggy and the Stooges was my bread and butter throughout the Joy Division era.'

In Joy Division's early days, they were first known as the Stiff Kittens, but then changed their name to Warsaw for their debut gig at the Electric Circus on 29 May 1977, supporting the Buzzcocks on the night of Andrew Lauder's visit, together with Penetration, John Cooper Clarke and John the Postman. Less than a month later Warsaw were playing at Rafters. DJ-ing there that night was Rob Gretton. He thought Warsaw looked 'dead weird', but they made a deep impression; 'I just thought they were the best band I've ever seen.'

Also impressed was Paul Morley. Paul worked on Hillgate in a bookshop and lived on Hawthorn Grove, Stockport. Visitors to the house in Hawthorn Grove included Howard Devoto and Linder Mulvey, Vini Reilly and Pete Shelley. The Negatives rehearsed in the back room. They did a version of the *Coronation Street* theme. Eventually Manicured Noise took to rehearsing there. The house was a hive of activity, Paul's sister Carol recalls: 'Once Paul got me and my sister to stick covers on bootleg Pistols and Clash LPs. In London they were selling for £5 without a cover and £9 with a cover.'

Morley took a well-trodden route to writing for *New Musical Express* when he attracted their attention through his own fanzine, *Girl Trouble* (4p a copy). Carol remembers what happened after a mention of *Girl Trouble* in *NME*: 'We were inundated with letters. I can remember Paul getting a telegram from *NME* offering him some work. He still had long hair then and when he came back from London he said to my mum, "I've got to get my hair cut".'

His first major *NME* assignment was a double page spread in the 30 July issue, trailed on the cover as 'MANCHESTER; THE TRUTH BEHIND THE BIZARRE CULT SWEEPING A CITY'S YOUTH'. In the piece Morley rounds up the story of post-punk Manchester. How much the groups minded sharing space with each other is debatable; despite his assertion that there's an 'undeniable sense of communal comradeship and involvement', the scene was riven by tensions, notably between Slaughter & the Dogs and the Buzzcocks. Between Slaughter & the Dogs and everybody else, in fact.

Slaughter & the Dogs never had much credibility with the tastemakers in Manchester during the punk era. The purists resented them for jumping on the punk bandwagon, and Buzzcocks fans, in particular, failed to mix well with the rough-hewn Wythenshawe types who followed Slaughter round the circuit. Furthermore, their onstage antics were far from cool, as Morley pointed out in the *NME*: 'Lead singer Wayne Barrett covers himself in talcum powder, which once was a neat idea, and guitarist Mike Rossi, who knows all the right moves, mercilessly crams them down the audience's throat.'

Slaughter still have their supporters, including, predictably, the man who put out their early records, Tosh Ryan: 'Bands like Slaughter & the Dogs, who were working-class kids from Wythenshawe, were the true embodiment of what punk was about; they were raucous, challenging and shouting at the Establishment', he claims. More support comes in Stewart Home's book on punk, *Cranked Up Really High*, which takes its title from a Slaughter & the Dogs single. His book celebrates the 'super-dumb sleaze-bag thud' of punk. For him (unlike the more cerebral Greil Marcus and Jon Savage), punk was a raucous, disposable, novelty genre. Using this as his criterion he asserts that Slaughter & the Dogs have a 'cult status as one of the greatest punk bands of all time. In this particular genre tackiness is greatness, and the Dogs are as cheap and nasty as they come ... Mike Rossi is a complete loser and this makes him a punk STAR.'

As Morley's sweep gets broader, he praises the Fall, namechecks Warsaw and mentions Ed Banger & the Nosebleeds – once 'directionless yobs' but now managed by Vinny Faal from the Oaks – and even Sad Café, Gags, Bicycle Thieves, Harpoon, Spider Mike King, and the folky Tom Yates – non-new wavers the lot of them – get a cursory mention. Morley also has time to mention John the Postman; 'A fan unable to merely spectate, his famous dance is a test for any visiting group; if the band's winning, he'll start twitching until eventually he'll be in full flight, playing imaginary guitar on his beer bottle, sweat pouring pints. He's also prone to climb on stage after a group's performance and deliver a solid a cappella version of "Louie Louie". Local rumour has it he wrote it.'

John was a postman from 1972 to 1980. It was the perfect job for helping him fit in gig-going, clambering onstage, drinking and recording: 'It was just the easiest job in the world. I was in the sorting office, and I'd been there so long that when I was on the late shift I could get out an hour or an hour and a half early; so even though it was an official 10 o'clock finish I'd be out by 8.30 or 9 o'clock, which gave me time to get to the pub, go to the gig, and then not have to worry about getting up in the morning.'

The group John grew to love most were the Fall. Within a year of Smith seeing the Sex Pistols, the Fall began gigging. In the summer of 1977 they played two gigs at the Squat. John the Postman first saw the Fall at their Squat gigs, including a Stuff the Jubilee special on 3 June with the Drones, Warsaw, the Worst and the Negatives (including Paul Morley on guitar, Dave Bentley on vocals, Kevin Cummins on drums; Richard Boon joined later, on saxophone). John couldn't keep off the stage that night, singing 'Louie Louie' with Warsaw (with Ian Curtis on backing vocals), after first appearing with the Negatives; 'I came straight off the street, out of the pub, and walked straight on to the stage. I still had my raincoat on.'

Meanwhile, the closure of the Electric Circus on the advice of fire safety inspectors was marked by two special nights at the beginning of October. One of the stars of the second night was John Cooper Clarke. A citizen of Salford and one-time member of the Vendettas, he was a stand-up poet who had begun appearing on punk bills in Manchester. His deadpan, deadbeat poetry, delivered at breakneck speed in a nasal Salford whine, heavy with rhymes and chock full of character, shared with punk a rough-cut urban harshness, but Clarke often found himself battling with punk audiences, or any kind of audience. Playing the Glasgow Apollo supporting Be Bop Deluxe he felt the loathing of 3,800 people. Onstage he was solo, bouncing on the spot, chewing gum, but on record for Rabid, and later CBS, he was backed by local session men and produced and managed (or perhaps 'supervised' is a better word) by Martin Hannett.

Very thin, with his drainpipe legs, all black be-suited garb, massive hair and dark shades, Clarke cut a curious figure when seen scuttling across Albert Square making for Cross Street. He seemed out of place most places though, especially among the pantheon of post-punk icons; up close to the everyday, the detail of dismal daily life, yet with his head mangled like a Martian with a bad education. He was at home at the Electric Circus though, with poems like 'Beasley Street' and 'Psycle Sluts', namechecking the Ritz, finding creative ways to communicate hate in 'Twat'. He pinned down life in the local environment, his characters drugged, their culture cut-price. A John Cooper Clarke set was always teetering between the tragic and the comic (it all depends where you're standing, of course). If Joy Division walked the shadowed side of the street, John Cooper Clarke provided the crazy paving. According to Michael Bracewell, 'Beasley Street itself, though recognisably northern, could be anywhere English and urban.'

Top of the bill on the last night of the Electric Circus were the Buzzcocks. At the end of their set John the Postman made his customary move onstage, greeted by a warm introduction from Pete Shelley:

'That's it from us, but the favourite of all Manchester, the one guy who never appears on the bill but is always there – John the Postman.' The album released by Virgin Records recording the highlights of the two days of gigs, *Short Circuit; Live at the Electric Circus*, includes 'Persecution Complex' by the Drones, reckoned by their aficionados to be their finest recorded work, and the Fall's first vinyl outing. John the Postman's performance is lost to history though; Shelley's intro remains, but the Postman's faded out just as he's about to begin.

For Warsaw 1977 and the early part of 1978 saw them finding a sound, stumbling towards greatness. Rob Gretton's interest, whetted by seeing them at Rafters, crystallised into full-scale management of the band by May 1978. By this time they'd changed their name to Joy Division (for a gig at Pips in January 1978), and made forays into the studio to do various versions of their songs. Undeterred by unsuccessful attempts to interest major labels, they took the DIY route, releasing five thousand copies of 'An Ideal For Living' EP made up of four songs recorded at Pennine Sound Studio in December 1977. Pictured on the fold-out sleeve, Peter Hook has a moustache, Bernard Albrecht has a tie, Stephen Morris a V-neck pullover, and Ian Curtis a raincoat.

Joy Division's fan base locally built steadily through 1978 – in June they played on the fourth Friday of the newly opened weekly Factory night at the Russell Club in Hulme – but by the end of the year they were yet to make a breakthrough nationally. In November 1978 the group made their debut London appearance; few more than thirty people paid 60p each at the Hope & Anchor in Islington. But by this time the Factory had become Manchester's key venue, and the fledgling Factory label took on Joy Division. Late in 1978 a Factory Sampler was released (a double 7"), and Joy Division provided two tracks, 'Digital' and 'Glass', both produced by Martin Zero. All five thousand copies of the sampler had been sold by February 1979, giving Factory an £87 profit, and getting Joy Division noticed.

1979 was Joy Division's year, the year they established themselves with the two most important champions of alternative music in the country at the time: *NME* and John Peel. A Peel session was recorded in January. In April 1979 they recorded their first LP for Factory at Strawberry Studios in Stockport. And by May they had won over another *NME* reporter, the previously sceptical Ian Wood: 'Feeble and pretentious in the past incarnation, Joy Division now sketch withering grey abstractions of industrial malaise ... Unfortunately, as

124

anyone who has ever lived in the low-rent squalor of a Northern industrial city will know, their vision is deadly accurate.'

Mike Pickering had known Rob Gretton in the pre-punk era, but had lost contact with him until he started going out to gigs at Rafters and the Factory. Pickering was engrossed in music at every level; he formed an alliance with a Manchester band called Fireplace who were in the Manchester Music Collective, and he used to get up onstage with them, manage them and drive them. In *Modern Drugs* Pickering reviewed Joy Division at the Factory, and he came back into contact with Rob and started hanging around Joy Division:

> There were a group of bands around in 1978, 1979, like the Pop Group – I really loved the Pop Group. They were intelligent. Clock DVA, Throbbing Gristle, Cabaret Voltaire; they were slightly arty, weren't they? There was a time with the Factory stuff when the covers were better than the vinyl a lot of the time. But I don't think Joy Division were arty in themselves. They just did what they wanted to do. I thought Joy Division were brilliant. If you liked them you became disciples almost. They were wonderful.

By June 1979 and the release of *Unknown Pleasures* Joy Division were carrying quite a burden, articulating anxiety and anger, defining Manchester, journeying well beyond the speeded-up rock riffs of punk, and with Ian Curtis, it seemed, in perpetual, furious panic, drunk with teen spirit. His onstage dancing has been likened to Iggy Pop's, but whereas Iggy has always bounced off the audience, taken a cue from them, goaded them, Ian Curtis's was a very solitary dance; it was like he was in his own world, and he couldn't touch us. It was inarticulacy made physical. And very scary.

The ambitions of Joy Division to reach beyond punk are well in evidence on the LP, from the slowed-down sound to the lyrics desperate to reach further into emotional heartlands than anything the largely terrace chant mentality of most punk had managed. I can remember hearing 'Transmission' and 'She's Lost Control' for the first time; it was the newness written into the very texture of the music that stunned, the spectacular uniqueness. Through the first album there was an unsettling battle between the controlling drums, the rippling bass, the downplayed monotone vocals, and the flailing guitars straining in and out of the mix. It was like a soundtrack to the aftermath of some urban disaster; which was presumably why it was connected so strongly with life in Manchester, England.

By August 1979 Paul Rambali in *NME* was proclaiming that Joy Division's was 'easily the strongest new music to come out of this country this year'. That month they played at Futurama One at Queen's Hall, Leeds, an event billed as 'the World's First Science Fiction Music Festival' and put together by John Keenan, which also featured A Certain Ratio and Cabaret Voltaire. The annual Futurama festivals in Leeds were landmarks in this era. In London the self-declared purists had cordoned off punk by the end of 1976, but the route post-punk took elsewhere in England, via milestones like Futurama and various Rock Against Racism festivals, took the music on a great creative journey. There were dead ends, but new possibilities as well. On the one hand, from Rabid Records came the throwaway everyday humour of Jilted John's 'Gordon is a Moron' and, on the other, punk was now embracing something intense, cold, as a sound emerged from a DIY Sturm-und-Drang gang, with Joy Division pre-eminent, alongside PIL, the Pop Group, Wire, Cabaret Voltaire, Subway Sect.

Some of the new groups in this era – the Cure, say – wore their intensity like a badge of authenticity, but for Ian Curtis it seemed like something he couldn't help and didn't court. Near the end of Joy Division – which, put more brutally, means near the end of his life – the fact that Ian Curtis was ill became clear onstage. He was on medication, his epilepsy was persistent, and the tangled threads of his private life were tightening around him. He was unable to perform at a gig in Bury in April 1980 and Alan Hempsall of Crispy Ambulance took over vocals from him on some of the songs, provoking a riot in the hall. Later in the month the band cancelled a series of gigs. I saw Joy Division at their last ever gig, at High Hall in Birmingham University in the first week of May. Ian Curtis gave a stumbling performance, and the band themselves appeared confused. At the time I thought the support act, A Certain Ratio, had played Joy Division off stage. On 18 May 1980, in the darkest hour just before dawn, Ian Curtis killed himself.

A Joy Division single, 'Love Will Tear Us Apart', had just been released, with Ian Curtis's unsettling vocal delivery sounding halfway between a Sinatra croon and an uptight Jim Morrison drawl. After the tragedy and the way these things work, of course, the sales curve steepened and the single reached the Top Ten in the national charts.

An album followed, *Closer*, a less uniform collection than *Unknown Pleasures*, juxtaposing a tense, clean-edged sound (on 'Isolation' and 'A Means To An End'), with a more frail and funereal sound ('The Eternal'). A further single, including both 'She's Lost Control' and 'Atmosphere', was released in September 1980. 'She's Lost Control' conjures a nightmare, the synthesised beats like a heart monitor on overdrive, the words like some traumatic episode snatched from the tranquilliser epidemic in Hulme. Joy Division and the clouds of myth and mystery swirling around them would live on.

The death of Ian Curtis shocked the city, but it didn't kill off creativity. Out on the fringes all kinds of Manc malcontents, unleashed by punk, were already making music, doing gigs, putting out records; the Passage, Durutti Column, the Distractions, Ludus. Ludus were founded by Linder Mulvey, an art student at the Poly whose strong female vision provided a vivid counterpoint to the perceptions of the music-making males who dominated the scene. She formed Ludus with Arthur Cadmon from Manicured Noise and Philip 'Toby' Tolman (an ex-drummer of the Nosebleeds), and the band shared rehearsal space with the Buzzcocks. As a designer she worked on material for the Buzzcocks, although her choice of title for their first LP – 'A Housewife Choosing Her Own Juices In A Different Kitchen' – was rejected in favour of the slightly less intriguing *Another Music In A Different Kitchen*. Linder also made mad jewellery, including a piece which was given a Factory Records catalogue number (FAC 8; a 'Menstrual Egg Timer'). Her artwork on the first Magazine LP is brilliant; disturbed, disembodied androgenes floating in a swirl of charcoal. Like Goya with lipstick.

In 1978, just as the Buzzcocks metamorphosed into a great pop singles band, with hits 'What Do I Get?' and 'Ever Fallen In Love (With Someone You Shouldn't've)', John the Postman got bored of them: 'The Buzzcocks didn't seem to be progressing at all, and I'd seen it all, unlike the Fall who were always different. I've seen the Fall about 125 times, about 90 of those times between about 1977 and 1981. Most of them were an occasion; they were always special, I thought.'

By 1978 the Fall were prominent among Manchester's post-punk groups, but there was no cosy music scene cronyism for Mark E. Smith, no one-dimensional views. The man had his own vision, the band their own sound. Smith admits disdain for the music around him: 'Manchester bands were like the Hollies, Freddie & the

Dreamers, 10cc, the Buzzcocks – it's all in the same fucking vein. All nice clean-cut lads singing about love. We deliberately went out of our way to avoid that.'

The backbone to the Fall has always been a fantastic rhythm section (line-ups often boasting two drummers), and Smith's pitiless lyrics, delivered with a distorted sneer, a sardonic rap. They'd followed up their contribution to the Electric Circus compilation with an EP featuring 'Bingo Master's Breakout' and 'Repetition'. In two early songs, 'Rowche Rumble' and 'Psycho Mafia', Smith slammed multinational pharmaceutical giants like Hoffman La Roche which escaped the censure reserved for the small-time dealer (while 'No Xmas For John Quays' portrayed the life of a junkie). The early releases introduced us to fantastic tales, masked biographies and vituperative rants against the music scene. 'We are the Fall, the white crap that talks back!' announced Smith on the first LP. He has subsequently stalked his wonderful and frightening world, with an occasional nod to fellow mavericks ('I like anybody who goes against the grain of mediocre mass thought', he once told me), becoming one of the most important figures in British rock music in the last twenty-five years.

It's an unmatched body of work; from the twisted tales and scratchy sound of the early *Live at the Witch Trials* LP onwards, there were some prime Fall years, right through and beyond *Bend Sinister* – with 'US 80s 90s' (built on a beatbox) and the yuppie-crushing 'Shoulder Pads' – via the bile of anger that is 'The Classical', the *Slates* and *Grotesque* purple patch (1980/81), and the un-put-downable put downs of 'Oh Brother'. Smith teases and tortures the English language until it tells the truth. This is the Fall country recognised by the trekking Dutch boys, the Manchester on the edge of industrial estates, sliced by rundown shopping streets, with beer monsters running amok, students trailing bad dope, dole-ites outside Kwik Save, bad TV, crap buses, crap bands, and those paranoid households in which mum, dad and the kids don't speak.

'Manchester was a very boring place to be', Morley had lamented back in 1976. Ten years later, a Factory-led week of events celebrating the decade since punk – the Festival of the Tenth Summer – culminated in a gig at G-Mex which included the Fall, New Order and the Smiths. Punk had triggered a wave of creativity in Manchester, England. The city had become synonymous not only with successful pop groups but questioning, original groups, groups fronted by larger-than-life characters playing cutting-edge music. Groups from

Manchester had what all groups have cherished: street credibility. Individuals were inspired, and the city was energised; of its own accord, uncontrolled. Paul Morley, meanwhile, had moved to London.

New Order headlined the G-Mex event. Their progress in the wake of Joy Division had been a phenomenal display of determination and genius. It had always been said that the Joy Division song 'Digital' (one of the first songs they released on record, and the last song they ever played live) earned its title on the whim of their producer, Martin Hannett, who had begun experimenting with digital technology at the end of the 1970s. It was therefore fitting that of all the groups formed in the wake of punk, New Order were the ones to move forward, despite the weight of the past, into music-making in the digital era. The New Order sound was based on drum machines, sequencers, computer-triggered sounds, synthesisers; it was a long way from power chord punk thrash.

In 1948 the digital era was inaugurated when Tom Kilburn and Freddie Williams at the University of Manchester ran the first program on the world's first stored program computer, or 'the Baby' as it became known. In the mid 1970s the German group Kraftwerk were pioneering the use of computers in music-making. The creative baton was passed back to Manchester when New Order so successfully meshed Kraftwerk's pure minimalist computer coldness, New York's dancefloor rhythms and confused Mancunian passion. The results, like the single 'Blue Monday', were astounding. Credible and commercial (a combination seldom found in pop music, but less rare in Manchester bands, M-People and Oasis among them), 'Blue Monday' spent thirty-four weeks in the charts in 1983 and became the biggest selling 12" single ever.

Shunning the usual things successful pop groups spend their earnings on (houses in the country, trout farms, David Hockney screenprints), New Order ploughed back the proceeds from their early singles into developing and maintaining the Haçienda club, a joint venture between the band and their Factory Records label which opened in May 1982. In the first years of the club a good deal of their royalties found their way to supporting the club's high losses. By 1986 the club had switched its emphasis from being a live venue to being a dance club. The gig at G-Mex marked the launch of a new Saturday night, and I was one of the DJs. At G-Mex I played 'Stoned Out Of My Mind' by the Chi-lites and then struggled round the corner to the Haçienda with my records in a cardboard box and my £40 wage in my pocket. It was the beginnings of a new era.

Meanwhile, the Smiths were at their peak in 1986. Morrissey and Marr came together after various escapades in other bands. Morrissey had friends from the punk world, had sung with the Nosebleeds and sent fan letters about the Buzzcocks to *NME*. Music was his first love. He discovered the New York Dolls while watching *The Old Grey Whistle Test* in November 1973, aged thirteen ('It was my first real emotional experience . . . The Dolls gave me a sense of unique-ness, as if they were my own personal discovery'). The rest of his life, he always claims, was very dull. His habit of communicating from his bedroom by letter he duplicated later in his music; his songs have often felt like epistles from one loner to another.

He had his music, and his imaginary life, a life peopled by James Dean, the New York Dolls and the works of Oscar Wilde. He bought his first record from the Paul Marsh record shop on Alexandra Road; 'Come And Stay With Me' by Marianne Faithfull. 'Rubber Ring', an elegy for a music-filled past, ends the Smiths' LP, *The World Won't Listen*. His was an adolescence in which music played a massive part, and later he expected his disciples to take music as seriously as him. Music means everything, he explained to me before he'd ever had a hit record: 'In the history of my life the high points were always buying particular records and hearing records and being immersed in them, and really believing that these people understood how I felt about certain situations. So that's the richness of records.'

If punk was about affirming an oppositional stance, and a reaction against polished pop and dreary industry cash-ins, then in these battles against the mainstream there's been nobody more animated than Morrissey. From the beginning of the Smiths' career, Morrissey's punk roots showed through, roots that went right back to 1976. Obviously upset at the bad press the paper was giving the Sex Pistols, Morrissey wrote to the *Manchester Evening News*. Many of his letters to the music press have been documented by his biographers; but this one escaped even the assiduous Johnny Rogan. Morrissey writes: 'The Pistols are speaking for the youth of today. Like it or not, they project rock'n'roll integrity, as do similar rock artists like the New York Dolls and Patti Smith – names which are hardly known to the media because the fawning masses choose to don their rose-coloured spectacles and ignore these artists for fear that they might disturb the routine of the day-to-day lives.'

The ideas he expressed in his letter about the Pistols were still being carried around by Morrissey ten years later, manifested in his disdain for slick pop, his opposition to videos, his battles with Radio One, his stands against disco music, his sloganeering, his suspicion that the media ignores outlaw ideas, that anything unsettling is shunned by the fawning masses, and, most importantly, his sense of the Smiths as real and grounded, not manufactured or plastic. 'This is real music played by real people', Morrissey proclaimed.

When I first met him, early in 1984, we went for a drink at the Grant's Arms. He told me how important a source for him his past was, a 'monotonous teenage existence' he called it, years of depression which he was happy to draw on in his songs. The world of school, job and domestic trivia seemed to make him shudder. But that time, and during most of our subsequent meetings, he was funny, clever, gossipy. Talking to Morrissey was always more than a trip down misery lane.

When the Smiths arrived in 1983, it was clear they had no allies among posturing Goth bands, the New Romantics, machine freaks like the Human League and New Order, or wine bar soundtrackers Sade, or Wham!, or anybody near the charts. Schooled in the tribalism of punk, Morrissey's self-belief bordered on arrogance, and his intense personality recoiled from compromise. He's never dealt in half measures, courting as much animosity as adulation. Morrissey described the Smiths as 'an absolutely closed society'; four boys against the world, speaking directly and emotionally, soul to soul, to his fans ('the private and extraordinary club', as he called them).

Morrissey's nonconformist attitudes and his willingness to articulate melancholia won over a huge constituency of music listeners. The music made a very personal appeal, something that reflected grimness, violence, loneliness. All this was communicated with a welcoming, quirky lightness of touch which Johnny Marr brought to the group. Often in pop music there is talk of 'manufactured' groups, but Morrissey and Marr were an unmanufacturable creative combination, a volatile alliance; like an early version of Liam and Noel.

With early singles like 'Hand in Glove' and 'This Charming Man', the Smiths made their mark in 1984 with a rush, a push and a shove. The *Meat Is Murder* LP of 1985 explored cruelty with a troubled eye – ranging from the dark excitement of 'Rusholme Ruffians' to the domestic violence of 'Barbarism Begins At Home' – and just prior to G-Mex they released *The Queen Is Dead*, which unleashed a more furious rock style from Johnny Marr and included one of the finest songs of the Smiths' career, 'There Is A Light That Never Goes Out'.

There was a certainly a good dose of cold reality in the kinds of subject pursued by Morrissey's lyrics; the language and tone were conspicuously very different to the mainstream. Unrequited love was the key thread in many of the songs, and a deeply melancholic longing. 'That Joke Isn't Funny Anymore', for instance, reveals his disdain for the plastic smiles of pop, yet Smiths songs were playful, coy and wry too. Though rooted in punk, Morrissey expressed anarchy more obliquely than a rabble rouser would; the one-liners were half-tame, half-Wilde.

Manchester bands were making a crucial contribution; in the decade after punk Ian Curtis, Mark E. Smith and Morrissey transformed the language of pop music. They also encapsulated new ways of describing Manchester, England. Morrissey was at home among the old black and white films of the early 1960s, *A Taste of Honey* especially. He namechecked Whalley Range and Rusholme. You sensed him as a character in the city, a modern Baudelaire with dreams of escape and paranoid nightmares. His was the loner's view of the city; Morrissey consciously rejected the street-corner gang in favour of more introspectiveness.

Misery was his muse but also seemed to suffocate him. He articulated discontent but couldn't seem to break free of it. If Mark E. Smith gives the impression that he meets the world with sleeves rolled up and a tongue-lashing on the way, Morrissey appears to run home and hide. His career is a progressive withdrawal, personal and cultural. When the Smiths split up, his solo work was blighted by the narrow, insular Englishness he advocated – anti-American and anti-change – and a further retreat into myth, to the past, to music.

According to Tim Chambers, sometime historian of Manchester's punk years, 'Punk was a passion borne out of imbalance, insecurity, the longing for something more'. If you were a dissatisfied outsider in Manchester before 1976 you grew up wanting to get away or get wasted; after punk, you dreamt of being a rock & roll star. Punk was democratic, like that; anyone could form a band. Noel Gallagher had those dreams and look where it got him; on *Top of the Pops*, deep in our hearts, and onstage at the Brit Awards slagging off corporate bullshit in second-hand punk style.

Punk changed Manchester, and established individuals key to the story since punk. What Anthony H. Wilson understood from the Sex Pistols was that the quickest route from street buzz to commercial success is via sensational media coverage. During the Madchester era he justified stoking stories of Happy Mondays' bad behaviour – the cussing, shagging, drugging – by the size of the headlines. It didn't matter if the coverage made the band look thick or obscured the music; 'It's all good copy', he would tell me.

Punk made Manchester a credible pop city, bred nonconformist attitudes, nurtured indie labels and gave us a DIY tradition, but it was the Madchester era in the late 1980s that opened everything up, bequeathed us a city of endless possibilities. Music in Manchester came out of the student unions, basement bars and rented pub back rooms and into a wider world, a less white world. Whereas punk had been a revolution within the confines of rock, part of a civil war fought with drums and guitars, rave culture grew out of clubs, dance-floors and discotheques.

In their response to disco music, the old wave and the new wave were connected even as much as they tried to diverge; wherever you stood in the rock wars, disco was still the enemy. In this, punk was no different to prog rock, or any other kind of rock for that matter. Discussing punk and disco, Jon Savage is bleakly adamant: 'There was no crossover.'

Madchester would change Manchester again, spiking the city with something stronger than punk: acid house. All kinds of precon-ceptions nurtured by the punk generation were turned on their heads. By then the principles that had underpinned the punk revolution had turned into narrow-mindedness and inflexibility. Punk proclaimed anarchy, but practised conservatism; cultural pluralism was denied, and soul music, Motown and rhythm & blues dismissed. The spirit of the rave revolution couldn't have been more different to punk; the exclusivity of the punk sneer was replaced by the embrace of the smiley face. The speed-induced aggression and paranoid edge of punk were supplanted by rave's soft-centred sociability, inspired by ecstasy, of course, the 'hug drug'. Enter the twenty-four hour party people, exit Morrissey.

The rise of disco music put intolerable strains on Manchester's punk era old guard. I remember DJ-ing one Saturday at the Haçienda sometime in 1986 when Morrissey came and settled himself down in the DJ box. I was all fired up; I pulled out that classic electro track 'Hip Hop, Be Bop (Don't Stop)' by Man Parrish. 'Remember this?'

I yelled to him. He didn't of course, and he didn't seem impressed. I didn't see why he wouldn't like the records I played; after all, I liked the songs he sang. Imagine if he'd gone round to Johnny Marr's the next day and said, 'I heard this great record last night, all drum machines, no guitars, no lyrics. Sack this gloomy rockabilly-tinged balladeering, we're going hip hop.' It was not to be.

Individuals moved on as the new era evolved. C. P. Lee remembers the Albertos toured until 1981, then claims, 'I don't know what I did after that; it's all a mystery!', and now writes and lectures at Salford University. Mark E. Smith and the Fall survived, according to Smith, through 'bloody-mindedness', and, acknowledged as an influence by the likes of Sonic Youth (and unacknowledged by scores more), the Fall have gone on to record an album a year for labels as diverse as the punk indie Step Forward (in the band's early days), to the multinational Phonogram (a relationship about which Smith remains bitter). One highlight was 1995's *Cerebral Caustic*, as witty, beaty and unique as any Fall LP, with raw bubblegum like 'Feeling Numb', the unhinged, improvised 'North West Fashion Show' and a cover of Frank Zappa's 'I'm Not Satisfied'. Smith has fallen in and out of favour and in and out with friends, but presently he stands alone, his work uncontaminated by showbiz.

Fans have become bands, consumers have become producers; that's always the Manchester way. In 1980 Mike Pickering moved to Rotterdam and became involved in putting on gigs in an old water-works there (he invited Joy Division over, and the Cure, Captain Beefheart and the Human League, as well as a Factory Records night featuring A Certain Ratio, Durutti Column and Section 25). By the middle of the 1980s even Mark E. Smith had started a record label. It was the same with Paul Morley and Rob Gretton. Gretton guided New Order, pursued a crucial role at Factory Records, was the prime mover behind the opening of the Haçienda, and remained crucial to the story until his death in May 1999. Paul Morley took a job at ZTT and directed the career of Frankie Goes To Hollywood.

Paul Morley, the ex-Stockport boy, and Holly Johnson – gay Scouser, man on the Eric's scene, former bass player in Big In Japan – was a bizarre partnership, but an alliance had grown between Manchester and Liverpool during the punk years. Roger Eagle, who had started out in clubland in Manchester by making his mark at the Magic Village, booked the bands at Eric's. A Manc–Liverpool collaboration took place in August 1979 when Factory and the Liverpool label Zoo (founded by Bill Drummond, later of KLF) organised an open-air festival in Leigh (commercially it was a disaster, but their hearts were in the right place). 'There was a lot of cross-fertilisation between the Liverpool and Manchester scenes', remembers John the Postman. There was none of the bitterness of the beat generation, and rivalry never degenerated into enmity. There was no aggro; 'No way. People into music are above that sort of crap; we'll leave that to football hooligans. I knew Julian Cope, Wylie, Ian McCulloch. They used to go and see the Fall; they were big Fall fans.'

Although the Festival of the Tenth Summer underlined the importance of Factory Records in the story and the city, there were other centres of activity, many of them, in fact, powered by a reaction against Factory, the big players, the media darlings. Both the Fall and the Smiths had consciously sidestepped their influence, for example, as had other groups making waves in the city in the mid 1980s, including the Bodines (one of Alan McGee's first signings to Creation Records; his love affair with Manchester would culminate in world domination with Oasis) and Big Flame. Big Flame were very much a product of their time; launched in an era of confrontational politics their songs were as uncompromising as barbed wire, three minutes of shrieking energy, unholy explosions fired at the monetarist, materialist Reagan–Thatcherite world.

By 1986 Factory had helped launch a younger generation of Manchester bands; James (who had subsequently signed to Sire Records), the Railway Children (who were also to decamp to a major), and Cath Carroll and her group Miaow. Cath Carroll had been a key element in the fanzine *City Fun* from 1980 onwards, with Liz Naylor. Years later, when Bob Dickinson asked Liz what motivated herself and Cath, she replied: 'I think it was our strange inner life. We had a world of our own really. You've got to remember Cath had this dreary upbringing in Romiley and a fascination with Mud and Frankie Valli, and I was stuck in Gee Cross, and we met each other at sixteen and we were each other's ticket to freedom.'

City Fun was a priceless publication in the first couple of years of the 1980s. Liz went on to work as a press officer in London, and played a notable (though underpaid) part in the rise of Sonic Youth and the Blast First label, and worked with the Sugarcubes and the Shamen. She also helped nurture the Riot Grrl bands Huggy Bear and Sister George. Miaow never broke out of the ghetto of the indie charts, and Cath Carroll went on to generate a huge bill for Factory as a solo artist. Her press photos were done by Robert Mapplethorpe. She's that kind of a gal.

Threads of today's Manchester wind back over the decades since punk. Mark Radcliffe secured a slot on Piccadilly Radio and named his *Transmission* programme after the Joy Division song. I remember listening to him one rainy Saturday evening in May 1983 just an hour after Manchester City were relegated. His playlist – the Blue Orchids, 'Flight' and 'Ceremony' – seemed to match the melancholic mood of the moment. By the end of the 1990s, Radcliffe was at Radio One, broadcasting to millions of listeners from Manchester, with his co-host Marc Riley, the Fall's guitarist from 1978 to 1982.

As part of the Tenth Summer celebrations in 1986 there was a fashion show at the Haçienda. I was DJ-ing on the night and given the job of sorting the music out. The show ended with a presentation by a young design shop in Back Pool Fold, Geese Clothing. Steve from Geese chose Joy Division's 'Atmosphere'. Jeff Noon helped me get all the records together and among those he insisted we had to use was 'Repetition' by the Fall. It lasted five minutes, Noon reasoned; long enough to get another dozen models on and off the stage.

Characters from these years have a hundred stories to tell. Jeff Noon had already been a published artist; one of his pieces appeared on the back of a Blue Orchids LP. After the Tenth Summer I next caught up with Jeff in 1995 on the publication of his second novel, *Pollen*. The sometime manager of Slaughter & the Dogs and Gretton's collaborator at the Oaks, Vinny Faal, went on to work in the fly-poster business, bred greyhounds and then became Manchester City Council's official dog catcher. Alan Hempsall ran a bar in Chorlton for a while until an armed robbery at the end of 1995. The Buzzcocks broke up and then re-formed. Mike Joyce from the Smiths took up drumming with them, and then left to work with Pete Wylie, doyen of the Liverpool scene and one of the original Eric's faces.

And so it goes on. Manchester became a city of high hopes and DIY determination, of record labels, record shops, fanzine writers. And musicians, of course, and rehearsal rooms, DJs and venues. People getting turned on. Bands making a noise. Music filling the air. Paul Morley described John the Postman as a fan unable to merely spectate. That's the story of all our lives.

PART **TWO**

CHAPTER 6

Playing to the Disco Crowd:

the Roots of the Rave Revolution

Every Saturday thirty thousand people are out on the town and out of their heads, the twenty-first-century versions of mad-for-it Mancunians, more drunk than Dronke, as sleepless as Sweeney; descendants of Victorian mill-hands stumbling down Oxford Street and audiences in Ancoats music halls; shadowy reminders of the scuttlers on turn-of-the-century street corners and the Vimto-swilling Cagneys and flighty Greta Garbos on the monkey run; children of the 60s set, the well-shaved Plaza regulars, and the twenty-four hour party people at the Twisted Wheel; the latest generation to trip down history-laden streets, painting the town red, missing the last bus home.

Manchester is the clubbing capital of England, the city with a renowned nightlife and dozens of important bands. Manchester is the city with the most highly developed music consciousness in the world, and sometimes you imagine you can reach out and touch it, a palpable buzz of a nightlife culture that's evolving, absorbing. Thread your way through Castlefield on a sunny summer Friday evening from Atlas past Nowhere, down to Quay Bar, or through Duke's to Barca and Jackson's Wharf; six bars and something like seven thousand people out on the bridges, the courtyards, the terraces, the cobbles. Take a trip down Canal Street, and marvel at the queues outside Praguefive, Manto, Metz. Turn the corner to Berlin or cross Piccadilly to the Roadhouse or Dry Bar. Then duck along Deansgate to Bar Coast, or South late on, drive back along Whitworth Street; on Oxford Street and Oldham Street clubs and bars are putting the 'sold out' signs up.

In Manchester the city's nightlife culture matters, and not just to the queues of club regulars – although it seems like life and death to a lot of them – or the DJs, the songwriters, the music moguls and nightclub owners. It matters because it's one of Manchester's key cultures, something living and thriving, something made in Manchester and the envy of the world. Nightlife also matters to the city in more prosaic ways; as a generator of jobs, for instance. The Haçienda, at its height, employed something like forty people on a Saturday night: cloakroom staff, DJs, pot collectors and bar staff, and doormen, and someone to put fluid in the smoke machine. Some academic will no doubt be researching this as I write, but for every person directly employed in running clubs and bars there must be four or five jobs in some way reliant on the scene, from taxi drivers to club wear designers.

The boom in the night-time economy since the rave revolution of 1988 has been responsible for rejuvenating previously bleak areas of Manchester; the Haçienda brought life to a dead end of Whitworth Street, Sankey's Soap from 1994 onwards was the first sign of new life in Ancoats, and Barca and Duke's 92 in Castlefield, the Boardwalk and Atlas in Knott Mill, and Dry in the Northern Quarter all moved into rundown areas and kickstarted the long process back to prosperity. From 1988 onwards Manchester's burgeoning clubland has brought cultural and economic regeneration to the city. Documented all over the world, Manchester's pop music and club culture has become a tourist attraction, as well as a source of re-employment, cultural expression, economic regeneration and international profile.

Every Saturday the sense of an event hangs over the city. It's not tidy, and only a certain kind of tourist will be impressed. Brent Hansen, President of MTV Europe, came to one of my nights at the Boardwalk once, and couldn't get in; there was a huge queue, jostling at the door, capacity and security problems. Nobody would listen to his pleas. He was left in the street outside. I got home at 4am and he'd left a message on my ansaphone: 'I tried to get in the Boardwalk tonight and it was chaos. I can assure you I won't be there again', he said. I was amazed. It was like that every week; living, breathing pandemonium.

Going out has a long history in Manchester, and a central place in the story of urban popular culture. Manchester's now well-established and unique night-time culture didn't begin with the rave revolution. It can be traced further back than that original moment when someone dropped an E at the Haçienda one Friday in February 1988 as 'Strings Of Life' resounded through the speakers. I remember telling a reporter from a Sunday paper that the explosion of 1989 and 1990 – the so-called 'Madchester' era – was inevitable. It had been inevitable since 1986, I thought. In retrospect 1982 might have been a more accurate start date; when New Order visited the Funhouse in New York. Or back further still, back to the 1830s when thousands of people poured into the first industrial city in the world and set about creating their own street culture and their own forms of entertainment.

The traditions that feed into the growth of Manchester music go back decades; there are the historic and cultural links between the city and the East Coast of North America, from the cotton trade to the jazz age, then via the Ship Canal, Burtonwood and John Mayall's tape recorder to the blues boom and the glory years of Northern Soul; thus when Detroit and Chicago started flinging out the first sounds of house and techno, Manchester tuned in, greedily importing it all. These traditions, and more – the hybrid nature of the local Mancs, the craving for drugs that goes at least as far back as De Quincey, the key role of entrepreneurs in the city's history, Manchester's independent spirit – all created the conditions that made Madchester inevitable.

However, despite our ability to chart decades of various cheap thrills and great moments in pop culture, the pace of change accelerated in the city during and after the rave revolution and the Madchester years. The house music explosion detonated in the city knocked Manchester, clubland and the world of music on to a new course. It's hard to conceive of just how much has changed in the dozen years or so since the rave revolution. That the city finally shed its ghost town image is confirmed by Jon Savage reminiscing in 1992: 'I lived in Manchester for several years in the late 70s. When I lived here the music was doomy and the city was a mess. Now the music has changed and the city has changed.'

We had more than a hundred years of street culture, devised by and for a hard-living urban populace, enhanced by the twentieth-century imports of the cinema and jazz. And then came rock & roll, an import that could be appropriated and refashioned. Early in the 1960s Manchester was renowned for its nightlife, its beat groups and basement venues, with nearly thirty clubs successfully operating in the centre of town. Manchester became a mod city by the middle of the decade; not self-consciously so, but soul was the big soundtrack to a night out. Then the club scene and the band scene went their separate ways in the late 1960s and early 1970s, when white youth took to lying in fields listening to guitar solos rather than crowding into basement clubs for rhythm-heavy soul or rhythm & blues. Prog rock fans followed bands on the college circuit, and the live scene remained the cutting edge in the punk era and beyond.

It all changed in the late 1980s when the dancefloor asserted its position as the focus of British youth culture. A product of the rave revolution, it was a huge, swift change, a wholesale scramble away from rock gigs and guitar bands and on to the dancefloor. These were the years of Madchester, Manchester's own reaction to house music, the sound of the rave revolution.

DJs selecting and mixing the records became the key figures in these years, positioned as the happy medium between the artists and the dancers. DJ-ing at the Haçienda, I got lucky, playing the right music in the right place in the right club in the most important music city of the era. Until then, DJ-ing had just seemed like the perfect hobby for a music fan and I hadn't considered it a career. A decade or so later, DJ-ing has become a hugely glamorous profession attracting the aspirations of countless people – as unreconstructed soul head Dean Johnson puts it: 'You go to a party and forty-eight people out of fifty are DJs' – and DJ-ing can mean big bucks, photo shoots, groupies, remixes, hi-tech equipment, a jet-set lifestyle. There's a culture, an industry and a network of supporting services surrounding the art of putting one record on after another.

Pre-rave, I'm not sure you would even confess to being a DJ; there were too many unpleasant role models, embarrassing characters hogging the nation's record decks. During the 1970s and early 1980s, when the mass of Mancunians went into town for middle-of-the-road discos and cabaret clubs, the average city centre disco was fronted by a so-called 'personality' DJ; a joker, a juke box with a chest wig. If you'd gone to Jilly's on Oxford Street in May 1982 you'd have stumbled upon two nights of Chicory Tip plus 'a non-stop disco'. It was par for a very dodgy course.

On the live music scene in the early 1980s music-making in the city was still one dimensional, with most Manchester bands working in a stolid rock tradition. Punk had changed the face of Manchester music in many positive ways. Importantly, it had gained Manchester's bands a certain amount of street credibility. Punk was a reflection of street culture, raw and meaningful, and one of the healthy legacies of punk was that bands like Joy Division and the Fall had held on to their Manchester roots and, in terms of the national scene, perhaps even played up their Northern 'otherness'. What was beginning to grow in those post-punk days was a strong attitude of staying real, doing things in an uncompromised Mancunian way; it was an attitude that later generations took for granted, shared by 808 State, Oasis and a host of others. This is in stark contrast to the earlier parts of the 1970s, when much locally made rock music, pre-punk, was root-less, bland, performed in a gutless style all too prevalent in British music of the time. 10cc were one example, Sad Café another. These groups were so over-stylised, so frilly, so blow-dried, it seemed like rock music had merely become a branch of bad hairdressing.

But whatever the fiercely independent attitudes and aspirations brought to Manchester music by punk, the business remained based in London, and the local infrastructure in Manchester was in its infancy. And if Manchester bands were a long way from the centre of power in pop, then black Manchester bands were further still. In music, as in life.

The achievements of the Manchester band Sweet Sensation, who had a Number One hit in September 1974 with 'Sad Sweet Dreamer', are therefore even more remarkable. The band revolved round the great singing voice of Marcel King, a young singer who was working at a quilt-making factory in Ardwick, but who had something of the young Michael Jackson about him; it was Marcel King's voice which dominated the band's debut album on Pye Records. The album included another single, 'Purely By Coincidence', a variety of spangly ballads (ideal smooching-under-the-mirrorball material) and a track in a Northern style ('Please Excuse Me'). Sweet Sensation took their inspiration from America for one obvious reason: there were no homegrown role models for black groups in Manchester, England.

At the time, there were few role models in England for the black community generally. Boxing would later deliver up some black British stars, but in the early 1970s, the high-profile British fighters were all white; champions like Henry Cooper, Joe Bugner and Pat Cowdell. Young black lads would have looked to black America for inspiration; Muhammad Ali, Joe Frazier and the other greats. And music mirrored boxing. It was no different to the way other English urban communities had looked abroad for important ingredients to give flavour to English popular culture. It's like the dockers getting turned on to American crime fiction, or the call of Hollywood, or the pulling power of John Lee Hooker. Oftentimes, the consumers and producers of English popular culture have had little to identify with among the accepted touchstones of insular, white, monolithic domestic culture.

'We had to look across the water to America actually; Marvin Gaye, Stevie Wonder, even the Jackson Five', remembers Sinclair Palmer from the group. Sweet Sensation were the first black British group on *Top of the Pops*. *Top of the Pops* had become one of the few places where black people were a visible and equal presence. From Motown and American soul, to Dave & Ansel Collins singing their Number One hit, 'Double Barrel', in 1971. Together with the slowly more frequent appearance of black players in the English football league – like Clyde Best of West Ham – these were some of the key moments of the decade for black people living in England; moments when the black community couldn't be ignored, downgraded.

In an era when racism was closer to the surface of white life, however, these breaks were not always welcome. Thin Lizzy made their debut in Manchester, supporting Slade at the Free Trade Hall in 1973. Phil Lynott from the group had grown up locally, attending Princess Road Junior School while his mother ran the Clifton Grange Hotel on the corner of Wellington Road in Whalley Range. Nevertheless, the Free Trade Hall gig was wrecked as racists showered abuse on the band. At Old Trafford in December 1978 West Bromwich Albion fielded three black players against United – Cyrille Regis, Brendan Batson and Laurie Cunningham – who were booed and abused every time they touched the ball. Regis recalled later how much more determined this made the players. West Brom won 5–3.

Sweet Sensation, however, were never in control of their destiny; this too was a sign of the times for black groups. Their songs were written and produced by svengali Tony Hatch – the Pete Waterman of his day – which perhaps deprived us of hearing the real sound of young black Manchester. It was like a version of Tin Pan Alley. Nevertheless, former band member Sinclair Palmer recognises that whatever the route they took, it took them a long way forward: 'People looked upon us later on as the British answer to the Jackson Five. Groups like Heatwave, Imagination, the Real Thing came after us. I'm pretty proud of what we did.'

It was primarily the Jamaican sound systems which provided the focus for young black Manchester in the 1970s. The black community had always had their own shebeens and drinking clubs, their own DJs cranking up Nat King Cole, calypso and sweet-voiced blues for the first generation, reggae and soul for the second. And elsewhere, away from the rock scene, there were other DJs serving specialist markets. This is where the best music-loving DJs from the pre-rave era could be found; in the underground scenes created after mod, the fragmented funk and soul fraternities where black music true believers who'd been turned on to Jimmy Smith, perhaps, or Marvin Gaye gathered.

The most visible and thriving fraternity was Northern Soul, which evolved directly from mod roots and attracted fans through the 1970s who, despite the disco craze and the rise of funk, took a purist dance stance and kept the old soul flame alive in old basement clubs and cellars in the North of England and the Midlands. The genre label 'Northern Soul' was originated by music journalist Dave Godin in 1970 after a visit to the Twisted Wheel in Manchester. He believed there were clear distinctions between the music favoured by soul fans in this area and those in London and the South which, in turn, mirrored the distinctions between soul music in the southern states of the USA and soul sounds from the urban northern states. But soul fans in Lancashire, West Yorkshire and North Staffordshire were attracted not just to the faster soul sound of Detroit; the music had become entwined with another ingredient in Northern Soul culture, the consumption of amphetamines. Speed was the drug of choice in Northern Soul circles from the early 1970s onwards; an upper for an all-nighter. Significantly, Northern Soul fans also relished the rarity of their music.

There was a time-lag; American soul records in the 1960s had been hard to get, but early in the 1970s imports began to be available. There was a lot of catching up to do, and the Northern Soul fan jumped in feet first. The appetite for rare records among Northern Soul fans turned many into collectors. Thus, since the early days, part of the furniture at Northern Soul all-nighters have been trestle tables covered with crates of old 7" singles. It was a hundred years since a trip to Shudehill lit up a Saturday evening; from a night out at the market, to having a market on your night out.

Dean Johnson believes that the Northern Soul scene was a self-conscious rejection of the predominantly middle-class long-haired hippy, post-Sergeant Pepper rock scene. It was about amphetamines, not acid; crisp drum beats and concise songs, not psychedelic meanderings; Northern basement clubs, not trippy festivals in Southern fields. 'The Northern Soul scene developed because the aesthetic angle up here was not into the "Summer of Love". Everybody wanted to be neat, sharp, urban – they looked good and they weren't going to be hippies.'

When the Twisted Wheel closed, other venues kept the Northern circuit alive: Up the Junction in Crewe and the Mojo in Sheffield, and the Torch in Turnstall (Stoke-on-Trent), which made a point of advertising its all-nighters throughout the North. A big contingent went down from Manchester to see Major Lance live in December 1972, with support from Bob & Earl (of 'Harlem Shuffle' fame); the night lasted the full twelve hours, from half eight in the evening to half eight the next morning. When the Torch was closed by the local council after the police had provided evidence of drug-taking in the venue, Wigan Casino, which opened on 23 September 1973, emerged as the new spiritual home of Northern Soul.

If Northern Soul was urban and Northern, it began to find its most dedicated followers not in the major conurbations – Manchester, Newcastle or Liverpool – but in more marginal, semi-urban places; small towns like Wigan and Stoke and Blackpool. The Mecca at Blackpool was another key venue, with DJ Ian Levine; it had a reputation for avoiding some of the populist excesses of Wigan Casino. The Northern Soul scene was self-contained, undiscovered and not media-led. It's a powerful example of the way street culture can create alternative communities away from the mainstream. It also paved the way for the contemporary soul weekender; jaunts to Caister or Southport, unfashionable seaside resorts on the very edge of England.

The Northern Soul scene maintained its underground status through the mid 1970s. Its dedicated followers lived for the weekend, self-consciously saw themselves as a community apart, and took their music very seriously. For them Northern Soul wasn't simply an escape; it was more real than the rest of their weekday drudgery. The scene demanded 'faith', and the soulsters talked in terms of keeping the faith, keeping the soul flame alive. Clear parallels with the rave generation of 1988 and beyond are there, but uniquely the Northern scene revolved around old records ('new' Northern records usually meant old records *newly* discovered). Thus the Northern scene was an anachronism from day one. The Northern fans who now follow the Black Lodge DJs, travel to Sunday sessions in out-of-the-way halls and big bank holiday Northern Soul gatherings at the Ritz are no less authentic than their early 70s counterparts; they share the same rejection of every other music since 60s soul and the same desire to dance all night. Perhaps it's no coincidence that the most dedicated followers are the white working class from the small one-industry towns; buffeted by economic and social change since the 1960s, a rejection of the last thirty years seems rational. Not that it has to be rational; dancing, being out on the floor, holding on, can mean everything.

Wigan Casino, the source of much of the mythology surrounding Northern Soul, had peaked by the end of the 1970s, and the scene had become split by raging arguments regarding the merits of 'classics' nights versus 'modern' nights; beat heavy 'stompers' versus vocal soul tunes; and accusations that clubs were being overrun by sightseers. The closure of Wigan Casino in December 1981 sent the scene back into the underground.

From the mid 70s to the mid 80s, city centre clubs ran occasional Northern Soul nights midweek or on bank holidays, but the rest of the week, and especially the weekend, the key attractions weren't to do with music. In 1975 the marketing campaign for Kloisters (16 Oxford Street, opposite the Odeon) was a list of drinks prices (Lager 18p, Pernod 20p). Other clubs offered other seductive enticements; Fagins (65 Oxford St, now Jilly's), for example, hosted a 'Nurses' night every Thursday. From the mid 70s to mid 80s the town was split between clubs playing naff music to pissed-up swingers, and inconspicuous, small-scale alternatives, little communities drifting around a DJ, a promoter, a collection of DIY party people.

Many venues around in the current era are descendants of earlier incarnations. For instance, in the early 1980s Placemate 7 at 6 Whit-worth Street took on the site previously housing the Twisted Wheel; later it would be known as the State, now it's trading as Follies and played host to 'Homoelectric', one of the city's most reputable nights. Tramps at 88 Princess Street became the Cyprus Tavern, and later the Granby. 42nd Street on Bootle Street – just down from the police station – was the Zoo in 1982 and the Playpen in 1984; formerly it had been Slack Alice's, owned by George Best. Best would stand outside from 10.30pm onwards, picking the best blondes out of the queue. As well as being the most famous footballer in the country, he had a playboy, pop star image and he was incredibly handsome. 'He had eyes like Jesus Christ', somebody once told me; a man, in fact, who'd gone to the club with a beautiful seventeen-year-old called

Sarah, but left on his own. Sarah had stayed with Best. But he bore Best no grudge: 'He was a star, Dave, a fucking star.'

Some clubs from the early 1980s have gone forever. Cloud 9 on Cross Street was in a basement opposite the Royal Exchange, next to the original site of the Spin Inn record shop. The Exit was on 8 Wood Street, just off Deansgate, where Fridays was jazz funk night in 1982, and on Saturdays DJ Marc Berry hosted 'Solitary Style' with club guru John Kennedy; the same partnership were involved with promoting early Smiths gigs. Midweek you'd find only a dozen or so people there, among them Johnny Marr. He might be sharing the decks with Marc Berry, alternating records by the Shangri-La's with tracks from a James Brown compilation LP.

Pips on Fennel Street has also disappeared. In its late 1970s heyday, with six dancefloors, each catering for different crowds, it promised 'Roxy, Electronic, Sixties, Disco'. It meant you could hear everything from 'Heroes' to 'Tears Of A Clown' in one night under one roof. In the era between the Electric Circus and the Haçienda, Pips was a favoured club. Joy Division's first gig as Joy Division was at Pips in January 1978. Bernard Sumner and Peter Hook from Joy Division were regulars, as was Johnny Marr; there were loads of regulars, in fact, especially in the Roxy room. Pips closed at the beginning of the 1980s, reopened briefly as the Playground in the summer of 1982, and was to play a role as Konspiracy in the acid house era.

Another club, Oozits, on the corner of Bradshaw Street and Newgate Street (in the network of Victorian streets between Shudehill and Victoria Station) was home to the Beach Club for a few months in 1980. Run by Richard Boon, its regular audience was drawn from among *City Fun* contributors and readers. Bands played, vaguely cult films like *Riot on Sunset Strip* were shown, and rumours always abounded that they'd be showing *A Clockwork Orange* which I don't think ever turned out to be true, although the rumours helped attract an audience. Most of the block of buildings housing Oozits have been demolished. Once big scuttling territory, it's an area that is now fast disappearing with newly laid tram tracks and redevelopment beckoning.

The early 1980s also saw the emergence of regular nights that attempted to cross over the soul scene, from the Northern fans on the one hand, and the modern soul and funk fans on the other; nights at Rafters, for instance – a basement club under Fagins (now the Music Box) – especially the occasional all-nighters with John Grant and Colin Curtis. Other popular, similar nights in the era included all-dayers at the Ritz with Richard Searling and Colin Curtis. The crossover was rarely successful, according to Dean Johnson, who recalls very regimented, segmented sets from the DJs. Soul DJs were catering for two distinct audiences: 'It would be a blacker and more Manchester audience who'd be into the jazz funk and a whiter, travelling-from-all-over-the-place audience for the Northern.'

These pockets of activity, these little communities – whether Marc Berry at the Exit, or John Grant at Rafters, or the Beach Club upstairs at Oozits – all required searching out. Good events were unstable and under-promoted, and nothing like today. The infrastructure of clubland was fragmented. The small scenes were happy to stay small – deriving their power from their insularity – but at the same time something more ambitious was being dreamt up by the team behind Factory Records. They went in search of possible permanent sites for a club in 1981 and considered a space on the corner of Oxford Road and Grosvenor Street (now the Flea & Firkin), and a carpet warehouse next to Oxford Road Station. Eventually, however, they settled on an old yacht showroom on Whitworth Street West. Mike Pickering recalls:

> When we found the site for the Haçienda, that part of town, Whitworth Street up to Deansgate and then back all the way along to the Ritz, was a ghost town, derelict. None of the railway arches were in use for anything apart from some garages. No one could understand why we wanted a place there. The Haçienda was right out of the way. But you look along Whitworth Street now and there's so much, the Boardwalk, the Venue, Atlas, Alaska; the whole of town has changed.

Although subsequent history made their choice of building perfect for the dancefloor revolutions to come – a club in a warehouse in the era of warehouse raves – in 1982 they were really looking for something more prosaic; a gig venue not a dance venue. Their choice had some logic to it. Under the bridge and right was Little Peter Street, the site of T. J. Davidson's semi-derelict rehearsal rooms where post-punk scene favourites the Distractions rehearsed in the late 1970s; Room 6 had housed Joy Division. Elsewhere in the building Mick Hucknall's punk band, the Frantic Elevators, rehearsed, as did a band featuring Gillian Gilbert (who would later join New Order). Just over the road from the end of Little Peter Street and directly opposite the Haçi-enda's building was the Gaythorn, a pub frequented by the rehearsal space bands and their cohorts. Round the corner from the Haçienda, G-Mex was being planned. The Haçienda was at the Hulme end of town, and – as the crow flies – not far from the PSV, the old Factory venue.

The Haçienda opened in May 1982, with Mike Pickering invited to join the Haçienda management by Rob Gretton. Pickering recalls the spirit of punk amateurism that surrounded the club. The bills weren't paid, and no money was made; 'None of us who started working there had ever worked in a club or a venue ever before. I didn't have a clue. But it was like one big party. I remember putting on Club Zoo with Teardrop Explodes and there were about a hundred people there and Julian and everyone took acid and had this fucking mad party in the middle of it all. It was all very irresponsible.'

The Haçienda in 1983 found it was still serving a community for whom disco music was anathema. It was a struggling live venue. The club was leaking money as predictably as the roof leaked rain during storms; on many occasions the club was late opening while the pot collectors helped mop up and clear away the buckets. Somehow they managed to be both out of tune and ahead of their time. In the early years there were probably only three big sell-out nights, when New Order played in June 1982 and January 1983, and the Smiths in November 1983. It was a great space in search of an audience.

It changed as dance music began to break down the walls of anti-disco prejudice erected by the post-punk generation. Punk had achieved much, but not the broadening of tastes. Punk, a reaction against dinosaur rock acts like ELP and Pink Floyd, shared rock's disdain for disco music. It sneered at anything outside its values (Tony Parsons has described it as 'Stalinist'). Among the post-punk generation any secret fondness for Donna Summer – in the case of Ian Curtis – was rarely communicated to the fans. Thus, the Buzzcocks' singer Pete Shelley proclaimed, 'I hate modern music, disco boogie and pop.'

In clubs punk and funk fans seldom met, unless it was to trade blows. The early and mid 1980s saw the birth of so-called 'alternative' nights, Goth nights, miserable affairs featuring hours of Spear of Destiny, the Cramps and 'Should I Stay Or Should I Go' by the Clash, cheap versions of the Bowie and Roxy rooms at Pips. As a mark of the stranglehold of so-called 'alternative' clubs in Manchester, the busiest club night at the Haçienda up to 1985 was their Tuesday night named, unambiguously, 'No Funk Night'. Graham Massey recalls that 'it was a cold, horrible place that you used to go to see gigs'. The club's acoustics were lamentable; it was the temple of boom.

The Haçienda was looking for a direction in an era when the rock music scene was jaded, struggling in the shadow of punk and Joy Division. The great days of Northern Soul looked to be over, and the black dance scene was halfheartedly pinning its faith in jazz funk. Ex-Velvet Underground collaborator Nico had settled in the city, and it was like we were all living in some large-scale version of the Chelsea Hotel; Manchester was living off the past, rundown, beset by bad drugs (heroin, cheap speed). Manchester's football teams couldn't repeat old glories. The plug had been pulled on the old industries; the big manufacturing industries, the mass employers, were being hammered by a Conservative government intent on radical restructuring of the economy (a restructuring, though, that offered nothing to those communities left broken and no future except welfare for those left unemployed).

But changes in the music scene were about to have profound repercussions on the image, the future and the regeneration of the city at large. The key catalyst was the advance in black dance music in the early 1980s; specifically the groundbreaking hip hop and electro scene in New York. Black dance music from America made extraordinary advances, flinging out ideas, discovering and using computer-reliant new technology (samplers, drum machines, sequencers), taking the creative cutting edge of music well away from rock artists wedded to their guitars and drum kits.

In New York, as the 1970s became the 1980s, on the street, in the recording studios and in the clubs, a new sound and a new style stirred, based around DJs, rappers, two turntables and a microphone. It was the birth of the hip hop vision; cutting, scratching, drum loops, video games, cosmic funk, graffiti art, breakdancing; rappers rocking the party or sending 'The Message'; DJs with their funky break beats, re-working 'Funky Drummer', 'Good Times' and 'Genius Of Love'. In the studio pioneers of the early electro scene like Afrika Bambaataa were searching for the perfect beat, taking inspiration from Giorgio Moroder, Kraftwerk and P-Funk, drenching their work with robotic vocoder vocals. Labels like Prelude and Salsoul were introducing harder, stripped down and electronic elements to disco formulae. At the Sugarhill label an in-house band (Doug Wimbish, Skip Mac-Donald, Keith LeBlanc and Duke Bootee, among others) created their own funky breaks and bass & drum collisions on releases like 'That's The Joint' and 'Rapper's Delight'. And then came more r'n'b-minded producers like Jam & Lewis promoting a heavy bass sound, thus blowing away the fluffier jazz funk, and often proving too raw for sentimental soul heads.

The repercussions of all this music-making in New York in the years up to 1984 went far beyond New York. Even before New Order had gone over to record there in February 1983, they'd co-opted cutting-edge New York disco rhythms in their massive-selling 'Blue Monday' single, recorded in October 1982. '"Blue Monday" was the turning point', remembers Bernard Sumner. 'Blue Monday' was initially released in March 1983, and kept selling all through the summer (on the back of its profile as a Euro holiday hit), peaking in October in the Top Ten. It achieved such high levels of commercial success that New Order were able to keep the Haçienda afloat during the pre-dance days, the uncommercial first era.

The creative impact of the black dance scene in New York was even more important to the survival of the Haçienda than the money raised by New Order's success; the black dance scene in New York began to give a direction to dancefloors all over the world; to Manchester, and the Haçienda, especially. The Haçienda was thus in pole position at the outset of the rave revolution – the big music and club revolutions of 1988 and 1989 – which in turn enabled Manchester to recover its creativity and achieve an unmatched reputation for youth culture.

That's what it amounts to: the cutting-edge New York musicians in the electro era energised New Order and gave their music-making direction, saved the Haçienda, sowed the seeds of the rave revolution, and changed Manchester. You can trace the current cultural state of the city (the recovery from the directionless dark days, the music-led regeneration of the city) back to New York at the end of the 1970s and the beginning of the 1980s; back to two turntables and a microphone; back to 2 September 1976 when Grandmaster Flash and Melle Mel played the Audubon Ballroom, 166 and Broadway. Grandmaster Flash has told the story of the night many times; how he took his turntable tricks – locking the beat, cutting, scratching, punch phasing – out of the little parties and small clubs like the Back Door, and filled the three thousand-capacity Audubon, with Melle Mel taking the mic. It was a night that turned on a thousand b-boys and launched the era of the DJ. The role of DJs as inane playboys was challenged by a new breed of DJs fathered by the New York vanguard; DJs as creators, music-lovers, taste-makers, remixers, producers, pop stars.

Greg Wilson's first proper job as a DJ, at the Golden Guinea in New Brighton, was a valuable apprenticeship, learning to work a crowd, trying to be radical without alienating the audience. In 1980 he took a four-nights-a-week residency at Wigan Pier, and for the first time had access to state-of-the-art DJ decks. DJs in Europe had become aware of American DJs mixing, but for the most part British DJs were making do with prehistoric Garrard turntables; turntable tricks just weren't possible. But at Wigan Pier the technology was there, and Wilson was able to combine new and old DJ techniques. 'For the first time I was working with vari-speed decks. I always had a big thing about announcing and back-announcing, and voices to vocals and all these old radio DJ techniques, but now I'd also been stringing a few records together or spinning the records back, or chop-mixing them.'

In the meantime, Legend had opened in Manchester (on Princess Street), under the same ownership as Wigan Pier. On Thursdays, it was 'Futurist' night – a night for the Goths and the New Romantics – which took over from Pips as Manchester's premier alternative night. Their successful Wednesday night jazz funk night was under the control of DJ John Grant until he moved across to 'The Main Event' at Placemate 7, which also pulled in Colin Curtis and Mike Shaft. With this high-profile black music night likely to kill off the Legend Wednesday, Greg Wilson was given a go at saving it. He dropped all his DJ verbals, sussed the audience – 'Black guys, black girls, a few white girls, very few white guys at first, an eighteen to twenty-five audience who knew the score', he recalls – and worked hard at getting the music, and the mixing, spot on. Once he'd pulled Legend up to about two hundred and fifty people the night just went into orbit. 'The Main Event' closed within three weeks.

According to Greg Wilson two main factors gave his night the edge:

> First, Legend was a superior venue in terms of equipment, sound and lighting. Previously the only places that black kids could go to were rundown clubs that had seen better times, but now they were going to Legend, which was way ahead of

everything else. Also I was going more down the New York electro road, tracks that were being ignored at 'The Main Event'. The conventional, established black music scene weren't into it. After a certain point in time word had got about that it was the place to go to hear these records.

Thus electro did for dance music what punk did for rock. The new era brought raw, bass-heavy music to the dancefloor; after the disco boom of 1976 and 1977 had thrown mainstream dance music into a variety of creative deadends, it took until 1982 for dance music to return to the streets. With a lack of clear harmony, hip hop and electro reflected the world well. 'Broken glass everywhere!' shouted Melle Mel on 'The Message'; he might never have been to Little Hulton, but his message made sense in Manchester.

Something was happening, and you can always tell something's happening because people start moaning about how things used to be better. Through 1982 and 1983 the electro funk sounds of In Deep 'Last Night A DJ Saved My Life', D-Train 'You're The One For Me', The Peech Boys 'Don't Make Me Wait', and the even more stripped-down, stinging, freaky fresh sounds like 'Planet Rock', 'Pack Jam' and 'The Smurf' were causing major ruptures all over the black dance world, with radio DJs in England like Robbie Vincent running anti-electro campaigns. The precious jazz funkers and the smoochie soul boys didn't like electro and hip hop, and the all-dayer circuit had stopped booking DJs like Greg Wilson and Pete Haigh who insisted on playing the new sounds. Greg Wilson was in the firing line; 'In *Blues & Soul*, the Northern correspondent Frank Elson wouldn't print the word "electro", he'd asterisk it. Manchester's dance import specialist record shop, Spin Inn, were happy selling the stuff but the records were advertised in the window on what they called an 'Electro Shit' chart. To some people I was seen as a heretic for playing it.'

Wilson's work on the decks every Wednesday drew the attention of Mike Shaft, who was then fronting a Sunday afternoon black music show on Piccadilly Radio. Although at first not a big fan of the new dancefloor sounds, he invited Wilson to do mixes for the radio show. These were probably some of the most taped radio programmes in Manchester radio history. According to Wilson's memory of events, they were the first ever live DJ mixes broadcast on radio in the country; 'Mike wanted it featured on his programme because he thought it valid, and I did those mixes for him, through 82 and 83, doing mixes every month, or six weeks, with a big end-of-year one.'

Electro was part of a whole hip hop culture, along with breakdancing, graffiti and new DJ techniques. With little radio coverage, almost no club play and the dance press divided, young Mancunians turned on to the hip hop lifestyle were living in an information vacuum. Charlie Ahearn's hip hop movie *Wild Style* and the video to Malcolm McLaren's 'Buffalo Gals' were two of the only visual aids to young Mancs looking to get into scratching or breakdancing.

Early in the 1980s hip hop came to Moss Side. It was the sound for a new generation. Sefton Madface is still a key face on the scene, DJ-ing, promoting, running a record shop in town. He knows everybody; go for a walk up Oldham Street with him and you're stopped every four yards by someone wanting to talk to him. He was young when he discovered bodypopping and breaking, coming to the music via his love for jazz funk and jazz funk moves. He followed his interests at a lot of under-eighteen clubs, but he also hung out with older kids. His cousins kept talking about Ali's on Alphonsus Street in Old Trafford, and one night took Sefton there; he'd put boot polish on his moustache to darken it up and make him look older. His crew also used to go to jazz funk nights at Rebecca's in Bury and the Tropicana on Oxford Street. At the same time, DJs like Chad Jackson and Greg Wilson were beginning to make waves in Manchester, but it wasn't about the DJs and the clubs at that time, says Sefton; 'It was just about us with our ghetto blasters. After school we used to get down to the park and get together. It was just escapism, get away from everything, and just practise your moves.'

In Manchester a bodypopping and breakdance crew called Reflex were one of the first to set up, but it was a crew calling themselves Broken Glass, derived from two Moss Side crews, DFK and the Scorpions, who made the biggest impact on the street. It was like a football squad. On a club date there might be ten or twelve, or, out on Piccadilly Gardens or Market Street on a Saturday afternoon, just half a dozen. The key crew members included Patrick Booth, Royston, Danny and Kermit (the same Kermit who, over ten years later, was to front Black Grape with Shaun Ryder). One Manchester bodypopper, Raymond Campbell, was so good he got picked up and taken by a New York crew.

A different dance crew, from a different tradition but with just as good a reputation, were the Jazz Defectors. They could be found throwing shapes on the dancefloor at gigs by the likes of A Certain Ratio. Sharply dressed, they were into coolly choreographed jazz dance, all the moves, and the suits, the look. Their recorded work – they released an LP on Factory – didn't come off; they couldn't sing and on record their jazz cool sounded like wine bar whimsy (another act from the same scene were Kalima, and the most successful were Swing Out Sister), but on the dancefloor the JDs made their mark in zoot suits in brown or slate grey and polo-necked sweaters. They were immaculate in fact, a bit beat, a bit mod, in brogues or spats and buttoned-down shirts. They were the sharpest-looking characters; Paul Cummings would take longer to get ready to go out than his girlfriend would. A basement club called Berlin on a Tuesday night was their weekly focus, and Colin Curtis was the DJ there that mattered most.

It wasn't all white boys with Lou Reed fixations in Manchester in the era after punk then, and it wasn't all doom and gloom. Factory and the Haçienda management tried their best to incorporate these various strands of black music and dance music into the activities. Ellie Gray from the Haçienda managed the Jazz Defectors, and alongside the gigs, the Haçienda also employed a DJ from the Reno on Princess Road in Moss Side; Hewan Clarke took the job as the Haçienda's resident DJ in 1982, and as the club was usually open every night – often it was free to get in – he was always busy. The club, though, never seemed to be. Graham Massey went to the Haçienda from the first; 'I started going there when it opened. People forget how empty the place was; for three years or something. It looked like it wouldn't survive.'

Back then the DJ booth was down below the stage and the disillusioned Hewan Clarke just used to sit reading magazines. If there was a way to embrace all elements of the fragmented Manchester music scene under the Haçienda's leaking roof, Hewan wasn't finding one. In 1983, even as a clueless punter, I could tell there just wasn't empathy between the DJ and the crowd. The Haçienda was usually less than half full, and it was cold. When Hewan played 'Don't Make Me Wait' in that kind of environment, the record didn't get anything like the reaction it got at Legend or the Reno. Thus, according to Mike Pickering, Hewan tried instead to play a style he thought suited the kind of people he thought the Haçienda were aiming to attract; 'He ended up playing records by Blancmange.'

By the middle of the 1980s – 1985 and 1986 – there was evidence that the scenes were converging. Many of the little club nights and one-offs were playing a broader selection of music than for years; it wasn't all ghettos and niche markets. Despite the way the dance music versus rock music battle was still being fought in the music press in the mid 1980s – Trouble Funk versus the Smiths, say, with the fires regularly stoked by Morrissey's negative pronouncements on discos and dance music – there was a genuine change of attitude among those going out in Manchester in the mid 1980s. The dormant strand – the one where musical miscegenation was welcome – began to reassert itself once the authority of the punk generation began to wane. For example, Greg Wilson remembers his crowd changing near the end of 1983. Most of the incoming white boys at Legend he now thinks were from 'the Factory side of town'.

Factory Records were key barometers of Manchester taste. New Order remained the label's key group, and from 'Blue Monday' to G-Mex and beyond, the inspiration of New York clubs like AM/PM and the Funhouse strengthened. They employed the talents of New York producer Arthur Baker on their 1983 single 'Confusion'. A former club DJ in Boston specialising in Philadelphia soul, Arthur Baker had produced 'Jazzy Sensation' on Tommy Boys Records, 'Planet Rock' with Afrika Bambaataa and 'Walking on Sunshine'. He had just finished 'I.O.U' for Freeez when he began work on 'Confusion'.

Other Factory favourites A Certain Ratio had always lived in a funkier realm than their contemporaries; Donald Johnson drummed with Cameo, they went on tour with Hewan Clarke as support, and memorably covered 'Shack Up' by Banbarra. Their twisted funk had a bitter, melancholic edge in the early days, though; their track 'All Night Party', for example, is the bleakest advertisement for staying up all night you've ever heard ('I work all day, I drink all night, my life is just an angry blur'), and the wonderful 'Flight' is equally troubled, despite its great rhythms. Other early Factory releases were less ambiguous, with a clear, more carefree embrace of soul and funk; 52nd Street 'Look Into My Eyes' in 1982, and one of Factory's finest moments, the return of Sweet Sensation singer Marcel King on 'Reach For Love' recorded in 1983.

At the Haçienda, Mike Pickering had been to New York and befriended Jellybean Benitez, as well as Mark Kamins (Madonna's mentor on the New York club scene); Kamins did some remix work for Pickering's group Quando Quango. As Hewan moved on, Pickering took on Friday nights with Marc (a.k.a. Andrew) Berry. These Friday nights had a messy genesis, but as the night began evolving, a young DJ, Martin Prendergast, took over from Marc Berry. By the end of 1985 the club was full. Pickering puts the success of the night down to the spirit of diversity in the music. Pickering has always felt that most of the established DJs in Manchester were too precious, then and now. He is adamant that you could play right across the board and do it in a credible way, breaking the barriers, going with the flow; 'It was just us playing the records we liked', recalls Pickering:

> The local DJs were telling us that you can't do this or you can't do that. It was like there were all these rules. I didn't know what the rules were, and I didn't care. In the end, me and Marc Berry said 'Fuck you, we'll do it'. We could play whatever we wanted to play. It was Manchester's first scally night. It encompassed all the scenes, so there were almost indie-type scenes, Perry boys, Motown, Northern Soul, tracks like Whistle 'Please Love Me'. It was a really good night, but it was really Mancunian. I think that had a lot to do with it. And it was happening at a club that half the audience hadn't been let into before. It was the first time Happy Mondays had gone out in town. And we used to get formation dancing, jazz dancers in. Foot Patrol, Zuzan and all them. Everyone was very happy, no one caused trouble.

At the Haçienda, new manager Paul Mason (who arrived in January 1986) took on a club which was still losing money and suffering a bad reputation as a live venue. Building on Pickering's successful Fridays, Mason made an accelerated switch to resident DJs and regular club nights. Economics played a part; if you can make a night featuring a DJ work, then there's more money to be made than booking bands with all their equipment, soundchecks, guest lists and managers. But, more importantly, the time was right.

Timing is everything in pop music, knowing how to tap into the zeitgeist. I remember 1985 going into 1986. I had been DJ-ing at the 'Wilde Club' at the Man Alive, a night promoted by Greg and Dil from Big Flame on Thursdays in 1985, featuring gigs by the Wedding Present, Chakk, That Petrol Emotion, the Age of Chance and – of course – Big Flame. In the summer of 1985 I also got the chance to do a Friday night at a small club about a hundred yards down the road from the Haçienda. Some friends of mine who ran a fly poster business round town, including the old Oaks promoter and dog breeder Vinny Faal, and Jimmy Carr, had briefly taken over the running of the club and had named it the Wheel; Jimmy had been a massive fan of the Twisted Wheel, and had an idea that together we might re-create the happiest days of his life. We didn't, of course (but we had a great first night when the whole of Moss Side piled in and I got too drunk to play).

The poster boys soon began to lose interest and moved on to more lucrative businesses, but the club owner decided to rename the club the Venue and install me as the resident weekend DJ – with no bands booked. At the Man Alive my box of Go Go, electro, Tack Head, early Creation releases and James Brown was occasionally more successful than the groups; at the Venue invariably so. All across town, it seemed, the clubs sacked the bands.

Nevertheless, the Haçienda's decision to go for club nights Thursday through to Saturday had an element of risk. Pickering's Fridays had yet to erase the club's remote image; there was still a gulf between its aircraft grey soul and the lively grassroots energy in the city. In addition, the city centre was underused, especially by students; apart from forays to the Cyprus Tavern, students stayed on their campuses. But at his previous club, Rock City in Nottingham, Mason had run a successful student-oriented night, and that became his first aim at the Haçienda. He and Paul Cons came to hear me playing at the Venue. On the strength of this visit I was given Thursdays at the Haçienda. The four-and-a-half year run of Temperance Club started on May Day 1986. I played whatever I liked, from the Smiths through Motown to endless New Order and big bunches of hip hop. Mark E. Smith bought me a pint because I played 'Little Doll' by the Stooges.

I still get people interviewing me about the Haçienda old days, and they're often under the illusion that everyone got together round a table with Tony Wilson, or New Order, or Paul Cons and worked out a music policy, a formula that would shake the world. It wasn't like that; Pickering's accidental stumble into DJ-ing was typical. The management had the foresight to employ DJs who understood the people in the queue, and then they let us loose (often, it has to be said, as a last resort). The only time I had to justify my playlist was during negotiations with the Haçienda just prior to the start of

Temperance Club. Paul Mason, the Haçienda's manager, read a list of my choice tracks; I'd included this fabulous funk record on 4th & Broadway by Donald Banks called 'Status Quo'. 'I don't think rock like that will be appropriate', he said (I think he assumed there was a song called 'Donald Banks' by Status Quo. Since then I haven't debated what I play with anyone).

The 'No Funk' fans and William Burroughs readers who'd lurked in the darker corners of the Haçienda since it had opened were soon alienated by the new generation. When Pickering played 'Love Can Turn Around' or I played 'Go On Girl' we were winding up the oldsters, the po-faced post-punk crowd, defining our culture just as be-bop had crashed against swing, and rock & rollers had chased off Pat Boone.

There's a story that when Mike Pickering first went down to London with his box of Chicago house in 1987 the floor cleared when he started playing and punters shouted abuse along the lines of 'get this homo music shit off'. There was an American tourist who berated me – this was probably about 1986 – I must have followed 'Blue Monday' with 'Let The Music Play' or something. He was very upset; 'Quit playing to the disco crowd', he demanded.

In the mid 1980s the live scene hadn't collapsed completely. Two valuable venues in particular filled all the gaps when the Haçienda changed course: the Boardwalk and the International. The Boardwalk opened on Little Peter Street in March 1986 in a building bought by Colin Sinclair and his father the previous year. It had been in a ruinous state, but they managed to get two floors into some kind of dry, working order. The basement housed rehearsal space, and the ground floor, previously a site used by Manchester's experimental Green Room theatre group, became a gig venue. In its first eighteen months the Boardwalk hosted gigs by Sonic Youth, A Certain Ratio and Laibach, and debut Manchester appearances by Primal Scream and the Shamen.

In the years since the Sinclairs took on the Boardwalk, many of the famous and not-so-famous local bands have been tenants of the rehearsal rooms. Simply Red and James were both around in the early days (for a while they shared management), with James working in a space on the first floor, where the rave era chill-out area behind the balcony bar is now situated. The class of 1986 – the Railway Children, the Bodines and the Happy Mondays – took rooms in the basement.

One of the keys to Manchester's continued success in pop music is the infrastructure of places to rehearse, small venues to play, record labels, sympathetic local media, studios, managers; the Boardwalk's part in that great story is fundamental. Since 1986 Colin Sinclair has also been involved in band management (with the Railway Children and A Certain Ratio), running record labels, and event management. Despite the Boardwalk's successful shift towards underground club nights in the 1990s, the venue still retains its place in the history of Manc rock & roll; it's where Oasis first took rehearsal space and then began their gigging career.

Live gigs were also the mainstay of the International on Anson Road. Run by Roger Eagle and Gareth Evans, it opened with Roger Eagle telling listeners to Radio Lancashire's *On the Wire* programme that it would be Manchester's finest dance club since the 1960s. After his twenty years in clubland – including the Magic Village and Eric's – we were prepared to believe him; he was a great DJ, with an unmatched soul, reggae and r'n'b collection. But things didn't turn out that way. Instead, until it closed in 1990, the International was one of the most important mid-sized gig venues in the area; Gil Scott Heron, Echo & the Bunnymen, Lee Perry, REM all played there. Gareth Evans became the Stone Roses' manager. That's how these things happen; what was supposed to be a dance club ended up doing all the gigs, and the Haçienda failed as a gig venue and ended up being a successful dance club.

The Haçienda's glory days were approaching. Gradually, more habitués of the specialist nights found themselves in there, as scenes diverged; old Northern Soul fans, New Order fans, Cloud 9's Friday night jazz and modern soul crowd, people from Dave Booth's psychedelic Tuesday night at the Playpen, regulars at 'The Revolution' upstairs at the PSV (the old Russell Club that had hosted Factory nights), graduates of Greg Wilson's nights, the jazz dancers from Berlin, soul girls, hip hop heads. The Haçienda had lost its remote image; the DJs had taken control.

CHAPTER 7

The Revenge of the Screwed-Up Places:

Madchester Raves On

In the long story of Manchester's urban popular culture there are creative booms and slumps, cycles of action and reaction. In some ways this pattern mirrors the economic cycle. As far back as the 1840s Frederich Engels had observed that the British economy was locked into a cycle that gives rise to a crisis every five or six years; a 'perennial round' of 'prosperity, crisis, prosperity, crisis'. So it was in the 1980s; we were about to go into a mini-boom stoked by Chancellor Lawson, and we'd just struggled out of a long, deep slump. The slump had claimed thousands of jobs and, in the miners' strike of 1984/5, we'd suffered the trauma of the last death spasm of the old ways; the old big manufacturing industries with their jobs for life and community-creating certainties had gone. In the mid 1980s, Manchester, like much of Northern England, was dragged down by high tides of disappointment and neglect. But by 1988 – the so-called 'Summer of Love' – we would be raving, not drowning. The energy and creativity of acid house music, buoyed by the use of ecstasy, resulted in repercussions far beyond the dancefloors of Manchester.

Through the mid 1980s, the dancefloor was reasserting itself as the focus for youth culture in Manchester, with records as diverse as 'Blue Monday', 'Rebel Without A Pause' and 'Pump Up The Volume' breaking down most remaining anti-disco prejudice. Every week at the Haçienda, new music from urban America was winning hearts and minds, whether New York's Beastie Boys or Trouble Funk from Washington. In the studio it was clear that computer-aided music was the dominating focus of creativity and excitement.

162

In 1948 Manchester had been the birthplace of the digital revolution, with engineers from the University successfully creating the first programmable computer. There was some historical symmetry then, that Manchester would embrace computer-aided music with enthusiasm. The city was also home to New Order, a band with a long interest in using whatever technology was at hand: drum machines, sequencers, synthesisers.

When house finally arrived, it changed the Haçienda, Manchester, England indisputably and forever. It came from America, on 12" import records, with minimal information, and principally from two cities: Chicago and Detroit. From 1986 we were beginning to hear Chicago 'jacking' records like 'Jack Your Body' and 'Love Can't Turn Around'. At the time it felt like these records were making a particular impact only in Manchester and one or two other cities. DJ Graeme Park, in the sleevenotes that accompanied *North* – Manchester's first compilation of homegrown house – later put the case that while London clubs in the summer of 1986 were exclusively exploring hip hop and go go, dancefloors further north, in Nottingham, Sheffield and Manchester, were 'crammed with people jacking to a new sound from Chicago called house, and for two years a North/South divide of a different kind was established'.

Graeme Park was writing in 1988, by which time things, he says, had moved on. While Northern clubs had retained their reputation for hedonism and dedication, house music had also, by then, hit nationwide. House music is here to stay, he writes; 'The Summer of 1988 reads very differently, with the whole nation rapidly becoming one jacking zone . . . A whole new culture is born.'

Also by 1988 we had a lot more than just jacking records from Chicago. The development of disco had continued through records like Class Action's 'Weekend' and Blaze's 'So Special' to records like Phase II's 'Reachin'' which would get regular play in garage-flavoured house clubs. And Detroit techno had become an integral part of the sound of what was now being called 'acid house', stripped-down and pulsing beats, squirts and bleeps, deep rhythms and undisguised computer sounds. Derrick May, Juan Atkins, Kevin Saunderson, among others, were a new generation of Detroit music-makers far removed from the old Motown sound. Moreover, they seemed plugged in to the atmosphere out on the streets of their city. As Derrick May told Stuart Cosgrove in 1988:

This city is in total devastation. It is going through the biggest change in its history. Detroit is passing through its third wave, a social dynamic which nobody outside this city can understand. Factories are closing, people are drifting away, and kids are killing each other for fun. The whole order has broken down. If our music is a soundtrack to all that, I hope it makes people understand what kind of disintegration we're dealing with.

In the mid 1980s, Manchester, of course, was dealing with its own kind of disintegration, and shared a similarly traumatic future as Detroit ('motor city', founded on the mass production of cars); collapsing industries, abandoned factories, lost jobs. Maybe there's some kind of empathy and some kind of link between the two cities which fuelled our mutual surrender to the sounds of techno and acid house. We communicated our shared desolation; but also, via music, we transcended it.

Somehow out on the strobe-lit dancefloor we felt we had something to celebrate; the music didn't bring us down, it was uplifting. Acid house was created at the intersection of Chicago's mutant reworkings of 70s disco and Detroit techno's totally modern, digital vision; giving us a future while acknowledging a past. The rave revolution was created out of the debris of post-monetarist disorder by and for people who were intent on survival. On the dancefloor there was a shared love of the music, and a collective spirit diametrically opposed to the view that there was 'no such thing as society'. And that crucially, magnificently, retrieved our sense of community.

At the heart of the Manchester story over the last two hundred years has been the city's international links, and its pluralist, radical outlook. In the 1830s the city's prosperity was built on overseas trade. In the 1980s the city's musicians had helped to create a network in the open-minded free trade of ideas. From Europe, New Order took the examples of Kraftwerk, Cerrone and Giorgio Moroder, filtered them through electro from America, and then began to influence music-makers in Detroit; New Order were namechecked by music-makers in Detroit like Derrick May who cherished the coldness of New Order's dancebeat.

The baton of creativity was being passed around the globe. Early in 1987 the London-based DJ Tim Simenon, making music under the name Bomb the Bass, copied artwork from a record by Miami act Maggotron for the initial pressings of his first single, 'Beat Dis'.

'Beat Dis' was a sampler-aided record made just as dancefloors were moving from hip hop to house, and during an era when homegrown releases were often dressed up to look like imports in order to filch some of the credibility of American dance records. The man behind Maggotron, James McCauley, was immersed in mid 1980s electro sounds, and went on to play a central role in what would soon be labelled 'Miami Bass'. One of McCauley's other songs went under the name 'Planet Detroit'. McCauley later recalled that he could have called himself 'Planet Miami', but instead defied geography and used the name Planet Detroit; 'We thought of another screwed-up place . . . Detroit. YEAH!'

Where the links began and ended made no difference; Chicago, Manchester, Berlin, Miami, Detroit, London all found the perfect beat. We had discovered a relay of urban creators living in disordered, disintegrating, post-industrial cities. Records like Reese & Santonio's 'Rock To The Beat' or 'Freedom' by the Children were travelling the world and changing the world. Records made in the North and East of America sounded perfect at the Haçienda, in the North West of England. Strangely, even the Haçienda sound system sounded good when we were listening to these import 12"s. It was like the revenge of the screwed-up places. House music connected us on the dancefloor and across the seas; even music that was superficially oblique and cold-hearted. Even a track called 'Washing Machine' that half-sounded like one.

The roots of rave are knotty and confused. Just as later the class of 1990 took a diversion from the indie route and got turned on to house music via Primal Scream remixes and Happy Mondays, so not all the first generation of house music fans in Manchester found the music via purist dance antecedents in New York, Chicago or Detroit. There were the twisted English versions of electro like Cabaret Voltaire, or mashed-up, spliffed-up versions of breakbeats released on On-U Sound. The variety of the Haçienda's customers was testament to this, reflected in the different trends incorporated into the three big nights of 1987. As well as Thursdays, I was doing Saturday nights at the Haçienda, with Dean Johnson playing his esoteric soul, Latin and jazz cuts alongside me in populist mode, playing whatever I thought would fill the dancefloor. Together we somehow reinvented the traditional Saturday night out; people got dressed up, got drunk, fell over and had a good time. By the middle of 1987 Thursday, Friday and Saturday were packed every week with twelve hundred people a night. My Thursdays were becoming the focus for the city's indie dance scene. Pickering's Fridays were then attracting a slightly harder, blacker crowd; 'It was like a twelve hundred-capacity shebeen', says Pickering. 'You could smoke copious amounts of pot and no one ever bothered you. No one took speed, or anything, it wasn't a drug culture in that sense. It was just dope and beer, dope and Red Stripe. It was a great atmosphere.'

What had begun to happen was a synthesis, a coming together under the leaking roof of the Haçienda, a coming together of working-class scallies and middle-class students; rap fans and indie kids; north and south Manchester; fashion designers and heavy drinkers; hairdressers and hooligans. The club gradually became home to most of the small scenes from the earlier part of the decade: the Man Alive crowd, the Venue regulars, Berlin's jazz dancers and people who'd never been to town before. The barriers began to come down, just a little, and maybe just at the weekend, but the city seemed ready for this transformation. Certainly, the bohemian, graduate belts and the working-class estates had come closer culturally, if not economically, by the end of the 1980s. Anthony Wilson always liked to see Factory Records as an agent of absorption, once congratulating journalist Stuart Maconie on a particularly apposite remark: 'You described us as somewhere between yobbishness and intellectualism and I think that's right. We are both. And I think this is the thing with Factory. We are very Mancunian. That's what makes us so special.'

By attracting everyone else's audience, by 1987 the Haçienda had at last found a role. House music was the penultimate piece in the jigsaw. Mike Pickering's Friday 'Nude' night had become the first night in Britain regularly to programme the first beginnings of Chicago house in 1986. The first house records he ever got hold of slotted in with Wally Jump Junior, JM Silk, Da Braxton's 'Jump Back'. It wasn't a sudden shift for him; techno had its roots in electro, garage had roots in New York disco, and hip hop breakbeats and electro synthesiser sounds had been filling the cavernous spaces at the Haçienda for years. Pickering is adamant: 'When people always say to me that I brought house music to Britain, I deny it. Things like that, they don't just arrive one day.'

The revolution wasn't plotted; in fact, it wasn't even expected. Labels came later: acid, Balearic, indie dance; I can remember Jon Da Silva in about November 1987 (before he'd become a DJ at the club) congratulating me on 'that last half hour of acid'. I really didn't know what 'acid' was. I was making it up as I went along. Most DJs working in the early days of DJ culture were working all kinds of records into dance sets, selecting the crucial tunes, learning how to programme a night, less interested in a seamless beat mix, more interested in good tracks. At the end of 1987 there was probably only half an hour's worth of decent 'acid' house around anyway; DJs had no choice but to be eclectic.

During the course of the Summer of Love, the trickle of house records became a tidal wave. House music became the sound of now, the bona fide party sound. When house had only been coming into Britain intermittently, we didn't really know where the scene was going. As it turned out, it was going overground. 1988 was the year 'acid' house hit the tabloids, 'We Call It Acieeed' went Top Twenty, and in Britain the media and the mainstream discovered house. And more house. And ecstasy. A little pill. The last piece in the jigsaw.

The metamorphosis of Manchester from raincoat city to a teeming town of twenty-four hour party people wasn't an overnight switch, but a conclusive change came with the arrival of ecstasy into the city. The drug had been around dancefloors since 1985, and by 1987 all kinds of influential club faces in London and all kinds of off-their-nuts Mancs in Manchester were using it. DJ Paul Oakenfold was quoted at the time: '1987 was probably the best year to date for Ecstasy. It takes you up and it gives you a feeling of freedom.'

These pockets of drug-taking in 1987 were nothing compared with the sudden surge in ecstasy use at the beginning of 1988. There were several reasons for this: ecstasy itself became easier to buy in and out of clubs in Manchester around February and March 1988; publicity was growing about the drug; and, in key synchronicity, the demand for the drug matched the demand for the music as house music and ecstasy began to lock themselves into a complementary alliance (the 70s-tinged laid-back sounds of rare groove which still dominated many dancefloors, and the slow, heavy beats of Soul II Soul, were both being replaced by stripped-down, spacey, 120bpm – later, faster – house records). The music buried itself deeply inside your dancing mind. It was something to do with chemistry, with heart beats and bpm's, with the ecstasy rush. On the Haçienda dancefloor all other stimulants – from lager to amphetamines – were discarded in favour of E.

But it was also something to do with Manchester itself, with the city's traditions of hedonism and drug use, traditions that went back to nineteenth-century drunks falling into the gutter in front of Frederich Engels, De Quincey losing himself in opiates and Jon Savage reminiscing about Section 25 playing at the Beach Club in 1981: 'The necessity and the impossibility of escape. Let's face it, Manchester is a great place to take drugs.'

Although reaching higher levels of drug infestation in the 1960s through into the 1970s, even before that popular culture and pop music had never practised temperance. In the 1920s and 1930s jazz and marijuana were inextricably linked in the pantheon of subversive behaviour, and jazz gave marijuana slang names ('weed', 'reefer', 'tea', 'muggles'), and jazz stars made coded reference to it. Later drugs followed similar patterns; cocaine (the 'Wacky Dust' of the song by Ella Fitzgerald), heroin (widespread among the jazz elite – and not so elite – during the 1950s, and the rock star drop-outs in the early 1970s), LSD (especially in the 1960s), and cheap amphetamines on the Northern Soul scene and during the punk years.

Despite these copious examples, pop music has usually been coy about its connections with drug-taking. The high-profile casualties – like Charlie Parker, Kurt Cobain and Jimi Hendrix – have been portrayed as one-offs. The infiltration of drug use into all parts of pop music – from black jazz to white rock, from club dancefloors to record company boardrooms, from the fan to the icon – is rarely acknowledged. On numerous occasions songs with anti-drug messages have been laying false trails; so Canned Heat sang 'Amphetamine Annie' even while the guitarist, Al Wilson, was mired in the barbiturate addiction which eventually killed him. Likewise, I remember Grandmaster Flash & Melle Mel's 'White Lines (Don't Do It)' played at the Haçienda while the DJ box was practically neck deep in cocaine.

Music journalists have been reluctant to grapple with the reality of drugs in pop. In the early 1940s *Down Beat* underwent internal debates on whether to acknowledge the widespread use of drugs on the jazz scene. Their hand was forced by exposure of the situation in the mainstream daily newspapers. Similarly, it was the tabloids that focused on the use of ecstasy in house clubs; it was cock-eyed and sensationalised coverage, but at least it blew open a version of the truth. However, exposure of the acid house scene in the media undoubtedly accelerated the spread of ecstasy. E soon became a key part of an underground clubbing lifestyle. Graham Massey felt the mood: 'I think the big change was drugs. Mike Pickering would be playing a few acid house records but nothing happened until the drugs. And then it happened over a period of weeks almost. The change took about a month and then it was full on.'

'Zumbar', the Haçienda's weekly Wednesday fashion show and camp-style cabaret night, was replaced by 'Hot' on 13 July 1988. 'Hot' became a big focus for the acid house scene and the quintessential Summer of Love experience, a mini midweek Ibiza, a swimming pool next to the dancefloor, nights of E'd-up airhorn madness. On Saturday nights Dean's Latin, jazz and soul got drowned in the cascades of house, and Jon Da Silva took over DJ-ing the night with me. My Thursday 'Temperance' night was usually a clubber's first port of call, enticing them into the Haçienda via the far-from-purist temptations of indie, house, hip hop and soul classics. Meanwhile, Pickering's 'Nude' night recruited Graeme Park, and exploded into the most important club night Manchester has ever staged.

The ultimate agent of synthesis was chemical. There is no doubt that the entry of ecstasy into dance clubs gave the scene a huge boost; it opened minds, loosened the crowds, fed the atmosphere, and undoubtedly contributed to the staggering rise of house music. Most importantly, it took conflict out of clubs. There were fewer bad vibes than in clubs in other parts of the city where lager was still the drug of choice. The vibe was so intense, the club so packed, the music just so pure, fresh and mind-blowing; DJ-ing at the Haçienda in 1988, 1989 and 1990 was fantastic. It wasn't forced, it had no models, it wasn't faked, it wasn't ritualistic, it was immediate. It didn't have the elite tag that the scene had in London. Nobody was excluded; shop assistants, secretaries, dole-ites, plasterers, thieves, gangsters, students. Everybody danced; on the stairs, on the stage, on the balcony and at the bar. They danced in the cloakroom queue. For all I know, they were dancing in the street outside.

If Manchester had just soaked up the rave revolution, it wouldn't have been unique. What made Manchester special – what made Manchester 'Madchester', in fact – was that from the very first sightings of the new culture, Manchester crackled with creativity. Sounds heard in clubs began influencing Manchester musicians just as rhythm & blues had in the early 1960s and electro in the early 1980s. Energy on the dancefloor matched with creativity, big time.

The creativity sprang from all kinds of sources. In 1987 the collection of renegade funksters, breakdancers and second-hand drum machine owners that would form 808 State began to gather in a dank basement underneath the Eastern Bloc record shop. With comrades Gerald Simpson (A Guy Called Gerald) and Nicholas William Dennis Lockett (MC Tunes) they experimented with hip hop, held parties, called themselves the Hit Squad, and took to the stage at the Boardwalk with drum machines and dodgy microphones. Among them was Graham Massey of Biting Tongues, a raging, saxophone-tinged noise band who had released a soundtrack album and some far-out singles for Factory, and recorded an unreleased LP for the short-lived Stockport-based Cut Deep label.

Graham Massey remembers the early days, late 1987, early 1988, making music to fill the spaces in Mike Pickering and Jon Da Silva's Haçienda sets. Often he'd work with Gerald, who was beginning to make waves as a solo artist. With his classic debut single 'Voodoo Ray', A Guy Called Gerald perfected this pattern; in the club one night and in the studio the next day, a cassette of the track in the DJ box the next weekend, followed by a test pressing a fortnight later, bedlam on the dancefloor for two months, and then, at last, the video on *The Chart Show*.

Feeding into the same network with 'Pacific State' – financed by Eastern Bloc through their Creed label (Martin Price from the shop was a full-time band member) – 808 State went all the way to *Top of the Pops*. It was the first of over a dozen appearances. Apart from their collaborations with MC Tunes, the singles were twisted instrumentals. It was one of house music's major contributions: to reinvent the instrumental, stripping music to rhythms, electronic noise, samples. It was refreshing to escape the prosaic verse–chorus–verse–chorus–guitar solo formula of rock music and enter a realm of noises, bleeps and electronica, echoes from the ether.

The beginnings of techno were raw, but other-worldly at the same time. It went straight to the consciousness of a generation, capturing something of the experiences of most kids born in the era of the Apollo moon landings. Ian Brown from the Stone Roses once confessed to me that he'd have loved to have been an astronaut. We were a generation living in urban chaos, our imaginations inspired by space travel, dreaming of flying high, teased by possibilities. We were bewitched by records like Moby's 'Go'; six minutes and thirty seconds of fast beats, dreamy melodies, atonal bleeps, thirty-seven shouts of 'go', and twenty-three shouts of 'yeah'.

In the confines of the music industry itself, the rave era felt like a genuine revolution. Clearly the technological changes of the 1980s –

especially the introduction of samplers – had redefined the rules of music-making. Samplers had underpinned the rise of hip hop and formed a key ingredient in the house sound. The potential democratisation of music-making unleashed by samplers threatened the big production values and guitar–bass–drums traditions that still dominated the music industry at the beginning of the 1990s.

House music also marked other reversals of prevailing music industry practices. Two aspects to house music were a return to the values of previous eras: its focus on the dancefloor (rather than the bedroom or the stadium) as the key site for the consumption of music mirrored the soul and rhythm & blues scenes of the 1960s; and the emphasis on cheaply produced singles rather than sprawling LP releases replicated one of the strengths of the punk era.

Aside from countering the individualistic thrust of Thatcherism by providing a valuable form of community on the nation's dancefloors, the rave revolution directly challenged the culture of the 1980s in other ways. It was the decade in which popular culture was in danger of becoming hypnotised by 'style', by form over content, by 'design' and packaging. Through Neville Brody socialism got a new typeface in the relaunched *New Statesman*. Teenage delinquency was given a neutering makeover in the film *Absolute Beginners*. West End values were everywhere. It was all too lifeless compared with the raw and direct appeal of a Saturday night in an acid house club. As if to emphasise the point that we didn't need designer packaging, dance hits were being made by DJs playing white label pre-releases; records with no label info, records relying purely on their ability to move the floor. Records would chart without airplay or advertising; purely on the back of sustained club play. No esoteric typefaces required.

The technology and the changing attitudes also boosted the potential of the lone music-maker. The new era buried the idea that making music required a group, stolidly practising every Sunday afternoon. It liberated some remarkable characters, real mavericks: the Aphex Twin, Moby, A Guy Called Gerald, the Hartnoll brothers in Orbital. Suddenly, one person with a sampler and a keyboard, or one person with a pair of decks, or one person on an Enterprise Allowance Scheme, could create, succeed and even change the face of modern music. You could be Derrick May just for one day.

The studio technology has continued to develop, each new advance opening up new possibilities. In November 1991 half the records in the British Top Ten were house instrumentals. By 1993 computer-aided music-makers like the Orb and Biosphere were producing chilled-out soundscapes of great expressiveness. By 1996, in the hands of groups as diverse as Leftfield, Portishead, Underworld and Scanner, computer-aided sounds were the bedrock of all kinds of music. Two acts well schooled in rap and the joys of techno breakbeats, the Prodigy and Roni Size, dominated 1997. Through 1998 and into 1999 the likes of Faithless and Daft Punk took the music further and filled live arenas as well as dancefloors. One of the decade's last stars, Beck, eulogised the creative potential of 'two turntables and a microphone' in his track 'Where It's At'. Through the 1990s, technology delivered music speaking in new languages, creating new realities, advancing way past Moby's 'Go'.

These changes have brought new life to pop music, but back in the early days of the rave revolution, the grassroots rise of this new generation of music-makers attracted open hostility from Establishment figures in the music industry (musicians like Roger Daltrey and George Harrison, music business executives like BPI big-wig Maurice Oberstein). The panic in the minds (and probably the bank accounts) of the old rock brigade as the rave revolution took hold recalls Bruce Mitchell talking about the older groups criticising the beat groups in the early 1960s for not being able to play their instruments. The anachronists are usually bitter, believing themselves to be the sole exponents of authentic, 'real' music. 'If that's music, I'm the Shah of Persia' is the kind of complaint that has echoed down the years, from musicians and fans too; witness the sensational moment at the Free Trade Hall in May 1966 when Keith Butler shouted 'Judas' at Bob Dylan.

808 State were unashamed believers in the new school, technophiles who went as far as naming themselves after a drum machine: a Roland 808. Celebrating a successful marriage between the primitive pull of rhythm and the sounds of the new era, Graham Massey confirms the status of 808 State's first hit, 'Pacific State', as another record inspired by the sounds the Haçienda was pumping out four nights a week, as another record finely tuned to the ecstasy era: 'It was definitely a Haçienda-designed record; it came out of Marshall Jefferson and things like that. It's an ecstasy mood piece, do you know what I mean? It's got all the bits that go with that.'

While sharing Graeme Park's sense that a new culture had been born, Graham Massey also revels in the way people had been triggered into doing their own versions of the house sound, making that inspired leap from consumption to production. His own work on 'Pacific State' was a case in point: 'It felt like that tune belonged to the whole culture. Something that a whole collective of people put a new value on. The empowerment of people was an important part of it, people doing things in groups. It felt strange, it was the first sense of community there'd been in years. We could define the culture, we could push the boundaries of the culture.'

The audiences at that time were filled with future DJs, including Justin Robertson, Pete Heller and Sasha. Sasha was a dedicated clubber in love with what he was hearing at the Haçienda – 'it was like a place of worship for me', he would recall later – and went on to become the most famous and highly paid DJ in the country. The Haçienda was crucial in 1988, he says: 'There really wasn't anywhere else, it was the total focus for the scene. It gradually spread as more people got into DJ-ing and more people got into putting club nights on . . . The first year was totally based around the Haçienda. I never really knew what was going on or who was DJ-ing. I guess no one really cared. The music was such a new sound, such a mad inspiration for people.'

What the music on the Haçienda dancefloor inspired, the technology facilitated. Those whose Haçienda experiences later became central to their successful music-making included: A Guy Called Gerald, 808 State, Happy Mondays, Johnny Marr, Bernard Sumner, Johnny Jay of the Development Corporation, Baby Ford, the Charlatans, the Chemical Brothers, Laurent Garnier and K-Klass. On the occasion of the Haçienda's fifteenth birthday in 1997, Paul from K-Klass told Radio One listeners: 'We met here. If it hadn't been for this club and the records that were played here and the records people related to this club have made, we wouldn't be doing what we're doing. I'd probably still be fitting telephones.'

Manchester was the epicentre of what became known as 'the house nation' in the years after 1988; attitudes and music influencing and influenced by Manchester spread through England, Britain and beyond. The house nation crossed borders and barriers, creating networks, laying the foundations of today's huge, commercialised house music scene, sowing seeds. The first sign of the harvest was the development of the 'rave' scene in 1988 under the influence of what was happening in Manchester clubs and London clubs, using old warehouses and open fields. Big out-of-town raves included 'Joy' at Stand Lees Farm in Rochdale in August 1989 and 'Live The

'Dream' in Blackburn a month later, both run by Anthony and Chris Donnelly with DJs including Mike Pickering, Paul Oakenfold, Paul Anderson, Tomlin and Chris Nelson (the Jam MCs), Steve Williams, Grooverider and Mr C.

Elsewhere in Manchester, activity had spread well beyond the Haçienda. The Thunderdome, at the Osbourne Club on Oldham Road in Miles Platting, was promoted by Eric Barker, Jimmy Muffin and John Kenyon. It became the new electro circus, with DJs including the Spinmasters and Steve Williams. Down at the other end of Shudehill, Konspiracy on Fennel Street was launched in November 1989 in the venue once known as Pips, with six bars and five dancefloors. Paul Uddoh and Marino Morgan were the owners, Chris Nelson of the Jam MCs the main man; it was also the club where Justin Robertson and Greg Fenton began their careers. The vibe spread through the North of England, jostling with influences from down South, from the key London club nights of the early rave era: 'Shoom', 'Future', 'Spectrum' and 'The Trip'. 'Shoom' took Monday nights at Legend on Princess Street, and although the night lasted barely two months, it cemented newly forming London/Manchester alliances. Glasgow too; it's said to have been at Legend that Primal Scream's Bobby Gillespie first took an E. Another time, Happy Mondays piled into Legend and filmed the video for 'Wrote For Luck'.

As the various records, histories, clubs and DJs met and mixed, there was no suddenly emerging fully fledged scene with a single musical formula. In contrast to the later development of mainstream house, in 1988 it was a case of almost anything goes. Experiment and unpredictability were both part of the scene's appeal. It was an ever-changing soundtrack; one minute you could hear 'Know How' by Young MC, the next 'Rhythm Is A Mystery' by K-Klass. In 1989 evolution was fast-forwarded, especially in the North, by the emergence of the Italian house sound – piano breaks and screaming divas – and, at the same time, the visceral brilliance of breakbeat-based hardcore rave multiplied house music's audience, especially around the M25 orbital.

All this marked the early years of modern commercial club culture. What had started out as an almost clandestine scene in a few clubs around the country had grown into a massive industry in a way that other clubland scenes (like Northern Soul) had never done. The sounds and styles and sites of pop music had shifted. In the Haçienda it wasn't so long ago that the club played host to a few hundred shiverers at the odd gig, and now there were six thousand people coming through the doors over four sold-out nights each and every week.

People were in clubs so much of the time, going out became a lifestyle and a career, and many people who were drawn deep into the culture weren't interested in going home and making records. Although some musicians created dance music from the inspiration of the house, there was something of a time lag – a year, two years – before the dancefloor devotees were turning in records that had a direct relationship to house music and a direct appeal to the dancefloor in any great numbers. It was left, instead, to the city's guitar bands to do most of the music-making. Thus was born the 'Madchester' sound, indie dance, the sound of young guitar bands with their roots in rock music but their hearts won over by the energy of house, their sense of rhythm unlocked and their creativity liberated by immersion in E culture. It was an unlikely fusion which flew in the face of traditional rock and dance rivalries, but according to Noel Gallagher, 'That's how the whole Roses thing kicked off; guys from guitar bands going to clubs.'

The Stone Roses and the Mondays were from a generation with great record collections; rap, psychedelia, reggae, soul, punk. Their evangelism dragged thousands of ordinary pop kids down a winding route through indie to house in the years after 1988. James fans became born-again ravers. Happy Mondays fans became rappers. Before this era gig-goers were prone to disappear for the support act or sit on the floor with pints of cider, but after 1988 live gigs had to raise their game to compete with the glorious delirium of the dancefloor. So the Shamen embarked on their 'Synergy' tour, and the Mondays, the Stone Roses and James all went on tour with DJs employed to warm up the crowd. When I played 'Good Life' by Inner City at the Stone Roses show at Alexandra Palace the whole crowd started pogoing. The Haçienda helped me understand them; I knew they liked to go out and listen to Inner City, go home and get stoned to the Velvet Underground.

The Manchester music scene in the Madchester years was chaotic; there were bands who embraced the new era, and those who rejected it; clubbers who found their life changed, and those who rejected the bandwagon (including many of the old soul heads who maybe preferred a spliff to an E, and who regarded rave as drug-led music and pure escapism). There were casualties among the hedonists, the ones who 'lost it', took too many drugs. There were career casualties also among the bands and groups and among the DJs. Some soul-based DJs fled the scene, and the shift in tastes left some great bands behind (King of the Slums), but helped propel other great bands (World of Twist, the Charlatans) into the limelight.

New Order's groundbreaking attempts to fuse influences had culminated brilliantly on their fifth studio album, *Technique*, recorded over twelve weeks in Ibiza in 1988 just as their culture reached a crossroads. The perfect balance of guitars and drum machines, raw post-punk anxiety and rave revolution warmth, clubbing and creating, made for a fantastic, fascinating record. New Order took all the baggage of their melancholic Manchester myths to a sunny Mediterranean holiday island and came back with something refreshed and positive, a relaxed, unforced mix of Ibiza and Manchester; blue skies and dark nights.

Technique was the first New Order LP to top the charts, helped by the strength of the record, of course, but also by a more commercial approach to marketing (including a billboard campaign and a TV advert during *The Chart Show*). It turned out to be their last LP for Factory, though they returned on London Records with *Republic* in May 1993. New Order's career had laid the trail for further incursions into funky rhythms by rock bands in the Madchester years, but once the rave years were full-on the band was torn apart, choices were made and solo paths taken, with Peter Hook taking a leather-trousered rock route with Revenge, Bernard getting housed up in Electronic, and the other two languishing in, well, the Other Two.

Similarly, the punk/rave schism split the Smiths. The personal divergence between Morrissey and Johnny Marr was reflected in their different musical directions too, with Marr, unlike Morrissey, fully won over by the podium heaven of the Haçienda's house nights. He joined Electronic, leaving Morrissey yesterday's revolutionary, confirmed in his role as today's reactionary. In March 1989 Marr told me just how suffocating the closed society of the Smiths had become: 'The one thing about any group who create a certain style and create a certain political aspect to what they do, it gets to be a club. And some things are in and some things are out. Towards the end of the Smiths, I realised that the records I was listening to with my friends were more exciting than the records I was listening to with the group. Eventually we'd got ourselves down a musical and political cul-de-sac.'

It was the first interview he had given since leaving the group, and yet it wasn't bitterness about the past that motivated his views, it was enthusiasm about what was then unfolding all around us in Manchester. He was immersed in the music of the moment, obviously inspired by the Daisy Age rap of De La Soul, and the Happy Mondays (or 'the best group on the planet', as he called them).

Happy Mondays, under the balcony at the Haçienda, were groovers and shakers, a little gang, all baggy jeans and eyes like flying saucers. On stage, like Ann Lee's Shakers they were speaking in tongues, high on ecstasy. Their music rolled with the kind of uncoiling, carefree, rhythm-heavy swagger missing from the swathes of purist indie bands around in the mid 1980s. Especially when collaborating with DJ Paul Oakenfold and his engineer, Steve Osborne, they produced some classic songs: 'Hallelujah', Step On', 'Kinky Afro'.

Singer Shaun Ryder and the rest of the group cultivated and communicated with what was effectively a private language; the privilege and currency of any gang. The title of their first LP was *Squirrel And G-Man Twenty Four Hour Party People Plastic Face Carnt Smile (White Out)*. Ryder's lyrics disrespected rock's formulae. In this at least he shared an attitude with the doyens of songwriting from the previous Manc generation – Morrissey, Ian Curtis and Mark E. Smith – that the language of their songs had to do something different to be real. Ryder followed no poetic formulae, instead he growled and scowled, filling his songs with fanciful dope talk, hot knife raps, street doodles, gossip and stories of drug dependency, teenage delinquency. It was the Manc rough edge set to music.

In 1986 Happy Mondays weren't considered by Factory, their record label, to be important enough to be given free tickets for the Tenth Summer gig at G-Mex. By 1990 they were serious Manc heroes. In 1986 they released 'Freaky Dancin', which – like titles of other songs of theirs ('Twenty Four Hour Party People', for instance) – proved to be an enduring slogan for their generation. It was produced by Mike Pickering, who picked up their potential early. He considered them clued-up representatives of the city's scally culture; working-class lads from the football terraces, the casuals, the Perry Boys. They brought a new style to Factory and the Manchester music scene, their distance from the old Factory summed up even by their sleeve designs. The bold, head-warping colours of Central Station were as far from Peter Savile's neo-classical work on early Factory releases as the Mondays' loose, raw, slangy music was from Joy

Division's tense minimalism. The Mondays were promiscuous in their influences; Ryder would reel off names like Funkadelic, Jimi Hendrix, Lou Reed. Bits of other songs kept echoing through their music; they were from a culture that survived by taking whatever you could lay your hands on for cheap, for free.

Stoned, rough, the Mondays looked more likely to be stars on CCTV than MTV; more likely to be arrested for loitering on street corners than picked out to be pop stars. They conformed to some of rock & roll's saddest clichés, chasing girls and chasing the dragon, yet there was something exhilarating about their rise. I did their first national music press interview. Most bands in that position are eager to make a favourable first impression, telling you what they think you want to hear. The Mondays were not like that; in fact only the bass player and the drummer turned up. Later I realised that meeting them early one morning in someone's living room was the wrong strategy altogether. Subsequent interviewers met Shaun Ryder late in the evening in a club and plied him with drinks. That way you got your interview and a lot more besides.

Happy Mondays were Salford street-corner society on a stage, carrying their friends around them, keeping their community close knit. Shaun's brother Paul was in the band, his father Derek worked behind the scenes, and Shaun's cousins Matt and Pat ran Central Station Design, the quintessential design team of the era (their work blossomed with the cover of the *North* compilation and Mondays' record sleeves, and dominated the 'Sublime' exhibition of Manchester design held at Cornerhouse in September 1992). All these Salford characters and extended Mondays family members partied with the band. How many times did you hear, after asking how a party was, or a new club night, 'Full of Happy Mondays and their mates'? It has to be said: this wasn't always a good sign.

The Mondays earned a reputation for outlaw activity. They were lads out on the piss, and out to take the piss. The press perhaps had a tendency to treat them like savages, buzzing off their roughness. It gave them a one-dimensional image which didn't do justice to the band. Shaun was, and remains, a witty guy. Bez was very clued up, with a great taste in music, and he always knew what was going on. But they weren't communicating in the language of the straight world. Once Shaun was photographed by Kevin Cummins unwrapping a Kit Kat. It was supposed to be one of his favourite things. I think the feature was for *Select*. It was the silver foil – a key item in a drug user's life – that was the subject of Shaun's veneration (he had wanted to be photographed brandishing Bacofoil but the message was deemed too explicit). No one seemed to pick up on this. When the picture was printed the grateful chocolate manufacturers sent a huge consignment of Kit Kats to the Happy Mondays office. It was my job to distribute the chocolates (their manager, Nathan McGough, had crashed a car he wasn't even licensed to drive). I took a handful to Eastern Bloc record shop and provided the staff there with their elevenses.

The Stone Roses were the other group that dominated the Madchester era. In their early years, they sounded surly and aggressive, and fell too easily into sub-Gothdom. Their first single, 'So Young', came across as halfway between a celebration and denigration of misery, with Ian Brown – then living among the battered Crescents of Hulme – unsure whether there was anything worth feeling positive about. But when they began to sound less like Theatre of Hate and more like Primal Scream they flowered.

There was a light Beatles touch to their second single, 'Sally Cinnamon', a brighter record in every sense. By 1987 singles like 'Elephant Stone' and new songs like 'Made Of Stone' (a mixture of 'Paint It Black' and 'Velocity Girl') won them not just a more discerning audience, but a much larger one, at least locally. They hadn't got marketing worked out, but their standing in small pockets of the country was huge; it was all word of mouth, the best kind of publicity there is. By the time they had unveiled the brooding, bolshy, magnificent 'I Wanna Be Adored' you could tell they had found their true direction; they were going to be massive.

Songs that were to form the basis of their first LP incorporated loud echoes of the 1960s, but the spirit of 1988 also gave them crossover qualities. Among the devoted early fans was Dave Simpson from *Avanti* fanzine in Leeds, who described them as 'the best band on the planet'. In a profile in the second issue, he described how the band were combining 'the dreamy beauty of 1960s pop with a feel for rhythm that shares its roots squarely with the acid and house parties of the burgeoning Manchester club scene'.

Like many Manchester bands, the Stone Roses gave the impression of being beholden to no one. They knocked back remixes, eschewed encores. Assured, direct and cocky, Ian Brown soon took to mooching onstage. Offstage, like New Order or Morrissey, he found it hard to play the music biz rules, describing the whole industry structure as a 'sausage machine'. Like the Mondays, he avoided giving interviewers an easy time, but unlike the Mondays he managed to progress beyond talking gibberish laced with 'fuck's. More talkative than guitarist John Squire, but less voluble than his hero, Muhammad Ali, Brown's interview speciality was the spacey soundbite; 'Man is weak. Woman is power', he declared in one interview, professing a disdain for the macho attitudes of rock music. 'Always say what you think and live for today', he told the readers of *Avanti*.

In light of the controversy that dogged his solo career in the late 1990s – especially his confused attempts to justify remarks he made in April 1998 which were widely judged to be homophobic – it's worth remembering how, in the Madchester era, valuably, Ian Brown put a positive political spin on the spirit of the musical times. He was all for breaking down barriers and opening minds, not just in music (backstage after gigs he would regularly exhort any assembled indie kids to listen to rap music), but he saw pluralism as a political aim too. In May 1988 the Stone Roses played with James at an anti-Clause 28 benefit I put together at the International II on Plymouth Grove; we were raising money to fund protests against the Government's plans to include an anti-homosexual clause in the Local Government Act. Two days later, Ian Brown went on the affiliated march and rally in Albert Square, barely conspicuous, another face in the crowd. Like his music, Ian Brown's attitudes seemed a cross-fertilisation of 60s and 90s, halfway between a hippy and a Bennite, a bit of a mod and a bit of a slacker; 'I never wanted to work on a building site or go to university. I didn't think what I was going to do, I just drifted, I'm still drifting', he said in 1988.

Ian Brown believed that rock music had been uncreative since punk ('I think pop music was saved by the advent of acid house and rap because whites have done nothing for ten years', he told *Rolling Stone*), and seemed to understand how an unchanging and uncreative popular culture could suffocate Manchester. Like the Mondays with their Central Station designs, the Roses, with their Paisley shirts and Jackson Pollock-influenced record sleeves, put a clear space between themselves and a Manchester past dominated by Joy Division and the Smiths. And their music soundtracked this difference, in songs as varied as the succinct 'She Bangs The Drums' and the stretched-out swirl of 'I Am The Resurrection'.

The Roses were vibey, strong and upbeat, like the best dance music. Although they didn't attempt to reproduce what they heard in clubs, they still seemed to catch the mood of the times. 'The past was yours, but the future's mine', Brown sings on 'She Bangs The Drums', their fifth single, which duly took its place at the heart of a Manchester scene that suddenly seemed alive with renewed hedonism, fresh colour and sexy swagger. Bands like Happy Mondays, the Roses themselves, James and others who had been working away for years, suddenly saw their moment. 1989 was a big year for the city. The mood in the clubs and among the bands was intoxicating. Living in Manchester never seemed so good; 'All Manchester's lacking is a beach. If there was a beach it'd be a great city', said Ian Brown.

Their grassroots following continued to grow apace, but it wasn't until they'd released their debut LP in May 1989 that the Stone Roses found themselves being championed by the music press. Their rise was clearly measured by a series of major gigs. In February they played the Haçienda – a key rite of passage in any Manchester band's career – and six months later they filled the Empress Ballroom in Blackpool. In October 1989 they stormed the seven thousand capacity Alexandra Palace, the band's first major gig in the South; barely six months before they'd been playing to two thousand in Manchester one night and the next playing somewhere like Brighton where next to no one turned up. They were now no Northern secret.

'Fool's Gold', released in November, took a funky breakbeat and produced one of their finest moments. It was their attempt to move forward from the early work and leave the 60s behind. Ian told me at the time: 'We need to be constantly changing. You've always got to change. When you realise it's not there any more, then you're chasing your tail. Then you stop.'

1989 ended a great year for the Roses, and 'Madchester' frenzy in the media was at its height. However, to some people 'Madchester' was about the clubbers, the parties, the DJs, the sounds of house and techno, the newness and the madness; to some that was the real deal. To them the indie bands with their fringes and second-hand dance sensibilities were the easy angle, too conventional. The Stone Roses and Happy Mondays were now on the front cover of music magazines worldwide, but to hardcore clubbers like DJ Darren Partington of the Spinmasters, the appropriation of house by the local guitar bands was peripheral: 'As far as the press were concerned, the Manchester scene was the Stone Roses and Happy Mondays. Bollocks, they had fuck all to do with it.'

The rock press, specifically, and the media generally, found it easier to understand the appeal of the bands. This skewed the picture of Madchester, certainly, and left huge currents of creativity undocumented, but the success of the guitar bands also brought attention to the city. The city's progress had been revolutionary and clearly soundtracked, but Madchester might well have gone unrecognised if the guitar bands hadn't hired London-based press officers like Philip Hall and Jeff Barrett. Through them, Manchester became front-page news.

Purists were right to be cynical of the way bands leeched off the dancefloor energy, but the bands were feeding the scene as well; when the Happy Mondays, Stone Roses, Inspiral Carpets, the Charlatans took over the airwaves, dominated the music papers, rocked *Top of the Pops*, they reached out of clubland, drew in more converts, creating more energy. The dancefloor action and the high-flying guitar bands; it was a highly combustible mix. Moreover, the guitar bands' feeling the need to acknowledge the music they were hearing in clubs showed that Manchester wasn't just passively sponging up new American dance sounds, but was making versions and hybrids of its own.

Aside from drummer Reni's feel for creative rhythms, the Stone Roses incorporated the mood rather than the mechanics of dance music. One of the 'Fool's Gold' remixes they'd refused was one by A Guy Called Gerald. Gerald himself had left 808 State, and the group had taken on two new members: Darren Partington and Andy Barker, the Spinmasters. With the Spinmasters – who had a residency at the Thunderdome on Oldham Road, where the playlist was harder than the Haçienda's, the music more aggressive, the club a different vibe altogether – 808 State began to shed the minimalist Detroit influences in evidence on *New Build* and take on darker sounds. After their second album, *Quadrastate*, 808 State signed to ZTT under the control of one-time *NME* writer Paul Morley (in a further twist, Morley left the label soon after).

There was a big Thunderdome record by Rhythm Device called 'Acid Rock', recorded in Ghent in Belgium. It's all heavy beats and mad clangs; you can hear the link with 808 State on one of their first hits for ZTT, 'Cubik'. Influences on music in this era piled in from all angles; breakbeats, those sampled snatches and drum loops which had been underpinning rap music since the end of the 1970s, for instance. In the early rave years in England there wasn't the strict demarcation between house and rap on dancefloors as was the case later. 'Pump Up The Volume', for example, was the first hit record of the new era – and its links with hip hop and house are strong. Hip hop tracks like 'Know How' and 'Back By Dope Demand' were strong dancefloor favourites in Manchester right through the early house years.

Sefton's career took a unique turn. In the park after school, breaking with his mates, he took to 'beatboxing' – imitating the noise of drum patterns, breakbeats and rhythms – by just using his mouth. It's a fantastic skill:

> Before we had any records, and before we had any turntables, we just did beats with our mouths. Even before I heard hip hop music, I was beatboxing at school. I was beatboxing at school, me and four other cats would beatbox all the time, with reggae chatting over it. It just came to us and we hadn't seen a video of someone doing it, and then did it, do you know what I mean? And I met up with Doug E. Fresh later and he was doing the same thing. But we hadn't heard that then.

In 1988 local rapper Prince Kool entered the national DMC Rapping Championships in London. Real name Robert McFarlane (his sister, Rachel McFarlane, was to be one of Manchester's singing sensations in the 1990s), Prince Kool took human beatbox Sefton down with him to lay down the rhythms. Against all the odds, the two guttersnipes from south Manchester won the event. Sefton believes it was because they were breaking the rules; 'Yeah, it was just different. All the other rappers came out with background music, tapes, records, whatever. We came out with just beatboxing and an MC. It just fucked everyone's minds up.'

Sefton did major European tours with Chad Jackson on the back of that victory (Chad had won the world mixing championship that year). The show started off with Chad DJ-ing, cutting, scratching, and then Sefton would start winding the crowd up. Then Chad would scratch and Sefton would echo the same scratch patterns, and more trickery unfolded for the next hour or so. It was a huge hit. Sefton continued touring for over two years, with other DJs like Cutmaster Swift and Pogo. It should be noted that at this point Sefton was still at school. He wasn't getting much work done.

During the Madchester era there were plenty of locally based rap and hip hop acts drawing on the sounds of New York, but pouring Mancness into the vibe. Unforgettably, there was MC Tunes whose 'The Only Rhyme That Bites', with 808 State, charted in 1990.

Other releases included the hard-to-find 'Hypnotizin' by Hybrid on Megablast built on the old b-boy favourite Tyrone Branson's 'The Smurf'. Another act mining the sounds of hip hop included the Ruthless Rap Assassins, whose roots went back to Breaking Glass, and who were managed and produced by Greg Wilson. Their classic dissection of the black experience in Britain, 'And It Wasn't A Dream', uses a break from Cymande's 'The Message' and a soundbite from Malcolm X; 'It wasn't a dream, it was a nightmare'.

What fuelled this process was the absence of any kind of insularity in Manchester. The music reflected cross-genre fusion. This was strengthened by music-makers, DJs and ravers as links were forged, barriers broken, new alliances created. At base, the scene seemed to be founded on open minds and an excited desire to share sounds. Thus the rave revolution wasn't just about Manchester or England; even before it went on to thrive in communities well beyond Whitworth Street West, it had drawn strength from a burgeoning international network of ideas, sounds, trends. A network from Manchester to Detroit, London to Berlin to Bologna, Milan to Japan, beyond and back again.

Thanks to its conspicuous role in the rave revolution, the Manchester music scene gained an international profile. Youth culture networks were buzzing with what was happening in Manchester in the years immediately after 1988; from fanzines to mainstream music weeklies (*NME* ran fifteen Manchester-related cover stories in 1990). From Japan to California, Manchester's music, attitudes, look and humour made an impact on the world stage. The world did its best to understand maverick Manc nonsense. America's finest style bible, *Details*, tried to get to grips with the latest fashions on the Haçienda's dancefloor as they began to establish themselves throughout Britain: 'The new look can best be described in its own vernacular in which BAF stands for "baggy as fuck" and sums up the stylistic aspirations of a generation.'

Later in the summer of 1990, four of us went on a DJ tour of America under a Haçienda banner: Paul Oakenfold (an honorary Haçienda DJ, I suppose, via his work with Happy Mondays), Graeme Park, Mike Pickering and me. We were there as the scene's representatives, trying to give a group of clubbers in Boston, say, just a little bit of Mancunian flavour. It was that tour, and one particular moment – me and Graeme and Paul Cons sitting in the back of a stretch limo driving to downtown Detroit, just grinning with the sheer excitement of it – when two things struck me. If Manchester could send DJs to Detroit (the home of techno, after all, and Motown, for that matter), we were either very cheeky or Manchester really was the pop culture capital of the world; and also it looked like DJs were going to be the new pop stars of the 1990s. We didn't stop grinning.

In America we discovered pockets of people, little communities on our wavelength. Networks were also being built between people in Paris and the Factory brigade in Manchester. The monthly magazine *Les Inrockuptibles* had been documenting music from Manchester assiduously for years, with a special penchant for Factory, James, New Order and Morrissey. I had a monthly residency at a club called La Locomotive, in the building next to the Moulin Rouge. The Stone Roses had headlined the prestigious annual festival at La Cigale in October 1989; it was the turn of the Charlatans a year later.

Newsweek in America carried a cover story on the swinging city. Manchester, England, was cool. But as the story of the city was picked up overseas, something changed in the translation. Attitudes became commodified, and sold as a style. Graham Massey remembers going to Tokyo with 808 State and being faced with venues full of clubbers wearing all the clichéd Madchester gear (Joe Bloggs flares and smiley t-shirts) and dancing like Bez. Manchester could have been flattered to have triggered imitations worldwide, but for Mike Pickering none of this rang true: 'What really got on my nerves was when I went abroad and I was in clubs where there were locals dancing and looking like scallies. They must have been to London or Manchester for a weekend and picked it up. I hated that. Here we are in Paris, Barcelona; have you not got a mind of your own?'

Sometimes it even felt that way in Manchester, to be honest. Nude Night's 'dope and Red Stripe' crowd were replaced by a whiter crowd, more predictable, more uniform. Individuality was swamped by the ubiquity of Joe Bloggs gear, distributed free to all the bands from Happy Mondays to A Certain Ratio. It was entertaining, but it wasn't youth culture at its most organic. Nevertheless, Manchester was the place to be. Or was it Madchester?

Madchester was a media and marketing version of reality. Its nearest equivalent in the real world – Manchester – has all the contradictions of every modern urban settlement: areas of poverty, leafy suburbs, posh department stores, boarded-up high streets and showcase buildings. Madchester, on the other hand, was a primary-coloured city full of seventeen-year-olds scurrying about in flares and ecstasy-inspired rock groups making a fortune putting out dance records.

It was amazing how quickly everybody bought into the myth. Dedicated followers of fashion poured into the city. And while it was fun to be at the centre of all this attention, there were dissenters, people with memories longer than fifteen minutes. Like Mark E. Smith: 'It's absurd now, you can't go into town for a drink. Big coaches from Wales – people camping outside the Haçienda. It's like San Francisco. It's worse now than it ever was. Like, Friday or Saturday night forget about going into town. Racks of people from all over the country, all trying to be part of a scene. It's fuckin' terrible. I find it fuckin' objectionable.'

As a gift at Christmas 1989 Factory Records sent out cards, photographs of Manchester landmarks, doctored. Manchester Piccadilly appeared as 'Madchester Piccadilly'. It was a clear and conspicuous sign of the qualitative difference Madchester had made to the imagination and landscape of Manchester; leading the city into a new era of international success and world profile, based not on manufacturing but on music, not on commerce but on leisure. It was a sign of just how important popular culture had become in the city.

The school-leavers of the late 1980s were no longer serving apprenticeships in factories or down at Salford docks, no longer using coal to make cotton; they were pulling scams on the DHSS, riding on Enterprise Allowance schemes, setting their sights on the pop charts, or borrowing decks and refining their DJ techniques. Madchester labelled the changes. Some American commentators – notably Greil Marcus – had long understood the special place of Manchester at the forefront of English pop music, but faced with the overwhelming evidence of Madchester, Manchester's creativity finally became more widely accepted. The city's impact was often overestimated; according to Andy Ross (Blur's record label boss) many in the American media assumed Blur came from Manchester (they were in their 'She's So High' and 'There's No Other Way' phase at the time). Manchester bands Happy Mondays and the Stone Roses were credited with marrying rock music with house rhythms, and giving birth to what was called 'indie dance'. It was a phenomenon that ended up drawing in any old guitar-based band with half a sense of rhythm; EMF, Jesus Jones.

Manchester's cutting-edge status provoked varying responses from the music industry in London. Some people – especially club promoters – took the opportunity to build links with Manchester. A&R men made flying visits up North. Others reacted as if profoundly threatened. *iD* magazine carried a story on new club bands from London, namechecking bands like Airstream, Natural Life, Deja Vu, If? and The Lazy, and quoted London club guru Charlie Chester's claim that 'the Manchester thing was over-hyped'. Over four pages the style bible sang the praises of London lads in bands; 'It's like Madchester never happened', trilled the journalist. This was September 1991. The bands, every one of them, sank without trace.

This isn't to deny creativity in London in this era – Soul II Soul, the Talkin Loud label, the Boy's Own posse, one-offs like 'Full Circle', the opening of Ministry of Sound – but that particular *iD* story was clearly desperate. You can't just invent a culture. Manchester had never forced it, and never faked it.

Perhaps young Manchester bands have an advantage over bands from London. In Manchester, one remove from the London-based press, bands can evolve at their own pace, make their mistakes in private (the Stone Roses, fortunately, weren't judged by their first single and early gigs). But every flicker of creativity in London gets distorted by media hype and pushed into the world half-finished.

Cities away from the capital often develop strong creative cultures. In America, Washington is the capital city, but you're more likely to place the creative centre in New York, Los Angeles or Detroit. In Spain, Barcelona rivals Madrid in every way, frequently ahead in energy and creativity. In Australia, Sydney leads Canberra. Capital cities have the legislators but not the innovators, whereas other cities literally can't afford to be so insular. In a city like Manchester, relations with other communities and other countries are more important; you need them to survive, and you can also learn from them. In Manchester, you're not surprised if great dance music comes from Chicago, Belgium or Leeds.

There's a spirit in Manchester which has learned to survive for decades away from the traditional centre of power. Significantly, via the rave revolution, it was the culture developed on the streets of the regional cities that was beginning to prevail nationwide. The revolution soon had important allies in London, and the Northern mill towns, and the new towns surrounding the M25; everywhere the alternative networks and underground alliances were making some noise. Rave culture was made, and thrived, out on the margins, the screwed-up places.

In Manchester itself the rise of rave culture was out of the control of the existing music community. Like the Chartists on Kersal Moor with the world watching, like the Red Megaphones giving voice to the dispossessed, ravers unlocked a spirit in the city. The rave revolution played a part in breaking the silence from the regions, pulling some kind of temporary shared identity together in Manchester. Being a part of Manchester is OK, but being a part of Madchester undoubtedly gave a certain kind of young person a sense of cultural identity and a sense of community; and what other towns in Britain could claim to generate such feelings? Normally we are fragmented and dispirited, united only in tragedy or a big football match. But no Haçienda regular or Spike Islander could doubt that the momentary diversion of Madchester gave us a little glimpse of utopia.

The influence of E culture on English culture affected our national sport, football. New Order's World Cup song 'A World In Motion' (with the chorus 'E is for England') caught the mood of the times. There were also, perhaps somewhat exaggerated, claims that inter-fan aggro had been curbed in a more loved-up, chilled-out atmosphere. Further evidence of a more tolerant mood between traditional enemies was the response in Manchester to the Hillsborough disaster in 1989 which claimed the lives of nearly a hundred Liverpool fans. Football fans in the two cities have a history of violent, hysterical animosity, but this was put to one side as Happy Mondays headlined a benefit for the Hillsborough victims held at the Haçienda.

The rave revolution changed music, and Manchester changed with it. It was a long process, a long revolution through the crucial years of creativity in New York, via 'Blue Monday', Greg Wilson, 'The Freaks Come Out At Night' and 'Let The Music Play', to Marshall Jefferson, Detroit, Chicago, the Haçienda, Mike Pickering. Thus in 1988, twelve years after Grandmaster Flash's first triumph, we got the rave revolution, and the birth of E culture. By 1990 Manchester had earned a reputation as the clubland capital of Europe. House music was the new underground – for about ten minutes – and then it went huge. Manchester itself had fresh attitudes, a new profile and a pioneering reputation.

The rave revolution even changed the look of the city; it literally made concrete the shift from the post-punk 70s and early 80s to the rave era late 80s and 90s. The Joy Division years were over. Clubs took over old buildings in rundown areas (often attracted by the low rents and rates, occasional refurbishment grants, and a lack of local residents and businesses likely to lodge planning objections) and thus achieved a trailblazing position at the forefront of city centre regeneration; the Haçienda on Whitworth Street, Sankey's Soap in Ancoats, the Boardwalk in Knott Mill. The Boardwalk's owner, Colin Sinclair, during the club and bar boom of the mid 1990s pinpointed the contrast between the era of Joy Division and the Smiths and the way the new club scene had begun to impose a new image on the city: 'What happened originally was that the landscape influenced the bands, and now we're seeing a change where the bands are influencing the landscape.'

A generation was empowered by rave in the same way that punk had spawned a thousand DIY fanzine-writers and countless bands. Former members of the house nation were less likely to join bands, however, than to become DJs, open record shops, design web sites and start labels. Key Manchester designers at opposite ends of the 1990s – Gio Goi and Matthew Williamson – were both indebted to the influence of dance culture on their work (Matthew Williamson's show during London Fashion Week in 1998 was entitled 'Disco's Revenge'). Manchester, England; the UK, as Matthew Collin neatly puts it, is an 'altered state'. By the end of the century, rave culture inhabited all spaces, its influence spread well beyond the dancefloor. The field of design, from flyers to clothes, has felt the change in spirit as slow-burning ideas from the rave generation reach the front pages. In 1996 fashion designer Alexander McQueen was asked where he got ideas from; 'I'm a bit of a raver, a bit of a clubber', he said. James Lavelle, who went on to run Mo' Wax – one of the most influential record labels of the mid 1990s – was just one of many creative characters around Britain who understood Madchester's ghetto-breaking, pluralist spirit as a product of a positive way of thinking. As he said in his early days with Mo' Wax: 'Music's been too formularised in the last few years. Back in the late 80s you had kids going out and buying an 808 State record, a De La Soul record and a Happy Mondays record on the same day. We haven't had that kind of shit happening for ages.'

We've always had a music-driven youth culture in Britain, but the alliance connecting acid house with ecstasy use back in 1987 and 1988 has boosted the impact of house and the profile of drugs. The rave generation has made drug-taking a conspicuous part of a new social landscape. The coyness of previous eras has disappeared. Writers like Irvine Welsh have documented, exposed, illuminated our drug era. Thus what started out in 1987 and 1988 as a trickle of records that enlivened a Friday night out has had maximum impact on the popular culture of Britain. Welsh himself acknowledges this: 'For me, the most important way of making sense of British culture is to see it in terms of pre- and post-acid house culture.'

Meanwhile, the drugged-up, pluralist delirium of the Haçienda in 1988 has been reproduced a million times every weekend in every city and town in the country. In the midst of the noise and the crowds, the dancefloor seems like the perfect escape, a radical alternative to drudgery, uniformity, and a perfect example of the real, raw, hybrid underground of English culture. Ten years ago we had no name for the wildness on the Haçienda dancefloor. But, as Tony Marcus in *Mixmag* was to put it some years later, 'Raving, in all its forms, is now as English as fish and chips.'

CHAPTER 8

Dancefloors and Door Wars:

Manchester's Clubland in the 1990s

In the 1990s Manchester's nightlife assumed an importance way beyond its standing in any previous decade. It became a source of city pride, routinely praised by the local Council and the official marketing and tourist agencies. But reputations are precarious, and Manchester clubs have simultaneously become the site of both fun and fear. They've come to be key barometers of the cycles and changes in music, yet also the focus for drug use, organised violence and a crisis in policing with repercussions for much wider society.

Peter Hook of New Order, one of the Haçienda's owners, had characterised the atmosphere in the club during the rave revolution as 'the closest you'll ever see to collective madness'. But the madness wasn't just a thrill. The powerful creative strength of the scene – that it was so out of control – was also a liability. Ecstasy use surged, and the drugs became wedded to the scene. For a generation of younger drug-takers, there was nothing to beat a night out with a head-full of pills. It was like a warped version of Belle Vue's first rollercoaster, a ride to physical and emotional heights; a new generation of highs and lows, and yours for a tenner.

On 14 July 1989, Claire Leighton, a sixteen-year-old from Cannock, visited the Haçienda. She took an E given to her by her boyfriend, collapsed in the club, and died thirty-six hours later; while noting that her reaction to the drug was unusual, the coroner concluded that 'This is the first [death] but regrettably it is not likely to be the last.' Unfortunately, his prediction turned out to be accurate. When fifteen-year-old Stacey Brown was killed by a reaction to a rogue batch of E bought outside Bowlers in Trafford Park in February 1994, the toll of ecstasy-related deaths in Greater Manchester had reached six. Claire Leighton's death had been followed by the death of Robert Parsonage from Denton in May 1991, Alasdair Burnett from Walshaw near Bury in July 1991, Paula Carrier from Marple in April 1992 and Ayshea Pero from Bolton in 1992. The unpredictability intensified these tragedies; for Alasdair Burnett it was the first time he'd taken the drug. He was seventeen.

What utopian hopes had been raised by the rave revolution had long since disappeared. For many people, Christmas 1990 marked the end of Madchester's natural lifespan. Manchester had gathered intense attention but, too long under the magnifying glass, the energy was burned out. Or so it seemed. Ian Brown: 'It was all over within a year. Then the merchandisers moved in, then the guns.'

By 1991 there were at least three good reasons to be disillusioned after the high of Madchester. First, the flagship acts, Happy Mondays and the Stone Roses, were sinking. The Mondays had made their mark by being shockingly good, but descended into seeking attention by being merely shocking; cavorting in porn mags and having a go at 'faggots' came across as self-indulgence. There had always been a larger-than-life element to the Mondays but the cartooning became predictable. Shaun Ryder slid into self-parody, and the songs on their LP, *Yes Please!*, sounded like lazy druggy dot-to-dot exercises. The edge had gone.

The Stone Roses got bogged down in legal and financial arguments when they left their record label, Silvertone, and attempted to move to Geffen in 1990. They then took so long to get down to recording a follow-up to their era-defining debut LP that creativity deserted them; *Second Coming* (1994) was a disappointing guitar drudge. It was no surprise to learn that the writing and recording of the LP had coincided with years of personal acrimony between the members of the group, and much drug use. Ian Brown admits smoking a lot of dope post-Madchester; 'it turned my head to mush', he now concedes. Meanwhile, early in 1995 John Squire admitted a heavy cocaine habit, and in July of the same year Mani went public with heroin troubles; the band's split was the result not so much of musical differences as chemical differences.

Second, the rave revolution had reflected open-minded, pluralist Manchester, but the success of the city brought different attitudes to the surface as Manchester pride turned back into insularity. Manchester was turning into London, getting too cocksure that it had everything, writing off the rest of the world. This flew in the face of one of the city's strengths, as the novelist Nicholas Blincoe has recognised, claiming that Manchester 'positions itself more readily in a global context – it's London that's parochial'. But in the early 1990s a whole slew of bands emerged in Manchester who believed that geography gave them a divine right to an audience; quality control was disappearing. As it turned out, the creative highlight of 1991 belonged not to any Manchester bands, but to Nirvana in Seattle, USA.

Third, it all got too serious, especially in the clubs. Bad vibes started seeping into the scene around the middle of 1989. The first signal was when the Gallery – a club on the corner of Peter Street and Deansgate, and a favourite venue for black youth – was closed by the police. The Gallery was rundown, but the club was relatively trouble-free despite various feuds erupting through 1988 and 1989 among some of the black gangs in the inner city. Promoters on the black street soul scene have always been wary of the police, accusing them of making all efforts to keep black people out of the city centre, alleging that the licensing police have a word with the owners of any club that begins to attract a black audience. As a consequence, the important black clubs were the underground ones. In town there was the Gallery, and in Moss Side there was the Nile and the Reno on Princess Road. They were close-knit and defiant. They were, as one punter described them to me, 'neighbourhood places; your face better fit'.

Friday nights at the Gallery, 'Groovers', featured Dean Johnson and John Tracey playing soul and jazz (the night ran from 1987 until the closure of the club), and Saturdays featured Soul Control playing to a blacker audience. The Gallery was maybe intimidating if you weren't used to it, and jeeps parked up outside the club on a Saturday night blocked the highway, but the music was pure gold – a purist version of Mike Pickering's pre-house playlist – and the club rocked. The Gallery was an unprepossessing venue but no one cared, as Dean Johnson recalls: 'The Gallery was a complete shit-hole and we could never get the sound system working until half past twelve, and when you arrived for work there'd be a moat because the toilets had been trashed. All these things are by-the-by, you just remember the good bits.'

There has been an unsubstantiated rumour that the Gallery closed down when someone involved with the management got jailed for dealing cocaine, but the truth is more prosaic according to Dean:

> They could have closed the Gallery for several reasons, but the actual law was no hot food on sale; that's actually what a nightclub licence is based on, the sale of hot food during opening hours, although obviously anyone ordering hot food in the Gallery would have been a braver man than me. And also, I think the police suspected that people were smoking marijuana; the fact that you couldn't see across the room was neither here or there, they *suspected* people were smoking marijuana.

The closure of the Gallery in 1989 didn't help the growing incidents of violence in the Haçienda. It displaced a crowd who in the Gallery had been self-policing, but once drawn into the Haçienda became a deadly addition to the cocktail of trouble. Nevertheless, no one could have foreseen the scale of the problems which were to engulf the Haçienda; aside from the enlightened music policy, the original appeal of the club in the 1980s was its friendly atmosphere. Even at the height of the rave revolution in 1988 it was probably more dangerous to be in a queue at a chip shop in Longsight after the pubs shut than it ever was being at the Haçienda.

Nevertheless, violent elements crept into the club, appearing under the balcony, round the stairs, behind the DJ box. A DJ can sense the vibe, your instincts are locked in to the atmosphere; riding and reacting to the crowd is a key part of the craft. Occasionally in those years you could sense there was going to be violence – there was tense unease in the club – but there was very little you could do about it. In fact, you'd want it to happen sooner rather than later, to clear the air. The fights in the club were usually between gangs of dealers vying for territory, rarely involving innocent customers. The customers were also well away from the behind-the-scenes intimidation faced by the management as various gang-led door teams competed for control of the club's security. Manchester clubbers, in their pursuit of great nights out, began to acclimatise themselves to the peripheral presence of intimidating characters in the city's clubs.

One night at the Haçienda I was threatened with a gun while I was DJ-ing. I thought it was someone wanting me to play a favourite record of theirs, but it was a guy with a different kind of request:

'Give me your records.' One night I'd had a girl come in the DJ box, take all her clothes off and lie down naked at my feet; she started untying my laces as I stumbled around for the next record to play. I'd seen boys battling with broken bottles one minute and hugging each other two minutes later. I'd seen hands in the air, smiling faces, total abandon, enormous pleasure and massive energy. I'd watched people climb up the pillars, dance on the bar, fight in the toilets. Having a gun pulled on me just seemed part of the carnival.

The Haçienda was receiving massive publicity, but in getting the praise and the plaudits, we got the problems as well. The club became a victim of its own success, as all kinds of undesirable elements appeared. There were also problems at Konspiracy and the Thunderdome. The Thunderdome closed after a series of violent incidents culminating in a drive-by shooting when doormen were hit in the leg in the summer of 1989. Konspiracy, the old Pips on Fennel Street, had gathered a huge following, especially on Saturday nights. Soon enough, dealers and gang members – especially black gangs from Cheetham Hill and white roughnecks from Salford – took up favourite spots inside the club, and had soon intimidated the staff to the point where they could stroll in unhindered, demand free drinks and openly deal drugs.

Manchester is a hard city with a long history of trouble on the streets, from the battles and the garrotting panics of the nineteenth century, to the scuttlers, drunkards, muggers and street gangs of the early twentieth. The city's entertainment venues can do no more or less than reflect the atmosphere of Manchester as a whole; frequently they've provided shelter from the chaos, depression and violence of the streets, but inevitably, the pubs, clubs, funfairs, dancehalls, bars and arcades have themselves been the focus of trouble. In recent years – probably the last decade and a half – old-fashioned violence has been amplified with the introduction of guns into the criminal community.

Ex-boxers had stood on the doors of venues in Manchester for over half a century. Up to the middle of the 1980s doormen would punish and deter violence by administering a swift beating, kicking the culprit all the way up the street and round the corner. But in the era of guns, the threat of armed retaliation has made the policing of nightlife almost impossible. On many occasions I've heard lads who have been denied entry to a club drop gang leaders' names and threaten to come back later with guns. Occasionally they have done;

it's even been known for doormen to be followed home by gunmen looking for revenge.

Another change in the late 1980s was that gang activity moved out of the neighbourhoods and into the city centre. Gangsters and criminals had plagued local communities for years, families and alliances of local hard men and nutcases taking their cut and controlling criminal activity. Up until the end of the 1950s the influence of a criminal gang seldom went further than a few streets and some pubs, but, as we've seen, these old communities were broken down by slum clearance, new estates and inner city demolition; the streets that provided established gangs with an income had literally disappeared.

Furthermore, unemployment grew through the 1970s as local manufacturing industries crashed, and divisive social policies and growing poverty in the early 1980s created desperate conditions. As unemployment rose kids without jobs took a route into crime instead, but the recession meant that what was left of local communities wasn't worth stealing. Instead, drug dealing became a lucrative business. If Manchester's city centre had been livelier through the 1970s and early part of the 1980s, then the gangs may have targeted businesses, but the night-time economy – such as it was – was then based around boozers, a couple of high street discotheques, live venues, and a handful of old clubs and gambling dens. But when clubland began to expand in the late 1980s, the gangs moved in. They wanted a piece of the action.

Another key factor in the upsurge in violence in Manchester's clubland was the way fuel for clubgoers underwent a huge change from alcohol to ecstasy in the late 1980s. This created markets for drugs in and around clubs, and a battle for control of those drug markets ensued. All drug markets are controlled by organised crime, by gangs operating on the streets and in estates. The way a gang could gain control of drug deals in a club was to take control of the front door and then hand pick the dealers inside.

Conflict between door security firms is commonplace in England, with its roots in protection rackets. The Manchester gangs developed a strategy: destabilise a club by sending in young wannabes to instigate brawls and cause mayhem, and then point out to the licensee that their firm is the only one capable of controlling the situation. And control of the door not only gives you control of the drugs trade, but puts the club owner in your pocket.

As the problems escalated, club owners, in their turn, attempted to develop ways of dealing with violent elements who latch on to clubs, but it's a battle that few clubs have ever come near to winning. As the problems at Konspiracy grew, one of the owners, Marino Morgan, said, 'Without Robocop on the door they are difficult to stop. This is the front line in a society which is getting more and more violent.'

Society had not only become more violent, but business had become more cut-throat and materialism had taken a grip. What was being played out in clubs in the early 1990s seemed like the chaotic result of attitudes that had prevailed for the best part of a decade, trickling down from a Government that prized the individual above community. In an era when the country's leaders were looking for a short cut and a quick buck it's not hard to understand how everyday life was being warped by the same sleaze. We'd listened to Government ministers justifying backhanders to the makers and dealers in weapons of mass destruction. If we believed anything could be justified in the pursuit of money, we'd been guided from the top.

Despite Manchester clubland making a huge and positive contribution to the international profile of the city, the police were suspicious; they saw clubs as the cause and focus of problems, fronts for laundering money, the focus for drink-fuelled violence. Even as late as 1998 senior policemen were going on record refuting the view that clubs were legitimate businesses that required police support. It was therefore not surprising that the 1990s were fraught with conflict between club owners and an entrenched police culture. A feature of police work in the city's nightclubs and bars was undercover officers gathering evidence of licence infringements in order to close the premises; in fact, other regular visitors were the so-called 'hush puppies', a squad of specially recruited out-of-town police engaged in deeper level investigations into criminal activities in nightclubs. One of the justifications given by police spokesmen seeking to explain spiralling violent crime in the city centre is the scarce resources of the force, and yet, in the case of one city centre club that came under scrutiny early in 1997, Greater Manchester Police are estimated to have spent nearly a quarter of a million pounds on covertly monitoring the premises. Closing clubs merely moves trouble on elsewhere; another lesson the police appeared slow to learn.

The pressure on the Haçienda intensified with the demise of the Gallery and the Thunderdome. In May 1990 the police advised the Haçienda that they were intending to revoke its licence and close the club, a move which the club challenged. The Haçienda won the case, with the help of the celebrated lawyer George Carman, letters of support from Manchester City Council and promises to clean up their act, but perhaps the police never forgave them their victory. When Konspiracy was closed just after Christmas 1990, more troubles were triggered at the Haçienda, and this time the management themselves decided to close the club. The disastrous publicity and the bad vibes had scared away customers, and the club was losing money which sapped morale; with guns being pulled on the door almost weekly, the management had no fight left.

This voluntary closure turned out to be temporary, and it was barely three months later that the club reopened, a decision made against the backdrop of a lull in gang wars in the inner city and the murder of one of the city's most notorious gangsters, 'White' Tony Johnson, killed outside the Penny Black pub in Cheetham Hill. But hopes that the Haçienda's problems were over were short-lived; one Friday, exactly three weeks after reopening, six doormen got stabbed when a gang tried to rush the doors. Publicity surrounding this new incident ensured that the club's reputation took a major hammering. Once again regulars stayed at home, numbers plummeted, and the club's PR supremo, Paul Cons, was left with nothing to enjoy: 'By the end of 1991 the best days of the Haçienda were over, and the crowd on a Friday and Saturday was horrendous, really ropey.'

These were the years sometimes referred to in the press as 'Gunchester', when Manchester gained a reputation for violence in the clubs and on the streets. Tension in town was heightened because of feuds between Moss Side factions Doddington and Gooch; thirty-five shootings were said to have occurred in the area in a six month period in 1991. Violence from Salford and Cheetham Hill gangs also started seeping into the clubs and bars. In May 1989 Factory had opened a bar on Oldham Street, Dry 201, and soon faced troubles similar to the Haçienda's. A minority of locals played up the image, getting some kind of rush from the situation, but others despaired as across town livelihoods, and – in the worst cases – perhaps even lives, were put at risk. One retailer who thrived through some good years selling flares, hooded tops and Madchester t-shirts felt the backlash when the scene went into decline, the recession deepened and criminality increased. He tells a fantastical tale:

> We had a manager kidnapped. 1990 and 1991 were bad years for everybody. Unfortunately I started bringing in all that LA Raiders gear. I loved it, but I didn't think enough about it. These guys appeared and lured him out of the shop pointing at something near the door and saying, 'There's no price on that jacket', bundled him into a car up to Ancoats, put a bag on his head, told him, 'We're turning the shop over tomorrow and unless you turn the video camera off you're a dead man.'

Eight or nine years after the events, the psychological scars were deep:

> It was a catalogue of nightmares. Shoplifting was horrendous, kids with handfuls of stuff opening up their jacket, showing a gun and saying, 'I don't pay for anything.' I couldn't get staff to work unless I had doormen. Christmas 1990 for the next twelve months it all went wrong. One gang threw a CS canister in the shop, steamed through; that was £12,000 of gear gone. I was locked into leases so I couldn't just walk away. It cost me more in security than the bloody takings.

The problems at the Haçienda didn't hinder all positive initiatives in the city, however, as promoters, DJs and club owners attempted to stay one step ahead of trouble. Under the dominating shadow of the Haçienda in its glory days, few promoters, DJs or club owners had managed to launch and maintain new nights in other venues, but the years after 1991 saw a welcome widening of choice, as creativity thrived in small clubs, new clubs and – in many cases – grotty old clubs.

The resurgence of a gay scene was the first big positive response to clubland's violent troubles. The city had got labelled – perhaps even libelled – by the blanket dismissal of life after Madchester as 'Gunchester', but once the media had caught on to a conspicuous rise in the profile of gay clubs and bars in the city, the label temporarily changed to 'Gaychester'. The glamorous, loud, proud and photogenic gay scene met the media's incessant demand for a new story, and somehow Manchester's image as city riddled with psychotic gangsters was, incredibly, swapped for one bursting with drag queens.

In the early 1980s gay club culture hadn't come out in Manchester. As can be imagined, there was no encouragement from the local

Chief Constable James Anderton, whose views on the subject were notorious, yet there were one or two tiny venues, often on the edge of old-time red light zones, which had developed a gay clientele; around Deansgate and King Street, for instance, Bernard's Bar (later known as Stuffed Olives), Manhattan Sound and Heroes. The scene in Heroes, in particular, had its roots among young dressed up, cross-dressing David Bowie fans. All three venues were kitted out in a plastic early 80s style – big carpets, potted plants and mirrors in fake gold frames – but enjoyed adventurous music policies. At Manhattan Sound one Tuesday in 1983 the Smiths played their first ever gig, supported by a Divine video. More usually the musical fare was a choice between nights with a New Romantic twist and hi-energy. In the early 1980s there were a couple of world-class DJs playing hi-energy in Manchester: Ian Levine and Les Cockell, who had both graduated from backgrounds as Northern Soul DJs.

A more hard-edged scene grew around the Archway on Whitworth Street, built under the railway arches with car repair shops as its only neighbours. Now it's a straight student-oriented club, the Brickhouse, surrounded by take-aways and café bars, but in the mid 1980s the Archway was a hardcore gay club, rudely furnished, the tarted-up damp bricks and steel beams from the railway arch fused with a few cold metal rails, a small balcony and a DJ box suspended on the back wall. Nothing was fake about the Archway, just stripped down and very dark, a bit claustrophobic. In 1985 it was one of the best clubs in Manchester. A few of us on a Saturday night, bored of the Haçi-enda, would go over to the Archway. If you were in by 1am, I think it was, you could stay till 8am, or longer. It wasn't mixed lesbian and gay like many of the better-known clubs of the 1990s; it was for the men only, the clones, in leather mostly, or lumberjack shirts. Many times there would still be guys coming out of there on Sunday lunchtime.

Around Canal Street, a gay scene had developed on the fringes of the red light area near Chorlton Bus Station, among the derelict canal-side warehouses, makeshift brothels and seedy old pubs. Some of the old pubs had been attracting a gay clientele for decades, and the area was a well known location for canal-side trysts. The New Union pub has been an unsophisticated gay hang-out for over half a century, as has New York New York on Bloom Street. Napoleon's, open since 1972, is one of Europe's oldest gay bars. There was also Le Rouge on the south side of the canal. Other gay venues in the mid 1980s included the Thompson's Arms and the Rembrandt. On Bloom Street there was a gay bookshop and café, and Clone Zone, a clothes shop that housed Les Cockell's record shop at the back. In the evening prostitutes and cruisers mixed business and pleasure, the scene like something from a painting by George Grosz, rent boys running in and out of pub doorways, transvestites tripping over the curbstones, the damp air filled with a cacophony of music, shouting, screaming and half-heard whisperings.

But the brief blossoming of small scenes around clubs like Heroes, the Archway and Nap's in the early 1980s had withered at the onset of AIDS. Harry and Wayne from the Archway were just two of the many men on the scene who didn't survive into the 1990s. Understandably, in the shadow of these tragedies, early 1990s gay clubbing was in the doldrums, and a revival was slow in coming; one of the first of a new breed of gay clubs in Manchester was the Number One club, which, thanks to DJ Tim Lennox, pursued a credible Haçienda-style music policy and attracted a young crowd, but the club was too small, stuffy in the summer and damp in the winter.

A new generation, though, began to lay the foundations of Manchester's so-called 'Gay Village' around the existing sites on Canal Street. A lot of the Manhattan crowd moved over when the owner sold up and took over the Rembrandt. A more conspicuous development came with the opening of Manto at the beginning of 1991. Manto was a softcore version of the Archway in its look, and immediately made its presence felt as a stylish bar, its huge windows giving the building brightness. It was designed as if it now had nothing to hide, a world away from the darkened dives around it. Fashionable straights also flocked to Manto, considering it an up-dated, safer version of Factory's Dry bar. Canal Street is now a major commercial gay area, but Manto was the key first part of the infrastructure. When it opened there wasn't even a club that catered for the kind of crowd Manto had invented. Then 'Flesh', a monthly night at the Haçienda devised by Paul Cons and Lucy Scheer, harnessed the desires of a new younger generation, drew on the energies of the house scene, and marked a major transition overground for both gay men and women in Manchester. The first 'Flesh' was amazing; thirteen hundred people, a lock-out.

'Flesh' was a major success story for the Haçienda in an era when the rest of the club's nights were falling behind. 1992 was a pivotal year, when the Haçienda lost its monopoly of good ideas and big crowds. Most significantly of all, the city's flagship independent label, Factory Records, went into receivership.

Yet other trends pointed to a positive future for the local scene, as we witnessed not just the beginnings of a new era for the gay scene but a new generation of emerging bands. Resurrection was in the air. Rob Gretton started Rob's Records, his own label (licensing the Beat Club's 'Security' and 'Dreams Are Made To Be Broken', two great pieces of housed-up electro from Florida). His partner at Factory, Tony Wilson, also emerged with a new project before Factory's liquidators had even had time to dust down the company's files. Thus two of the old guard joined a host of younger enthusiasts, entrepreneurs, DJs and musicians who were already developing new labels, new club nights, new groups. The collapse of the Factory empire scattered the seeds of creativity.

There is no great mystery behind Factory's financial collapse in November 1992; they had been spending more than they earned in almost every year since the Haçienda was built. In their last years they signed second division guitar bands, lost Haçienda and Dry regulars weekly, and faced a slide in the fortunes of the Happy Mondays. Furthermore, the Madchester years had coincided with Nigel Lawson's 'boom'; the nation was high on credit, and the consumer frenzy in that era had undoubtedly fuelled the entertainment sector in the city. Nationwide, it was an era when property developers became the consumer society's latest saints. The demand for shiny new buildings reflected the continued 80s fashion for style and image. It was in this atmosphere that Factory Records left their offices on Palatine Road and invested heavily in a new headquarters on Charles Street.

However, by the end of 1992 things looked different. The economy was suffering in the middle of new Chancellor Lamont's slump, and the entertainment and property sectors were both hit hard. Coupled with the independent record label sector losing credibility in the wake of changing music tastes, the Factory empire came under pressure. Without a steady flow of albums from New Order, Factory's most bankable act, with no one willing or able to get a grip on the flailing career of Happy Mondays, and with debts piling up – not the least of which was the building on Charles Street – fundamental weaknesses in Factory's position appeared when the economy slumped. As the experts say, 'You can't tell who's swimming naked until the tide goes out.'

In an astounding display of hype and brinkmanship, in October 1992 Anthony H. Wilson launched In The City, an annual music business convention, even while his own business was going bankrupt. Delegates travelled from around the world to talk through new ideas, marketing angles, product development and sales strategies. In The City has become an ongoing success, but for Factory Records it was all over by Christmas. Throughout the last year of the label, Wilson affected all the trappings of a mover and shaker. At the time he used to tell me, in a fit of businessman bluster, that his favourite reading was the *Wall Street Journal*. I didn't realise until later that he was probably scanning the situations vacant.

The Manchester music scene has been powered by accidental entrepreneurs. Whereas the personal and emotional investment of businessmen in other industries may be strong, accidental entrepreneurs just fall for the music, the scene, want to be involved. Unable merely to spectate, their involvement in it all as a business venture creeps up to them, grabs them unexpectedly. You do a fanzine, sell some t-shirts, put on some parties, manage a group, put out a record. Next thing you know you're filling in your first VAT return.

This new blood awash with energies pouring time and ideas into the music scene brings ceaseless activity to Manchester, but there's not necessarily a lot of business acumen behind the creative imaginations. The jobs are insecure, the scene is built on shifting sands. Factory is a prime example of friends falling into business together. There was always strife. Factory always was a volatile combination of street suss and bad accounting.

The financial crisis at Factory in the autumn of 1992 was complicated by continuing problems at the Haçienda. The creative sharp-edge seemed blunted, and while 'Flesh' ran as a successful monthly for five years, other nights at the club struggled through 1992 and 1993. The situation was exacerbated by recurrent violence setting back attempts to rebuild a safe reputation for the club. The management employed a door firm controlled from Salford, some of whose employees were alleged to have taken part in the violence, and charged, though cleared, with matters relating to the killing of Tony Johnson, Wilson reasoning that the only effective security firm was one unafraid of anybody or anything. The doormen maintained a hard reputation but believed in giving leeway to certain characters in order to keep the peace; there were one or two untouchables. The bad vibes hung around. The continuing violence after the reopening was a key factor in Mike Pickering's decision to leave the club in May 1993: 'I continually asked for something to be done about it. There was nothing I could do; I don't really know how all these gang things work, maybe there wasn't anything that could have been done anyway, but in the end I said to Paul Mason, "I can't work here when I'm even telling my friends on the guest list not to come".'

Despite serious problems of continuing violence and intimidation, rumours of the death of Manchester's clubland were greatly exaggerated. Even in the dark days of 1992 and 1993, the seeds of clubland's successful survival into the late 1990s were still growing. Nights like 'Most Excellent' tuned in to the so-called 'Balearic network', featuring a fun-filled eclectic playlist and building links with clubs like Full Circle in London and Venus in Nottingham. In 1992 'Most Excellent' could be found at the Wiggly Worm on West Mosley Street (a club previously known as Millionaire, under the ownership of Peter Stringfellow). But the 'Gunchester' label stuck as the continuing violence took attention from the positive trends for several more years. We were left to comfort ourselves with the thought that the best things happen when no one's looking.

Within just a few years of the beginning of rave culture, enough myths had developed to warrant a growing demand for nights that billed themselves 'reviving the spirit of 88'. Ironically, the audience for these was dominated by younger clubbers who had actually missed the reality of 1988, but threw themselves wholeheartedly into house culture, usually with a predilection for the hardcore house championed locally by DJs like Moggy, Jay Wearden and Steve Williams at venues like the Hippodrome in Middleton early in 1992, and nationally at mega-raves by DJs like Carl Cox and Grooverider.

Ecstasy victims were often from the younger end of clubland; for these second-generation ravers, getting into the accelerated bpm's of techno and hardcore, drug use appeared mandatory. In Scotland, the majority of ecstasy deaths were teenagers, concentrated at hardcore house venues like Ayr's Hangar 13. A similarly young crowd took residence at 'Life' at Bowlers in Trafford Park which started in April 1992 and went on to develop as Manchester's quintessential rave night, all piano breaks, white gloves, whistles and Liquid's 'Sweet Harmony'.

A feature of clubbing in the early 1990s, in addition to fragmentation and niche marketing, nostalgia, escalating drug use and increasing commercialisation, was the rise of DJ culture. The biggest name,

Sasha, came to prominence DJ-ing at Shelley's in Stoke in 1990, and at clubs like Shaboo in Blackpool and Venus in Nottingham. In 1988 he'd been a Haçienda regular, driving over from Wales every weekend and dancing for five hours on the podium; he started DJ-ing by picking up some of the gigs Jon Da Silva was too busy to do. His rise to DJ superstar was swift; he graduated from enthusiastic Haçienda punter to *Mixmag* cover star in less than three years. The buzz about certain DJs spread by word of mouth, and once the media got hold of the 'DJ phenomenon' the trend accelerated. In the early 1990s thousands of clubgoers were on the move, following DJs, travelling to nights at Liverpool's Quadrant Park, the Arena in Middlesbrough, 'Back to Basics' in Leeds and 'Golden' at Liberty's in Stoke, which, in the wake of the closure of Shelley's, first opened its doors in March 1992.

The idea of a DJ circuit was nothing new – Manchester's Northern Soul fraternity had travelled down to the Torch in Stoke and the soul crowd had followed Colin Curtis from Blackpool to Bournemouth – but the circuit opened up by the Boy's Own DJs and the Venus/ 'Most Excellent' axis revived and extended the network, although the first people to feel the benefit of a nationwide dance scene and a new demand for guest DJs were the Americans. The circuit became a gravy train for American DJs. Although they started out playing small venues – Todd Terry made his Manchester debut at the Boardwalk in June 1992 and got paid £800 – David Morales, Danny Tenaglia, Tony Humphries and Todd Terry would go on to earn many thousands of pounds guesting in big clubs all over Europe. Their domination of clubland was another feature of the time; by the end of 1995 Todd Terry's fee for a Manchester gig was said to be £12,000.

As in most other types of culture, however, in club culture the best work is away from the mainstream and out, instead, among the adventurers and accidental entrepreneurs. Two music lovers who had come to Manchester as students – Tom Rowlands and Ed Simons of the Chemical Brothers – started out DJ-ing at 'Naked Under Leather' in 1992. They were the resident DJs and the organisers, along with Phil South and Alex Kohler, and hosted their night at a selection of uninviting, unlikely, mostly damp, very cheaply hired venues (including Consorts, the Swinging Sporran and the Mineshaft). Following a playlist veering wildly from old skool block rocking hip hop (LL Cool J, Public Enemy) to Renegade Soundwave and Flowered Up, the Chemical Brothers soon moved into music-making;

their first single, 'Song To The Siren', was released by Junior Boy's Own in 1993.

In the spring of 1993, small-scale nights across the city were doing great things; 'Hoochie Coochie' at Oscars and the 'Glory Hole' at Bar Kay, for example. Making their way towards a career DJ-ing worldwide were the Luv Dup DJs, Adrian and Mark; early in 1993 they were hosting 'Hell' at the Number One on Friday nights. At the Planet on Back Piccadilly, Mike Chadwick mixed and matched with guests like Coldcut. The Planet had very little going for it, but pro-moter Andrew Stratford, in a typical example of someone trying to make something happen despite overwhelming odds, took one night a week, and thus, at 'Teutonic' at the Planet in 1993, Richie Hawtin and C. J. Bolland first played Manchester.

The shift of interest away from the Haçienda after the reopening, as well as a new-found confidence in Manchester's future, was under-lined by the arrival of purpose-built clubs like Paradise Factory in May 1993 and Home in September 1993. The survival of the scene was further guaranteed by music-makers inspired by Manchester nightlife delivering massive hits in these years, most notably M-People. Mike Pickering had made music in Quando Quango and T-Coy as well as DJ-ing; but with M-People in the 1990s he struck gold. In the early part of the decade, as house music fragmented, many cutting-edge DJs championed progressive house, a kind of chugging instrumental techno. Pickering made a conscious decision that M-People would avoid that particular flavour of the month: 'I was saying to DeConstruction about how I wanted to keep hearing songs; they went, "Well write some; you can do it."'

M-People started out as a series of collaborations with different musicians, but with singer Heather Small in place the line-up became permanent in 1991 during the recording of *Northern Soul*, the band's first LP. In 1992 the LP was released and then re-released as interest grew, and through 1993 M-People were chart regulars with songs like 'One Night In Heaven' and 'Moving On Up'. Heather Small's was a voice there was no escaping as the decade developed and the band had hit after hit. The choice of singer was key.

A stream of great local black female singers vibed up Manchester music in the 1990s. Rachel McFarlane sang with Family Foundation and Loveland, and Diane Charlemagne (who had started out with 52nd Street and Cool Down Zone) sang on 'The Key, The Secret' and with Goldie. Another, Denise Johnson, had sung with Fifth of

Heaven – her first live performance with them was supporting Maze at Wembley Arena – then ACR, and on to Primal Scream (featuring on their *Screamadelica* and *Give Out But Don't Give Up* LPs), as well as finding time to guest with Electronic and the Joy. Bad experiences with major labels held back her solo career, but late in the decade her own releases included 'Inner Peace', released in July 1997.

Perhaps just one of many reasons for the great number of black female singers is the huge part played by gospel music in the lives of young black kids (especially girls) growing up in a swathe of south Manchester, from Old Trafford, through Chorlton and Whalley Range, to Moss Side and old Hulme. Those who made a direct leap from singing in gospel choirs to joining local groups include Cordelia Ruddock from Serial Diva (their 'Keep Hope Alive' single was released on Ministry of Sound's label) and Veba (signed to Mark Rae's Grand Central label), who served an apprenticeship in the evangelical churches of Old Trafford, going on to star in some classic tracks made in Manchester in 1998 and 1999 – like 'Spellbound' and 'All I Ask' and 'Swan Song (For a Nation)' – and freestyling mesmerically at Mark Rae's club, Counter Culture. Occasionally the influence of gospel on M-People is conspicuous, as on the live version of 'Another Surprise' on their 1998 tour.

M-People built their career in classic clubland territory, appearing on flyers with Sasha and Dave Seaman, and playing at nights like 'Kaos' in Leeds, but relentless ear-kissing hit-making won them a big, adult, mainstream audience. Their rise is a reminder of how versions of the up-front can become acceptable mainstream in a very short time. It's also a reminder that there's nothing uniform about Manchester-based bands; from Morrissey's bedroom introspection, to N-Trance's headless dancefloor ramraids, to the maverick Mark E. Smith.

But there's also a tradition of Manchester acts working solely within the confines of commercial formulae. M-People's hits have given them similarities with acts like Simply Red and Lisa Stansfield. Dig deep, though, and there may still be some roots that cling to them, remind us and them of where some of their strength is drawn. Deeper than Mick Hucknall's support for Manchester United and Lisa Stansfield's obsession with *Coronation Street*, and even beyond M-People's 'Angel Street' single set in Ancoats (the video underlines this connection). Perhaps right down to the fact that they reflect something of the local mix of communities, particularly as all three clearly work in the local tradition of Manchester music inspired by black American soul music, a tradition which goes back at least to the beat groups of the early 1960s. The soul connection can't be overstressed; even in 1982 when Mick Hucknall was fronting a rockabilly-tinged punk group called the Frantic Elevators he was name-checking the likes of Bobby Bland, Aretha Franklin and James Brown as influences.

Some of the city's mainstream acts were having spectacular success in the early 1990s. When Manchester was post-Madchester, the city supposedly dead, Simply Red's *Stars* was, incredibly, the best-selling LP in the UK in both 1991 and 1992. At the same time that Simply Red dominated the adult pop market, Take That were dominating the teen market. They were Manchester's most manufactured group, as manufactured as the Monkees, as safe as Herman's Hermits. Put together by a Manchester-based management team, Take That had two LPs in the top-selling twenty LPs of 1993 and a record-breaking eight Number One hit singles.

At the other end of the commercial scale, the house scene was thriving, and there was more variety in Manchester music-making than probably ever before. As well as the commercial giants and the piano break merchants, there were rap, breakbeat and Balearic tracks, including Krispy 3's 'Stereotypes', Franschene's 'Go Sister', and Greg Wilson's brief return to the scene producing a take on Maze's club hit 'Twilight' called 'Lost In A Maze'.

Manchester Underground record shop began financing releases, as did Dead Dead Good in Northwich – who moved beyond the Charlatans with Bowa's 'Different Story', eventually developing Transworld, a subsidiary label specialising in hi-octane house anthems – and Eastern Bloc. Their label, Creed, had debuted with the 'Hit Squad' EP, and released the early records of 808 State. Eastern Bloc (who had started out as a cooperative venture on a stall in Affleck's Palace trading as Earwig) had become a focus for the rave generation in their first proper, but cramped, Oldham Street shop (now housing Exit in Affleck's Arcade) – where they held legendary all-night parties and jammed non-stop in the basement – and, from 1990 onwards, in a bigger shop over the road. Working behind the counter in the shop proved to be a useful step in the DJ careers of Richard Moonboots, Mike Kirwin, John Berry and Justin Robertson. Robertson and Andy Ellison (Dub Federation), as well as Mike Kirwin, were among those who also combined working at Eastern Bloc with music-making.

Oldham Street had grown tatty in the 1980s. Two decades earlier it had been the most thriving shopping street in central Manchester, but the building of the Arndale shifted activity towards the redeveloped Market Street. The arrival of underhyped shopkeepers selling clothes, accessories and records in the warren of stalls in Affleck's Palace from 1984 onwards was an early glimmer of life. Eastern Bloc became another of Oldham Street's most important attractions, as did Factory's Dry bar, but there was still a lot of economic uncertainty around. A hugely successful operation during the height of Madchester, Eastern Bloc went into receivership in July 1993.

The demise of Eastern Bloc was seized upon as another sign that the Madchester vibe was in retreat. For Martin Price, it had bigger implications; in his apocalyptic vision, the grassroots had been trampled to death, with mainstream clubs playing a greatest-hits version of house and big retail chains like HMV moving into what had been specialist territory and winning the commercial battle. In an interview in *Jockey Slut* he claimed that the local dance scene had been wrecked by an invasion of students: 'It's Hawkwind for a new generation. I want out when it's like that. It's lost its way – it's too up its own arse. It's done exactly the same that punk did, because the British psyche can't do anything except follow disasters.' He told *Jockey Slut* readers there was only one way forward: 'Get off drugs and look at the real world.'

In September 1993 Eastern Bloc found a new backer: Pete Waterman, a former DJ who had found fame as part of the Stock, Aitken & Waterman writing partnership churning out catchy chart fodder by the likes of Kylie Minogue and Rick Astley. But like most old soul boys, Pete Waterman's heart was in the right place. The shop gained a new hip hop section, but naturally lost the last vestiges of its original cooperative status. The Eastern Bloc record label became part of Pete Waterman's PWL group, and subsequent releases included, in April 1994, a big hit for Loveland (featuring Rachel McFarlane) with 'Let The Music (Lift You Up)'.

Despite the loss of major players like Factory and Eastern Bloc through 1992 and 1993, the music business infrastructure was being extended through huge activity at the grassroots; record labels (like Bush and Rob's Records), producers and engineers, studios, and a host of DJs and remixers to fill them. King of the Manc remixers in these years was probably Johnny Jay. His Development Corporation remixes created the defining sound of Urban Cookie Collective, and his remix of 'Joy' by Staxx went Top Twenty in November 1993. Great Manchester DJs also continued to proliferate; in October 1993, according to one magazine, seven out of the top hundred DJs in the world were based in Manchester.

Activity in the less constructive spheres of clubland unfortunately also thrived. Promoters and party people had tried to stay one step ahead of the hoodlums, but once a new night becomes successful and gets a wider audience you get the kind of problems that attached themselves to the Haçienda. There's a 'honeymoon' period when a club can be busy, fun, successful, and undiscovered by the hooligans. Gradually, there's an element in the club who refuse to pay in, then deal drugs, hassle girls, pick fights with the students, and tax the bar. The pattern has been repeated all through the 1990s. 'Most Excellent''s honeymoon came to an end one Thursday night in June 1992, when a group of Salford lads were turned away from the Wiggly Worm and returned in a stolen car and rammed the entrance.

Manto's owners opened Paradise Factory in May 1993 in Factory's old building on Charles Street. There was some justice in the building's new role as a gay club, as the homophobia revealed by Happy Mondays in their later interviews was regarded as a key reason for their slide from public esteem; on the opening night the partygoers fancied that they were literally dancing on the grave of lad culture. Unfortunately, the club hasn't quite lived up to its ambitions. Paradise Factory's survival was only achieved by giving space to straights: Luv Dup's 'Jolly Roger' in 1993 and Justin Robertson's 'Sleuth' in 1994.

We were into the era of corporate clubbing. Home – opened in September 1993 – was the Haçienda's first big purpose-built competitor. Unlike the informal, stumbling origins of the Haçienda, however, the launch of Home – owned by Tom Bloxham, managed by Joe Strong and run by Paul Cons – was backed with money and experience. It formed part of Bloxham's development of Ducie House into a club, café bar and studio office facility. Home struggled to find big regular crowds at the weekend, and one-offs in the hands of outside promoters often drew the biggest crowds. Among the best were the garage-oriented 'Seconds Out', and the most essential night at Home, 'Foundation', promoted by Simon Calderbank. The night launched the DJ careers of Dean Wilson and Bobby Langley, and provided rare treats, like Kenny 'Dope' Gonzalez DJ-ing in the club's café bar in August 1994. In a one-off at Home the previous month, DJ Shadow made his Manchester debut on the Mo' Wax tour.

House music had become a serious money-making opportunity for well-run clubs. There were versions of house music out on the margins, but rave culture had become accepted, neutered. That the culture was now mainstream was underlined by the arrival of a shelf-load of new dance music magazines. Their biggest advertisers were the so-called 'superclubs' – Ministry of Sound, Cream, the Haçienda – who were supposedly doing it best, big barns playing safe, paying big-name jocks. There were still small independent promoters, but promoting seemed to become more about design and marketing as the commodification of house ushered in new obsessions about style rather than music. As Dean Johnson told me in 1995, 'You've actually reached a point now where there are graduates in marketing running nightclubs. In some cases they might succeed because they're really good at the promotional side, but in any case the soul of it is actually dead.'

Dean Johnson's complaints were answered even as they were being made, by other club promoters trying to renew the underground and reintroduce an uncommercial feel in clubs. Two such nights were 'Pollen' and 'Herbal Tea Party', both launched as a direct challenge to what the promoters perceived as a small clique of clubs in Manchester. 'Pollen' began at the beginning of 1993 with resident DJ Crispen Somerville at various venues in the south of the city, settling eventually at the New Ardri in Hulme. Controversy came their way when it was alleged in the press that fruit spiked with LSD was being given out free at the Ardri, but the promoter, Rollo Gabb, merely played up the controversy, dressing up their next flyers like a wrap of whiz. 'Herbal Tea Party' entered the fray from October 1993 fortnightly at the New Ardri. The club was decked out with lightshows and drapes, the entertainment occasionally included face-painting and festival-style stalls, and the refreshments included herbal highs. The atmosphere at 'Pollen' and 'Herbal Tea Party', and the hard techno, appealed to another new audience that had joined the rave nation: a cross-section of students, Hulme squatters and 'crusties' (as they were affectionately known).

Both nights reflected and intensified the spirit of Hulme in the early 1990s. The failed 60s housing blocks – including the notorious Crescents – were marked for demolition from the beginning of the 1980s, but in the absence of money to do the job or any vision of what a new Hulme could look like, the area remained blighted for the whole decade. Families had long gone from the Crescents –

moving out in the mid 1970s when the design faults first became apparent. By the early 1980s Hulme had attracted a growing community of musicians, artists, drop-outs, students and squatters. By the end of the decade, the buildings were slowly collapsing and another generation of punks, anarchists and travellers moved in. Stray dogs roamed the wastelands; Jeff Noon's vision of Hulme as Bottletown in *Vurt* was becoming uncomfortably close to reality. And one group of music-lovers and artists, Dogs of Heaven, came together to create trailblazing spectacles.

Dogs of Heaven had spent a few years of madness on the margins – dragging burning Viking longboats through Hulme, setting fire to a gigantic effigy of Margaret Thatcher – but took centrestage at 'Safe As Houses', the official celebration of Hulme's demolition in 1993. William Kent Crescent was turned into a huge circus arena filled with jiving six foot cockroaches, forty foot skeletons, bonfires, blasting techno and cars falling from the top floor. The event bemused the dignitaries but perfectly encapsulated the renegade creativity apparent among the last inhabitants of high-rise Hulme, many of them denizens of the free festival network, a new house nation fringe of political activists and travelling techno heads who were at the forefront of campaigns against road-building and the criminal justice system. Theirs was a culture only displaced by the rebuilding in the late 1990s.

Elsewhere in the city, changing patterns of nightlife brought the era of the café bar, spreading regeneration into new areas, and encouraging changes in social habits which were to have as big an impact on going out in Manchester as ecstasy had. Two bars opened in December 1993: Isobar bringing further life to Oldham Street, and Atlas providing a gateway to Castlefield. Throughout the 1990s the regeneration of derelict city centre land has quickened, but when the Phoenix Initiative, a private enterprise launched in the early 1980s, had attempted to bring the owners of derelict land together with developers to begin reconstructing parts of the city, the financiers hesitated from making any first moves. It was largely the music venues which moved in first and led the way: the Haçienda had gone alone on to Whitworth Street in 1982; Manto rejuvenated Canal Street; Duke's 92 set the renaissance of Castlefield in stone; the Boardwalk and Atlas turned Knott Mill around; Affleck's Palace, Eastern Bloc and Dry brought some life to Oldham Street. Clubs and bars were the pioneers, capitalising on the availability of cheap land, subsidised rates, and local, national and European grants.

By-passed by urban regeneration in the 1980s, Ancoats had continued to confirm all preconceptions about what a battered post-industrial city should look like, but once Sankey's Soap took occupancy of the ground floor of Beehive Mill on Jersey Street in June 1994, for a couple of nights a week at least, the club was besieged with cars and coaches from out of town, and a buzz had returned.

Although the early days at Sankey's were a struggle, a key turning point in their fortunes came in October 1994 with the opening of a new Friday night, 'Bugged Out!', promoted by Paul Benney and John Burgess from the magazine *Jockey Slut*. Within three months, the established Stoke-based promoters, 'Golden', took over running Saturday nights. This not only secured Sankey's Soap's immediate future, but also opened another chapter in Manchester's club-going relationship with Stoke (going back to the Torch in the Northern Soul era and Sasha's nights at Shelley's during the rave years).

The post-acid fragmentation continued, with clubs playing different permutations of house and old traditions reasserting themselves after an era out of the limelight. At Parker's, from 1990, Dean Johnson and Richard Searling kept the soul flame alive, and in 1992 I went back to funk with my 'Yellow' night at the Boardwalk. The dressed-down baggy look of Madchester was replaced in clubland as Gaychester attitudes filtered into straight clubbing on a number of levels, including the unleashing of more sexy, flamboyant clubwear styles, which girls especially took to at nights like 'Yellow' and at bars like the Athenaeum. A focus for a mixed generation of exhibitionist ravers, models and trannies was established during the early months of 1994 when 'Manumission' started, under the direction of brothers Andy and Mike McKay, with a one-off series of Friday nights at the Athenaeum and Equinox. In the summer they threw the first of their Ibiza parties, which have now grown into huge eight thousand capacity weekly events on the island, attracting much tabloid notoriety in 1998 when Mike and his girlfriend took to having sex on stage.

Cycles, revolutions and reactions keep pop music alive. The creative revolution – each generation doing its own thing – is accentuated by the demands of capitalist commerce as new markets are exploited, new big things hyped. 'Acid House Killed Rock & Roll' was the title of the debut single by Factory Too's Space Monkeys, and certainly 1988 had the feel of a Year Zero about it as the staple diet of rock music – live bands, guitars, singer-songwriters – was shunned. But in Manchester by 1993 and 1994 house music was becoming mainstream, and the Haçienda had become the Establishment. Other nights, other venues, other sounds were seizing the moment, and rock music reasserted its presence; marked by the rise of Oasis.

'Shakermaker' entered the Top Ten in July 1994. It was a fantastic coupling of timing and talent. It not only heralded the band's swift rise to stardom, but also brought dormant rock values back to the fore. The cycles of pop music had turned so often and so far that we'd come back to the Beatles. Oasis were taking their cue from the past, from before punk. And if their rise was a direct reaction against the modern sounds of the post-rave era, it also serves as a reminder that, on the one hand, while Manchester is the birthplace of the computer, it was also home of the Luddites.

Noel Gallagher, back in 1989, had grabbed a sampler and a keyboard and began, and then shelved, some dance tracks. Even once Oasis had taken off he seemed to keep an open mind, guesting on a track by the Chemical Brothers, and promising that, despite what he agreed were the band's 'pub rock' tendencies on the first three LPs, he would one day work more experimentally. One of many ingredients in the tension between Noel and his younger brother is that Liam, too young to have felt the rave revolution vibes, seems a whole lot less enamoured by either dance music or musical experimentation. He's never even seemed to understand clubs. Oasis used to rehearse in the Boardwalk basement and afterwards they'd turn up on Friday nights for 'Yellow', but Liam rarely moved from near the cigarette machine.

Even though Oasis, in going back to basic rock formulae, were rejecting the prevailing mood among Manchester musicians in 1992 and 1993, they still had strong local traditions to tap into; perhaps even in the way they initially managed to capture in their music the euphoria of the classic rave experience. More obviously, according to Liam Gallagher, Oasis are the latest in a line of Manchester bands represented by the Smiths and the Stone Roses; he's always said the Roses 'were the last group to do anything'. Noel Gallagher's guitarist role models are clearly Johnny Marr and John Squire, and Liam has inherited Ian Brown's pouting arrogance. He was inspired by the Stone Roses: 'I went to see the Stone Roses play at Spike Island and it changed my life. I saw Ian Brown on stage and he was singing off key and everything, but it just got to me. After that I was mad for getting into music.'

The emergence of Black Grape in 1995, a new group featuring

Shaun Ryder, was another reassertion of the non-stop creativity of the city's musicians. After the demise of Happy Mondays Ryder appeared lost, his only foray back into the business a terrible single with Intastella. But despite a host of bad rumours about his health, Ryder resurrected his career, teaming up with Kermit from the Ruthless Rap Assassins and sticking with Bez, the original vibemaster from the Mondays. The Black Grape debut LP contained several great songs, 'Reverend Black Grape' and 'Yeah Brother' among them, mad ideas bristling with energy. On 'Tramazi Party' Ryder revived his reputation for songwriting embracing outlaw attitudes.

Even in guitar music, the Manchester talent pool still had much to offer. Way back before the Gallaghers got their music together, the Stone Roses had inspired other bands, notably the Charlatans, who had strong Manchester connections and shared the 60s touches of the Stone Roses, as well as drive, rhythm and a singer, Tim Burgess, with a slouch and a pout the equal of anything Ian Brown could muster. Younger bands like Northern Uproar and Puressence then emerged in 1995 and 1996 as Oasis briefly gave Manchester rock press credibility again. Another band making their mark through the late 1990s were Audioweb, signed to U2's label, Mother. Fronted by Martin Merchant, they mashed up musical genres, with a take on indie warped by reggae, drum & bass and ragga. It took time for it to come together, but after a disappointing first LP, they flourished when they began working with ex-Black Grape associate, Stephen Lironi. The Freestylers' mix of Audioweb's single 'Policeman Skank' was one of the highlights of 1998.

In clubland the ambition of DJs and promoters motivated by a desire to break the domination of the house scene in Manchester was growing. Mark Rae was foremost among the new clan. He'd moved to Manchester from Newcastle in 1987 to study and to immerse himself in music. He took a job working behind the counter at Spin Inn, helped establish 'Feva' at the Man Alive in 1988, went on to do two nights at Precinct 13 – 'Daisy Age' and 'Optimistic' – and restarted 'Feva' in 1991, this time at the State on Thursday nights. 'Feva' featured live musicians, soul and hip hop in one room, house downstairs and rare groove in the other room ('We got seven hundred in regularly', remembers Mark Rae. 'We had a good two year run with that, and then the MC tried to shoot the bouncer so that finished that! Terrible!'). With 'Feva' and his other forays into clubs, like 'Half Steppin' at Home, Mark Rae wanted to provide an eclectic antidote to mainstream house: 'Clubbing was about all types of music originally: soul, ragga, go go, funk, electro. There was a massive break with house. Now the lowest common denominator rules nationwide.'

Mark Rae's vision sharpened when he started a record shop, Fat City, in 1993, his interest in new stuff complemented by Ed Pitt, his business partner who had a London background dealing in rare records. The first Fat City was in a small unit in Affleck's Palace, selling breaks, old soul and funk, and new import CDs. Originally dominated by American releases, Fat City began to satisfy the market for trip hop, acid jazz and jungle as more British alternatives to house began to emerge. Subsequently the shop moved on to bigger premises before settling on Oldham Street.

Mirroring the role of Eastern Bloc in the rave era, Fat City provided a focus for activity triggered by Manchester's renewed interest in hip hop-related sounds and the return of the breakbeat. Beats per minute slowed as new sounds reached parts of the imagination dancefloor house had neglected. It was a small but influential scene, and rolling a joint replaced dropping an E, and head-nodding replaced raving. Some of the local musicians who benefited from the new ideas were Jake Purdey from Strangebrew (signed to Rob's Records), and two lads from Bury, Rob Brown and Sean Booth of Autechre, masters at melding new electronica and old breaks, signed to Warp in Sheffield. In 1994 the club scene was enlivened by nights like 'One Tree Island' at Jabez Clegg. 'Don't drink from the mainstream' exhorted the flyers, the emphasis on world music and the leftfield, with bongos, drapes, jugglers and an ambient room attached, and DJs including Guy Gondwana, Stefano and Jake from Strangebrew.

These trends were musician- and DJ-led, as the soundtrackers looked to free themselves from the house-dominated mainstream. Their quest was assisted by the growth of café bars as favoured new spaces, Isobar, Atlas, Alaska and the Athenaeum among them. It's a different kind of DJ-ing in bars; in a club always having to satisfy the dancefloor is like a tyranny over the DJ, but in a bar a DJ can work more freely. One Sunday night in 1993 I went to the Athenaeum and the DJ was playing old dub records and his mate was playing a didgeridoo. A new generation of DJs was emerging, not from the mega-raves and the superclubs, but from the bars, the intimate little clubs, and the best back rooms. The DJs were testing the barriers, selecting and, in many cases, creating a new market for a different kind of music-making. Mr Scruff began DJ-ing in bars and clubs with a mellow, free-ranging playlist. His progression to music-making resulted in witty, idiosyncratic tracks like 'Chicken In A Box'.

At the big clubs, door wars continued through the mid 1990s, including a series of drive-bys and death threats at Home, but most of the police attention still seemed to penalise rather than protect the owners. One Saturday in June 1995 the police raided Equinox, Cheerleaders and Home, where they stopped the music and searched the customers for drugs. Simon Calderbank, who had done so much to boost Home's reputation, moved over to Code, a new club – underneath another café bar, Generation X – opened by Manto's owners on New Wakefield Street on the edge of Little Ireland. The last straw for Home's owners came when the police and nearly two dozen balaclava-wearing Salford hooligans battled it out on the dance-floor and through the bars. Tom Bloxham closed the club in September 1995.

For the rest of the decade, the city's reputation for violence and trouble in and around clubs naturally proved a big disincentive for people planning a night out in town, especially when the situation was often exaggerated, producing lurid headlines in the press. In this context, it's a wonder that Manchester has maintained a reputable nightlife at all through the 1990s. That is has, is down to the work of a core group of promoters, DJs and venues who have survived the hype of Madchester, the fads, the crazies and the nightlife scandals.

Through 1996 and 1997 well-organised new promoters like David Vincent, Sacha Lord, Joe Akka and Kenny Goodman began working in a largely commercial house market but successfully found ways of working with the problems. Other promoters tried to reinvent club-land, looking to create intimate, eclectic vibes in small venues. From the 'Feva' team came 'Frying the Fat' in 1996 (a monthly at the Haçienda featuring appearances by the likes of Grandmaster Flash and Mushroom from Massive Attack), which built on Steve Smith's 'Headfunk' at Time on Princess Street (the big success in 1995 with DJ Chubby Grooves taking the honours with an eclectic mix of old school breakbeats and future funk).

Many of the best nights continued to be those where the people promoting the club on the street were also DJ-ing; there's a great creative strength about such a set-up, the promoters close to the crowd, the producers of the culture barely distinguishable from the consumers. Barney Doodlebug continued to turn even the most deadbeat venue into a happening space. The Unabombers – Luke

Cowdrey and Justin Crawford – originated 'The Electric Chair' monthly at the Roadhouse. They were joined at the Roadhouse by Jayne Compton, whose 'Stepper's Delite' showcased female DJ talent, and, with 'The Electric Chair', became one of the key nights for the post-house brigade, and another success for the under-capitalised independents.

It was getting harder to hold a club night together, though, with set-up costs rising and high-profile nights targeted by wannabe gangsters. On Fridays I was DJ-ing at 'Yellow' at the Boardwalk, which, by rights, should never have survived. We drew in such a mixed crowd we'd be praying they would all get along, but that's Manchester for you. Over seven years our regular crowd would include black kids, white students, trainee solicitors, dental nurses, models in short skirts, football players, jazz dancers, single mothers from Droylsden, the singer from Olive, the songwriters in Lucid, Morrissey's sister, Cleopatra's manager, actor Christopher Eccleston, window-dressers from Kendal's, Galaxy 102 DJs, Atlas bar staff, pissheads, soul girls. We had regular visits from all the gangs: Doddington, Gooch, Salford and Cheetham Hill. The police kept telling us about 'known criminals' in the club. That we held it together for seven years, all through the 1990s, was down to vigilance, luck and, judging by the devotion of our core audience, the power of the music.

Those of us involved in clubland also learned from each other, from mistakes or through cooperation. Superficially we were in competition, but if the gangs and the police could get organised, so could the promoters and DJs. In March 1998 I was talking to 'Golden' promoter Jon Hill after one particularly problem-strewn weekend. As it turned out, he was just weeks away from pulling his night out of Sankey's Soap. Like dozens of other people we'd got into clubs for the buzz, for the love of music. Perhaps we'd been naive thinking it was all going to be glamour and good times, but here we were, worrying for hours, about door policy and club security mostly. 'None of this was in the job description', he sighed.

Clubland is never still, that's for sure. From the acid house madness onwards, the club scene had powered Manchester into a different age; from black and white to dayglo, from miserabilism to cosmopolitanism. It had produced unexpected repercussions economically and culturally, and driven local design and fashion industries towards success. The local Council, civic leaders and local PR companies hailed clubland as an example of Manchester's vitality; the authorities perhaps weren't sure why or how, but they had come to realise that Manchester's music scene marshals the energy of the city in a way no official institutions have ever done. But the early euphoria was being eroded by violence.

Those who understood the long view weren't writing the city off – from the 60s beat boom, the Northern Soul years, through electro, hip hop and house, Manchester had focused a spirit, stood for something, and even at the height of the door wars, club commentators understood the particular intensity of clubs in the North of England – but the final years of the 1990s saw clubland struggling and fragmenting. It was mirroring the city's own story in the 1990s; a deep down desire for good times, commercial and cultural forces clashing, recurring violence, hopes dashed, a surprise round the corner, a bittersweet symphony. The successes always in jeopardy.

CHAPTER 9

Hard Times and Basslines:

the Moss Side Story

Walking townwards, just before the brewery, there's an area of wasteland on the corner of Princess Road and Moss Lane East. Huge
advertising hoardings are sited there to catch the eyes of drivers
snarled in traffic making their way to and from the city centre. The
hoardings stand on the former site of a club, the Reno, now levelled,
gone. Hewan Clarke, the Haçienda's first resident DJ, worked there
in the early 1980s; Tomlin – one half of the Jam MCs – was one of
the Reno's DJs in its final months. Sefton was a Reno regular too when
it closed, getting on the microphone at every opportunity, MC-ing,
beatboxing. Above the Reno was another drinking club, the Nile. At
the time Sefton was still a schoolboy at the Holy Name on Denmark
Road; 'Basically I shouldn't have been in the Reno. I was one deviant
child, and I'd have my school uniform on and I'd zip up my jacket
to hide my uniform and I'd go in the Reno and come out of there
at 8.30 in the morning, go get some breakfast and go straight to
school.'

The Reno was an established focal point in the Moss Side community going back decades, alive with the noise of drinking, dancing
and hustling; you could get a little smoke, do your thing or sit gambling in the back. The Reno – 'basically just a den', according to
one regular – was about as far from a corporate, clean, mainstream
nightclub as you can get. It wasn't always trouble-free, but the vibe
was good. I used to go in about two in the morning at weekends,
usually when I was too drunk to have second thoughts. You might
be offered weed on the stairs, but there was no major security (just

one old African man behind a counter and a little letter box that you looked through and where you paid your money, and if you didn't pay, you didn't get in, simple as that). The mix of people was incredible, especially as the clock crept towards 4am: middle-aged Irish women, old domino players always wearing hats, young black guys off the street, girls with beautiful hair, jazz dancers, people slumped drunk over the tables. The music – Whodini's 'The Freaks Come Out At Night', Michael Jackson's 'Thriller', lots of disco, Barry White and the Gap Band – was predominantly good rare grooves and black street soul; like the crowd, a good inner city mix. A Guy Called Gerald has two tracks, 'Reno' and 'Nile', on his *Black Secret Technology* LP named in tribute to the venues. Sefton is glad he's always mixed with older kids otherwise he would have missed out. For him 'the Reno was probably the best club in Manchester ever. There's nothing like it now. You can meet fifty-year-old men and they'll tell you stories about the Reno and how they'd go in there with their best gear on; in fact, I think the older people back in the 60s and 70s, they had the best time.'

Moss Side is an area full of history rubbed out, the kind of place promises are postponed, good times fade and new beginnings are made every decade; hopes, like battered buildings, are regularly demolished. Over the road from the hoardings is the site of one of the big disasters in the story of attempts to boost Moss Side in recent decades: the shopping precinct. The precinct was built in the early 1970s, but soon struggled as successive recessions sucked away the already limited spending power of the local population. Escalating unemployment among the young contributed to the precinct's problems, and it became a focus for conflict between shopkeepers, police and black youth. The situation had spiralled far out of control by 1990, with dealers stashing drugs behind panels in the walls of the Post Office. In October 1991, the Cottage Bakery – you can imagine someone dreaming up the name in the hope of evoking cosy English traditions – was the scene of the savage killing of Darren Samuel. He was chased through the shopping precinct by a gang on mountain bikes who cornered him in the Bakery and shot him dead. He had a five-month-old son, Keaton.

Attempts were made to erase this unhappy history. The precinct was torn down and eventually replaced by a new Asda supermarket and an extension to the Pressmain plant (one of the biggest employers in the area).

Moss Side needs special attention in our story for a number of reasons. Away from the city centre, the major shopping streets, the concert venues, and the Northern Quarter and Castlefield youth pop cult spaces there's a whole other Manchester; and the patterns of hope and despair that are apparent in Moss Side are replicated in many other areas. Moss Side, in that sense, can stand for Seedley or Mersey Bank, Beswick or Wythenshawe. This is the sharp end of Manchester life. But all these places have their own identities, problems and escape routes. Moss Side, for its part, is a name synonymous with Britain's black community in the same way as Brixton in London and St Paul's in Bristol. In that sense, its history and destiny also reflect that of the black community in Britain as a whole.

Moss Side has also been subject to decades of negative media attention, so much so that the area now has a fearsome reputation for gun-filled gang wars and multiple drug-dealing. This part of its history, sadly, has been played out in the glare of sensationalist headlines. Moss Side also provides graphic evidence of the centrality of music in Mancunian lives, and also the key part played by black music in shaping popular culture, from jazz, blues and soul: the Moss Side jazz clubs of the 1950s which brought fresh rhythms to the dancefloor, featuring far rawer sounds than the mainstream jazz dominating the rest of the Manchester circuit; the sound systems, moveable feasts of bluebeat and blues, which sustained the roots of the black community in the 1960s; through to the heavy dub years in the 1970s and the breakdancing era in the early 1980s.

And Moss Side is also the inspiration for one of the clearest, most concise demonstrations of the power of music to reflect and define Manchester: *Moss Side Story*, an LP released in 1988 by Barry Adamson. Adamson's music career grew out of Manchester's post-punk era; he was the bass player in Magazine with Howard Devoto and later went on to play with Nick Cave in the Bad Seeds. *Moss Side Story* is like a *Bladerunner*-tinged version of Harlem jazz, with bits of Gershwin, John Barry and Lee Perry heard through a dark, oppressive filter, conjuring a sound that not only clearly comes from the streets of Moss Side but carries resonances of city experience worldwide; souls struggling to be heard, urban exhilaration, paranoia, Berlin, New York.

The dynamic mix of influences in Adamson's first LP – jazz, reggae, punk noise, movie soundtracks – reflects something of the variety of Moss Side and Mancunian backgrounds. The city's wealth has been based on migrants to the city, from as far back as the early nineteenth century, when an enormous influx of families from the English shires, Scotland, Ireland and Europe fuelled the industrial revolution. When Elizabeth Gaskell set *Mary Barton* here – around Denmark Road and Great Western Street – Moss Side was mostly boggy fields, but soon became populated as the city grew. In the middle of the nineteenth century Engels lived at various addresses, short-term lets on the edge of the town, around Moss Lane East and Denmark Road; a rich German merchant with his poor Irish lover. Up to the late 1930s Moss Side was closely associated with Manchester's Welsh community. The politician and most thoroughbred Welshman David Lloyd George was born in the area in 1863 (his father was a teacher at a local school). But in recent decades it's been the Afro-Caribbean community that has found a home in Moss Side.

Some of the roots of Manchester's black community go back to West African, Somali and Indian seamen settlers working for British shipping companies in the first decade of the twentieth century. They were mostly based near the Manchester Ship Canal, living around the docks and around Greengate. One of the highest profile was Len Johnson, the son of a ship worker from Sierra Leone who earned a living boxing in touring shows (despite being one of the most skillful boxers of his generation, Johnson couldn't enter official British championship contests because of the colour bar operated by boxing's Board of Control). And the early black community in Manchester also included a lawyer, Edward Nelson, and a doctor, Peter Milliard, both from Guyana. During the war technicians and engineers from the West Indies and black servicemen from the USA increased the profile of Manchester's black community. This was resisted in some areas; the Mecca-owned Ritz ballroom on Whitworth Street barred blacks during the Second World War.

In the post-war years there was a labour shortage in Britain, and workers in building, engineering and manufacturing were urgently required. New jobs became available also in the new National Health Service and public transport. There were more migrations of people looking for work, a re-jigging of city populations, and various Government initiatives to bring over workers from the Caribbean to work on the rebuilding of Britain. As the boom years of the 1950s developed, further recruiting of West Indian labour took place, often to fill jobs which indigenous workers weren't willing or able to do.

When landlords pursued shamelessly racist policies and turned the new immigrants away, the black community was hounded into just a few areas. They began to find security by living close to others in the same position; thus certain streets and certain districts became favoured by the new immigrants, and Moss Side became home to many of the Afro-Caribbean community simply because housing options were at a premium. Munian Moonsamy, a black South African from Durban, came to Moss Side in 1949 as a merchant seaman. He made for Moss Side as the area was known then as one where you could be 'guaranteed to get a room'. He worked in the docks and in a foundry, and later married an Irish woman.

As the new immigrants began to settle in Moss Side, there were conflicting views on their effect on the area. There was a novelty factor at work, at first, and Moss Side began to be described as 'the city's most cosmopolitan district', but negative views surfaced as the area gained a reputation for crime and prostitution, with a concentration of brothels around Denmark Road, many controlled by black immigrants. Crime levels began to rise, and the area was further unsettled by a chaotic housing situation. Some of the new immigrants got involved in shady or illegal activities in preference to the poorly paid menial jobs they were expected to take. A web of exploitation grew in the neighbourhood, reaching from the slum landlords, through the bed sits, to the Moss Side streets.

An infrastructure developed by the black community in Moss Side and around Oxford Road and the University had been established by the end of the 1940s, and included welfare centres, cafés and clubs. Ghanaian Jimmy Taylor ran the Cotton Club at 28 Ducie Street in Manchester (he also owned clubs in Cardiff, Liverpool and London), Nigerian John Bassey started the Merchant Navy Club on Princess Road, and Ras T. Makonnen (from Guyana) owned a string of establishments including a restaurant (the Cosmopolitan on Oxford Road), the Orient curry house at 64 & 66 Oxford Road, a nightclub (the Forum) and another restaurant (the Belle Etoile), and played host to stars like Joe Louis and Nat King Cole. Significantly, entrepreneurs like Taylor and Makonnen were also in the vanguard of social welfare and pro-African activism; their desire for liberation cut all ways, and their venues were often the centre for political meetings, as well as drinking, dancing and music.

In the 1950s the black population of Manchester discovered they were unwelcome in many local pubs and clubs, and organised their own entertainment instead, establishing cafés and clubs, and commandeering various private houses for what were locally called shebeens or blues. These all-night parties brought problems for other residents and often attracted the attentions of the police, but they endured, providing somewhere to socialise and a way of raising money for those who hosted them. A friend of mine grew up in a household where her mother hosted blues on a regular basis, for fun but also to raise funds for the family; eventually her mother was shopped to the police by her Gran, who had become worried that too often the children were not getting enough sleep.

The new immigrants into Britain from the Caribbean faced a horrifying degree of overt racism in the 1950s. Newspapers, politicians and police were all guilty of stereotyping and slander. In 1957 the local *Evening Chronicle* launched a clean-up campaign in Moss Side after four violent deaths on its streets in as many months, describing the district as 'Manchester's hot-bed of vice and corruption' and calling for 'a united effort to sweep up the dregs of Moss Side'. An editorial made much of the negative changes over the previous decades, clearly pinning the blame on the new black community. The racial dimension to the campaign was highlighted by constant references in the paper to 'Manchester's Little Harlem'.

Historically, though, Manchester had a reasonably good reputation for tolerance. Despite large communities of Protestants and Catholics, there was less sectarianism than in cities like Liverpool and Glasgow. Manchester's radical middle class subscribed early to anti-slavery causes. And despite the fact that local Lancashire cotton workers' jobs were under threat from the burgeoning cotton mills of Ahmedabad and elsewhere in India, when Gandhi visited Manchester in 1931 he was greeted with great enthusiasm as he walked barefoot through the cobbled streets. Meanwhile, black activists had a number of organisations in the city calling for freedom for the African people under colonial rule and providing services for the local black population. The New International Society, formed by three communists, including Len Johnson, led various campaigns in the 1940s, supporting sacked black workers, fighting racism and raising awareness of international issues. The finest hour for anti-colonial, pro-black organisations in the city was the Pan-African Congress held in Manchester in October 1945 in All Saints. Powerful and emerging international figures from the world of black consciousness were drawn to Manchester by the local organisers, including Amy Ashwood Garvey (the widow of Marcus Garvey), the African-American writer and social critic W. E. B. Du Bois, Kwame Nkrumah (the future Prime Minister of Ghana) and Jomo Kenyatta. Kenyatta lived in Manchester for a while, lodging at one of Makonnen's houses and working at his Cosmopolitan restaurant. Returning to Kenya and imprisoned by the colonial Government, his National Union party later won the first election after independence and he became the republic's President. In 1963 Kenyatta recalled the Pan-African Congress in Manchester as 'a landmark in the history of the African people's struggle for unity and freedom'.

Out on the streets, though, the 1950s and 1960s continued to provide flashpoints over housing and socialising, battles in the media and discrimination in the jobs market. Housing problems were exacerbated by Manchester's slum clearance programme in the 1960s. Moss Side's housing stock was decrepit, old and ill-used, and, as in Hulme, the old terraced streets were demolished to make way for new developments. The blueprint for a new Moss Side was unveiled in April 1967 and featured the shopping precinct surrounded by a complex of deck-access housing and high-rise blocks. It soon became clear that many people in the local community were unhappy with the plans; the number of residents in the area would be reduced by a quarter, families would be relocated and friends dispersed, and suspicions of a covert attempt by the Council to end the strong black identity of the area were hardly helped by remarks by Alderman Richard Harper – Chairman of Manchester's Housing Committee – predicting that after redevelopment the area would probably retain 'no more than a sprinkling of coloured people'.

The authorities refused to listen to the demands of the people, even in the 1960s, supposedly the era of civil rights. The Town Hall only conceded that consultations with local people might be useful after three months of lobbying by Moss Side's Housing Action Group and a three thousand-signature petition. Even then no information was forthcoming. An editorial in *Moss Side News* reflected the anger: 'We have, for generations been told what to do, where to live, very nearly what to think . . . It is high time that those who make decisions which affect hundreds of thousands of people should be made to listen to what those people want. And not just to listen, but TO TAKE NOTICE.'

The developments of the 1960s and 1970s were a disaster. In April 1972, just two months after the high rises were completed, a petition signed by local residents was delivered to the Town Hall protesting at slum conditions in their new homes in Hulme. Prompted by the clear failure of phase one, the planners switched to low-rise housing for the second stage of the redevelopment and the building of the Alexandra Park Estate, but more mistakes were made: shops on Alexandra Road and down the west side of Princess Road were demolished, destroying key local amenities, and Princess Road was widened, which drove a wedge between the new Estate on one side and the older terraces and remnants of the established shops on the other. The Estate itself became a network of streets, crescents and closes, with squat, sandy-coloured brick houses each with a patch of uncultivatable back garden. The outer ring of houses backing on to Princess Road and Quinney Crescent were given tiny slit windows; the Estate today still gives the impression that it's some kind of a stockade, adrift and hostile.

The redevelopment of Moss Side had aimed to replace a decaying ghetto with a new blueprint for urban life, but the delivery of the vision was undermined by a combination of major social pressures and defective planning. As the national and local economy fell from the prosperous heights of the 1960s to the recession-torn 1970s, so the social and physical fabric of redeveloped Moss Side collapsed. There were escalating problems in the high rises, the leisure centre was underused and the launderette vandalised. An ugly precinct had replaced lively Moss Side shopping streets.

Irvine Williams was picked up by police in the precinct and charged with shoplifting. He was fifteen at the time, out of school early. He was accused of being part of an organised gang of shoplifters, but of the seven charged with him he'd only ever met two. The case was thrown out of court, but the incident wasn't forgotten by Williams, who recalls that police harassment was virtually an everyday occurrence for black youth at that time: 'In the late 1970s, early 1980s people were getting harassed for all kinds of reasons, young people were being criminalised and a lot of people in the community were being targeted. We resented the way the police were acting, the manner they were policing the area.'

The economic problems of the 1970s triggered sharp hostility on the streets. The National Front incited racist scapegoating of the black population, tacitly assisted by Margaret Thatcher, who complained about English people being 'swamped by an alien culture'. Larry Benji came to England from Jamaica in June 1977 and lived in Levenshulme. His first attempt to get a job floundered. In Jamaica he'd been a custom broker, but when the Job Centre sent him to a Manchester company who had claimed to be desperately in need of an experienced custom broker, it was clear that they weren't interested in employing a black man: 'They told me the job had gone. They told me they'd given it to the guy who'd just been in. There was no guy in front of me, I knew that. I realised that getting a job was going to be hard.'

It was an era of raw, polarised politics. In October 1977 the police allowed the National Front to march through Levenshulme – almost literally on Larry Benji's doorstep – while helping to deflect media and Anti-Nazi League protesters to Hyde where a much smaller, simultaneous march took place. Groups opposing the National Front – notably Rock Against Racism and the Anti-Nazi League – managed to mobilise considerable support for anti-racist causes all over Britain. In July 1978 a march against the National Front culminated in a rally in Moss Side's Alexandra Park, where the crowd – estimated at around twenty-five thousand – was entertained by X-O-Dus, Steel Pulse and the Buzzcocks.

As well as sharp hostility on the streets and defamation in much of the media, the black community in Moss Side had a specific struggle in the wake of the flawed developments. The mismanaged and insensitive slum clearance programme had left many Moss Siders suspicious of outside agencies and so-called 'experts' and 'planners'. 'We were the subject of an experiment', according to youth worker Ken McIntyre. 'What the authorities did was to try to convert a ghetto into something more acceptable for the image of the city – without properly taking the local community into account. Moss Side was a community, if not geographically, psychologically – the shopping precinct and the council estates destroyed it.'

Against this background, the Moss Side riots of 1981 were not unexpected. Unchecked harassment of black youth, especially in the operation of stop-and-search laws, had brought anger in the black community to a head in other cities, and it seemed inevitable that Moss Side would be one of the flashpoints. In 1980 there were riots in St Paul's in Bristol, and in 1981 riots in Brixton.

Moss Side rioted just a few days after Southall in London and Toxteth in Liverpool. In the early hours of 8 July 1981, a group of black and white youths who had just left the Nile Club attacked shops along Princess Road ('the front line'). A pawn shop was petrol bombed on Raby Street. By the afternoon a crowd had gathered on the grassed area in front of Quinney Crescent. There were high spirits as well as anger; implausibly, ice-cream vans and hot-dog vendors arrived on the scene. Things got heavier in the evening as police in riot gear confronted the crowd, who responded by throwing missiles and jeering. An hour or so later the local police station on Greenheys Lane came under attack by both black and white youths. From the police station, a contingent of rioters rampaged down Princess Road attacking and looting shops, and then moved up Claremont Road. Manchester City Social Club was unscathed, but in Rusholme cars were vandalised and shops set on fire. The police had disappeared from the streets, a situation which caused much controversy later; local traders were scathing about the poor protection they were given, and there were widespread allegations that the police had decided to let Moss Side burn.

In the area the following day, Thursday 9 July, any lingering beliefs in police neutrality evaporated as police vans toured the area with officers leaning out of the back shouting racial insults at black youths and taunting them. Despite this provocation, trouble petered out. There had been over two hundred arrests during the three days, for crime and public order offences; and, undermining police theories blaming outside agitators for the trouble, only seven of those arrested were from outside the Greater Manchester area. Despite the stand-offs, the prolonged fires, the widespread devastation, and melodramatic press and media coverage, there were very few police casualties. Threats of extensive violence never materialised.

Nevertheless, the riots were an angry, perhaps overdue response, to decades of frustration and oppression in Moss Side. Locally, the riots are known simply as 'the uprising', underscoring their political significance. The Report of the Moss Side Inquiry Panel to the Leader of the Greater Manchester Council suggested that the poor design of the new accommodation, the lack of consultation and the depressing state of the general environment had deepened the community's unhappiness. It also highlighted the effects of unemployment (among black school-leavers estimated to be as high as 70 per cent) and endorsed the view that resentment against the police was widespread, especially among young blacks. The Chief Constable refused to give evidence to the Panel, but let it be known that such 'resentment is confined to thieves and robbers'. Unable to comprehend the serious grievances of Moss Side's population, Anderton always stuck to his statement that outside influences were behind the violence. Slogans in support of the IRA on defaced walls on the Alexandra Park Estate led to claims that the IRA were active in the area, although there was graffiti everywhere in Moss Side and Hulme. On the end wall of William Kent Crescent someone had painted a phrase from a Lou Reed song recorded by Nico; 'Wrap Your Troubles In Dreams', it said. However, no one was blaming the Moss Side riots on the Velvet Underground.

The repercussions of the riots were various. Even though the participants included many white people as well as black (and, indeed, many girls as well as young men), the riots fed the racist stereotypes linking blacks and crime and contributed to Moss Side's lawless reputation. Yet without the riots the problems faced by the inner city populations of areas like Brixton, Toxteth and Moss Side might never have been addressed.

Despite unemployment remaining a major problem, the mid 1980s are remembered almost fondly in Moss Side. In a sense, it was the calm before the storm. The police had heeded some of the lessons from the riots and community policing came into vogue. A network of self-created agencies in the area thrived, and social life in the area was strong, with a plethora of shebeens, all-day drinking at the Volta, and all-night dancing at the Nile and the Reno. In Karline Smith's novel, *Moss Side Massive*, the early days of the Sphinx and the Vegas – her fictional equivalents of the Nile and the Reno – are remembered by one old Moss Sider not just for keeping the community in touch with the music from 'back home', but for providing a haven from life's problems; 'From Monday to Friday they would work for "the Man", but the weekend was theirs and they knew it.'

For the youth, music was a lifeline. This tradition spanned several generations. One of the first passengers to disembark from the *Empire Windrush* – a liner which brought four hundred settlers from Trinidad and Jamaica to Britain in 1948 – was Granville Edwards, a carpenter by trade and a mean tenor saxophone player too. He drifted to Manchester via Coventry, Birmingham and Huddersfield, eventually making his way to Moss Side, in part attracted by the black-dominated jazz clubs which thrived in the area. He formed a band soon after arriving in the city, multi-racial in make-up, and including Lord Kitchener on bass. Kitchener (real name Aldwyn Roberts) was a calypso star who frequented Ras T. Makonnen's Forum Club, recorded for Melodisc and became something of a mod icon in the 1960s. Edwards himself made his way as a musician via marching bands; in the 1990s, in his seventies, he could be found on the New York street mock-up on the Granada Studios Tour with Dave Dona-hue's Hi Life marching band, with a repertoire that included ragtime, Ray Charles and Fats Domino.

The 1970s were a glorious time for reggae, building on advances in blue beat and ska, studio trickery and a plethora of righteous creators: King Tubby, Lee Perry, Jacob Miller, Bob Marley. The musical, political and spiritual vibes were having an impact inter-nationally. In Moss Side, sound systems – a DJ set-up including a mixer, turntables, an amp and as many speakers as you could get in the back of a Ford Transit – had been a focus in the black community since the late 1950s, run by various charismatic individuals with the help of devoted crews. They'd play local venues, support live bands, plug in anywhere, anytime. It was all about bringing the music and the people together. Moss Side sound systems operating through the 1970s and early 1980s included Bushman, Killa Man Taurus, Baron, Cabbi Youth, Papa Cas and President. According to Larry Benji, 'President had the biggest bassline that you can imagine. When they played outside Manchester we'd all go down, you know, and President would say "Jus' watch this, jus' watch this, watch the bassline now" and when the bassline started bulbs would start blowing.'

The sound systems would travel to Bradford, Wolverhampton, Birmingham and occasionally to London, and crews from other parts of the country would come to Manchester. This was the era of the soundclash, when two or three big sounds come together in one big arena. The sounds might all be playing the same records but it's the way each sound plays its version of a record that generates the vibes; tweaking the sound, piling on echoes, hammering the bass and treble, throwing down the dubs and rewinds. They'd be using primitive, ear-bashing effects in the 1970s, or what Larry calls 'real back-in-the-days effects'. He remembers one dance: 'The guy had a little kiddie's toy and he was pressing the buttons to make funny little sounds, like little bleeps, sound of thunder, shots. And he was pressing this against the mic and everything was distorting. I went up to see how he was making the noises and it was just a toy! Yeah, made in Korea!'

Live bands would play in Manchester at venues like the Mayflower, PSV and the Polish Club on Shrewsbury Street. The Nile and the Western were also reggae venues. Early in the 1980s Larry Benji, together with Chris Paul, began to promote large-scale reggae shows in the city, bringing over many musicians he had grown up with and around in Jamaica: Dennis Brown, Mighty Diamonds, Big Youth, Yellowman, Half Pint and Freddie McGregor. Local reggae bands operated all round Hulme and Moss Side, including X-O-Dus and Shadrock. The music meant everything. One of the guys from Shadrock explained at the time: 'Nobody can get a job so they learn an instrument. I'd be lost without it. Around this area you need the sounds. Without music you'd crack up – you'd get so depressed you'd turn into a zombie.'

In the mid 1980s, the annual Moss Side Carnival in Alexandra Park featured reggae, but also breakdancers. Some of the breakdancers had no decks, just a ghetto blaster set up on the side of the grass or by a bench. The culture was changing, the music shifting, the generations taking different paths. School kids like Sefton were spinning on their heads; on Carnival day the spirit was carefree. This was before the explosive devastation wrought over the next decade by drugs and guns. Music was taking over Sefton's life; he was discovering music as a medium for self-expression, entertainment, and an escape and a way of socialising. Sefton acknowledges how important music has been to the black youth, but he's not convinced it's just a black thing, though: 'It's rhythm. It's something that's going on around you, everything's musical. Music brings people together. You don't have to know all about it, you can just feel it.'

Music was also a physical means of escape as well as a way of imagining or pleading for change. Even before jazz and ragtime, even before the arrival of the *Empire Windrush*, for Afro-Caribbean immigrants into Britain pursuing a career as a musician was both a way of making money and a way of making a life. In Sefton's case, he was beginning to make a career beatboxing, away in Europe, or at home on the mic with Tomlin at the Reno. They were there together on the last night of the club. One day it was gone, demolished. Sefton remembers the shock felt: 'I'm not too sure of the politics behind it, but it was a serious blow to everyone in the hood, know what I mean?'

1986 and 1987 now seems like a lost age in Moss Side. Back then Moss Side was 'different' to how it is now; of that everyone is agreed. The Reno was rocking, blues were unchecked and weed was plentiful. Its reputation for vice remained, around the Broadfield Road and Great Western Street and out on the Whalley Range border, but there was a freer, far less tense atmosphere. Sefton doesn't claim the scene was ultra-safe, but incidents weren't hyped; 'I mean I saw things in the Reno that would make some people think they'd never go there again, but that's just part of the hood. You see things happening, but you just become so fucking immune to all that stuff.'

The era is captured in the work of Clement Cooper, a local photographer who grew up in Longsight in the 1970s when Longsight and the surrounding districts were predominantly white working-class areas, with an established Irish presence (it wasn't until the early 1980s that Longsight opened up to colour). From a mixed-race background, Cooper went to school at Ducie High on Denmark Road, where an interest in photography was encouraged by a teacher who gave him a camera. He used to go to the after-hours clubs in the area – the Reno, the Nile and the Volta on Great Western Street – where he began to plan and research 'Presence', an exhibition of photographs shown at the Cornerhouse in 1988.

'Presence' has three sections; the first includes photographs from the old Robin Hood pub on Lloyd Street. In the early 1980s I went in there a few times, late on Sundays, the pub dominated by the loud clacking of dominoes being thrown down, the sound echoing round the room; one or two shifty-looking guys coming and going; the half-light filtering through big, dusty, stained-glass windows; no one buying drinks, just Coke or Red Stripe behind the bar. The domino players of south Manchester would congregate in bigger numbers at the old Man Alive on Grosvenor Street or the West Indian Sports & Social Club on Westwood Street, taking a coachload of supporters down to Birmingham or Bristol for serious competitions. There's a big national network still thriving.

The other two sections of 'Presence' feature the congregation at the Church of God, and portraits of the local youth, including pictures taken in and outside the Hideaway Project on Moss Lane East. The Hideaway started in 1965, the first voluntary Church-led youth provision in Moss Side, established in the crypt of the Moss Side People's Church. The church was set on fire and then vandalised while repairs were being carried out, so it was demolished in 1968 and a square-block building for the Hideaway was purpose-built. The volunteers at the time were members of the church but in the early 1970s the church volunteers evolved into a small team of paid workers. Work at Hideaway continued to be differentiated from youth clubs locally, like the highly successful Moss Side Youth Club, by concentrating on issues, including work around the criminal justice system and unemployment, and drugs.

The young people in the photographs from the Hideaway, Procter's Youth Club in Hulme, Birley Youth Club and Longsight portray a range of emotions, and a good deal of unity and strength. They appear less tense than the older people at the Robin Hood. But looking back at the photographs, Clement Cooper regrets the changes, and the losses. Many of the people photographed in the book have since died, through illness or violence. The memories make him unhappy: 'It's gone, it's all gone. See those lovely kids in the picture of the sound system, and right near the back of the book, the photograph of them all walking home. It's all gone. It's awful.'

The change in the drugs blew the lid off everything, and changed the atmosphere forever. Cocaine and crack replaced marijuana, alcohol and tobacco. The soundtrack to Moss Side changed; Grandmaster Flash, Teddy Riley moved over. Music embellished the changes, gathering darker, meaner styles through the 1990s; fierce gangsta rap led through to frenzied bad-bwoy ragga. The music is so deep in the consciousness of local youth, that it's impossible to say whether the music was reflecting what was going on or encouraging it. Perhaps it was a bit of both.

Some of the dealers out on the street are desperate, reckless people, while some of the more established 'heads' have intricate business minds, the ones who first dealt heroin in Moss Side in the late 1980s, for instance, deviously taking on the established heroin trade in Manchester. On the streets in 1985 or 1986 you'd have had to go to Wythenshawe or Salford if you wanted to score heroin, and wholesale the only source was via elements in Manchester's Pakistani community. But the Moss Side gang sourced the drug in Amsterdam and opened up a new route, bringing the drugs in via Ostend using an elaborate network of decoys and couriers. The effect was to launch Moss Side into a dangerous era, precipitating ferocious gang warfare. Once heroin became prevalent, and big money started being made, there was a lucrative market and turf wars began. Up to the late 1980s Moss Side, Cheetham Hill, Salford and Wythenshawe – districts with active criminal gangs – kept their distance, and there were few internecine conflicts. In the late 1980s, on the back of the rise of heroin, two major gangster groups on the Alexandra Park Estate emerged, and became known as Gooch and Pepperhill, the former taking their name from Gooch Close, the second from the Pepperhill pub on the Estate.

The drugs drew other criminals into the area, and the Gooch and

Pepperhill split was exacerbated by a series of alliances. One known criminal, Delroy Brown, had moved from Birmingham to Manchester in 1986. He lived in Longsight but involved himself with Pepperhill. In turn, Gooch and Cheetham Hill factions teamed up against Pepperhill and Brown. In 1988 this stand-off led to a spate of shootings on the southside of Hulme, at the PSV and on Alexandra Park Estate. Brown's council house on Roker Avenue in Longsight in June was blasted with shotgun rounds. The Pepperhill pub lost its licence, and the gang regrouped and became known as Doddington.

The gangs quickly developed thorough organisations with the head guys wielding complete control, like generals, controlling the lieutenants and the young kids, the foot-soldiers. The kids growing up in Moss Side are aware of what's going on; it's their big brothers, it's the guys up the road with the nice car who are doing the business. Resisting the criminal fraternity is a harder option than joining, and from an early age kids get sucked in. The gangs involve the kids as runners and look-outs, and then extend their role to dealing the drugs on the street. Unwittingly, they're then on the front line, and become targets in street wars. Even those at the very fringe of the scene are targets, a kid who fetches a can of coke for someone, or helps out his older brother or half-brother, or even somebody unconnected. Kids die. It's all too conspicuous. What's more, dealing is done indoors in Wythenshawe and Salford – if anyone wants something they come to your house and you're prepared for a knock on the door – but in Moss Side people were dealing on the street. It was a mix of fearlessness and foolishness; their activities attracted the ever-eager media and eventually provided easy pickings for police surveillance cameras.

High-profile police operations destroyed the hierarchy in 1990, took lieutenants and a couple of generals out of the picture, and left the kids with nothing to do. Other ringleaders backed off and in the power vacuum the shooting rate went up by three or four hundred per cent as the younger gangsters fought to gain big reputations, not through graft or earning, but purely through violence. There were revenge attacks in the aftermath of the Cottage Bakery incident. It was in this era that some of the first fictional attempts to document the atmosphere in Moss Side were produced, including the novels *Lick Shot* by Peter Kalu and *Moss Side Massive* by Karline Smith.

Moss Side Massive began as a play sent to Channel Four in 1984, then evolved into a short story. Karline Smith had two children, then took the project up again and by 1992 five chapters had been written. As the project evolved, Moss Side changed. The 1984 play was more centred around family life than it was around gangs, but the rewrites from 1988 onwards coincided with an escalation in gang activity; 'The book began to write me, in the end. I couldn't ignore what was going on around me; I thought it was important to put it in, although I had to take the obviousness out and try to interweave fact and fiction.'

The novel opens with the shooting of Fluxy, a killing that destroys the fragile peace between two rival gangs and brings the middle-aged matriarch Queenie face to face with a nightmare. Her son, Storm, helps spin a fatal web of drive-bys and violent attacks, as old heads in their flash motors and kids on the street fight it out for deals, money, respect and revenge. It's a frantic crime story, with a cast of characters mostly with nothing to look forward to and a regretful past piling up behind them; the older ones muse endlessly on Jamaica, the old days in the social club, and how Moss Side and Manchester have changed (not for the better, inevitably).

The pace of *Moss Side Massive* vividly reflects the way that violence in Moss Side seems to take on a life of its own and situations spiral out of control. In an early twist, no witnesses for Fluxy's death come forward. This, too, was becoming one of the key problems for crime in Moss Side and elsewhere in Manchester. After the Cottage Bakery killing witness intimidation reached new heights: shots were fired through the window of one witness's house in Smalldale Avenue; a witness was given money by Gooch to take a trip to Tunisia; one took a drugs overdose to avoid giving evidence. Other cases collapsed: in April 1992 the four men charged with the machete murder of seventeen-year-old Carl Stapleton walked free from Manchester Crown Court when the prosecution's primary witness, supposedly in protective custody, went missing. She subsequently changed her evidence.

Once guns took a grip in the community, disputes seemed to escalate rapidly; shots were being fired over who-did-what, who-knows-who, who-said-what. On the streets there are automatic pistols, and even sub-machine guns. At one time Gooch were even rumoured to be in possession of a grenade launcher. Exactly where these weapons have come from is naturally not easy to work out, although possible sources include IRA connections, raids on gun shops, and a nation-wide network for guns which is generally accepted to have grown hugely after the Falklands War and the break-up of the Soviet Union.

According to one person close to the action, another source for Gooch's weapons was alleged to be a rogue insider at an international arms company's warehouse. From there Gooch's contact was able to pass on weapons boxed, new, greased up; 'It was all brand new kit, bullshit stuff at first, then it got serious: sixteen shot automatic handguns, and another one, a Russian version of a Magnum but more powerful. It's just a fucking huge thing. Gooch have got their hands on some serious shit in the past.'

Through the 1980s the British Government actively promoted the arms trade. One company, Interarms, based in Regent Road in Salford, was run by Sam Cummings, a former CIA spy who became a British subject in 1972. He is reputed to have sold more weapons than any other individual in world history, and counted General Franco and the Shah of Iran among his friends. In 1995 Sam Cummings was estimated to be the tenth richest man in Britain.

By 1997 and 1998 there was talk of a truce among Moss Side's gangs. Police and community relations were improving. Early in the 1990s the police initiated the idea of regular meetings with local people to talk through issues arising from the gang troubles, and that evolved into the Moss Side & Hulme Community Forum in which local people discuss concerns among themselves, including dealing with issues around policing but also housing and media representation. There are still monthly meetings with the police. Police tag vans now carry conspicuous code letters so individual patrols can be recognised. Informal stop and searches are now logged and records kept. Dialogue has been maintained and harassment and resentment are generally perceived to have dropped.

Irvine Williams is now a youth worker based at Hideaway, two decades on from his days hanging around the precinct:

> If the police arrest people for the crimes that they've committed using legitimate procedures and without using unnecessary brutality and force, then the police are doing the job they're paid to do. I haven't got a problem with that. In general I think we have got over the bad old days and one of the best things that happened in policing around here was having Superintendent Lilian King who had a lot of understanding of the issues. That period, and with the Forum, seemed to change the police's perception of certain individuals and organisations in the community.

In an ever-changing situation, many of the older criminals had developed semi-legitimate activities, moved from Moss Side, pooled resources with one-time enemies, split shipments in half. When this happens the young ones are left battling it out for new positions in the hierarchy, looking for respect, proving themselves through violence, relishing the huge headlines, even emulating the glamorised gangster images of films and media. A lot of it is about front. Even some of the old Moss Side heads deplore the mentality of the younger kids, not just in Moss Side, but elsewhere: 'You get a lot of kids in their baggy trousers, NFL jackets, baseball caps. These guys are nothing, but they still carry on with all that "Who are you looking at?", "Do you know who I am?". It's straight out of the rap videos and the movies; these guys are taking on the whole hype, trying to bring off the whole attitude.'

In *Moss Side Massive* some of the gangsters are portrayed as sensitive – or, rather, sentimental – guys, prone to get a tear in their eye when they hold their baby children. The genuinely mad evil bastards involved in gang activities around Manchester aren't really represented in the book. Karline Smith claims there's a balance: 'I wanted to show that there were people out there who weren't really enjoying being criminals. They had to do it because for them it was the only way they were going to make money, to deal with drugs. At the same time I wanted to show that there were people who didn't give a damn and were quite prepared to shoot anybody, be violent to people, to get where they wanted to go.'

The unpredictability of the situation as new players appear, old heads disappear, is accentuated by the drugs. Kids on crack aren't rational. On occasions in the last few years the violence has died down, only to return in another savage cycle of killings. Alliances are formed, only to break down. Successful police operations and prosecutions have continued to bite away at the dealers – for instance, in August 1996 thirty dealers received sentences ranging from three to ten years after being caught on surveillance cameras selling crack cocaine and heroin around Grierson Walk on the Alexandra Park Estate – but a long-running feud between Gooch and Longsight marred the second half of the 1990s. Like Moss Side's, Longsight's drug economy is based on selling crack into the community, and heroin to outsiders.

In October 1996 Orville Bell was shot at point blank range by two teenagers on mountain bikes. They rode up behind him as he sat in his car in Linnet Close in Longsight with his fifteen-year-old girl-friend. Bell, just seventeen, and a suspected drug dealer, had his £850 gold necklace taken from him. Leon Kenton of Brassington Road, Chorlton, was arrested for the attack, and in June 1997 was sentenced to life imprisonment.

The killing triggered a horrific round of local shootings. In March 1997 Zeus King was shot dead on Langport Avenue in Longsight. He lived in Chorlton, and was the son of Marcel King, the Sweet Sensation singer in the 1970s who had also recorded for Factory Records in the 1980s (Marcel King himself had died tragically at the end of 1995 following a brain haemorrhage). Three weeks after Zeus King's death, Kevin Lewis was killed on Crondall Street, and through 1997 and into 1998 many of the violent incidents in south Manchester were said to be connected with an ongoing feud, many featuring an increasing use of powerful machine pistols. There were more deaths and shootings, including incidents on Claremont Road, and the murder of Julian Wagaba on Monica Grove, Levenshulme in March 1998. The violence was enveloping new areas, and bystanders seemed increasingly at risk. In January 1999 eighteen-year-old Leon McKenley was shot dead on the doorstep of his family home in Old Trafford. The police started using this phrase to describe the young gangsters: 'trigger happy'.

Unfortunately these battles have ensured that Moss Side has kept its bad reputation for crime and violence, while problems in other districts have kept a lower public profile. Protection rackets and armed robberies are greater in number in Salford than in Moss Side, for instance. But for people in Moss Side representation – in films, on television, through the media – has always been tainted. From the start, the local black population realised that criminal activity in the Moss Side area stirred up more interest than crime in other areas. The *Manchester Guardian* quotes one man of African descent way back in 1957: 'Many English cities have more crimes than Moss Side. Our crimes are written about much more than others. One day there are twenty similar cases at the Manchester court and only one is reported – the one by a coloured man from Moss Side. But there is a lot of crime in Moss Side, a lot of it, and living here you can be drawn in if you wish or you can keep out.'

Over the last forty years Moss Side's reputation has taken even more of a hammering. In one sense, it's comforting that people are still shocked enough by killings that they still reach the front pages, but the area is in danger of being locked into a cycle of violence. The more sensationalised the coverage, the more distorted the representation of life in Moss Side becomes. For people trying to halt the violence, anything that feeds negative views of the area demoralises. This presents particular problems for anyone trying to document the area. When Clement Cooper's 'Presence' photographs were exhibited at the Cornerhouse, he'd shown all the prints to key people in the community and exhibited many of them in small groups, but early enthusiasm turned to violent opposition; his photographs were stolen off the walls and he was forced into hiding. When I talked to him about his work in Moss Side, I kept using the word 'community', but he eventually interrupted me. For him, there are no supportive, identifiable, shared values and aims in Moss Side. Karline Smith suffered a similar backlash when her novel was published: 'The idea of the book was to give people an insight into what I felt was happening in the area but when it came out I got a lot of criticism for exposing what was going on. I think there was a lot of shame as well. Some people in the so-called community said that I was reinforcing negative stereotypes.'

For local artists, photographers, film-makers, rappers and writers the urge to portray life in Moss Side can conflict with attempts to talk up progress. They're easy targets, of course, easily scapegoated for communicating messages people may not want to hear. Irvine Williams was among Karline's critics; for him the book was another knocking exercise, the latest example of over forty years of negativity. He feels that a community has been criminalised, and that this has held back progress. There's a new millennium, and another fresh start, and therefore a desire to accentuate the positive. According to Maria Kafula, 'Moss Side has been stigmatised and stereotyped by people from outside the area for years now. The media takes a negative image of the area which needs challenging.'

The Alexandra Park Estate certainly has a negative image, and money and social projects are making their way there in an effort to reverse the downward spiral. The City Council's 'Moss Side Initiative' includes plans for Moss Side, Rusholme and parts of Fallowfield, and is funded by £12.3 million from the Government. From this source there's money for new and existing education drives, crime prevention and sports projects, plus funds for Council action on three fronts: the environment (transforming wastegrounds into playgrounds, for example); safety (from household security to traffic-calming measures and panic alarms for the elderly); and community liaison. Maria Kafula is employed to provide full-time support for tenants' groups and residents' associations, and to encourage tenant involvement with new schemes.

Other European and Government funds have gone towards other projects. 'City Challenge' money funded the rebuilding of Hulme, and the Moss Side & Hulme Partnership was set up by the Council to build on regeneration in the area, to provide a new £2.8 million Powerhouse youth centre on Raby Street, and to work towards making Princess Road important and viable again. For decades now, the main artery through Moss Side has looked so unhealthy that it's hard to believe that Alexandra Road and Princess Road were both once thriving shopping streets. In the 1920s and 1930s when Anthony Burgess grew up in the area, his father and stepmother ran three shops in and around Princess Road. In the late 1950s, Princess Road still attracted shoppers from all over south Manchester, but by the end of the 1990s there were just a few successful businesses, including a garage, a dentist and a funeral home, and a couple of brave shops, including Peace & Love selling designer children's clothes. The economics of the situation – notably poverty in the area – had produced more complete destruction than the riots of 1981. Over half the shops were closed, trashed or boarded up.

Schemes and plans can go awry. Just as the economic and social problems of the 1970s undermined the last chances of the precinct, so advances into the new century will depend on jobs for local people and a long-term, stable economic future. Big social issues, such as community breakdown and mistrust of authority, as well as the effects on generations locked into poverty and crime, will also take time to resolve.

Intermittently, politicians express their desire to help. In 1993 Paddy Ashdown visited the Alexandra Park Estate. As he arrived a house on the Estate was being raided by armed police in riot vans. They were puzzled to find him in the locality, and the following morning his wife got a telephone call from the Chief Constable telling her there was a man in Gooch Close masquerading as her husband. She had to tell him that, no, it really was her husband.

Politicians think they have power, but not in Moss Side they don't. Sefton doesn't believe that the kids on the street would ever listen to a politician. They look at politicians and experts of most kinds across a huge gulf of mistrust. They walk a different walk. 'I don't think there's much Tony Blair can do to sort that situation out. I mean, they're only going to listen to someone who's lived it; you need to be a part of that situation for anyone to pay attention to you; and he's not. That's the final answer.'

For Sefton, real change has to come from within:

> Personally I think it's down to the older heads who have been involved in certain situations and who the younger ones still respect. I don't think the young kids get into all this because they want to, it's just because it's what every other seventeen-, eighteen-year-old is into. But they need to see the alternatives. If they saw all the older guys working in town or setting up organisations it might show them how to direct that energy and power they're putting out every day to do illegal things and channel that into doing something constructive.

Much of the real positivity has always come from inside the community, where networks of self-help and support have grown, usually out of desperation rather than after official encouragement. And Churches are involved, and charities and trusts. Moss Side & Hulme Development Trust, next to the brewery on Moss Lane, was established in 1989 in order to track down opportunities and jobs, and to boost prospects for local businesses. But the positives aren't just imperilled by unpredictable and merciless market forces in the global economy, but also on the ground by young kids buying into the untamed drug culture. Confidence shatters at the sound of gunfire. Even here, though, the situation may be improving. Sefton believes that increased police powers and increasing violence may one day deter people from getting involved: 'They've got to wake up or they'll learn the hard way. I know a kid who's doing life, man, and he ain't even killed someone, he's just got tangled up in it and he ain't even from the hood. It's just bullshit. If you really try to be a part of all that, you'll go to jail for it.'

Until other options are clear, practical and within reach, the temptations of criminal life will remain. It's a buzz brandishing gold chains, and to kids growing up in Moss Side, Salford, Cheetham Hill, the gangsters appear immune and untouchable. Kids are hungry, they don't want to live a poverty-stricken life. They see the police stand by while some guy in a council house who's seventeen or eighteen drives a big car, lives the life; they want it. Conspicuous consumption has a very strong hold in England. Powerful cars, women, an apartment full of lavish furniture and designer clothes bring respect in the neighbourhood; all neighbourhoods, from Cheshire to Cheetham Hill. Ours is a society in which possessions signify power and authority. Karline Smith thinks that there's a 'fuck you' mentality born in communities denied so much for so long: 'All right, we've got no jobs, and you're going to work nine to five, but what you earn in a week I'm going to earn in a day. Showing society that they can have it all.'

Family breakdown and generational conflict take their toll. In the masculine world of the gangster depicted in *Moss Side Massive* women struggle to be heard. 'In real life, the women don't really have much', is Karline's view. She doesn't much like my flippant remarks that I've seen women buzz around gangsters; 'Most of the women that I know wouldn't entertain a gangster. The glamour's there, and you can get the clothes and whatever, but it's a dangerous life. No woman wants to go through the pain you go through when you lose a boyfriend or a brother.'

Again in her second novel, *Balancing Acts*, and in conversation, it's clear that Karline is concerned about fathers absenting themselves from their children and leaving the local youth to find role models among the high-rolling gangster fraternity. It's a crisis developing throughout Britain, but Karline's perspective is very personal: 'There's only so much a woman can do, speaking from my own experience. I've had problems with my son since he was two and a half. I'm concerned my little boy needs his Dad there for him. I can see my son in a few years from now out on the streets, and I won't have any control over him.'

Larry Benji is concerned that a large minority of the generation now in their teens have been 'lost'. They're rebelling against their own community, education, the police, the system. 'They may never come back', he says. Many Moss Siders worry that ever younger kids are becoming involved in crime, locking them early into gangster fantasies, enticed by a sense of excitement and the buzz of violence as much as anything that can be rationalised. As one person I've spoken to put it: 'There's no reason for half the shit that goes down.'

The Chrysalis Project on Westerling Way is a lifeline for desperate people, a family advice centre which occupies two council houses knocked together. When the Pepperhill pub lost its licence, it was refurbished and reopened by St Edmund's church in 1994 for use as a drop-in centre, café and youth club known as the Saltshaker. Hideaway, despite problems with funding and resources, continues to initiate new projects close to the needs of the community. The Powerhouse is an ambitious scheme, but the effects on the community are yet to be evaluated. Jackie Burton at Hideaway hopes it will mark the end of short-term remedies for long-term problems:

> They come in with this short-term funding for you to do a certain project for three years, but what happens after three years? They close us down and a similar project opens somewhere else when the need becomes acute and it's starting all over again. Short term is like they just want to be seen to be doing something. You'll find that right throughout inner city areas. And of course the workers and the young people become disillusioned.

Larry Benji has moved on to establish a printing company and a magazine, *Flexi*, distributed free around the area through letter boxes and left in corner shops, doctors' surgeries, youth clubs; a pile left in the Chicken Run or Douggie's disappears in a matter of hours. Karline Smith is now working on her third novel. Clement Cooper followed 'Presence' with 'Deep' – portraits from mixed-race communities in Bristol, Liverpool, and Cardiff – and 'Stated', a project exploring the relationships between adults and children. Dealers swarmed over the Robin Hood in the late 1980s, and the pub closed. It's now been transformed into Greenheys Appliances, selling second-hand and reconditioned washing machines and fridges. In 1997 the Interarms warehouse was demolished as part of the extension to the Manchester–Salford inner relief road. By this time Sam Cummings had amassed a £1,100 million fortune. He died in May 1998. At the time his thirty-five-year-old daughter was facing charges after shooting her lover, a polo player. It transpired she'd used one of her father's guns, a Walther automatic pistol.

The decision taken to improve Princess Road made at the end of the 1990s promised a new chapter, and renewed hope. While welcoming all attempts to bring good vibes back to the area, for Irvine Williams most encouraging was the drive towards peace self-imposed by the gangs in the area. 'No youth worker, no agency, no one called the truce except the young people took it on themselves. A few workers encouraged it, maybe, but those young people realised it was their community and they were destroying it, and that they weren't going to go on living like this. It didn't stop it, but it's nowhere on the scale it used to be.'

But there's nothing to replace the Reno. In the shadow of the Crescents in Hulme, the PSV – where Factory hosted nights back in 1978 – went through a bewildering series of revamps and reincarnations. There's been rave and reggae – sometimes at the same time; one upstairs, the other down – as well as punk and jungle. The PSV hosted some massive jungle nights; at this point the club was known as the Lighthouse. DJs like Nicky Blackmarket, Jack Frost and Goldie played there. The scene had a ghetto feel; the world of bad boys, gangsters and guns was interwoven with the music. I've got some fantastic tapes off the pirate station Love Energy from 1995: the harshest, most uncompromising drum & bass pounds and breakdowns, with the DJs and MCs incessantly dissing and discussing, pure fuck-abouts and shout-outs, wind-ups, role-playing, rapping throughout (time and again they challenge the badmen, namecheck guns, take it darker). Gunfire became a feature of massive jungle nights at the PSV; shots fired into the air to hype up the vibe. The club was never very plush, and this trend didn't help much; management complained that the bullets were bringing chunks of the ceiling down on the dancers' heads. The guy running the jungle nights went on to serve time. The PSV is now a second-hand shop.

The music scene in Moss Side lacks venues, but that doesn't seem to stop the musicians, bands, rappers. Audioweb's Martin Merchant was born on the Rusholme side of Moss Side; a Manchester United fan born a street away from the Man City ground. Barry Adamson moved to London in the mid 1980s. New acts with connections with Moss Side include Subliminal Darkness, Parrish and Elavi. Moss Side, also, can take pride in producing Cleopatra, one of the biggest new acts to come out of Britain in 1998. The band grew up in Moss Side, three out of a family of four sisters brought up by their mother. Their first brush with success came when they took the stage for the very first time, at a local Valentine's Night dance, and sang a perfect version of En Vogue's 'Hold On'. When they signed to Warner's in 1997 the eldest sister, Zainam, was sixteen, Cleo was fourteen, and Yonah was just twelve. In an era when other girl groups appeared to gain fame without even being able to sing, Cleopatra were authentically talented, the genuine article, singing a cappella on chat shows and breakfast TV; all those years in church choirs were paying off.

Come the first stirrings of success for the band, the girls were happy to take the role of ambassadors for the city and the area they grew up in. 'We're here to prove that lots of good things come out of Moss Side', promised Zainam. The debut single, 'Cleopatra's Theme', was a self-confident manifesto and a big hit. Two more hit singles were taken from the first LP, *Comin' Atcha*. 'Cleopatra are putting the record straight', proclaimed one interviewer, trying to convince himself that it was possible that Cleopatra – bright, bouncy, young, and full of positivity and wit – could redefine, perhaps revive, Moss Side. Transformation is unlikely to be achieved solely by three girls and a handful of hit singles, but it surely helps. Every step counts.

Hideaway used to run dances but it's reticent about doing so at the moment. 'I would feel terrible if we put on a disco night and something happened – whether it would be on the way home, here, or whatever', explains Jackie Burton, who knows full well the demand. 'We've got to go beyond it at some stage because we can't let a few spoil it for the rest because at the moment there's just nowhere for them to go. I drove through the city centre the other night and there were tons of white kids coming out of all the different clubs, and driving back into Moss Side it was like a ghost town. There's nothing for us, nothing at all.'

It's not just a Moss Side problem. Perhaps it's lack of money that holds the scene back, or police intervention, or licensees playing it safe, too wary to allow any events that even remotely threaten to draw in trouble, but it also seems like any dance or club in the city is a challenge to certain people to wreck the night. Small steps towards positive change are gratifying, but there's still a long way to go. Jackie Burton can sound close to despairing:

> I don't know if they've got that understanding to say, 'Hang on a minute, look what's happening, while we're fighting, killing each other, the man at the top is just laughing at us.' I don't know when they're going to get a wake-up call to say enough is enough. As a woman I say to myself how many more mothers have to cry, how many more mothers have to go through that pain of standing by a graveside and burying a child because of this stupidity?

OUTRO

The Building of the City:

Keeping the Pop Cult Dreams Alive

Occasionally on a Sunday some of us would have a beer in the Peveril of the Peak and then go down into muddy, decaying Castlefield. This was some time in the middle of the 1980s. We wouldn't see a soul as we wandered under viaducts and along canals, sometimes dreaming of gangster films we'd one day set there or choosing sites for warehouse parties that never happened, peering into broken-down workshops and climbing over rusty pipes and fractured girders, the debris of industry and history piled up all around us.

It was a site of bleak industrial decay like Ancoats, across town; ruins, scrap value and nothing more. The Romans built a fort in Castlefield, where the Medlock and the Irwell rivers meet. Two hundred years ago the area became an inland port when canals opened up trade routes from Manchester across to the Atlantic Ocean and beyond. Come the railway age, the city's trading potential increased, and the world's first passenger railway station was built on Liverpool Road. Thus as Manchester became the first industrial city in the world and the richest place in England, Castlefield became a bustling junction of canals and railways, warehouses and workshops. Through the twentieth century, though, the city slumped and export markets vanished, manufacturing industry faded. Producers and consumers moved on to other markets, and by the early 1980s Castlefield was derelict.

Yet within just a few years of our Sunday treks, Castlefield witnessed a massive style makeover. First came museums – the Museum of Science and Industry in the old Liverpool Road Railway Station, the Air & Space Gallery in Lower Campfield market – and reconstructions of gatehouses and walls on the Roman site. At this point, Castlefield was designated the country's first Urban Heritage Park, but even with these developments it was still dead in Castlefield; it was death sentence heritage. It was as if we were all destined to no better future than re-creating a tourist version of the old days; Manchester as hygienic industrial theme park.

Injections of new life began in the late 1980s, coinciding with the Madchester era and the emergence of pop culture as a major force in the city. Madchester not only unveiled a new way of imagining the city, but broadcast these changes. It brought a thriving sub-culture to the surface, and marked the point when it seemed the city was no longer carrying the baggage of a hundred and fifty years of preconceptions, about the weather, the environment, the misery. Manchester talent was not only successful commercially, riding high in the charts, but embodied an attitude which struck a chord worldwide.

In Castlefield there were already some key developers in the area, looking to give new uses to old warehouses; notably Jim Ramsbottom, who had made his fortune owning a string of bookmaking shops. His property company turned the broken-down stables next door to Manchester's oldest canal-side building, the Merchant's Warehouse, into a thriving pub, Duke's 92. Up the cobbles towards Deansgate, Ramsbottom also transformed a rundown warehouse into the Eastgate office block. Once the area was being used not just by tourists, but by people working in offices, visiting bars, making their homes in quayside residential developments – once Castlefield became peopled again – it came alive again.

As well as the perceived change in the city's fortunes and the involvement of successful entrepreneurs, a further catalyst for regeneration was the Central Manchester Development Corporation (the CMDC), set up in 1988 to help develop strategies, and to secure and channel funds for developers in key areas of the city centre. An agency of central Government, the CMDC claimed to have attracted over £500 million of investment to key areas of Manchester city centre up to 1996 when it disbanded, and its input into Castlefield was huge. The CMDC's final report was one of 1996's most glossy brochures, stuffed with contrasting photographs taken before and after regeneration. In all the photographs of the city centre from the 1970s, the sky is overcast and grey, but on pictures of the new and improved Manchester the sun is shining. Miraculously, even Manchester's infamous bad weather had been regenerated.

After the CMDC was wound down, regeneration still continued apace. With a £1.7 million grant, the Middle Warehouse was restored as a complex of apartments, and became home to Key 103. During 1998 big breweries built new canal-side café bars like Quay Bar (owned by Bass Brewery) and Jackson's Wharf (owned by Greenall's). Castlefield became increasingly busy, especially on warm summer evenings. Occasional music events boosted the area's profile.

Developments also prospered on the edge of Castlefield – including an old church restored by Pete Waterman for use as a recording studio, the building of Atlas café bar, and the opening of the V&A Hotel – as well as an area on and just off Whitworth Street, where housing in old warehouses became a feature. The CMDC were wary of flaws in past schemes for redeveloping Manchester, and encouraged sensitive use of the existing buildings. The CMDC also favoured the use of degraded ex-industrial land rather than greenfield sites; the British Council on the site of the old gasworks opposite the Haçienda, for example, or the establishment of 144 homes in the new Piccadilly Village development on degraded land bordering the Ashton Canal near Ducie House. At the dissolution of the CMDC only one minor project remained undelivered: an attempt to transfer a statue of Engels to Manchester from the Eastern bloc.

This idea had come to the CMDC's Christine Derbyshire at the beginning of the 1990s, stimulated by TV images of statues being taken down in the old Eastern bloc. Investigating, she discovered that in St Petersburg, Manchester's official twin town, the authorities were well aware of how Engels had used his knowledge of Manchester to underpin communist theory. They also understood the importance of drawing strength from history, rather than merely erasing it, and pledged to help the CMDC in the search.

Possible sites for a statue were discussed. The favoured spot was the triangle of paving in front of the Fire Station where Whitworth Street splits two ways. An enormous statue would fit with the scale of the buildings in that area, and would overlook the Whitworth Street warehouses, those old palaces of capitalism now transformed into housing. 'But they couldn't find a statue', says Christine Derbyshire; 'The main debate was that an Engels is a very hard statue to get, that Engels may not exist.'

Engels in modern Manchester would indeed find little trace of his former existence. An extension of the M602 motorway from Eccles to Salford goes through much of the site of Ermen & Engels's Victoria

Mill. On the last day of 1968, trading at the Royal Exchange ceased, and the Hall then became a theatre. Among the few reminders of Engels in Manchester is a plaque on a wall on Marlborough Street marking the centre of Little Ireland, and the only trace of the various official and unofficial homes Engels had in Manchester is a blue plaque on the wall of Aberdeen House commemorating the fact that he lived on the site. At the CMDC's dissolution in 1996 no available statue had been found, and within weeks a big chunk of Manchester's city centre was devastated by an IRA bomb. Political violence had an even more instant effect on the built environment than economic change, and the search for a statue was dropped down. But while Engels may not be getting a memorial, another famous German émigré in nineteenth-century Manchester, Charles Hallé, was being very well looked after.

Hallé was born at Hagen, near Elberfeld, in 1819, and Engels was born in Barmen in 1820, less than ten miles away. Hallé worked at the Conservatoire in Paris, but left Paris in 1848, fleeing the French Revolution. Engels, on the other hand, had been thrown out of Paris some months earlier for encouraging anti-Government activity there. Despite these clear differences in attitude, within a decade they had both enrolled as members of the Schiller Anstalt, a social and cultural club set up in 1859 for Manchester's German middle-class merchants, manufacturers, bankers and businessmen. Hallé had brought various musicians together for the Arts Exhibition of 1857 and subsequently guided the Hallé Orchestra to world renown. In the mid 1990s, while a fruitless search for a tangible memorial for Engels took place, a new concert hall for the Hallé Orchestra was built at the Bridgewater Hall at a cost of £42 million, with the money coming from various sources: the Council, the CMDC and the European Regional Development Fund.

Although Hallé directors were vocal in their view that the Orchestra had outgrown its previous home at the Free Trade Hall, it was clear that the building of a new concert hall was also motivated by a desire to compete with other cities. Birmingham had spent a lot of money around Broad Street, including a new Symphony Hall for Simon Rattle's CBSO, and Glasgow had developed new conference centres and concert halls. These cities were felt to have seized the initiative from Manchester.

New buildings have become an accepted way of measuring a city's progress, but it's possible that the obsession with grand schemes is warping perspectives on regeneration. Sometimes it's necessary to remind the planners, civic leaders and local hype-merchants that these buildings are only buildings; the key to the cultural, economic and social health of Manchester doesn't lie in piling up shiny new halls or instigating new developments.

But those 'marketing' the city love these big new buildings; nationally, in fact, civic leaders and local political figures are obsessed by them. It's a version of some primitive impulse; but instead of invading a neighbouring tribe, local leaders build a bigger skyscraper, a neater wharf, a wider dome. The terms of the first National Lottery awards to arts organisations, where the funds made available could only be spent on capital projects (i.e. buildings), further intensified this trend. Two new theatre buildings – a major refurbishment of the Green Room and a £4.5 million rebuilding of the Contact Theatre on Devas Street – were major capital projects in the late 1990s, but I'm not sure that sparkling new theatres guarantee the good health of the city's drama scene, improved ideas or performances.

There are also practical reasons to be wary of the way new buildings can affect the life of a city. New construction incurs high costs and only highly capitalised operations can afford to carry the costs of new construction, so new buildings tend to house corporate, mainstream businesses: Planet Hollywood, Tesco and UCI. But the creative, local, young groundbreaking popular culture activity in Manchester we've been tracking in the last few chapters – small record labels, young designers, leftfield record shops, rehearsal studios – as well as small community-based initiatives like youth centres, co-ops, drop-in centres, are all low-yield, risky, underfunded operations. No matter how profitable or successful some of them may prove to be, in their early days they aren't suited to, or welcome in, the high-overhead environment of new buildings.

The suspicion remains that many of the big building projects are motivated by the need to buy Manchester some prestige in the overhyped world of inter-city competition. Locked into a marketing agenda, these initiatives are more about image than reality; they're about providing brochure fodder rather than an enhanced civic culture. Manchester has been widely publicised competing with other cities in recent decades to host Olympic and Commonwealth Games. It's also, less obviously but just as intensely, been competing with other cities for investment, business and tourist profile.

For those marketing the city, shopping opportunities – like new buildings – have a high status. Manchester had always juggled manufacture and trade, making and marketing, even in the Engels era – remember the exultant religious metaphors used to describe the shopping experiences provided by Lewis's and other major department stores – but since 1995 there's been a relentless, unprecedented series of major shopping developments in the Manchester area. Investment in out-of-town building in Cheshire, including John Lewis and Sainsbury's in Cheadle, and Marks & Spencer and Tesco at nearby Handforth Dean, topped a billion pounds. Fearing the loss of customers from town centres, Manchester City Council and seven other local authorities opposed a development on the M62 at Dumplington, but to no avail, and the Trafford Centre opened in September 1998, including the first Selfridge's store outside London. Manchester retaliated with the biggest Marks & Spencer shop in the world on the site of the IRA bomb, complemented on the other side of the road by the biggest branch of Boots in Britain; the very bigness of the projects enough, we suppose, to bring a warm glow to the heart.

The city also pressed ahead with a £100 million retail development at the Great Northern Warehouse. One of the buildings demolished to make way for the development was the Gallery on the corner of Peter Street and Deansgate. Thus another landmark venue in Manchester's nightlife history disappeared, just as the Magic Village had when the Arndale was built. When Selfridge's opened it advertised the huge array and variety of its goods with the phrase 'A Perfect City'; the shop was turning itself into a city, and the city was turning itself into a shop.

It has now become accepted that shopping and tourism have key roles in the future prosperity of the city. For the young, especially, Manchester is becoming a must-see city, a cult pop city, and it was probably the Madchester era that brought the first big influx of tourists. When the Stone Roses played to nearly thirty thousand people at Spike Island, near Widnes, in the summer of 1990, they drew people from all over Europe and beyond. Spread among the locals strolling up and down Oldham Street that weekend were more than a few pop sightseers. We'd met the odd Dutch Fall fan, but this was a big, baggy army. Here they were, paying homage to the city, come to feel the noise. 'Are my flares wide enough?' they asked.

To boost the city's profile, the City Council and Manchester Airport devised Marketing Manchester. Its £2.5 million budget was to be spent on selling the city to potential business investors and to tourists, complete with a press office and funds to send delegates around the world. Manchester had become a product. Through 1997 there were months of wrangling over the right image and the best logo. Marketing Manchester was dogged by a group of young entrepreneurs who dubbed themselves the McEnroe Group, professing 'you cannot be serious' when confronted with some of Marketing Manchester's more embarrassing attempts at branding the city.

But if Manchester was a product, it seemed wise to ask: why prioritise the design of the logo over improving the product? A gap was developing between what the marketeers wanted to claim about the city and the reality of everyday life; a gap that was being filled by cynicism. It was like the old Tory claim about having put the 'Great' back into Great Britain, conveniently ignoring massive unemployment, rising debt and increasing social conflict. But it also owed something to the New Labour mentality of spinning the right message and giving the presentation of the message a higher priority than the message itself. This was the late 1990s. Locally and nationally we were all dressed up but going nowhere; we were becoming a fur-coat-and-no-knickers society.

Controversy over £2 million spent on the Old Moat estate in 1998 is typical of the way these conflicts impacted on the ground. Throughout estates in Manchester, as elsewhere, there are major problems of vandalism, intimidation and burglaries – and Old Moat is a long way from being the worst – but when the Council put the money towards repairing buildings, re-roofing and new chimneys, some local people complained that the real problems weren't being met. One resident spoke anonymously to a local paper: 'It is the community that needs the development not the houses. The money should be spent on increased security and community improvements.'

The McEnroe Group didn't question the need to market the city. However, they put forward their own design-led marketing ideas, including a neat series of designs based around the theme of Manchester's role in revolutions; the industrial revolution of course, and also the sexual revolution (focusing on the Pankhurst connection). The city's place at the forefront of the rave revolution was incorporated, as was Manchester's claim as the starting point for the digital revolution ('the most transformative invention since Gutenberg's printing press was born', according to the McEnroe Group's deposition to Marketing Manchester).

A festival was organised to celebrate the fiftieth anniversary of the digital revolution during the 'Digital Summer' of 1998, including the building of a replica of the Baby, screenings, installations, webcasts and D-Percussion (a twelve hour celebration featuring 89 DJs and 17 bands on 8 stages around Castlefield). The D-Percussion event coincided with the tenth anniversary of acid house. If jazz was 'a symbol of modernity, the machine age, a break with the past' – to recall Hobsbawm's words – then acid house was a symbol of the digital age, the moment computer-generated dance music went overground and blew a hole in the music Establishment. D-Percussion also signalled the changes in Castlefield. The event's prime mover, Steve Smith, said at the time: 'The Bridgewater Canal is where the industrial revolution started. Here we have a celebration of the second industrial revolution, or the digital revolution, in exactly the same place as the first one started.'

Drawing a link between these revolutionary moments underlined Manchester's traditions of creative, social and scientific innovation and revolution. 'It again proves that Manchester is ahead of the game in terms of ideas', said Steve Smith, going on to focus on lessons to be drawn from more recent years: 'The main revolution in the last twenty years has been music and fashion.'

Over the last couple of chapters we've seen just how important this recent explosion of interest and success in music and fashion has become to Manchester. We've traced the long revolution, the two centuries of popular culture in the city, the music hall, variety shows, jazz, dancehalls, Northern Soul and rock & roll, Mancunians cultivating their own resources, improvising and soaking up every influence, creating a culture as fluid as the changing population. Manchester's story echoes that of cities like Bristol, Liverpool and Birmingham, sharing a popular culture that reflects urban, confused, hard-faced, noisy, hedonist, multi-racial life. A culture that embraces the geographical and political margins, a pop culture long ago divorced from the dominant culture.

The cultural alienation of the city is extreme because our national identity is still so bound up with what has been described as 'Deep England'; the idea that real England is rural, peaceful moors, fields and streams. By implication, cities are a defacement. Manchester has been marooned in a culture that denies the value of urban industrial life. But traditional views of English national identity – fine arts, the country house, green fields – have continued to marginalise the mass of the English people. The pop cult city has offered an alternative.

It's been a battle of the rulers versus the ruled; the nostalgia of peace and privilege versus the reality of noise and chaos; a national identity that's scared of change versus a pluralist popular urban culture; a refined reverence for tradition versus a raw embrace of the new. The country house versus acid house.

Other aspects of our national identity – Parliament, the BBC, the tourist sites of olde England – are connected with the centres of political power in London, and have a less than tenuous hold on the Mancunian imagination. Mancunians have tended to react against London's haughty domination of our national affairs, and the symbolic, social and economic gaps between Manchester and London and the North and the South have helped nurture Manchester's independent spirit; from the Anti Corn Law League to Factory Records. Mancunians have the same raw, noisy lives as many inner city Londoners, but, in general, Manchester seems to have more in common with Glasgow than with England's capital; the Glasgow of Alan McGee and the writer James Kelman, that is. McGee signed Oasis to his independent record label Creation but, earlier, in the late 1980s, had rented a flat in Manchester just to be near the epicentre of music energy. Kelman – who understands how it is to be marginalised geographically and culturally – once took a few years out of Glasgow working in a Manchester factory. As a writer he claims to have found nothing of interest in the established canon of English literature, so he looked elsewhere, to life in the Glasgow dole queues and the works of Beckett and Kafka.

Manchester has often found inspiration from America, but often not from mainstream, corporate America; it's outlaw American culture that's fed into Manchester culture. From the cinema, through jazz, to rock & roll and rap, the Manc pop cults have seized on disruptive American culture – ragtime, James Cagney, Northern Soul, blues, Public Enemy – and taken it to their hearts. It's as if there's a huge constituency of people in Britain who can identify with creative voices from the American margins. In the 1960s, the first signs that black music could appeal to a white record-buying public came when the British took to black American music in a way which the segregated American market never had; not just the way blues inspired the likes of John Mayall, but the way that Motown stormed the charts. In the 1970s Mark E. Smith got into the Velvet Underground, he says, because their New York sensibility matched his Mancunian life. Morrissey wrote a book on the New York Dolls. In Manchester in the 1980s, thousands understood hip hop culture; it rang more true than the traditional symbols of English identity.

Our versions of rock & roll and house music have then gone on to loosen the giant hold America has had over British popular culture. The way Britain has sold the Prodigy and the Chemical Brothers back to an America that had been deaf to its own house sounds, mirrors the way the Stones and the Beatles first introduced the blues to the American mainstream. Looking back, Sefton remembers how the appeal of hip hop culture was strong, but didn't preclude fashioning the lifestyle to fit a Mancunian vision: 'We were watching America, and everything that was coming new to us we were adapting, and changing around.'

Perhaps Lancashire's cotton trade – renowned for importing cotton, then colouring and reworking it, and then selling it on – is the pattern for this kind of non-precious, non-purist attitude. And perhaps the city's non-parochial attitudes were also born years ago, in the mix thrown up by the industrial revolution: Irish immigrants, German and Jewish businessmen, Scottish engineers and Lancashire mill girls. The more recent links with Jamaica, West Africa, Pakistan and India have built on this, opened the city's eyes to new experiences, and increased the hybrid nature of modern Manchester.

In the pluralist city there's a babble of voices, and in the fragmented world of the twenty-first-century music business there's no single, one-dimensional, definable Manchester sound. However, by the end of the 1990s, in the area around Tib Street and Oldham Street known as the Northern Quarter, a community, of sorts, had developed around music-makers steeped in breaks and beats and wedded to experimentalism, from Andy Votel to Waiwan, nurtured at club nights like Graham Massey's 'Toolshed' and Mark Rae's 'Counter Culture', two of the benchmark nights of 1999. Mark Rae's Grand Central label reflects this activity; on collections like *Central Heating* and Rae & Christian's *Northern Sulphuric Soul* there's a mix of unsegregated sounds as hip hop beats meld with quiet psychedelia, and transatlantic rap voices share space with Veba's south Manchester gospel-tinged vocals. The music also reflects a certain kind of Manchester experience well; it's slo-mo with a barely buried paranoia, head-nodding music, dope head, downbeat, drawn out.

Pop music has reflected and also created Manchester, in the same sense that the Beach Boys intensified a view of California and Public Enemy magnified a version of New York. The big pop cult groups like Joy Division, New Order, the Smiths, the Fall and Happy Mondays have changed perceptions of Manchester, even if that was never their intention, and few Manchester-based musicians can deny the influence of the city on the music. Whether there's a conscious attempt to catch the essence of the city (as with Lionrock's *City Delirious* LP) or not, more musicians than ever are clearly absorbing and reflecting Manchester vibes. Waiwan confesses:

> I'm sure that if I was sat on a beach in the Bahamas I'd be writing things a little bit differently. When you live in the inner city, the general landscape definitely has some sort of subconscious effect on you. I like to push a feelgood vibe in my music but I also like to contradict that with harsh reality in order to reflect what's going on around me. 'Revenge' was the first track I wrote while living on Whitworth Street. Every night I'd hear the sound of sirens bouncing between the tall buildings.

Successful music from the city travels well. A compilation of Manchester dance records released in 1996 included New Order's 'Blue Monday' remixed by Richie Hawtin. A track originally created under the influence of New York disco and German electronica, remixed by a star of Detroit's second generation of house-makers, it's an international record rather than a provincial one, so much so that it seems daft to include it on a compilation of 'Manchester' records. We've seen throughout this story the way urban life cross-references internationally, how, via film, radio and recorded music, city speaks unto city, how disenfranchised urban populations are more likely to forge alliances with foreign cities than with villages in their green belt. And Richie Hawtin does a great job, rebuilding the original into a fierce technoid track, ironically – given New Order's reputation – turning it into something even more industrial than the original, and more neurotic. Not so much Manchester as Don DeLillo meets exploding anti-matter inside a dodgy car alarm.

Culture soon dies if it's confined to one city or one country. Artists of all kinds need to leap intellectual or emotional border controls; thus Henry Moore, arguably Britain's finest sculptor of the twentieth century, found a way to express his vision via the influence of Aztec sculpture and the works of the French sculptor Brancusi, and for decades Manchester's musicians have drawn upon a shared international musical currency. While our political leaders prevaricated over the propriety of the country's overseas alliances during the late 1980s, the direction youth culture was taking was progressively more open-minded, international, cross-border. It was a role the youth had maintained for generations, further back even than the early 1960s when Colin MacInnes had noted how teenage sounds and styles are carried over Europe 'by a sort of international adolescent maquis'.

So a culture is created that's not about museums and national purity; it's a living culture which absorbs new things, remains open to new, old or foreign influence, and to new technology. Indeed, the international rave community was strengthened by the advances in 1980s computer technology, the internet, ISDN. The fact that the internet found its place as a pop cult tool – before big business and national corporate institutions – is testimony to this.

This street culture is not about civic pride and marketing initiatives. It's about ideas, self-expression and escape. It can, and will, thrive in crappy coffee bars, under leaking roofs or down unlit roads. It's uncontrollable, uncomfortable and never far removed from the problems of everyday living. Yet it's survived – and, at times, prospered – because it's had to; the alternative to this independent Manc pop culture is silence.

More by accident than design this activity has created a tradition, jobs and a commercial infrastructure; most conspicuously, a small, but powerful, music infrastructure, more compact, less corporate than London's. It also benefits from In The City every year; Tony Wilson's annual music conference has grown and prospered since 1992 and gives an annual energy boost to the city and an important endorsement of what goes on in Manchester. Towards the end of the 1990s this infrastructure was extending on many fronts, including café bars and record shops. The boom in small record shops providing something more than the mainstream was a product of music's fragmentation. The all-encompassing rave scene had fractured into specialisms. In 1992 Martin Price had lamented the fate of the independent record shop, yet within five years there were a slew of new record shops in the Northern Quarter: Fat City, Piccadilly Records, Vinyl Exchange, Beatin' Rhythm, Beat Street and Slam Jams among them, as well as Dean Johnson's Expansions nearby on Shudehill. Sefton set up Slam Jams with DJs Owen D and Leaky Fresh. 'It was something that I never thought I'd be doing in a million years', he says, 'but there's no record shops owned by our own people breaking into that black music market in Manchester. But I thought there was a hunger for rap, soul, bit of jazz, garage; and it's been proved as the shop has grown and developed.'

Whenever economists and politicians talk about regenerating the North West, their first thought over recent decades has been to offer inducements to foreign-owned companies to invest in new factories in the area. Car giants and new technology – particularly run by Pacific Rim companies – are favoured targets, but attracting these companies isn't necessarily healthy for the economy, or the culture. Samsung, Fujitsu and companies like them come to Britain to exploit the low wages and the new casualised work ethic, to snap up Government incentives and to get into the European markets. It's a regeneration policy fraught with danger; millions can be spent creating jobs in a foreign-owned factory, only to see those jobs disappear when the world economy falters.

We would do better to sow seeds in the grassroots, encourage and nurture independent, even oppositional, cultural activity. That activity could possibly grow into jobs, perhaps self-employment or cooperatives, but it draws on the desire to be involved, to participate rather than merely to consume, to live to work rather than work to live. We're talking about designers, promoters, musicians, fanzine editors, pirate radio crusaders, film-makers, DJs, writers, artists. We're talking about difficult people who may not have commercial nous. People who have successful small-scale, independent businesses in Manchester – shops like Arc, Identity, Westworld and Wear It Out; designers like Hooch and Gio Goi; magazines like *Jockey Slut*; promoters like SJM, Doodlebug, Lee Donnelly at MCR; record labels like Grand Central, Paper Recordings and Blood & Fire; graphic designers like Via and Jai Moodie; organisations like Kinofilm, Potential Development, Ear to the Ground and the Buzz Club – have worked against all odds; how much more energy could be harnessed, how many more ideas could blossom in an environment that actively encouraged them?

These young creative characters continue to draw strength from their own self-belief and the city's traditions of DIY youth culture. Perhaps there even lingers in them the spirit of the old street hustlers, amateur Houdinis, and hawkers living on in the modern-day grafters in Salford, Manchester and beyond, selling a bit of this, pushing stuff, moving in.

Club culture is a problematic area, with its roots in old gambling dens and its recent history shot through with dodgy dealings, where even the most timid clubber may be passing on a bit of weed, some pills. An illicit economy thrives off the back of club culture. There's money to be made, and organised and disorganised crime hasn't waited to move in.

Problems with gang violence continue to plague Manchester's nightlife. Just as there remain grim areas of real, deep poverty a world away from the sites of civic splendour, so violence in Manchester is always just beneath the surface. On Sundays my phone starts ringing at four or five o'clock in the afternoon as the clubbing community starts waking up; there are tales of fights, bar brawls, threats, rumours.

Among the rumours that turned out to be true was the final, irrevocable closure of the Haçienda in June 1997, a month after the club's fifteenth birthday. Despite the club's high profile and history, there had been a succession of year-on-year losses. FAC 51, the company set up by Rob Gretton to run the club, went into voluntary liquidation. The perennial door troubles had ensured that the high running costs were exacerbated by massive security bills. Following the closure, a war of words blew up between the club and various police spokesmen, who phoned local papers rubbishing the club's management and planting lurid tales of gang violence. I'd been DJ-ing on what turned out to be the last night of the Haçienda, Saturday 28 June 1997; it was full and it was totally trouble-free.

A late run of successful Saturdays hadn't been enough to turn the club's fortunes around. The Haçienda, a huge name in Manchester's music history, had dropped off the map. I swear there are people who've not been to a club since.

After widespread dismay following the Haçienda's closure, the City Council intervened to encourage a series of policing initiatives. This was also a reaction to fears of a crime wave in the city centre generally. As cash in clubland became scarcer, designer clothes shops had come under renewed attention from the criminals. Retailers suffered ram-raiding, steaming and intimidation. Within the space of a week in November 1996, a Vauxhall Astra was reversed through the window of Jigsaw on King Street, a Ford Fiesta went through the front window of Vivienne Westwood on St Mary's Gate, and a red Mazda crashed through another shop on St Ann's Square. As the quality of Manchester's shopping choices increased, so did the range of stores hit by the organised gangs, with Emporio Armani and DKNY both targeted through 1997 and 1998.

Policing problems in the retail sector had, paradoxically, strengthened the case that clubland was just another magnet for trouble, not the cause of trouble, in the city. When DKNY, rather than a major club, was the site of gang activity, it wasn't so easy simply to blame the premises. It was reported that a major city centre hotel had been invaded by a large contingent of Salford gangsters one Sunday lunchtime, and Planet Hollywood were rumoured to have pulled out of an investment in the Great Northern Warehouse complex because high-status bars and restaurants in Manchester weren't being adequately protected by the police, or so they claimed. Pressure on the police to act increased.

In the city centre, the arrival of big-name designer shops had been celebrated as a boost to tourism and trade. However, it seemed that some of these success stories were destined for unhappy endings. A local paper received a copy of a letter sent by the Leader of Manchester City Council, Richard Leese, to the Chief Constable of Greater Manchester Police, David Wilmot. Leese acknowledged that clubland's problems with 'thugs and gangsters seem to have escalated, spreading to other areas of business activity within the city centre. And now they are seriously undermining investor confidence so vital for the city's regeneration.'

Years before, I'd cornered Richard Leese at some bar opening, keen that the Council would maintain its support for clubland; the issues didn't seem so urgent then and we ended up talking about Motown and one of his favourite records, 'Tears Of A Clown'. Now he was on record demanding police action to defend the city's nightlife. He described 'rampant lawlessness' in the city centre. It was 'a crisis', he wrote, 'that your officers seem either unable or unwilling to address'. The biggest shock was the change in tone. While the city had been bidding for international sporting events, inward investment and a place among the elite European cities, he'd always been upbeat about Manchester. But the remarks addressed to the Chief Constable sounded positively apocalyptic. The marketing mask had slipped.

Tragically, on 4 April 1998, just days after the publication of Richard Leese's letter, Chorlton bank worker Nick Cenci was stabbed to death near the corner of Whitworth Street and Deansgate. He was the fifth person to be killed in Manchester city centre in twelve months. The situation was clearly deteriorating. There were problems in and around some of the highest-profile licensed premises, and representatives from Manchester's DKNY and Armani stores were forced to call a meeting with the Council and police.

The police managed to make some advances in the weeks that followed the killing. At the end of April mass arrests of doormen from one particular firm were aided by evidence from video cameras. On the streets, the police pursued known troublemakers with an active campaign of road blocks, body searches and club visits. However, it's apparent that inside information may well be available to organised crime; one police surveillance operation, planned for months, was scuppered on its first Saturday. Associates of the suspects drove a huge removal van to the club and parked in front of the building, thereby obscuring everything that went on at the door.

The effect of this increased criminal and police activity was the erosion of Manchester's reputation for cutting-edge nightlife. DJs and clubbers alike were increasingly staying at home or travelling away from town. After fourteen years in Manchester clubs, I started work at Cream in Liverpool. Ironically Cream was inspired by trips the club's founders, Darren Hughes and James Barton, had made over to 'Most Excellent' and other Manchester club nights in the early 1990s.

Manchester in those early years had also been ahead of Leeds; 'Kaos' started at Leeds Warehouse in 1989 after promoter Tony Hannon had visited the Haçienda (his first resident DJ was Steve Williams from the Thunderdome); 'Kaos' in turn became an inspiration for other nights in Leeds. Similarly, clubs were playing a part in reviving other cities. In Birmingham, the huge commercial success of 'Miss Moneypenny's' boosted the infrastructure of shops, bars and clubs, and justified the claim of promoter Jim Ryan: 'In our own way we've put our city on the map.'

These were organic changes, cities expressing and changing themselves without the intervention of big business or Government initiatives. Planning is an inexact science anyway, and attempts to improve the quality of life can go awry; just think of Hulme and Moss Side in the 1970s.

The City Council chanted a twenty-four hour city mantra through the 1990s, pledging to turn Manchester into a chic European city; people sitting in pavement café bars drinking cappuccino, eating late and dancing till dawn. In one sense, it was a very unambitious vision for a new Manchester, perhaps even misguided, especially as the Council stuck naively to the notion that Manchester could become Barcelona simply by enacting liberal licensing laws. Magistrates were encouraged to grant extended licences to café bars and new licences were virtually unopposed.

This policy had three unintentional side effects. First, it collided with the drive to attract new residents to the refurbished loft and warehouse apartments; venues and clubs which had initially helped make the city centre attractive to young homeowners were threatened with closure by environmental health inspectors after a surge in complaints about noise from new city dwellers (presumably the excitement of living in a twenty-four hour city wanes after a few weeks of sleeplessness).

Second, the huge increase in licensed premises in the city centre – from 250 in 1996 to more than 400 in 1998 – outstripped the ability or resources of the local police to protect them, with serious public order consequences.

Finally, the growth in post-11pm licences for café bars had a detrimental effect on demand for clubs, and returned a drink-fuelled, rather than music-fuelled, nightlife culture to Manchester. The city centre attracted drinkers rather than ravers, and on Saturday nights the streets were besieged by swaggering gangs of lads wandering around Deansgate, pissed up and singing 'Suck My Cock, Suck My Cock' to the tune of 'Here We Go'. In the words of one local: 'It's certainly very continental out there, but less like Paris, more like the Somme.'

Conspiracy theorists pointed to the huge power of the breweries to influence policies via donations to political parties and highly paid lobbyists. The breweries were aware that the pill-gobblers of the rave era weren't drinking alcohol, and lobbied for an increase in opening hours for bars and pubs to decrease the demand for clubs. Bars, leeching off the clubs in the mid 1990s, were killing them off by the end of the decade. As a recession spread through the North of England, triggered by further problems in the manufacturing sector, the leisure and service industries were hit; the proliferation of free-entry bars open late had led to a fall in the number of regular clubgoers, security bills were rising, dance music was fragmenting, and the spending power of the local audience was diminished. In August 1998 Sankey's Soap and Kaleida both closed. Independent operators who had taken creative risks were being squeezed out by blander, corporately owned venues better able to ride the recessions. In March 1999 at least four clubs were for sale, including the Boardwalk, and I called a halt to my seven year stint at 'Yellow'.

The club scene remains unpredictable and insecure. When the Haçienda closed, Manchester nightlife lost its flagship. In January

1998 I gained access to the building, and spent a good hour wandering around being photographed for a book celebrating ten years since acid house. All the DJ equipment had been ripped out. The only things left in the DJ box were some bare wires and a packet of Rizla. Behind the bar the spirits hadn't even been cleared away. Cash books were stacked in boxes, and rubbish was piled on the stage and at the side of the dancefloor. There was no energy, nothing. The photographs of me sitting on a dusty, deserted dancefloor in the crumbling shell of the Haçienda were never published.

Some months later it was announced that the club had been sold to developers who were set to demolish the building to make way for luxury flats. 'I'm not into a museum culture', said Tony Wilson, refusing to shed a tear at the news. Wilson had a point; despite the fantastic memories so many of us had of the Haçienda, the spirit of underground creativity had moved on to other clubs by the end of the 1990s: 'Guidance', 'Rinky Dink', 'Electric Chair', 'Counter Culture', 'Tropical Hotdog Payday', 'Havoc', 'Tangled', 'Spellbound'.

These club nights are not household names, not backed with huge money, and long ago divorced from the mainstream nights at the corporately owned clubs and bars. Similarly, among musicians, it's the characters on the margins of pop culture, divorced from rock formulae and commercial imperatives, who turn out the most creative work. Following his wonderful 1988 debut LP, *Moss Side Story*, Barry Adamson has continued to dig deep into self-mythologies, pursuing a vision shot through with paranoia, eroticism, breakbeats and the influence of John Barry. Autechre are another example; new electronica they may be, but somewhere I can hear echoes, reverberations, the sound of falling chimneys and flying shuttles. These two soundtrackers, in particular, have captured something of the city's sense of conflict, cynicism and melancholy. In Manchester there's always melancholy.

Oftentimes, ways of working in Manchester seem to reflect the history of the city. The city's role in the early days of trade unions and the founding of the Cooperative movement just down the road in Rochdale are just two markers on the road of cooperation. In the music business this has extended to a degree of cooperative work between clubs and bands that you don't get everywhere; make a phone call offering somebody a part in a project and they don't often ask 'What's in it for me?' Mark Rae at Grand Central makes a point of nurturing a collective spirit: 'For me, the most important thing is people working together. Whatever your talent – as a programmer, a great musician, if you have good ideas, or are a good singer – it's about realising those talents. It's not about using other people, it's about working with people. It's the right attitude that matters.'

The accidental entrepreneurs I've been talking about have needed to draw strength from other people. It's practical as much as ideological soundness; away from the bigger business and media structures of London, Manchester's creative types have needed to band together to get things done. Much of what has happened in the story of the last two centuries in Manchester – the Chartists, the suffragettes, Salford strikers, Jamaican sound systems, In The City, credit unions and club nights – is evidence of something that Ian Brown pointed out in a radio interview with Key 103's Pete Mitchell: 'People getting together to do things and make things better, that's what Manchester's always been about.'

On the other hand, there are plenty of less positive experiences: pure go-getting greed, claims of innate Northern friendliness banished by a poke in the eye in a rundown pub or outside some café bar. And there are many less positive ways of working than the cooperative spirit. 'More like "fuck you, I don't give a fuck",' says Mark Rae, who consciously reacted against some of the arrogance around during the Madchester era; 'Too many people bought into that Shaun Ryder style – followed that as a way to be and a way to behave – aggressive, truculent.'

Also many artists are by nature born mavericks, not readily given to joining groups, or gangs, or committees. It's noticeable how many Manchester bands have given off a maverick air, and the story told over these chapters has been littered with great discontented visionaries, from Ann Lee to Mark E. Smith, Liz and Cath at *City Fun* to A Guy Called Gerald. Manchester-born writer Jeff Noon has often told me how cut off from the city he feels. Some chilly July afternoon on the terrace behind Atlas he even explained where the word maverick came from: 'It's from cattle-raising in America, it's the word used to describe the stray, the animal that won't run with the herd.'

In a city with long traditions of independence and nonconformity, many creative people in Manchester have become mavericks in a maverick city. Photographer Clement Cooper is one of the most wary people I have ever met. His alienation from the city, even from the creative leftfield communities in the city, is complete. 'Everyone's got their own agenda. They come in, take what they want, and then you never see them again. When you talk about Manchester you're talking about the world out there, and that's really nothing I'm a part of. I don't operate in it.'

That's the irony undermining the phrase 'the creative industries'; many of the truly creative voices in the city don't want to be part of an industry. They may be idealistic, unrealistic or cynical, but they don't want their work filtered through a marketing process, and don't want to be commercial in a way an industry demands. You could argue that the Stone Roses were blown apart by their unwillingness or inability to come to terms with life in a marketplace.

One of the current local stars, Badly Drawn Boy, appears to be another uncompromised indie maverick. Performing onstage alone, his sets meander like Patrik Fitzgerald taking Beck out busking with a beatbox and getting lost on the way home. Starting his career releasing two 7" singles on the Twisted Nerve label he helps to run with Andy Votel, Badly Drawn Boy (real name Damon Gough) took a couple of steps towards local recognition with gigs at 'Black Eye' at Kaleida and at the Boardwalk, and then guested on the UNKLE album *Psyence Fiction*. His idiosyncratic style and rapid rise was soon picked up by *The Face*. He seems to belong to that long succession of Manchester bands, clubs, labels and musicians who have appeared less compromised, more honest, less hypnotised by the desire for fame than their counterparts elsewhere. Manchester's function is to deliver street credibility to British youth culture. The first Oasis front cover run by the *NME* was headlined quite simply: 'TOTALLY COOL'.

Although being in Manchester gives you more credibility, the location of all the major record labels, music publishers, magazines and media in London creates something of a glass ceiling: 'In the end you're going to be shagged if you're not in London', says Mark Rae. But people still come to the city to ride the vibe, to make films, make music, design sleeves, promote clubs, make clothes. This is another similarity with New York; Manchester draws people who want to make it. In the cult pop city there's incessant grassroots activity which buoys aspiring stars, and constant attempts to build infrastructures which also furthers careers. DJ and music-maker Waiwan emigrated from Hong Kong with his family in the 1960s, went to college in Leeds, and then moved to Manchester; 'I arrived here with not much more than my portastudio, some decks and a pile of records.'

One of the key strengths of Manchester's music community is that now there's the legacy of the past to draw on, role models that can incite inspiration or reaction. The new breed can define themselves against previous generations who've walked the same streets in the search for success. It's like living history, the Manchester music scene; you can feel that energy from the past. It's not only something you can feel when you work in the city, but it's a direct contrast to the way our lives are presented by the media and the marketing men. The agenda of public discourse denies the importance of our links with the past, edits the past in order to simplify the here and now.

Marketing loves the idea of the new, the fresh initiative, the opportunities for social trend-spotting. The media, so often mistaking advertising for culture, discover a few people in a few bars with some opinion or habit which rapidly gets labelled and sold. Political parties launch and re-launch, trends eat up trends, planners demand demolition and fresh starts. The relentless pursuit of the new is symptomatic of a way of thinking about who we are; in the words of the American novelist Tobias Wolff, 'Our culture so depends on novelty, it exhausts subjects so quickly, that after a time everything gets lost.'

The past isn't one thing and the present another. Patterns from the Engels era are still being replicated, there is still a massive gap between the wealthy, flash Manchester and the everyday life of many citizens. Misery and grime are still concealed from the monied classes, as car owners speed into town along widened roads and extended motorways. A generation ago, Moss Side's Princess Road was a busy shopping street. Now it's a dual carriageway, with the local community paying the price in terms of numerous tragic traffic accidents and struggling local businesses. Engels noted how many main roads in Manchester were bordered by large, ornate buildings which effectively hid the mean streets behind, but, ironically, the tall shopfronts which line one side of Princess Road no longer efficiently conceal the poverty behind them, they advertise it; many are abandoned, their broken facades shuttered.

Engels wouldn't find poverty so conspicuous in the city centre now as it was in the nineteenth century. He'd see shoppers and hordes of power-dressed young women in the day, deserted streets in the week, and thronging drinkers at weekends. He'd find street sleepers in shop doorways, of course, although their numbers have steadied after sharp increases in the mid 1990s; schemes, hostels and shared lodgings have alleviated the problem. An embarrassment to a go-getting city, most poverty is out of sight; the working and not-working poor don't go near the new glittering spaces around town. The benefits of regeneration are a long way from reaching the whole community. The poorest and most marginalised are unlikely to book into the hotels, visit the Concert Hall or move into what they would see as 'yuppie flats'.

The kinds of housing development provided in the city centre don't make for a varied social mix, and Gordon Hood, once of the CMDC, admits that city centre homes – lacking local schools and parks – aren't appropriate for families. He also talks about a psychological and social barrier between areas like Hulme, Moss Side, Ardwick and Ordsall, and the city centre; the people in those inner city areas are yet to be convinced that they have any kind of 'ownership' of the city centre. 'Perhaps that's one of the criticisms of UDCs – whenever we attempted to get into community-related issues we got our fingers rapped', he says.

There are still two nations, still grim areas of real, deep poverty a world away from glittering sites of civic splendour; anyone living a walk away from the Royal Exchange is now more likely to be living in a top-security canal-side residential development than anything even half-resembling old Ancoats or Long Millgate. It's still all about mill-owners and mill-hands.

Manchester provides an exemplar of urban living that's all too familiar in modern Britain; it's the same in Glasgow, Newcastle, Sheffield. On the one hand huge investment is being made in new shopping malls, sporting stadia and concert halls, while at the same time a large proportion of the population live in struggling poverty. In Glasgow, the £50 million invested during the city's euphoric year as 'City of Culture' has since been undermined by recession, violent crime and drug abuse; the economic downturn has left one in three families dependent on income support and unemployment among men of 25 per cent, yet retailers like Lacroix, Versace and Katherine Hamnett, and restaurateurs like Terence Conran have moved in, there are new and refurbished art galleries and a new concert hall. In Newcastle there's a mind-boggling juxtaposition of boarded-up houses and fading life in Scotiswood and Benwell on one side of the river and the Metro Centre at Gateshead on the other. The city has mean streets and posh shopping 'boulevards', and a reputation for hedonism on a par with Manchester's. Sheffield has a dedicated Cultural Industries Quarter and a new £15 million National Centre for Popular Music, but six hundred thousand jobs were lost in the area in the 1970s, and it's a long haul to recovery; in the interim it's been granted EU Objective One status, labelling it one of the most deprived areas of Europe alongside Sicily and the former East Germany.

In Moss Side the infrastructure is crumbling, in stark contrast to the city centre's rejuvenation. There's now just one bank – a Nat West on the corner of Claremont Road and Lloyd Street – a result, no doubt, of 'rationalisation' by financial institutions in search of bigger profits elsewhere. Meanwhile, in Davyhulme, after a machete-wielding gang raided the Nat West in August 1997 the branch did not reopen, leaving the local customers to make a trip to Urmston town centre. Local communities are battling to keep convenient, local services in an era of out-of-town supermarkets and major malls.

This remains one of the contradictions of Manchester, England, old and new, and most of the cities of the world: some of the world's most cool, chic and privileged citizens often live amidst the deepest divisions. In Paris the Right Bank shopping streets are worlds apart from the city's far-flung *banlieu*. In Barcelona the beggars on the Ramblas are only part of a wider polarisation between rich and poor that's simply summed up in the differences, both cultural and material, between *arriba* – the area above Placa Catalunya – and *abajo*, the lower half of the city. In Chile, the big glass bank buildings and the penniless ghettos in Santiago are planets apart. In Manchester there's often this juxtaposition. A cul-de-sac of £300,000 houses within spitting distance of a sink estate. A few yards from the glam surroundings of Mash & Air feeble teenage prostitutes trip down Minshull Street. Step out of the Holiday Inn and you'll be accosted by beggars. You can't escape the poor; there's always something there to remind you.

Late one night I chanced upon a Channel Four chat show featuring people discussing the state we're in. All the talk in part one was of 'new sensitivity' (evidenced by national mourning after the death of the Princess of Wales), and then some of the panellists went on to describe 'the new decadence' (evidenced, rather thinly, by a Prodigy video and a new Damien Hirst animal in formaldehyde). But much more shocking than the idea that everything is new is the idea that everything stays the same. Out here, away from the London media scrum, little changes and every day can feel the same. Never mind the new sensitivity, what about the old emotions, felt daily by lone parents, struggling school-leavers, the jobless, the homeless; tears of rage, frustration, boredom and loss? Never mind the new decadence, what about the perennial problems on the nation's housing estates, the jellied up, the skag heads, the piss heads?

In a world of words distorted by spin and counter-spin, marketing speak and media sensationalism, pop culture, at its best, gives voice to the real deal. It isn't about marketing a positive world-view. Pop music at its best has no illusions, and, progressively, it's played an important role in stripping the spin from real life. In 1995 I interviewed the American music critic Greil Marcus, who has lauded post-punk in England over and above just about every other music from any other time and place. He admired 'the frightening seriousness' of English punk and post-punk bands, he told me, and seemed genuinely excited to be doing the interview in Manchester (where the post-punk era, especially the music of the Fall and Joy Division I guess, so clearly summed up his description). Although not so one-dimensional that it excluded exuberance or having a laugh, music in this era brought to Manchester a way of dealing with the struggle to survive, a way of making a culture and having a say. Manchester has spawned more great and influential lyric-writers in the last two and a half decades than any other city in the world, and it's not just lyrics that change lives; music can worm a wordless way in too. All it takes is a bassline that pops a bulb.

Over the last few generations music has been the outlet of choice, the prevailing means of self-expression, but this may change. Writing in Manchester and Salford has strong, independent traditions among playwrights and novelists especially: Annie Horniman's Lancashire school, Elizabeth Gaskell, Walter Greenwood, Shelagh Delaney, Mike Leigh. Like many of the city's best songwriters, they are independent, awkward people, who value saying something real, maybe harsh, rather than taking flights of fancy. In recent years it's perhaps been the young comedy writers – Caroline Aherne, Henry Normal, Craig Cash, Steve Coogan, Fiona Allen and Dom Carroll among them – who have challenged pop music's dominating definitions of Manchester. Manchester is also making its presence felt as a backdrop to novels – especially the crime novels of Val McDermid, Cath Staincliffe and others – and as a bigger player in other stories and poems. The city is deeply ingrained in the work of Jeff Noon, Karline Smith, Nicholas Blincoe, Peter Kalu and Lemn Sissay.

Many of these younger writers have come out of, or been part of, Manchester's music scene. Lemn Sissay has collaborated many times with some of the city's leading jazz musicians. One-man pop cult Jeff

Noon played in Manicured Noise, hung out with the Blue Orchids, took inspiration from 'Herbal Tea Party' and 'Pollen' (of course) in his novel *Pollen*, and has gone on to explore DJ culture in the collection *Pixel Juice*. Music in the city has had all kinds of influence on wider culture in Manchester, but it's curious how acid house – that most unliterary of music forms – has influenced a new generation of storytellers nationwide. Many of them, of course, were first collected in *Disco Biscuits* (a compilation of rave-influenced writings edited by Manchester-born journalist Sarah Champion). In today's corporate atmosphere – in which a cultural revolution becomes a commercial opportunity in less time than it takes for the flyers to be printed – it's easy to be cynical of any great claims made, for example, about the cultural influence of the rave revolution, yet Irvine Welsh swears by it and the music critic Simon Reynolds gives the scene big political credibility: 'Rave equals bohemia – but bohemia as people trying to achieve through art what others achieve through political revolution.'

If Reynolds is right, then Manchester's role as a key rave city reinforces my idle speculation in the introduction that there may be some connection between chart hits and the Chartists, that pop music and political activity both provide a vehicle for self-expression and escape, for anti-Establishment views voiced in a mass movement. Clearly pop music is a commercial activity, but at its source – the grassroots – the scene is driven by a desire to be different, to strip away market forces and communicate directly, heart to heart, soul to soul. It's a reaction against corporate mainstreaming that motivates most valuable cultural activity. This isn't just a music thing; this unites Mike Leigh with Mark E. Smith, Lemn Sissay with Slam Jams. Throughout this book we've seen how grassroots activity is spurred by cultural, rather than commercial, desire. Furthermore, pop groups who calculatedly attempt to cash in are usually forgotten. The anti-commercial acts – the Velvet Underground, Curtis Mayfield – survive. The best clubs are often not the obvious ones but the ones who want to do things differently; so too bands. This is why New Order and the Fall – rather than the Hollies or Oasis – are probably Manchester's two most important bands ever.

Popular culture has reinvented itself, mutated and survived in Manchester, in a long revolution created by the desire of successive generations to make something of their lives in the world's first industrial city. Peopled by strangers arriving with nothing, Manchester has made things happen. I suppose, throughout this book I've been trying to reclaim popular culture for the people, uncover its roots, follow its threads, to reclaim the culture of xeroxed fanzines not glossy brochures, and to understand what is lost when the underground goes overground. Cycles, loops, patterns from the past return and develop in music, as in history. It's like a remix; when an original track is passed to a producer, DJ or writer and re-worked, maybe with a harder drum pattern, madder noises, more pianos. Since the quarrelsome, chaotic arrival of the industrial era over a hundred and fifty years ago, Manchester is recognisably the same, but new elements have appeared, disguising, reinforcing or extending the original version.

One day in the Central Library I was looking through newspaper archives for reports of a fascist rally that took place at Belle Vue in 1933. My attention was grabbed by something else: a news item about three Salford teenagers who stole a motor car and took it on a 'joy ride'. One of them had been convicted of a similar offence just three months previously; 'I do it for the thrill', he explained. This was back in 1933. The spate of such incidents provoked the local Chief Constable to warn motorists in the Salford area not to leave vehicles unattended.

Nearly seventy years later such warnings are still issued, echoing down the years. If there's no history, then no lessons are learned and the reaction to them is nothing more than crisis management. One example is the way authorities deal with drug use. Waging wars against drug users, threats to close the clubs; none of this means anything in a world where a five second high seems more appealing than a humdrum life. When the authorities – governments, police, Churches – ask what is to be done, they should ask themselves this: what is it about their society that makes it, by contrast, so unappealing?

Crime and poverty have stormed through our story like gate-crashers at a party, and yet, for centuries, those who wish to boost the city in the eyes of the world have failed to confront these problems. Politicians often ignore the long view; their short-term quick fixes are often better vote winners. Meanwhile, a sense of mistrust of the authorities and so-called experts passes through generations of Mancunians. There's a collective consciousness, and a sense that many of the traumas of the past live on; the legacy of the slum clearance before and after the war, for instance, or the equivocal attitudes to the black population in Moss Side. Even further back, Thomas Carlyle forecast that the suspicion and bitterness in Manchester arising from the deaths at Peterloo and the smothering of free speech would live on, a 'treasury of rage, burning hidden or visible in all hearts'.

Carlyle's use of the word 'treasury' is ambiguous, probably unintentionally. He no doubt saw the legacy of Peterloo wholly negatively, yet creativity has sprung from the well of rage, as in the life of Ewan MacColl, forever dogged by a 'thread of anger', as he called it, a reminder of the social unrest, poverty and hard days of the 1930s. But certainly, you can sometimes sense a collective rage in the Mancunian air which can often burn destructively. It can be a hard-faced city. In 'Salon de 1846' Baudelaire described the black undertaker's garb as the uniform of his century. If Manchester in our era has a uniform it's the big jacket with the hood up, covering the face; the anonymous lad, hooded and hidden from the watchful gaze of CCTV.

There's also collective cynicism, the result of the conspicuous gap between the hype and the reality of city life. Marketing doesn't like a downside, and marketing speak can't be ambivalent or complex, so agencies like Marketing Manchester are left to make claims which will always ring a little hollow in the real world. Massive funds are found to meet Commonwealth Games expenditure on infrastructure and marketing, but provision for sport in local schools is piecemeal and patchy. Manchester has a fantastic new swimming pool for the Commonwealth Games, while pupils at many junior schools only have access to swimming lessons once a week every other year. The city boasts one of the richest football clubs in the world, yet many local schools have no provision for organised football training.

The limits of Manchester's vision of urban regeneration are clear. The penchant for sexy projects – grand buildings and enhanced leisure opportunities – ignored the needs of the grassroots. In the 1990s Manchester was becoming some kind of clone of South Kensington circa 1985, all al fresco, design-led bar snacks; PRs and PAs on their mobile phones clogging up the café bars; shops selling luminous kettles and see-through toasters. Style obsessions amounted to repackaging rather than regeneration. Regeneration was something to do with image and marketing rather than a medium for delivering enhanced lives for the ordinary majority of Mancunians.

Before it becomes a dirty word, there's an urgent need to find a less glamorous but more profound definition of 'regeneration'. A host of other criteria should be added to the equation – reversing the city's poor record in education standards, mental health, housing, childcare, public transport and crime prevention, for instance. Most of all, it should be a long-term strategy directed towards creative and social empowerment, and enhanced opportunities. It should dismantle the barrier between the city centre and the rest of the city, filter the benefits of city centre investment to the inner city, and bond the themed tourist quarters with those parts of the city the tourists never see; the parts of Hulme wracked with drugs and crime, the Langworthy area of Salford blighted by vandalised houses and violence, the shuttered-up shops of Wythenshawe.

Into the twenty-first century, as the city centre is further zoned, themed and quartered, Ancoats is finally in line for serious spending. Plans for Moss Side look capable of delivering some genuine improvement for local residents in the inner city, and a tourist infrastructure in Rusholme – built on the back of successful Indian restaurants (Oxford Road's so called 'Curry Mile') and the tireless work of Daood Akram and others from the Rusholme Traders' Association – is also likely to generate and retain revenue in the local community. Meanwhile, a £90 million super-stadium built for the 2002 Commonwealth Games in a decaying area in east Manchester has created four thousand jobs and is good news for the local area of Beswick, an area of perennial housing problems, devastated by the loss of thousands of local manufacturing jobs in the 1970s and 1980s. How beneficial this will be, and whether there will be a long-lasting and positive effect on local communities, is yet to be seen, and, to an extent, is out of local control; a significant upturn in the national economy is required. It's certain that when shudderings on the far reaches of the global market impact on a neighbourhood street, there's only so much even the most enlightened City Council can do.

There are other problems for the city to address, including a steady flow of talent from Manchester to London, especially of people making their way through creative or media jobs. Not only does this deprive the city of a chance to develop the kind of advanced media and cultural infrastructure the ideas in the city warrant, but over-reliance on representation via the London-based media can mean life in Manchester is easily distorted. For decades, the idea that Mancunian life is accurately rendered by *Coronation Street* has had a traumatic effect; through the 1970s and 1980s the soap portrayed a backward, insular, monochrome world which fed the cobbled streets and cloth caps stereotypes. Subsequently, in their eagerness to prove that Manchester is (to quote the BBC blurbsters launching a series of

Manchester-oriented programmes in May 1998) 'Britain's most happening city', new clichés have emerged. There's the Liam Gallagher lad – almost a self-parody – all swagger and blag, Manc-ing it up for the cameras. And, more recently, there's been a fixation with Manchester as a location for crime dramas, docu-dramas and undercover investigations, and Manchester is becoming a director's shortcut, a quick way of signifying violence, grime and crime, and this is the strangest thing; in the city you can sense we are turning our role into the reality, falling into line behind the stereotypes, clinging to someone else's cliché of who we are.

Another problem for Manchester to confront is the suicide rate among men aged between fifteen and thirty-five – it's twice the national average – and the numbers of young men who suffer from severe depressive illnesses: one in ten. This sort of statistic runs counter to the upbeat image of Manchester and sits uneasily with the braggadocio of the Manc lad, but clearly underlines that many people are untouched by the hype about hope and prosperity in the city. Depression is isolation; for these isolated people agencies provide help-lines and counselling of all kinds, but identifying the causes – let alone rooting them out – is harder. Drug use is known to have a negative impact on mental health, for example, and poverty can quickly dismantle a mind. Manchester also has more children in care than any other city, and being taken into care heightens the effects of isolation. Problems of social exclusion go back decades in the city, but some particular pressures faced by men are newer; to do with changing roles and increasing job losses.

There have been dramatic rises in the number of crimes of violence in recent years, but although Greater Manchester Police deal with more crimes per head than almost any other metropolitan force, the fact is that in many parts of Britain life wears a hard face. The story over the last ten chapters confirms that Manchester has never been a safe city. Its current problems with organised crime are far from unique; in Manchester, Glasgow, Liverpool and London there are criminal families who have tried to control and exploit communities, shops, pubs and clubs for generations. And there are policemen who are off the pace or who aren't interested in rooting them out. That Manchester is tempted and tortured by crime is part of a general national experience exacerbated by a proven link between crime and the use of illegal drugs. Users take to thieving to feed habits of up to £400 a week; 78 per cent of suspects held in police stations in

Trafford in 1997 tested positive for illegal drugs (27 per cent for crack cocaine, 32 per cent heroin). That Manchester has also witnessed massive recent rises in heroin use is also part of a general pattern. Opium is the religion of the people.

Bad news for the city deflects attention from the attempts to boost and market Manchester, and locally – as nationally – there's a tendency to deny or ignore problems in favour of hype, but it's hard to ignore the statistics as they stack up: Manchester leads league tables for levels of school exclusions, under sixteen pregnancies, male suicides, single mothers and children in care; Manchester has the lowest number of cars per household than any other city, yet through-traffic, climate, geography and heavy industry have conspired to create a pollution blackspot; 'Manchester is the asthma capital of Britain', according to one doctor living locally. Life expectancy in cities like Manchester is demonstrably less than in quieter, more prosperous areas of the country. The patterns of inequality in wealth, like health, are becoming more, not less, pronounced.

Yet in Manchester, like Liverpool, Detroit – other places with similar problems of poverty and crime – music has given the city a voice, broken the silence, woven itself deep into the fabric of life. In the main, this has been an organic process, the intervention of independent, maverick operators with ideas, desperate to express, unlikely to be corporate. We've followed the travels and travails of an urban culture generated by people looking to make something of their lives, and create the means to express and entertain, meet, socialise, escape and enjoy. We've seen how activity in Manchester is an exemplar of how urban popular culture in Britain has developed away from the country's mainstream culture, thriving even in spectacularly unprepossessing surroundings: Hulme Boys' Club, Gotelli's, the coffee bars, the Twisted Wheel, the Gallery, the Reno. We've seen how what goes on in Manchester still has the power to throw light on Thomas Carlyle's mission to uncover the Condition of England.

As part of the fresh start in the new millennium, Manchester has created Urbis (the Building of the City), a gallery and exhibition space in the new Millennium Quarter on the site of the June 1996 IRA bombing. It overlooks the old Thomson House print building (now part of the Printworks), deep in the heart of Medieval Manchester, near Hunt's Bank (named after the hero of Peterloo), across the street from the site of Ben Lang's, round the corner from where the ravers spilt out of Konspiracy (the old Pips nightclub), and next to Chetham's Library where Engels sat by a window and wrote his brilliant exposition on the first city of the industrial age. Urbis validates and celebrates this history, an exhibition space intent on exploring the growth of the modern history, Manchester's place as the prototype, the vanguard city, and the common strands that unite Manchester and other cities of the world (from New York and Chicago to Barcelona and London).

As warehouses are gutted and turned into hotels, factories into nightclubs, and green spaces into runways and shopping cities, it's clear that leisure and pleasure have become big business. The power of commercial forces in our society is massive. Even the most creative underground activity is eventually assimilated, taken from the streets, neutered and fenced off, and then sold back to the populace as product. 'Be part of Manchester United', one of the TV adverts exhorts; it turns out that the way to do this is to buy something from the club's mail order catalogue.

This is part of a wider drift towards passivity, the way that market forces and vested interests encourage us to consume rather than create. Pop music's traditions of participatory activity have the power to reverse the passivity of sheer consumerism. From skiffle through punk, to cut-and-paste sampler technology, the DIY element has been strong, empowering the young. One of the things about Manchester is that people accidentally become entrepreneurs; we've met them all through the last few chapters. Their activities – club promotions, opening a bar or running a record label – are now blessed with a label: the creative industries. But for many people working in this scene, the involvement is triggered often by a simple motivation: to build a scene, to participate. Take pirate radio; for the people operating the stations, there's nothing in it for them, just a desire to spread the word, share songs, communicate. Since the early 1980s the pirate radio stations have had something of the effect of the American Forces Network in the 1960s, feeding the underground, spreading the vibes you don't get in the mainstream, often based on black American and Caribbean records, or the raw, marginalised sounds of UK soul or drum & bass. The transmission sites of stations like Love Energy, Soul Nation, Frontline and Sting FM are regularly raided by the DTI, often at the behest of the local, official, corporate radio stations desperately trying to preserve their listening figures and advertising revenue. But commercial muscle is being flexed in all fields of activity, and powerful, safe, single-vision leisure corporations, retail chains and food franchises are snuffing out the independent operators.

Corporate culture, big business and market forces press down heavily on pirate voices, mavericks and underground activity. Rejecting what's sold to us and questioning what's told to us have never been harder. But out there people with nothing can turn it around. Remember Joy Division getting it together upstairs at the Black Swan near the bus depot and going on to change pop music forever. Or Robert McFarlane and Sefton Madface – a rapper and a human beatbox – inspired by music, going down to London with nothing but their own way of doing things, taking on the world, winning and making a life. We're living in an uneasy city in a very tough world; life, let alone creativity, is threatened. The bad man is looking for a chance to wreck the joint. The bad vibes are slamming the ghettos shut. But someone, somewhere is getting up, not giving up. The corporate merchandisers, the so-called experts, the planners, the politicians can't stifle the desire to break the silence, to be heard, to make some noise. There's anger, hate, desire and hope. The end of the story is yet to be lived, let alone told.

Acknowledgements

Being part of a great community of dancers, drinkers, DJs and thinkers gives me much pleasure. I owe a massive debt of thanks to dozens of people for inspiring, aiding and abetting me over many years, and these are just a few of them: Bob Dickinson, Rachel George, Johnny Jay, Anthony H. Wilson, Colin Sinclair, Tosh Ryan, Andrew McQueen, Rebecca Goodwin, Tim Chambers, Nathan McGough, Carol Morley, Adrian Thrills, Donald McRae, Sheryl Garratt, Jean McNicol, Allan Campbell, Steve Barker, Pete Mitchell, Janet Reeder, John Peel, Erik Rug, Jason Boardman, Elliot Eastwick, Pete Tong, David Dunne, Gareth Evans, Paul Cons, Martine McDonagh, Tim Booth, Geoff Travis, Alan McGee, Mike McCormick, Linda Cheater, Melanie Smith, Steve Redhead, Andy Spinoza, Chris Sharratt, Sarah Champion, Andrew Berry, Elizabeth Taylor, Terry Christian, Fritz, Pat Karney, Kath Robinson, Keith Patterson, Paul Lambert, John McCready, Darren Hughes, Jon Whaite, Jayne Casey, Brenda Kelly, Sue Ferguson, Lew Starr, Michael & Linder, Mike & Denise, Ursula & Phil, Jane Bradish Ellames and Andy Miller.

Special thanks to my family, and especially to Catherine for love and support.

To all the interviewees whose words I've used and abused, thank you, especially C. P. Lee, Alan Lawson, Bruce Mitchell, Mike Pickering, Sefton Madface, Stan Whittaker, Clement Cooper, Graham Massey, Greg Wilson, Rob Gretton, John the Postman, Ian Brown, Morrissey, Mark E. Smith, Maria Kafula, Irvine Williams, Jackie Burton, Larry Benji, Jimmy Savile, Mark Rae, Mike Sweeney, Dean Johnson, Leo Stanley, Jeff Noon, Karline Smith, Bernard Sumner and Johnny Marr.

Key Texts

Marshall Berman, *All That Is Solid Melts Into Air; the Experience of Modernity* (Verso, 1982).
David Boulton, *Jazz in Britain* (Jazz Book Club, 1959).

Michael Bracewell, *England is Mine: Pop Life in Albion from Wilde to Goldie* (HarperCollins, 1997).

Asa Briggs, *Victorian Cities* (Penguin, 1968).

Anthony Burgess, *Big Wilson, Little God* (Penguin, 1988).

Jerome Caminada, *Twenty Five Years of Detective Life* (1895: Prism, 1982).

Thomas Carlyle, *Past & Present* (1843: Minerva, 1898).

Sarah Champion, *And God Created Manchester* (Wordsmith, 1990).

Nik Cohn, *Awopbopaloobop Alopbamboom* (Paladin, 1970).

Matthew Collin, *Altered State; the Story of Ecstasy Culture and Acid House* (Serpent's Tail, 1997).

Andrew Davies, *Leisure Gender & Poverty* (Open University Press, 1992).

Shelagh Delaney, *A Taste of Honey* (Methuen, 1960).

Bob Dickinson, *Imprinting the Sticks; the Alternative Press Beyond London* (Arena, 1997).

Frederich Engels, *The Condition of the Working Class in England* (1845: Panther, 1969).

David Fowler, 'Teenage Consumers', in Andrew Davies and Steven Fielding (eds), *Worker's Worlds – Cultures & Communities in Manchester & Salford 1880–1939* (MUP, 1992).

Sheryl Garratt, *Adventures in Wonderland; a Decade in Club Culture* (Headline, 1998).

Elizabeth Gaskell, *Mary Barton* (1848: Penguin, 1970).

Charlie Gillett, *The Sound of the City* (Souvenir Press, 1983).

Paul Gilroy, *There Ain't No Black in the Union Jack* (Hutchinson, 1987).

Robert Graves and Alan Hodge, *The Long Weekend* (1940: Four Square, 1961).

Walter Greenwood, *Love on the Dole* (1933: Penguin, 1969).

Robert Hewison, *Culture & Consensus* (Methuen, 1995).

Eric Hobsbawm, *Industry & Empire* (Penguin, 1969).

Eric Hobsbawm, *Age of Extremes* (Michael Joseph, 1994).

Richard Hoggart, *The Uses of Literacy* (Penguin, 1958).

Stuart Home, *Cranked Up Really High* (Codex, 1995).

Stephen Humphries, *Hooligans or Rebels?* (Basil Blackwell, 1981).

Jane Jacobs, *The Death and Life of Great American Cities* (Penguin, 1964).

Winston James and Clive Harris (eds), *Inside Babylon; the Caribbean Diaspora in Britain* (Verso, 1993).

Mark Johnson, *And Ideal For Living; an History of Joy Division* (Bobcat, 1984).

Joe Kay, *Chronicles of a Harpurhey Lad* (Neil Richardson, 1987).

Alan Kidd, *Manchester* (Ryburn Publishing, 1993).

Alan Lawson, *It Happened In Manchester; the Story of Manchester's Music 1958–1965* (Multimedia, 1992).

Ewan MacColl, *Journeyman: An Autobiography* (Sidgwick & Jackson, 1990).

Colin MacInnes, *England, Half English* (Penguin, 1966).

François Maspero, *Roissy Express; A Journey Through the Paris Suburbs* (Verso, 1994).

Mick Middles, *From Joy Division to New Order; the Factory Story* (Virgin, 1996).

Jeff Noon, *Vurt* (Ringpull, 1993).

Jeff Noon, *Pollen* (Ringpull, 1995).

George Orwell, *The Road to Wigan Pier* (1937: Penguin, 1962).

Frank Pritchard, *Dance Band Days* (Neil Richardson, 1988).

Jeffrey Richards, *Stars in Their Eyes* (Lancashire County Books, 1994).

Robert Roberts, *The Classic Slum* (Penguin, 1973).

Johnny Rogan, *Morrissey & Marr; the Severed Alliance* (Omnibus, 1992).

Dave Russell, *Popular Music in England 1840–1914* (MUP, 1987).

Nicholas Saunders, *Ecstasy and the Dance Culture* (Nicholas Saunders, 1995).

Jon Savage, *England's Dreaming; Sex Pistols and Punk Rock* (Faber and Faber, 1991).

Lemn Sissay, *Rebel Without Applause* (Bloodaxe, 1992).

Deyan Sudjic, *The 100 Mile City* (Flamingo, 1993).

T. Swindells, *Manchester Streets & Manchester Men* (J. E. Cornish, 1906).

Roy Whitfield, *Frederick Engels in Manchester* (Working Class Movement Library, 1988).

David Widgery, *Preserving Disorder* (Pluto Press, 1989).

Raymond Williams, *The Country & The City* (Chatto & Windus, 1973).

Edmund Wilson, *To The Finland Station; A Study in the Writing and Acting of History* (1940: Penguin, 1971).

References, Notes and Discographies

INTRODUCTION

p. ix   'The inhabitants are of a good sort . . .'; the William Stukeley quote from 1724 is reproduced in the sleevenotes to Various Artists *Palatine* (Factory LP).

p. ix   'The city does not tell . . .'; Italo Calvino, *Invisible Cities* (Picador, 1974), p. 13.

p. xi   'A great day for Manchester . . .'; BBC, 11.9.96.

p. xii   John Schlesinger is not the only film-maker to have faked Mancunian rain. When the BBC were in Manchester filming the ten-part police drama *City Central* one day in January 1998 the storyline required rain, but this time, too, the weather was dry and unhelpful. And, again, the Fire Brigade were called; 'They have some pretty specialised equipment that can produce realistic-looking rain at the drop of a hat', said a BBC spokesman.

p. xiv   'Two Nations . . .' was a phrase popularised by Disraeli (see Asa Briggs, p. 64).

p. xv   'Where the ill paid curate . . .'; *Manchester Figaro*, 3.12.1880.

p. xvi   'What most human beings like . . .'; Arthur Shadwell, *Industrial Efficiency* (Longmans, 1906), p. 66.

p. xvi   'Manchester is very English . . .'; Shadwell, p. 67.

p. xix   'It stands out like a sore thumb . . .'; Norman Morris quoted in the *Daily Telegraph*, 7.6.76.

p. xix   Manchester *Faces & Places* report on the Boys' Club in vol. 10 p. 103ff. Written in March 1899 (by which time the Hulme Lads' Club had moved to a site next to the Procter Gymnasium in Silver Street, and their facilities amalgamated), the article begins: 'It is quite unnecessary to enlarge upon the dangers by which the city youth is surrounded, or even to point out that the specious attractions of town life tend to lower the standard of conduct; but it must not be forgotten that it is only the provision of counter attractions that the evils arising from the causes indicated can be avoided.' The Adelphi Lads' Club, founded in October 1888 out of the Adelphi Ragged School, made its home in an old mill on the corner of Arlington Street and Pine Street in Salford.

p. xx   'I have been out of business . . .'; Avril quoted in the *Manchester Evening News*, 30.8.96.

p. xxiii   Shirley Baker, *Street Photographs* (Bloodaxe Books, 1989). The quotes in this chapter are variously taken from pp. 16 and 17. Her introduction pointedly avoids any sentimentalisation of pre-clearance Hulme.

p. xxiii   'They would just like to have . . .'; Ralph Ellison quoted in Peter Wilsher and Rosemary Richter, *The Exploding Cities* (Andre Deutsch, 1975), p. 84.

p. xxiv   Slotted together 'like a child's construction kit . . .'; *Manchester Evening News*, 18.8.67. Rod Hackney, *The Good, the Bad & the Ugly* (Frederick Muller, 1990), charts the deterioration of Hulme: 'Le Corbusier's notion that a street atmosphere could be nurtured in the sky proved a desperate and tragic mistake' (p. 45).

p. xxiv The details regarding Hulme in 1977 come from *Manchester's Hulme*, published by Hulme People's Rights Centre, October, 1977.

p. xxv 'Warhol had this building in New York . . .'; Alan Erasmus quoted in FAC 229, a *Music Week* supplement, 15.7.89.

p. xxv 'Hulme found its own identity . . .'; Jim Glennie in conversation with the author.

p. xxvi 'I'd had quite a lot of loss in my life . . .'; Bernard Sumner quoted by Jon Savage in *Mojo*, July 1994.

p. xxvii 'The greatest name in the world . . .'; *Newsnight* (BBC2), 26.1.95.

p. xxvii 'I am Jeane', quoted in Gallagher, Campbell & Gillies, *The Smiths; All Men Have Secrets* (Virgin, 1995), p. 102.

p. xxviii 'That's my only contribution'; Noel Gallagher in *Red Pepper*, March 1995.

p. xxviii Phyllis Dare, *From School to Stage* (Collier & Co., 1907), and the Manchester correspondent's letter is on pp. 122/3.

p. xxviii 'The main issue for me . . .'; Irvine Welsh in the foreword to the text of the plays *Trainspotting* and *Headstate* (Minerva, 1996).

p. xxix 'When my generation left school . . .'; Noel Gallagher in *Red Pepper*, March 1995.

p. xxxi 'Disneyland for drugs . . .'; Shaun Ryder in *Q*, July 1996.

p. xxxi 'I tell them it's a shit-hole . . .'; Martin Moscrop in *Debris*, issue 13.

p. xxxi 'LISTEN!'; Andrew Kopkind, *America: The Mixed Curse* (Penguin, 1969), p. 21.

p. xxxi 'They just think you are a madman . . .'; Jeff Noon quoted in *Pulp* magazine (November 1995). Like *Vurt*, Manchester is full of mad dogs; according to documents in the Central Library, there was a panic about roaming mad dogs in 1794. The Boroughreeve and his two constables issued a proclamation warning: 'There have lately been many Mad Dogs in this town & neighbourhood. We hereby give Notice, that we have appointed proper Persons to pursue & destroy all such as are suspected of being Mad.'

p. xxxiii 'The rushing, shoving, screaming, shouting . . .'; Stephen Kingston in the *Manchester Evening News*, 26.5.95.

CHAPTER 1

p. 5 'Street Arabs'; *Manchester Guardian*, 2.8.1868.

p. 9 'This English Nation . . .'; *Past and Present*, p. 7.

p. 9 'Arguably the most grim place . . .'; Edmund Frow in *The Battle of*

Bexley Square (Working Class Movement Library, Salford, 1994), p. 5.

p. 11   'We pile up their fortunes . . .'; *Mary Barton*, p. 45. There was a social, economic and physical division which reflected the shape of industry; masters and men.

p. 11   'A panacea for all human woes'; Thomas De Quincey, quoted in Grevel Lindop, *The Opium Eater; A Life of Thomas De Quincey* (Weidenfeld, 1993).

p. 11   'Manchester's deepest thinker . . .'; R. W. Procter in *Memorials of Manchester Streets* (Thomas Sutcliffe, 1874), p. 63.

p. 12   'Accorns, Beans, Bones . . .'; J. P. Earwaker, 'Constables Accounts of the Manor of Manchester' (1891), quoted in E. P. Thompson, *Customs in Common* (Merlin, 1991), p. 211.

p. 12   'All public disturbances . . .'; the *Leicester Journal*, quoted in M. I. Thomis and J. Grimmett, *Women in Protest* (Croom Helm, 1982), p. 30.

p. 14   Coverage of the events at and around Peterloo can be found in various histories, including Samuel Bamford, *Passages in the Life of a Radical* (Heywood, 1842); Archibald Prentice, *Historical Sketches & Personal Recollections of Manchester* (Charles Gilpin, 1851); Robert Walmsley, *Peterloo; the Case Reopened* (Kelley, 1969); and Robert Reid, *The Peterloo Massacre* (Heinemann, 1989).

p. 14   'Their sabres were plied to hew . . .'; *Passages in the Life of a Radical*, p. 101.

p. 15   'The greatest poem of political protest . . .'; Richard Holmes in *Shelley; the Pursuit* (Weidenfeld & Nicholson, 1974), p. 532.

p. 15   It 'did not seem to meet with favour . . .'; quoted in Walmsley, p. 34.

p. 17   'Divided, ill-organised . . .'; E. J. Hobsbawm, *The Age of Revolution* (1962: Abacus, 1977), p. 153.

p. 17   Napier had no sympathy for the people of Manchester. He described them as 'drunken ragamuffins and prostitutes'; see Sir William Napier, *The Life & Opinions of General Sir Charles James Napier* (John Murray, 1857), p. 56.

p. 17   'The provinces spoke in the name of England . . .'; Briggs, p. 119.

p. 18   The Disney analysis was included in *Working Lunch* (BBC2), 19.2.97.

p. 18   Industrial accidents and disasters (and more) are detailed in William Axon, *The Annals of Manchester* (Heywood, 1886).

p. 21   'The relation of the manufacturer . . .'; Engels, p. 302.

p. 21   'A compact group . . .'; Engels, p. 51.

p. 22   'A new spirit came over the masters . . .'; Engels, p. 23. When Queen Victoria visited Manchester in 1851 she was moved to comment on the submissive citizens: 'The order and good behaviour of the people, who were not placed behind any barriers, were the most complete we have seen in our many progresses through capitals and cities.' The subdued mood of the populace on this occasion may well, in part, have been down to the weather, however. It 'rained poikels' according to an eye-witness among the crowd.

p. 23 'Hard-headed shopkeepers . . .'; quoted in Briggs, p. 109.

p. 24 Lewis's in *Manchester Faces & Places*, 11.8.1890.

p. 24 Bovril in *Manchester Faces & Places*, 10.6.1890. Meanwhile, the Nichols family business has come a long way since Vimto was first distributed from Granby Row; currently annual turnover is approximately £75 billion.

p. 27 Exploring Ancoats, MacColl became aware of the importance of Engels in mapping the territory: 'Engels' book became our Baedeker to the city. Crossing the bridge in Ancoats, over the scabrous water of an old canal bordered by abandoned cotton mills where broken windows revealed shattered weaving frames and rusted overhead drive shafts, we felt a strong kinship with Frederich.' *Journeyman*, p. 183.

p. 27 More on the Red Megaphones and their metamorphosis into the Theatre of Action can be read in MacColl's introduction to Howard Goorney and Ewan MacColl (eds), *Agit-Prop to Theatre Workshop* (MUP, 1986). MacColl and his comrades took the theatre to the people, performing in parks, at factory gates, rallies and occasionally outside the entrance to Manchester City Football Club. In *Journeyman* he recalls one particular performance of 'The Mask of Anarchy' on the stage at Hyde Socialist Sunday School.

p. 27 'Debarred from expression . . .'; from the Theatre of Action manifesto; see *North West Labour History*, issue 17 (1992/3).

p. 27 Engels translated Shelley's poem, 'The Sensitive Plant', into German.

p. 28 'Singing and politics . . .'; *Journeyman*, p. 23.

p. 28 Robert Owen arrived in Manchester in 1788, worked in a draper's shop in St Ann's Square, went on to manage a textile mill, and left Manchester twelve years later. Like Ann Lee, he formed his own 'model' community; in New Lanark, Scotland (on principles he later replicated in New Harmony, Indiana). His views inspired the Cooperative movement founded in Rochdale.

p. 28 'Superabundant humour . . .'; Engels in *Neue Rheinische Zeitung*, 9.6.1843.

p. 28 'Take it easy . . .'; quoted in Whitfield, p. 104.

p. 28 The Smiths 'Hand In Glove' (Rough Trade).

CHAPTER 2

p. 29   'Time flies, time crawls . . .'; Magazine, 'The Light Pours Out Of Me', from *Real Life* (Virgin Records LP).

p. 30   'Summer leisure for men . . .'; *The Classic Slum*, p. 49/50.

p. 31   'The street was our stage . . .'; *Journeyman*, p. 60.

p. 31   'An open-air society . . .'; *The Classic Slum*, p. 156.

p. 31   'Seeing a crowd of youths . . .'; *Salford City Reporter*, 28.8.20.

p. 32   'Their only resource . . .'; William Cooke Taylor, *Notes of a Tour in the Manufacturing Districts of Lancashire* (1842: Frank Cass, 1968), p. 239.

p. 33   'Operatives, publicans, mendicants . . .'; in Leon Faucher, *Manchester in 1844* (1844: Frank Cass, 1969), p. 27.

p. 33   'The tide of life . . .', 'Pauperism, vice and misery . . .'; Shadwell, p. 66.

p. 34   'On Saturday evenings . . .'; Engels, p. 157.

p. 35   'A district crowded with men . . .'; *Statistical Report on Public Sunday Tippling in Manchester* (William Tweedie, 1854).

p. 35   'If one counts up . . .' and 'tea-parties where young and old . . .'; Engels, p. 157.

p. 36   In Paris in the winter of 1846, while under surveillance from the local police who feared the German communist was spreading sedition, Engels paid trips to the Montesquieu, Valentine and Prado ballrooms. He wrote to Marx: 'Life simply wouldn't be worth the trouble if it weren't for the French girls'; letter from Engels to Marx, 9.3.1847.

p. 36   'I hit out with an umbrella . . .'; Engels to Marx, 22.9.1859.

p. 36   'Drunk as usual . . .'; Engels to Marx, 10.6.1854.

p. 36   'Grab at a female . . .'; Engels to Marx, 20.7.1854.

p. 36   'The superior class of thieves'; Angus Bethune Reach, *Manchester & the Textile Districts in 1849* (1849: Helmshore Local History Society, 1972), p. 55.

p. 37   'Idle profligates and practised villains . . .'; Revd. J. Clay quoted in J. J. Tobias, *Crime and Industrial Society in the Nineteenth Century* (Batsford, 1967), p. 67.

p. 37   'Female immorality in the mills . . .'; Reach, p. 19.

p. 38   'None of the girls . . .'; Ellen Reece, quoted in Tobias, p. 94.

p. 38   'These plague spots . . .'; Caminada, p. 18.

p. 39   'The neighbourhood of Deansgate . . .'; Caminada, p. 16.

p. 39 'I was sought after . . .'; Polly Evans (a.k.a. Madame Chester), *Memoirs of Madame Chester of Manchester* (G. Vickers, 1868), p. 9.

p. 39 'All his friends were young . . .'; Polly Evans, p. 10.

p. 40 'Son of a very rich cotton lord . . .'; Polly Evans, p. 34.

p. 40 The American writer Nathaniel Hawthorne came to visit Manchester for the Exhibition (which was inspired by the Paris International Exhibition of 1855), and pronounced himself well pleased with it, although he lamented that, 'The Exhibition does not reach the lower classes at all'. The presence of Polly Evans must have passed him by. Nathaniel Hawthorne quoted in C. P. Darcy, *The Encouragement of the Fine Arts in Lancashire 1760–1860* (Chetham Society, 1976), p. 153.

p. 40 'Being fond of display . . .'; Polly Evans, p. 34.

p. 40 'I have known my house . . .'; Polly Evans, p. 151.

p. 41 'The annoyance it is to be feared . . .'; quoted in S. J. Davies, 'Classes and Police in Manchester', A. J. Kidd and K. W. Roberts (eds), *City Class and Culture* (MUP, 1985).

p. 41 'An adventurous life . . .'; *Manchester Evening News*, 1.2.33.

p. 42 'In returning, last Sunday night . . .'; Reach, p. 61.

p. 43 'In no place in England . . .'; *Manchester Courier*, 2.8.1868.

p. 43 'Manchester's Improving Daily' was written by Richard Baines, who was buried in an unmarked grave at the lower end of Harpurhey Cemetery in 1852.

p. 44 'After the labours . . .'; *Manchester Courier*, 2.8.1868.

p. 44 The inquest took place on 12 August 1868.

p. 45 'To cultivate a taste . . .'; *Popular Music in England*, p. 33.

p. 45 'Shopkeepers and publicans . . .'; *The Classic Slum*, p. 148.

p. 45 'Of a wretched quality . . .'; *The Classic Slum*, p. 151.

p. 46 'Swells who did not mind paying . . .'; Caminada, pp. 17/18.

p. 46 'Working lads . . .' and 'Gangs, twenty or thirty strong . . .'; Charles Russell, *Manchester Boys*, 1905 edition, p. 114.

p. 46 'Deprived of all . . .'; *The Classic Slum*, p. 156.

p. 47 'You were born in a gang . . .'; Henry Grimshaw quoted in *Humphries*, p. 178.

p. 47 'Disgraceful scuttling cases . . .'; *Manchester Courier*, 21.5.1892.

p. 48 'Three main points of attraction . . .'; Charles Russell, p. 115.

p. 48 'Preliminary mating ritual'; *Journeyman*, p. 74.

p. 48 The boys 'exchange rough salutation . . .'; Charles Russell, p. 116.

p. 49 'The daughter who was of our age bracket . . .' and all other quotes are from an interview with Stan Whittaker conducted by the author.

p. 50   'Going far?' and 'Fancy a walk?'; *Journeyman*, p. 74.
p. 50   'You know the toreador hats . . .'; quoted in Davies, p. 105.
p. 51   'All up Regent Road . . .'; quoted in Davies, p. 103.

CHAPTER 3

p. 55   A 'symbol of modernity . . .'; *Age of Extremes*, p. 184.
p. 56   'From the days when they . . .'; Charles Russell quoted in Kidd p. 131. Attendances at football matches in Manchester rose sharply in the first twenty-five years of the twentieth century. There was a lot of money floating around in football, then as now, evidenced by more than just the building of large stadia. The successful Manchester City team of the mid-1900s collapsed in a bribery scandal centred around Billy Meredith (who was suspended for nine months for attempting to bribe an Aston Villa player).
p. 57   'One thing laughing at another . . .'; Joe Kay, p. 35.
p. 57   'Stifling parochialism . . .'; Robert Roberts, *A Ragged Schooling* (Fontana, 1978), p. 52.
p. 57   'The world suddenly expanded . . .'; *The Classic Slum*, p. 175.
p. 59   The Kinemacolor closed at a cinema in 1933, when it was turned into a furniture store. It was later converted into a porn cinema. After a few years of disuse in the early 1980s, it was incorporated into the Cornerhouse, currently housing their Screen One.
p. 60   'Short skirts, lipsticks . . .'; *Manchester Guardian*, 2.10.26. T. S. Eliot's long poem 'The Wasteland' (published three years earlier) includes a typist 'home at teatime' to 'Stockings, slippers, camisoles, and stays' piled on her divan, and an empty embrace with a clerk. The defenders of high culture considered short skirts and jazz dancing as evidence of spiritual emptiness. Unfortunately, for Manchester higher hemlines meant lower demand for local cloth.
p. 61   *The Musical Mail* quoted in Boulton, p. 167.
p. 61   Sir Dyce Duckworth quoted in Boulton, p. 172.
p. 63   Pat Sykes's article appeared in the *Manchester Evening News*, 1 January 1929.
p. 63   'In the explosive dancing boom . . .'; *The Classic Slum*, p. 232.
p. 63   'A more raucous tone . . .'; Pritchard, p. 23.
p. 64   'Be bop . . .'; Bruce Mitchell quote from an interview with the author.
p. 64   'To break the tradition . . .'; Terence Blanchard quoted in *Straight*

No Chaser, issue 21, Spring/Summer 1993.

p. 64   'Ironical cheers . . .'; Pritchard, p. 10.

p. 65   'I'm the Shah of Persia'; *Journeyman*, p. 73.

p. 65   'Flighty pieces . . .'; Joe Kay, p. 35.

p. 65   'She was considered by Dad'; Joe Kay, p. 35.

p. 65   'Radio transformed the life of the poor . . .'; *Age of Extremes*, p. 195.

p. 66   '. . . frequented by first class dancers'; Pritchard, p. 11.

p. 67   'American razzmatazz . . .'; Arthur Donbavand quoted in Maryann Gomes, *The Picture House – A Photographic Album of North West Film and Cinema* (North West Film Archive, 1988); an important source of information regarding the early days of Manchester's cinemas. See also William Shenton, 'Manchester's First Cinemas', *Manchester Region History Review*, vol. IV, no. 2.

p. 68   'One of the major artistic experiences . . .'; Burgess, p. 73.

p. 68   Deyan Sudjic, *The Guardian*, 27.9.94.

p. 69   'One lad adored Maurice Chevalier . . .'; Burgess, p. 104.

p. 69   The work of researcher Joan Harley in the 1930s is discussed in Fowler, p. 137ff.

p. 69   'Slatternly synonyms . . .'; the *Manchester Evening News*, 10.9.37.

p. 69   'If you could afford it . . . and a jazzer's haircut' quoted in Davies, p. 104. The jazzer's words were echoed half a century later by Martin Prendergast, a DJ at the Hacienda, talking in the spring of 1988 about being stared at wearing flares to London's Wag Club: 'I didn't even have my widest bottoms on, they were only sixteen inches.' Flares and bellbottoms make perennial returns to the wardrobes of young Mancunian males. Is it something to do with the city's yearning to be a port? Is it the dock connection? The hard man (Cagney in the middle third of the twentieth century and LA gangsters in our era) is often a fashion leader, and the bell-bottomed sailors in the first third of the twentieth century probably had something of a rough reputation, drinking, fighting, been there, done that.

p. 70   The variety circuit had become heavily reliant on top stars who had established themselves in local communities by playing up local accents and behaviour (promoters on the variety circuit held to the view that humour had a regional bias; in Lancashire the humour was character-based and anecdotal, with less verbal gags than Liverpool and more self-deprecating than London). Films featuring the variety stars also tended to have heavy regional flavours.

p. 71 Les Dawson was born in Collyhurst in 1931. His debut on the comedy stage was at a grimy hall on Deansgate, an occasion he used to mention in his act: 'You could tell how dirty it was, the vandals were breaking in and decorating it.'

p. 73 'People coming home from work . . .'; Joe Kay, p. 55.

p. 75 'I frequented the dances . . .'; Joe Kay, p. 35.

p. 75 'If you went there . . .'; MacColl in 'Theatres of Action, Manchester', in R. Samuel, E. MacColl and S. Cosgrove (eds), *Theatres of the Left* (1985 History Workshop). Even in the comparatively leafy area of New Mills, organisers hiring the Town Hall were requested to hire a police officer to run the door and keep order after vandalism and other incidents during dances in February 1933.

p. 75 'They did all sorts of things . . .'; Henry Grimshaw quoted in Humphries, p. 191.

p. 78 'The century of the common people . . .'; *Age of Extremes*, p. 192.

p. 78 'The cathedrals and minsters . . . thousands of rows of little houses . . . the England of arterial roads . . .' J. B. Priestley, *English Journey* (1934: Penguin, 1977), pp. 397–9, 401.

p. 79 'Plaster and gilt . . .'; D. H. Lawrence at his most twisted: 'The stacks of soap in the grocers' shops, the rhubarb and lemons in the greengrocers'! The awful hats in the milliners! All went by ugly, ugly, ugly, followed by the plaster-and-gilt horror of the cinema with its wet picture announcements, "A Woman's Love" . . . This is history . . . One England blots out another.' *Lady Chatterley's Lover* (1928: Penguin, 1960), p. 158.

p. 79 'Shiny barbarism . . .'; Hoggart, p. 193.

p. 79 'Developing a greater knowledge . . .' Hewison, p. 43.

p. 80 'What intrigued me . . .'; William Keal quoted in Ken Worpole, *Dockers and Detectives* (Verso, 1983). 'They were talking the way we talked', Keal says, 'What came through with the Americans was really a brutal and realistic attitude to language' (p. 30).

p. 80 '"Garbo" coats . . .'; quoted in Fowler, p. 138. George Orwell – not perhaps known for his interest in teen fashion – was even moved during a visit to Wigan to note that a change in the look of the younger generation had taken place, although he captures little of the variety and invention of some of the era's fashion followers. *The Road to Wigan Pier* (1937: Penguin, 1962) p. 79.

CHAPTER 4

Unless otherwise stated, all quotes attributed to Jimmy Savile, Bruce Mitchell, C. P. Lee, Mike Sweeney and Alan Lawson are from various interviews conducted with the author.

p. 84 Bruce Mitchell remembers Hughie Flint as a drummer on the same circuit as he was: 'He was a much better player than me. He was from a family that had become religious. Hughie's father was dying and he was saved, they always thought, by a priest, and made a dramatic recovery. Their way of thanks was to send Hughie to train as a missionary in Ireland. But Hughie couldn't cut it as a missionary and became a drummer instead.'

p. 84 More on the Phil Moss Band in Phil Moss, *Manchester's Music Makers* (Neil Richardson, 1994).

p. 87 Most information about Jimmy Savile in Manchester and various quotations are from an interview kindly given by Mr Savile to the author. In Savile's autobiography, *Love Is An Uphill Thing* (Coronet Books, 1976), his Manchester years are chronicled on pp. 42–52 (from which some quotations used in this chapter are taken). In 1976, a minor furore erupted when it was discovered that Jimmy Savile had been maintaining a £10 a week council flat on the top floor of Ascot Court on Bury New Road. The Chair of Salford's Housing Committee, David Lancaster, criticised Savile for having a council flat when he already had two other homes in other parts of the country. Said Savile, 'I am there more often than people think, but I usually come and go late at night because when the kids see me or my car there, there is a hullabaloo.'

p. 87 Ray Teret quoted in *It Happened In Manchester*, p. 14.

p. 90 Vic Farrell quoted in *It Happened in Manchester*, p. 15.

p. 91 Rick Dixon's recollection of the poor turnout at the first Manchester gig by the Beatles is in *It Happened In Manchester*, p. 55.

p. 92 The power shift in pop to the regions post-Beatles is addressed in *The Sound of the City*, p. 262.

p. 93 'From here to America . . .'; MacInnes, p. 54.

p. 93 'The battle for a place . . .'; MacInnes, p. 18.

p. 94 'Merseybeat was huge . . .'; Cohn, p. 149.

p. 100 'The great social revolution . . .'; MacInnes, p. 56.

p. 104 There's more on this stage in the life of Ewan MacColl in Robin

Denselow, *When the Music's Over* (Faber & Faber, 1989). On the folk scene MacColl's status in Britain was on a par with the American figures like Woody Guthrie and Pete Seeger (following his marriage to Joan Littlewood, his second wife was Peggy Seeger, Pete's half-sister). In a twist of fate, he ended up having a massive commercial hit with a love song – 'The First Time Ever' – which, sung by Roberta Flack in the film *Play Misty For Me*, was a Grammy-winning, million-selling Number One in America in 1972. MacColl earned huge royalties for the song, written, he used to say, 'in eight or nine minutes' while on the phone to Peggy Seeger in 1956.

p. 106 For much more on the Dylan appearance at the Free Trade Hall see the invaluable C. P. Lee book, *Bob Dylan; Like the Night* (Helter Skelter, 1998). You are warned that there are numerous obsessive web sites covering Dylan updates and controversies. The Keith Butler episode features on many of them.

p. 106 'There was a gentler time . . .'; *It Happened In Manchester*, p. 1.

p. 107 'It has been my good fortune . . .'; Pritchard, p. 34.

p. 107 'Innocent times had been consumed'; *It Happened In Manchester*, p. 105.

p. 107 'The only key . . .'; George Melly in the introduction to *Revolt Into Style* (1966: Oxford Paperbacks, 1989).

p. 107 'The most electrifying single moment . . .'; Richard Williams in *Mojo*, November 1998.

p. 107 A mere slip of a lad at the time, C. P. Lee hung around outside the *Top of the Pops* studio on Dickenson Road one afternoon Jimi Hendrix performed there and was awestruck when the man himself appeared and began a conversation. Hendrix invited him back to the hotel for a drink, but unfortunately C. P. Lee had to decline; 'I've got to go home, my Mum's expecting me back for tea', he confessed.

For this chapter, and the succeeding ones, some records for suggested listening are listed. Some are discussed in the text, some are from Manchester; the aim is to provide an ideal soundtrack for each era.

Recommended Soundtrax for Chapter 4

The Animals – 'We've Gotta Get Out Of This Place' (Columbia).

Joe Turner – 'Shake Rattle & Roll' (Atlantic).

Elvis Presley – 'Hound Dog' (RCA-Victor).

Howlin' Wolf – 'Smokestack Lightnin' (Chess).

John Mayall's Bluesbreakers with Eric Clapton – *Blues Breakers* (Decca LP).

The Beatles – 'A Hard Day's Night' (Parlophone).

Jimmy Smith – 'Got My Mojo Workin'' (Verve).

Junior Walker – 'Shotgun' (Motown).

The Four Tops – 'Reach Out (I'll Be There)' (Motown).

The Supremes – 'You Keep Me Hangin' On' (Motown).

James Brown – 'Papa's Got A Brand New Bag' (King).

The Shangri La's – 'Remember (Walking In The Sand)' (Red Bird).

Spencer Davis Group – 'Keep On Running' (Fontana).

The Yardbirds – 'For Your Love' (Columbia).

Bob Dylan – *Live 1966; the "Royal Albert Hall" Concert* (Columbia LP).

The Beatles – 'Tomorrow Never Knows' (from *Revolver*, Parlophone LP).

Jimi Hendrix – 'Hey Joe' (Polydor).

Rolling Stones – 'Sympathy For The Devil' (Decca).

CHAPTER 5

Unless otherwise stated, all quotes attributed to John the Postman, Morrissey, Mark E. Smith, Tosh Ryan, Mike Pickering, C. P. Lee, Rob Gretton, Carol Morley and Bernard Sumner are from various interviews conducted with the author (including some Morrissey material from interviews previously published in *Debris* and *Melody Maker*, and some Tosh Ryan and Carol Morley material which first appeared in *City Life*).

p. 110 Manchester was a very boring place to be . . .'; Paul Morley in *New Musical Express*, 30.7.77.

p. 110 'My life changed . . .'; Howard Devoto in Savage, p. 153.

p. 111 'The 70s incarnation . . .'; Boon in *Sublime,* catalogue accompanying 'Sublime; Manchester Music & Design' exhibition at Cornerhouse, September 1992 (p. 10).

p. 111 'I didn't know what the fuck was going on . . .'; Wilson, in Savage, p. 204.

p. 112 'Their language . . .'; Ron O'Neil in the *Manchester Evening News*, 3.12.76.

p. 112 'I have booked them in for one night . . .'; Mr Anwar in the *Manchester Evening News*, 9.12.76.

p. 112 'Detectives in denims and pop gear . . .'; unnamed reporter in the *Manchester Evening News*, 10.12.76.

p. 113 'They made a lot of noise . . .'; Mr Anwar in the *Manchester Evening News*, 10.12.76. The Arosa was demolished in January 1999.

p. 113 'I'm sickened by . . . punk rock . . .'; *Manchester Evening News*, 9.12.76.

p. 114 'Dolls/Patti fans wanted . . .'; advert in *Sounds*, 11.12.76.

p. 114 'Mickey-mouse, fake Cockney . . .'; Devoto in Savage, p. 297.

p. 115 'England's second Punk city . . .'; Savage, p. 298.

p. 118 'I remember I had made my mind up . . .'; Andrew Lauder quoted in Tony McGartland, *Buzzcocks; the Complete History* (Independent Music Press, 1995), p. 47.

p. 122 'Undeniable sense . . .', 'once a neat idea . . .', and 'fan unable merely . . .'; Paul Morley, *New Musical Express*, 30.7.77.

p. 122 'Cult status . . .'; Stuart Home, p. 48.

p. 123 For a celebration and loving dissection of 'Beasley Street', see Bracewell, p. 178.

p. 124 'Feeble and pretentious . . .'; Ian Wood, *Sounds*, 26.5.79.

p. 126 'The strongest new music . . .'; Paul Rambali, *New Musical Express*, 11.8.79.

p. 130 'It was my first real emotional experience . . .'; Morrissey quoted in the endpiece of Steven Morrissey, *The New York Dolls* (Babylon Books, 1981).

p. 130 'Speaking to the youth . . .'; Morrissey, *Manchester Evening News*, 10.12.76.

p. 132 'Passion borne out of imbalance . . .'; Chambers in *Sublime*, p. 5.

p. 133 'No crossover'; Savage, p. 583.

p. 133 The narrow-mindedness and inflexibility of punk was its undoing. There's a story Lester Bangs used to tell about guesting as a DJ to a punk crowd devoted to Devo, Richard Hell and the Clash. He couldn't get away with playing soul, Motown or rhythm & blues. Punk had excluded, precluded too much. Bangs was having none of it: 'I like cultural pluralism, everybody just getting together and sharing stuff, and I thought that that was what any kind of avant-garde or alternative or utopian thing was supposed to be about. It turns out the punks are just as bad as the rest of them assholes' (interview in *Puncture* magazine, no. 17).

p. 135 'I think it was our strange inner life . . .'; Liz Naylor quoted by Bob Dickinson during a Cornerhouse talk (April 1997).

Recommended Soundtrax for Chapter 5

The Stooges – 'I Wanna Be Your Dog' (from *The Stooges*, Elektra LP).

Patti Smith – 'Piss Factory' (Sire).

The Sex Pistols – 'Anarchy In The UK' (EMI).

Buzzcocks – 'Spiral Scratch' (New Hormones EP).

Various – *Lipstick Traces* (Rough Trade LP).

Various – *Short Circuit; Live at the Electric Circus* (Virgin LP).

Joy Division – 'Transmission' (Factory).

Joy Division – *Unknown Pleasures* (Factory, LP).

John Cooper Clarke – 'Beasley Street' (from *Snap, Crackle & Bop*, Epic LP).

The Fall – 'Repetition' (Step Forward).

The Fall – 'Slates' (Rough Trade EP).

Tapper Zukie – 'MPLA' (Front Line).

Pere Ubu – *Dub Housing* (Chrysalis LP).

Suicide – 'Dream Baby Dream' (Island).

Joy Division – 'She's Lost Control' (Factory).

Magazine – *Real Life* (Virgin LP).

The Smiths – 'That Joke Isn't Funny Anymore' (from *Meat Is Murder*, Rough Trade LP).

CHAPTER 6

Unless otherwise stated, all quotes attributed to Dean Johnson, Graham Massey, Sefton Madface, Greg Wilson, Mike Pickering and Bernard Sumner are from various interviews conducted with the author (including some Mike

Pickering material from an interview for *Cut* and Graham Massey material from an interview for *The Wire*). For more of my DJ-ing experiences, relevant to this and the following chapter, see 'DJ Culture', in S. Redhead. D. Wynne and J. O'Connor (eds), *The Clubcultures Reader* (Blackwell, 1997).

p. 141 'I lived in Manchester . . .'; Jon Savage on *Celebration* (Granada TV), 27.8.92.

p. 143 Bands from Manchester playing music in a kind of rootless trans-atlantic style also included the Bee Gees. They grew up on Keppel Road in the Manchester suburb Chorlton-cum-Hardy. The Gibb family, however, emigrated to Australia when the brothers were barely teenagers. Though sentimentally still much attached to Manchester, their roots in the city have never been made obvious. The Gibb brothers attended Oswald Road Infants School, and made their performing debut at the nearby Gaumont Cinema, miming to 'My Boy Lollipop' (the cinema, incidentally, is now a funeral parlour).

p. 144 'We had to look across the water . . .'; Sinclair Palmer on *NWA* (Granada TV), 25.8.94.

p. 144 Phil Lynott's connections with Manchester are fully described in Philomena Lynott, *My Boy; the Philip Lynott Story* (Virgin, 1995).

p. 144 'People looked upon us later . . .'; Sinclair Palmer on *NWA* (Granada TV), 25.8.94.

p. 145 For more on Northern Soul see Garratt, and also Katie Milestone, 'Love Factory; the Sites, Practices and Media Relationships of Northern Soul', in *The Clubcultures Reader*; Pete McKenna, *Nightshift* (ST Publishing, 1996); and Russ Winstanley and David Nowell, *Soul Survivors; the Wigan Casino Story* (Robson Books, 1996). There are many great web sites for information, background, news of revival events, bank holiday all-nighters, and so on (including http://members.tripod.com/mickfitz and www.frizbee.demon.co.uk/soul). Likewise, there are dozens of compilations (anything released on Goldmine Soul Supply will be good-quality stuff). Should you find yourself on a shopping trip to Manchester, a trip to Beatin' Rhythm on Tib Street is recommended.

p. 150 'Stalinist'; Tony Parsons quoted in Marcus Gray, *Last Gang in Town; the Story & Myth of the Clash* (4th Estate, 1995), p. 204. Reggae was associated with the punk movement, however. There was a perceived ideological connection, enhanced by the power and influence of Bob Marley in the mid-1970s and the work of the Anti-Nazi League and Rock Against Racism. Groups like the Clash and the Ruts incorporated reggae sounds in their music. On Rock Against Racism stages, Misty in Roots and Steel Pulse shared space with the Buzzcocks and the Jam. Factory Records released 'English Black Boys' by the Moss Side-based X-O-Dus in 1979.

p. 150 'I hate modern music . . .'; Pete Shelley in *Plaything*, issue one.

p. 150 Punk against funk. On 21.12.83 the front page of the *Manchester Evening News* reported a battle between 'skinheads and body-poppers' (bodypoppers, the paper explained, were 'followers of the latest dance craze') at St Dominic's Youth Club in Alkrington; 'Chairs flew as skinheads and punks fought with bodypoppers'. Following the fight a car-full of skinheads drove at speed into a crowd, injuring three people including Donald Farrer, who explained how the fight started: 'It all flared up after a bodypopper's jacket was torn'.

p. 152 Bernard Sumner; '"Blue Monday" was really influenced by four songs', he once told me. 'The arrangement came from "Dirty Talk" by Klein & MBO, the beat came from a track off a Donna Summer LP, there was a sample from "Radioactivity" by Kraftwerk, and the general influence on the style of the song was Sylvester's "Mighty Real".'

p. 152 The Audubon on 166 and Broadway, New York, where Grandmaster Flash and Melle Mel were working in tandem on 2 September 1976 was also the site of Malcolm X's assassination.

p. 154 Through 1982 and 1983 not everybody on the *Blues & Soul* scene reacted against the new electrosounds. A DJ beginning to make his name at the time was Pete Tong. At the start of 1983 he wrote in the magazine: '1983 will be a very special year. A year for the birth of something new, something exciting – although undefinable at the moment. There is a fad brewing out on the dancefloor and in the home that's waiting to break out. The hi-tech disco is here to stay, as is hi-tech music (electro and disco grown nearer and nearer).' *Blues & Soul*, issue 372, November 1983.

p. 157 The video for 'Confusion', filmed on location at the Funhouse and Paradise Garage, re-enacts New Order's first and successful foray into New York's club sounds. Back in Manchester, Greg Wilson incorporated 'Confusion' into his end-of-year mix for Mike Shaft, overlaid, fittingly, with the a cappella from 'Walking on Sunshine'.

p. 157 New York and Manchester connections are there, somewhere in the ether. They're both go-getting cities, with wide social divisions and an urge to create independent identities away from their respective capital cities. 'Manchester is England's New York', *Gutter-*

snipe writer Phil Thornton once told me. The spiritual bond has been cemented by music collaborations and connections: Danceteria provided a model for the Haçienda; pioneering group ESG recorded for Factory; New York DJ's David Morales and Todd Terry had a huge influence in Manchester in the early 1990s; and Grand Central have since built more links with New York rappers and musicians. The mutual admiration society formed by New York and New Order reached its apotheosis when the band were signed by Quincy Jones for his Qwest label in February 1985; 'They're beautiful', he said (*Select*, September 1993).

Recommended Soundtrax for Chapter 6

Sweet Sensation – 'Sad Sweet Dreamer' (Pye).

Various Artists – *Out On The Floor* (Goldmine Soul Supply LP).

Various Artists – *It'll Never Be Over For Me* (Stateside LP).

Bob & Earl – 'Harlem Shuffle' (Sun).

David Bowie – 'Heroes' (RCA).

Earth Wind & Fire – 'Fantasy' (CBS).

The Peech Boys – 'Don't Make Me Wait' (West End).

SOS Band – 'Just Be Good To Me' (CBS).

Parliament – 'Flashlight' (Casablanca).

Afrika Bambaataa & the Soul Sonic Force – 'Planet Rock' (Tommy Boy).

Funky Four + One × 'That's The Joint' (Sugarhill).

New Order – 'Confusion' (Factory).

New Order – 'Blue Monday' (Factory).

A Certain Ratio – 'Do The Du' (Factory).

Keith Le Blanc – *Major Malfunction* (On-U LP).

Fonda Rae – 'Touch Me' (Streetwave).

Shannon – 'Let The Music Play' (Emergency).

CHAPTER 7

Quotes from Mike Pickering, Johnny Marr, Graham Massey, Ian Brown and Sefton Madface are from various interviews conducted with the author (including some Mike Pickering material from an interview for *Cut*, Johnny Marr from *Debris* and *New Musical Express*, Ian Brown from *Recoil* and Graham Massey from an interview for *The Wire*).

p. 162 'Perennial round', Engels, p. 117.

p. 163 'Crammed with people . . . one jacking zone . . .'; Graeme Park in the sleevenotes to Various Artists, *North* (DeConstruction LP).

p. 164 'This city is in total devastation . . .'; Derrick May in *The Face*, May 1988.

p. 165 'Detroit. YEAH!'; James McCauley in *Grand Royal*, issue 5.

p. 166 'Yobbishness and intellectualism . . .'; Tony Wilson in *New Musical Express*, 30.11.91.

p. 167 'The best year for ecstasy . . .'; Paul Oakenfold in *New Musical Express*, 13.8.88. In the same issue Sean O'Hagan described the burgeoning acid house scene via references to Northern Soul: 'Back in frontline clubland, the Ecstasy habit has become an underground encoded lifestyle with its own music, dress, meeting places and street slang. You have to go back to the hard core Northern Soul scene to find a club culture so wrapped up in its clandestine identity.'

p. 168 'A great place to take drugs . . .'; Jon Savage in the sleevenotes to Various Artists, *Palatine* (Factory LP).

p. 170 Ian Brown's space travel fantasies were explored in his 'My Star' single in 1998.

p. 171 One feature of the recession years was the Enterprise Allowance Scheme, set up by Margaret Thatcher's Government to get people off the dole and into self-employment. If you'd been unemployed for a while and could muster £1,000 capital, for a year the government would pay you £40 a week and cover your housing costs. For a time, the Enterprise Allowance Scheme acted like an arts subsidy on an accidental, grassroots scale. Many people borrowed £1,000 for a day or two, and armed with a bank statement as proof, signed up as budding writers or musicians. The authorities then left you alone for a year while you perfected (or not) your art.

p. 172 In 1991, Roger Daltrey hailed his protégé Chesney Hawkes as the saviour of 'real' music. However, Hawkes disappeared after just one hit – delightfully it was entitled 'The One And Only' – as house music marched on.

p. 173 'The empowerment of people . . .'; Graham Massey quoted in *Altered State*, p. 150.

p. 173 'A place of worship . . .'; Sasha in *UK Club Guide*, issue 5, p. 106.

p. 173 'There wasn't really anywhere else'; Sasha quoted in Saunders, p. 205.

p. 173 'We met here . . .'; Paul from K-Klass on Radio One, August 1997.

p. 175 'The whole Roses thing kicked off'; Noel Gallagher in *NME*, 4.6.94.

p. 179 'The best band . . .' and '. . . burgeoning club scene' from *Avanti*, issue 2.

p. 180 'Say what you think'; Ian Brown in *Avanti*, issue 2.

p. 181 'As far as the press were concerned . . .'; Darren Partington in *DJ* magazine, August 1994.

p. 184 'Baggy as fuck . . .'; quoted in Jane Bussmann, *Once in a Lifetime; the Crazy Days of Acid House and Afterwards* (Paradise, 1998), p. 86.

p. 186 Andy Ross on Blur moving to Manchester; *Q* magazine (March 1995). In 'Playing for England' – in Anthony DeCurtis (ed.), *Present Tense; Rock & Roll and Culture* (Duke University, 1992) – Paul Smith unforgivably moved the home of the Farm from Liverpool to Manchester (a scenario which would have much displeased all the parties concerned, I would have thought).

p. 187 The unfortunate article, 'Like Madchester Never Happened', was printed in *iD* September 1991.

p. 189 'Bands are influencing the landscape'; Colin Sinclair on *Celebration* (Granada TV), 27.8.92.

p. 189 'I'm a bit of a raver'; Alexander McQueen on *The Frank Skinner Show* (BBC1), 23.1.97.

p. 189 'Music's been too formularised'; James Lavelle quoted in *The Face*, December 1995.

p. 190 'Pre- and post- . . .'; Irvine Welsh in the foreword to the text of the plays *Trainspotting* and *Headstate*; he continues: 'Far from being a simple rejection of individualism, house culture is about broadening the basis of that individualism. It is about individual spirituality, about attempting to understand the entire psychic terrain an individual operates in. It'll never be recognised as such: the bourgeois cultural fascists of the media and arts establishments could never bring themselves to concede that an 18-year-old unemployed person with a set of decks and some good friends might be far more adept and advanced in the whole life process of exploring their social and spiritual identity than they could ever hope to be . . .'

p. 190 'As English as fish and chips'; Tony Marcus in *Mixmag*, August 1995.

Recommended Soundtrax for Chapter 7

Ce Ce Rogers – 'Someday' (Atlantic).

Rythim Is Rythim – 'Strings Of Life' (Transmat).

A Guy Called Gerald – 'Voodoo Ray' (Rham).

808 State – 'Pacific State' (Creed).

New Order – *Technique* (Factory LP).

Inner City – 'Good Life' (10).

Orange Lemon – 'Dreams Of Santa Anna' (Bad Boy).

Rhythm Device – 'Acid Rock' (Music Man).

Sweet Mercy – 'Take Me Away' (10).

E-Lustrious – 'Dance No More' (M.O.S.).

K-Klass – 'Rhythm Is A Mystery' (DeConstruction).

Happy Mondays – 'Hallelujah' (Factory).

The Stone Roses – 'I Am The Resurrection' (Silvertone).

The Charlatans – 'The Only One I Know' (Dead Dead Good).

Asha – 'J.J. Tribute' (Discomagic).

Moby – 'Go' (Outer Rhythm).

CHAPTER 8

All Dean Johnson, Mike Pickering, Paul Cons, Ian Brown and Mark Rae quotes (unless otherwise stated) are from interviews with the author (some of the Paul Cons interview appeared in *City Life* and Ian Brown was interviewed for *Recoil*).

p. 191 '. . . Collective madness'; Peter Hook on Radio One, August 1997.

p. 191 'This is the first . . .'; quoted in *Altered State*, p. 159.

p. 192 'It was all over within a year . . .'; Ian Brown on *Jo Whiley* (Channel Four), 22.4.98.

p. 192 Once Manchester became Madchester it became a commodity. A trademark by which we could sell anything, our souls even. We'd started out loving music, putting music in the centre of our lives, an escape, a soundtrack, a reflection of how we live and think. It was transformed into more, and less, than that. Wrote Ernst Fischer: 'The artist in the capitalist age found himself in a highly peculiar situation. King Midas had turned everything he touched into gold; capitalism turned everything into a commodity' (*The Necessity of Art* (1959: Penguin, 1978), p. 49).

The final part of the process is that once the commodity has been bought and sold, the market moves on and hypes the new big thing. Madchester gets dumped, Manchester with it. This frustrating process misunderstands and undervalues the importance of the long view, the way ideas, experiments and creativity travel down avenues and by-roads before hitting the headlines. It misses the web of influences that surround a culture. Madchester was a trend rather than a living, changing city; it meant that for a few months what was happening in the city was overvalued, then, for several years, ignored.

p. 192 'It turned my head to mush . . .'; Ian Brown in *Q*, March 1995.

p. 192 Mani went public with regrets about heroin in *Select*, July 1995.

p. 193 'It's London that's parochial . . .'; Nicholas Blincoe in *City Life*, 29.4.98.

p. 197 'Robocop . . .'; Marino Morgan, *Manchester Evening News*, 13.12.90.

p. 200 Manhattan Sound, January 1983 was only the second gig by the Smiths. James Maker appeared as a dancer, in stilettos banging a tambourine.

p. 202 While Factory acts New Order and Happy Mondays were moving rock music forward by manipulating dancefloor rhythms, and while Factory part-owned the best and busiest house music club in the world, the record label missed out on signing anything significant from the dance scene. Instead they signed The Wendys. The oversight was hard to fathom, given the confessions of many hit-making Manchester-based groups that they were influenced by visits to the Haçienda. Sub Sub, for example, described their origins to me thus:

'We used to meet up in the queue outside the Haçienda, spend all night on the dancefloor, and then we started making music.'

p. 209 'It's Hawkwind for a new generation . . .'; Martin Price in *Jockey Slut*, issue 5.

p. 210 The seven Manchester DJs deemed by *DJ* magazine to be among the top hundred DJs in the world were Haçienda stalwarts Mike Pickering, Graeme Park and myself, plus Stu Allen, Justin Robertson, Paulette Constable and Sasha (issue 100, October 1993).

p. 214 Liam Gallagher loved the Stone Roses but Ian Brown couldn't find it in himself to return the compliment: 'When we started we wanted people to see the band and be influenced enough to start their own thing, and not copy it. I think Oasis have set music back twenty years. Oasis are babies taking coke and pretending to be the Beatles. They're wasting all of our time.'

p. 217 Another casualty in the shake-up around 1995 and 1996 was my 'Freedom' night at the Boardwalk which had started in 1990, a real community; the crowd came early, danced all night on the podiums, went back to each other's houses. By the end of 1995 I could tell that it was time to move on, though, as house music careered further towards the mainstream and attracted less friendly crowds. We got out while the going was good, though, and the end of 'Freedom' was marked on 25 May 1996 with an unforgettable guest appearance by Robert Owens.

Other club figures moved on. Simon Calderbank from 'Foundation' stopped promoting and became a restaurant manager. Crispen Somerville from 'Pollen' fronted a show on MTV interviewing film stars, then left and opened a bar in Mexico. His colleague, Rollo Gabb, worked at the Stock Exchange. Paul Cons from the Haçienda and 'Flesh' bought the old Bar Kay, renamed it South, then moved to London promising to start a club down South called North.

Soul Control are still one of the most dedicated teams of promoters and DJs. After the Gallery, they moved to the Mall, and then the X-Club. In 1993 they launched Soul Nation 104.6FM. Launching 1999, they ran one of the best New Year's Eve parties Manchester has ever seen, and started a residency at Club Havana.

The Unabombers went on to host spin-off nights from the 'Electric Chair', including 'Electric Blue' at Kaleida and 'Homoelectric' at Follies. At the end of 1998 the 'Electric Chair' moved to the Music Box.

Recommended Soundtrax for Chapter 8

The Beat Club – 'Dreams Are Made To Be Broken' (Rob's Records).

Bizarre Inc. – 'Playing With Knives' (Vinyl Solution).

Electric Choc – 'Shock The Beat' (Hi Tech).

Degrees of Motion – 'Shine On' (Esquire).

Staxx – 'Joy' (Champion).

M-People – *Northern Soul* (DeConstruction LP).

New Order – *Republic* (London LP).

Lionrock – 'Packet of Peace' (DeConstruction).

Veba – 'Spellbound' (Grand Central).

A Guy Called Gerald – *Black Secret Technology* (Juice Box).

DJ Shadow – *Endtroducing* . . . (Mo' Wax LP)

Ian Brown – 'My Star' (Polydor).

The Chemical Brothers – *Dig Your Own Hole* (Freestyle Dust LP).

Scarface feat. Ice Cube – 'Hand Of The Dead Brother; Goldie Remix' (Virgin).

Genaside II – 'Narra Mine' (London).

CHAPTER 9

Unless otherwise stated, all quotes from Clement Cooper, Karline Smith, Irvine Williams, Larry Benji, Jackie Burton and Sefton Madface are from interviews with the author. For various reasons, a number of other interviewees asked to remain anonymous.

p. 223 For more on the Welsh community in Moss Side see the *Manchester City News*, 27.8.35.

p. 223 For more background to the Afro-Caribbean community in Manchester see Marika Sherwood, *Manchester and the 1945 Pan-African Congress* (Savannah Press, 1995).

p. 223 For more on black immigration in the immediate post-war period – a solution sought by what Paul Gilroy (p. 37) calls 'an ailing industrial

Jimmy Cliff – 'Many Rivers To Cross' (Mango).

Junior Delgado – 'Blackman's Heart' (Island).

Tappa Zukie & the Aggravators – *If Deejay Was Your Trade* (Blood & Fire LP).

Parliament – 'Flashlight' (Casablanca).

Change – 'Change Of Heart' (Atlantic).

Marcel King – 'Reach For Love' (Factory).

Grandmaster Flash & The Furious Five – 'The Message' (Sugarhill).

Roxanne Shante – 'Def Fresh Crew' (Pop Art).

Kid Frost – 'Terminator' (Electrobeat).

Run DMC – 'Peter Piper' (Profile).

Whodini – 'The Freaks Come Out At Night' (Jive).

Joyce Sims – 'All And All' (London).

Barry Adamson – *Moss Side Story* (Mute LP).

A Guy Called Gerald – 'The Reno' (from *Black Secret Technology*, Juice Box LP).

Audioweb – 'Policeman Skank (Freestylers remix)' (Mother).

OUTRO

Unless otherwise stated, all quotes from Clement Cooper, Jeff Noon, Gordon Hood, Christine Derbyshire, Mark Rae and Sefton Madface are from interviews with the author.

p. 251 The scarcity of memorials of Engels perhaps symbolises the choices made about the history deemed appropriate to celebrate. The uncomfortable, dissenting moments are excluded. See also the disappearance of Peterloo from official histories and the lack of major recognition of the Theatre of Action.

p. 254 For the exultant religious metaphors see Chapter 1.

p. 255 'It is the community that needs the development . . .'; unnamed resident quoted in the *South Manchester Express*, 2.4.98.

p. 256 'A symbol of modernity . . .'; *Age of Extremes*, p. 184.

p. 256 'A celebration of the second industrial revolution . . .'; Steve Smith quoted in *City Life*, issue 357 (June 1998).

p. 256 'Ahead of the game . . .'; Steve Smith quoted in *City Life*, issue 357 (June 1998).

p. 256 For a fuller explication of the phrase 'Deep England' see Hewison, p. 22.

p. 259 '. . . sat on a beach in the Bahamas . . .'; Waiwan interviewed by Paul Mahoney, *Manchester Evening News*, 1.5.98.

p. 260 'International adolescent maquis . . .'; MacInnes, p. 59.

p. 263 'Thugs and gangsters . . .'; Richard Leese letter revealed in the *Manchester Evening News*, 12.3.98.

p. 264 'We've put our city on the map . . .'; Jim Ryan quoted in *DJ* magazine, December 1996.

p. 268 'I arrived here . . .'; Waiwan in the *Manchester Evening News*, 1.5.98.

p. 269 'Our culture so depends on novelty . . .'; Tobias Wolff quoted in the *Independent on Sunday*, 30.10.94.

p. 272 Greil Marcus interview in *Puncture*, issue 29.

p. 273 'Rave equals bohemia . . .'; Simon Reynolds quoted in *Uncut*, September 1998. See also his *Energy Flash; a Journey through Rave Music & Dance Culture* (Picador, 1998).

p. 275 A 'treasury of rage . . .'; *Past & Present*, p. 13.

p. 276 The trend for cutting the city into quarters is a major feature of public policy. There are, therefore, more than four quarters. The current campaign in Ancoats (just north of the 'Northern Quarter') is inspired by the notion of a 'Little Italy'. Urbis is sited in the 'Millennium Quarter'. Then there's 'Petersfield' near the Great Northern Warehouse shopping development, drawing on its geographical proximity to Peterloo (the ideological irreconcilability of dissenting versus shopping is sidestepped). As witnessed by the way Oldham Street deteriorated when the building of the Arndale shifted activity towards the redeveloped Market Street in the 1970s, there are problems with a piecemeal approach; one area's gain is another area's loss, like shifting the deckchairs as the ship goes down.

p. 278 Early in the Urbis project, scale models had already been exhibited, and drawings reproduced in the newspapers. The building looked scintillating. I contacted Andrew Nicholls at the project to find out more: 'We know what the building will look like, but we don't know what's going in it yet', he said. All very 1990s.

Recommended Soundtrax for the Outro

Golden Girls – 'Kinetic' (R&S).

Curtis Mayfield – *Superfly* (Buddah LP).

Mark Stewart – 'Hypnotised' (Mute).

Rae & Christian – *Northern Sulphuric Soul* (Grand Central LP).

Finley Quaye – *Maverick a Strike* (Epic LP).

UNKLE feat. Ian Brown – 'Be There' (Mo' Wax).

Barry Adamson - *Oedipus Schmoedipus* (Mute LP).

Waiwan – 'Revenge' (Autonomy).

Veba – 'All I Ask' (Grand Central).

Salt City Orchestra – 'The Book' (Paper Recordings).

Autechre – *LP5* (Warp LP).

Autechre – *Peel Sessions* (Warp LP).

Faithless – 'Insomnia' (Cheeky).

Massive Attack – 'Unfinished Sympathy' (Circa).

Index

Index

Brighouse, Harold: *Hobson's Choice*, 72
Bristol: mixed-race communities of, 244; popular culture of, 222, 256; riots (1980), 228
Brody, Neville, 171
Broken Glass, 155
Brown, Dennis, 232
Brown, Ford Madox, 15
Brown, Ian, 98, 170, 179–81, 192, 214–15, 267
Brown, James, 77, 148, 159, 208
Brown, Nacio Herb, 66
'Bugged Out', 213
Burdon, Eric, 85
Burgess, Anthony, 68–69, 241; *A Clockwork Orange*, 68, 148
Burgess, Tim, 215
Burns, Mary, 20
Burroughs, William, 160
Burton, Jackie, 244, 246
Bush (Records), 209
Bushman, 231
Butler, Keith, 106, 172
Buzzcocks, xxvi, 110–11, 113–15, 117–19, 121, 123, 127–28, 130, 136, 150, 228; *Another Music In A Different Kitchen*, 127

Cabaret Voltaire, 125–26, 165
Cabbi Youth, 231
Cadmon, Arthur, 127
Café Pop, x, xxi
Cagney, James, 57, 69, 75, 80, 139, 257
Calderbank, Simon, 210, 217
Calvino, Italo, ix
calypso, 145, 230
Cameo, 157
Caminada, Jerome, 38, 46; *Twenty Five Years of Detective Life*, 38
Campbell, Raymond, 155
Captain Beefheart, 110, 134
Carlyle, Thomas, 9, 10, 274–75, 278
Carmen, George, 198
Carr, Jimmy, 159
Carroll, Cath, 135
Carroll, Dom, 272
Cash, Craig, 272
Castlefield, industrial decay and regeneration, 249–51
Cave, Nick, 222
Cenci, Nick, 263
Central Manchester Development Corporation (CMDC), 250–52, 270
Central Station Design, 10, 177–178, 180
Cerrone, 164
Chadwick, Mike, 206
Chambers, Tim, 132

Champion, Sarah: *Disco Biscuits*, 273
Charlatans, the, 173, 176, 182, 185, 208, 215
Charlemagne, Diane, xxxiii, 206
Charles, Ray, 85
Chartist Movement, xv, xxxi, 17–23, 25, 188, 267, 273
Cheerleaders, 217
Chemical Brothers, the, 173, 205, 214, 258
Chevalier, Maurice, 69
Chicago, 279; music, 141, 165, 187 [blues, xxx, 97; disco, 164; house, 160, 163, 165, 166; rave revolution, 188]
cholera epidemic (1832), 8–9
Churchill, Winston, 26
cinema(s), role of in cultural life of city, xxviii, 4, 41, 54–82, 141, 257
Circuit 5, 105
City Fun, 116, 135, 148, 267
City Speaks, A, xviii, 15
Clapton, Eric, 95, 105
Clarke, Hewan, 156–58, 220
Clarke, John Cooper, 116, 121, 123
Clash, the, 114, 121, 150
Clegg, Pauline, 86, 96
Cleopatra, 218, 245–46; *Comin' Atcha*, 246
Clock DVA, 125
Cloud 9, 98, 148, 161
Cobain, Kurt, 168
Cobbett, William, 8, 69
Cobden, Richard, 16, 18
Cockell, Les, 200–1
Code, 217
Cohen, Leonard, 111
Cohn, Nik, 94
Cole, Nat King, 145
Collier, John, 86, 91
Collin, Matthew, 189
Collins, Dave & Ansel, 144
Compton, Jayne, 218
Cons, Paul, 159, 184, 198, 201, 210
Consorts, 205
Contact Theatre, 253
Coogan, Steve, 272
Cooke Taylor, W., 32
Cooper, Clement, 233–34, 240, 244, 267
Cope, Julian, 135
Cornerhouse, 59, 178, 233, 240
Corn Exchange, xx
Coronation Street, xi, xii, 58, 71, 81, 97, 121, 207, 276
Cosgrove, Stuart, 163
Cottage Bakery killing, 221, 235–36
cotton manufacture and trade, ix, x, xviii, xix, 5, 22–23, 25,

37, 55, 141, 258; industrialisation of, 6–8
'Counter Culture', 207, 266
Cox, Carl, 204
Cramps, the, 150
Cream, 211, 264
Creation (Records), 114–15, 135, 159, 257
crime, xv, 12, 22, 32–37, 41, 80, 144, 196–97, 224, 230, 236, 239, 241, 243, 262, 264, 270–78; organised, 196, 264, 277; *see also* drug(s); gang(s); violence
Crispy Ambulance, 126
Crosby, Stills, Nash & Young, 105
Cummings, Paul, 156
Cummings, Sam, 237, 244
Cummins, Kevin, 123, 178
Cure, the, 126, 134
Curtis, Colin, 149, 153, 156, 205
Curtis, Ian, xxx, 120, 123–27, 132, 150, 177
Curtis, Kevin, 85
Cusick, 'Nipper', 75
Cyprus Tavern, 147, 159

Daft Punk, 172
Da Silva, Jon, 166, 169–70, 205
Daltrey, Roger, 172
dance hall(s), role of in cultural life of city, 52–53, 55, 59
Dare, Phyllis, xxviii
Davidson, T. J., 149
Deansgate Picture House and Café Rendezvous, 59
DeConstruction (Records), 206
Delaney, Shelagh, xxxi, 77, 272; *A Taste of Honey*, xi, xxx, 73, 81, 84, 132
De La Soul, 177, 189
De Quincey, Thomas, 141, 168; *Confessions of an English Opium Eater*, 11
Derbyshire, Christine, 251
de Tocqueville, Alexis, 9
Detroit, 165, 185; as creative centre, 187; industry, collapse of, 164; music, 97, 141, 164, 182, 184 [house, 163, 165; MC5, xxxiv; rave revolution, 188; role of in popular culture of, 278; soul, xxx, 145; techno, 93, 163, 164]
Devine, Lex, xix, 32
Devoto, Howard, 29, 110–11, 114, 121, 222
DFK, 155
Dickinson, Bob, 135
Dietrich, Marlene, 69
digital revolution, 163, 255–56
Digital Summer (1998), 256
Dingwall, Chief Superintendent, 101

313

Index

disco: era, 103, 145, 154; music, 131, 133, 150, 163; New York, xxix, 93, 152, 259
Discothèque Royale, xviii
Disraeli, Benjamin, 9
Distractions, the, 119, 127, 149
Divine, 200
Dixon, Rick, 91
Dogs of Heaven, 212
Dole, Len, 81
Domino, Fats, 90
Donbavand, Arthur, 67
Donegan, Lonnie, 85, 93, 104
Donnelly, Anthony, 174
Donnelly, Chris, 174
Donnelly, Lee, 261
Doodlebug, Barney, 217, 261
Douglas, William, 8
'D-Percussion', 256
Drones, the, 118, 123–24
Dronke, Ernst, 36, 139
Droylsden, xxxii, 218
drug(s), xxviii, xxxi, 167–68, 191–92, 204, 274, 277–78; acid, 145, 150; amphetamines, 100–1, 133, 145, 151, 166, 167, 168; cannabis, xxii, 101, 168, 194, 216, 232, 234; ; cocaine, 168, 192, 194, 234 [crack, 234, 238, 278]; dealing, and crime, 234; ecstasy, 133, 162, 167–69, 172, 174–77, 186, 188, 189, 191, 192, 196, 204, 212, 216; heroin, 151, 168, 192, 234, 238, 278; LSD, 168, 211; opium, 11; -related deaths, 11, 191, 192, 204; see also crime; gang(s); violence
drum & bass, 215, 245, 279; jungle, xxxiii, 216, 245; ragga, 215–16, 234
Drummond, Bill, 135
Dry bar, 139–40, 198, 201–2, 209, 212
D-Train, 154
Dub Federation, 208
Du Bois, W. E. B., 226
Ducie House, 210, 251
Duke's 92, 139, 140, 212, 250
Durutti Column, 104, 127, 134
Dylan, Bob, 97, 105–7, 172
Dyson's (aka The Jig), 75

Eagle, Roger, 104, 134, 161
Eastern Bloc, 170, 179, 208–9, 212, 216; Creed, 170, 208
Eccleston, Christopher, 218
Echo & the Bunnymen, 161
Edwards, Granville, 230
808 State, xxvi, 143, 169–70, 172–73, 182–83, 185, 189, 208; Quadrastate, 182; Spinmasters, 174, 181–82
Elavi, 245

'Electric Chair', 266
Electric Circus, the, 112, 115, 117–19, 121, 123, 128, 148
electro, 93, 133, 151–52, 154–55, 159, 164–66, 169, 202, 216, 219
Electronic, xxvi, 176, 207
Ellington, Duke, 80
Ellis, Glynn (aka Wayne Fontana), 86, 97
Ellison, Andy, 208
Elson, Frank, 154
Engels, Frederich, xiii, 19–22, 24, 26–28, 34–36, 68, 162, 168, 223, 251–52, 254, 269, 279; Condition of the Working Class in England, The, 19, 22, 26–27; & Karl Marx, Manifesto of the Communist Party, 19
Equinox, 213, 217
Erasmus, Alan, xxv, 116
Eric's (Liverpool), 104, 115, 134, 136, 161
Evans, Edward, 108
Evans, Gareth (aka Eric the Mod), xiii, 104, 161
Evans, Polly, 39–40; Memoirs of Madame Chester, 39
Exit, 148, 149, 208

Faal, Vinny, 117, 122, 136, 159
Fabulous Thunderbirds, the, 105
Factory Records, xxv, xxvii, 104, 114–15, 118, 124, 127–29, 134–35, 149, 156–57, 166, 170, 176–77, 185–86, 198, 201–3, 209–10, 239, 257; club night, xxv, 124–25, 134, 150, 161, 245
Factory Too, 213
Fagins, 147–48
Faithfull, Marianne, 130
Faithless, 172
Fall, the, xxvi, xxvii, xxxii, 110, 120, 122–24, 127–28, 134–36, 143, 254, 259, 272–73; Cerebral Caustic, 134; see also Smith, Mark E.
Family Foundation, 206
Farrell, Vic, 90
Faucher, Leon, 33
Fenton, Greg, 174
Festival of the Tenth Summer (1986), xx, 128, 135–36, 177
Fields, Gracie, 71
Fifth of Heaven, 206
Fireplace, 125
'Flesh', 201, 203
Flint, Hughie, 84, 105
Flowered Up, 205
Follies, 147
Fontana, Wayne (aka Glynn Ellis), 86, 97

food riots, 12–13, 15, 19
Foot Patrol, 158
Formby, George, 70–71, 93
42nd Street, 147
Forum Club, 230
'Foundation', 210
Frankie Goes To Hollywood, xxi, 134
Franklin, Aretha, 208
Franschene, 208
Frantic Elevators, the, 149, 208
Freddie & the Dreamers, 92, 94, 97, 105, 107, 127
Free Trade Hall, xvi, 14–15, 23, 26, 106, 112, 144, 172, 252
Freeez, 157
Freestylers, the, 215
Frontline, 279
Frow, Edmund, 9, 26
'Full Circle' (London), 204
Funhouse, the, 141
funk, 145, 148, 150, 157, 160, 213, 216
Funkadelic, 178

Gabb, Rollo, 211
Gaiety Theatre, 72–73, 81
Gallagher, Liam, xxxi, 83, 131, 214–15
Gallagher, Noel, xxviii, xxix, xxxi, 27, 83, 131–32, 175, 214
Gallery, the, 24, 193–94, 197, 254, 278
gang(s), 47, 193; criminal, 37–38, 195–96, 199, 235 [Cheetham Hill, 75, 198, 218, 235; Doddington, 198, 218, 235; Gooch, 198, 218, 234–38; Longsight, 238; Moss Side, 75, 234, 237; Napoo, 75–76; Pepperhill, 234–35]; raids on designer clothes shops, 262–63; Salford, 75, 198, 218, 263; wars, 198, 222, 234]; street, 3, 29, 31–32, 46–47, 52, 69–70, 75, 195 [Bradford Street Gang, 47; and fashion, 70; Lime Street Gang, 47; and violence, 74; wars, 47–48]; see also crime; drug(s); violence
gangsta rap, 234
Gap Band, the, 221
garage (house) 163, 166, 261
garage (rock), 118
Garbo, Greta, 57, 139
Garnier, Laurent, 173
Garvey, Amy Ashwood, 225
Garvey, Marcus, 225
Gaskell, Elizabeth, 9, 11, 73, 272; Mary Barton, 223
Gaye, Marvin, 144–45
Gaythorn, 150

314

Index

Index

Index